Confucian Ethics in Western Discourse

Also available from Bloomsbury

The Bloomsbury Research Handbook of Chinese Philosophy and Gender, edited by Ann A. Pang-White

The Bloomsbury Research Handbook of Chinese Philosophy Methodologies, edited by Sor-hoon Tan

The I Ching (Book of Changes), Geoffrey Redmond

Confucian Ethics in Western Discourse

Wai-ying Wong

Bloomsbury Academic
An imprint of Bloomsbury Publishing Plc

B L O O M S B U R Y
LONDON • OXFORD • NEW YORK • NEW DELHI • SYDNEY

Bloomsbury Academic
An imprint of Bloomsbury Publishing Plc

50 Bedford Square
London
WC1B 3DP
UK

1385 Broadway
New York
NY 10018
USA

www.bloomsbury.com

BLOOMSBURY and the Diana logo are trademarks of Bloomsbury Publishing Plc

First published 2017

British Library Cataloguing-in-Publication Data
A catalogue record for this book is available from the British Library.

ISBN: HB: 978-1-4742-8587-2
ePDF: 978-1-4742-8586-5
ePub: 978-1-4742-8588-9

Library of Congress Cataloging-in-Publication Data
Names: Wong, Wai-ying, author.
Title: Confucian ethics in Western discourse / Wai-ying Wong.
Description: New York : Bloomsbury Academic, An imprint of Bloomsbury Publishing Plc, 2017. | Includes bibliographical references and index.
Identifiers: LCCN 2017010085| ISBN 9781474285872 (hb) | ISBN 9781474285865 (epdf)
Subjects: LCSH: Confucian ethics. | Philosophy, Confucian. | Philosophy, Comparative.
Classification: LCC BJ1289.3 .W66 2017 | DDC 170.951—dc23
LC record available at https://lccn.loc.gov/2017010085

Cover design: Irene Martinez Costa
Cover image © INTERFOTO/Alamy Stock Photo

Typeset by RefineCatch Limited, Bungay, Suffolk
Printed and bound in Great Britain

To my teachers: MOU Zongsan, TANG Junyi and LAO Siguang

Contents

Preface

Confucianism is a philosophy, yet it is not merely a philosophy. As a grand and profound system of thought, it is manifest at different levels of human existence, and should therefore be understood with regard to those levels accordingly. Otherwise, assertions and criticisms, like "Confucian moral rules suppress human desires and so violate human nature," or "Confucian ethics legitimizes class, age, and gender discrimination," or "Confucian ethics gave rise to capitalism in East Asia," cannot be validated. By the same token, confusions and mistakes in discussion will arise if one is not aware of at which level questions such as the following are being asked: "Does Confucian ethics refer to a bundle of conventions which Chinese people (in the ancient world as well as in the present) consistently and habitually follow?"; "Is it a set of social norms established and enforced by emperors?"; "Does it consist of virtues wedded to various roles?"; or, "Is it a system of moral principles derived from certain metaphysical claims?" Therefore, it is of utmost importance to clarify and distinguish among the different levels before discussions are made and this constitutes the core theme of this book.

In Part One I attempt to divide Confucian ethics into four levels:

1. The level of heart-mind
2. The level of ethical virtues and moral maxims
3. The level of institutional moral norms
4. The level of customs and etiquettes.

This division can facilitate academics for the study of Confucian ethics in their respective disciplines, such as philosophy, ethics, anthropology. But apart from this, Confucian ethics can be treated from a completely different perspective, viz. not as a subject-matter of thoughts and beliefs, but as a system of insightful directives for self-transformation. This is not a novel idea. Ancient Chinese thinkers as well as many contemporary Chinese philosophers have already claimed that Confucianism is "a teaching for becoming virtuous" (*chengdezhijiao* 成德之教), whose aim is to search for ways of transforming the self. It follows that the knowledge one attains through learning is not of primary value, but it is valuable only when it contributes to this proposed aim. From this perspective, the above four levels can be viewed as corresponding to different realms of human existence, and the focus of teaching might vary in each realm:

A. The spiritual/metaphysical realm
B. The realm of moral life
C. The socio-political realm
D. The realm of daily life.

Confucianism believes that, through practice, every human being will have a better life in each realm. Everyone will eventually become a sage when he or she keeps on perfecting himself or herself in each of the realms and all realms has attained a state of equilibrium. Undeniably, the central concern of a Confucian is practice. Nonetheless, Confucianism also involves a set of beliefs in each realm, and these sets of beliefs inevitably generate theoretical questions. For instance, one may ask: "What constitutes sagehood?"; "How is morality possible?"; "What is a good life?"; "What is the relationship between Heaven and human?"; "Is political principles an extension of moral rules?"; "Does a virtuous person define virtues?"; etc. If one scrutinizes these questions in a philosophical way, it is obvious that conceptual thinking and logical reasoning must be made use of. Here, we need bear in mind that, for Confucianism, philosophical searching is only one approach among many to the aim, and it is thus only *instrumental* in this sense.

The theoretical questions just mentioned refer us further to some wider and more general areas of investigation, such as that of the attribute of human nature, the logical property and meaning of moral judgments, the presupposition of moral reasoning and its validity, the ultimate/highest accomplishment of moral practice, the overriding nature of morality, or the transcendental ground of the moral, etc. These dimensions of investigation were not confined only to Confucian ethics in particular, nor to Chinese philosophy in general, but they have also been undertaken in Western philosophy too. Obviously, even though the approaches and conclusions may differ, Confucianism and Western philosophy have certain common interests. For example, the issue of moral dilemma has been discussed in both traditions since ancient times. The status of empathy in the making of moral judgments is another important common issue. It is this that renders dialogue between the two traditions possible.

In tackling the apparently same issues for the two different traditions, some "common" concepts may have to be employed. Take "universality," for example. For Confucianism, "human nature is good" is a universal claim applicable to every human being. On the side of Western moral philosophy, it is claimed that moral judgments should possess the logical property of universality (or universalizability, as advocated by R.M. Hare). Before we utilize the same notion to characterize the two different traditions of thought, we need to clarify the meaning of that notion and its implications. Similarly, the same task should be done with regard to the notions of "virtue," "empathy," etc. I have taken up this task in many chapters of this book and found that there are discrepancies in the meaning of these notions between the two traditions, sometimes to such an extent that applying the meaning of one tradition to that of another (usually when applying the Western meaning of a concept to Confucianism) would lead to completely wrong conclusions. The same happens in the attempt to translate some essential notions of Confucian ethics, such as *ren*, *yi* and *li*, by some common concepts in Western philosophy. For example, *ren* is often translated as benevolence. This might not be totally wrong, if it be considered at one level of its meaning, namely, as a virtue. Nevertheless, it would neglect the more important meaning of this term which signifies the heart-mind. Bearing this in mind, I have chosen to leave these notions untranslated.

Conceptual analysis is undoubtedly very important in philosophical investigation. Notwithstanding, it should not be just grasping the meaning of a concept through definition and its logical relation with other concepts within a theoretical system. It is common in comparative philosophy to argue that, if there are common concepts shared by two schools of thought, then these schools belong to the same category. It is tempting to argue this, since it is easier to understand a foreign and remote tradition in terms of a familiar one. But the point is: it is not essential whether two traditions do possess a common concept, for it is rather the role the concept plays and the way it functions in the two systems that make up the similarity or difference between the two traditions. For example, it is far from adequate evidence to claim that Confucian ethics is virtue ethics basing merely on the fact that the former puts tremendous emphases on virtues, value assessment of an agent's character, good life and empathy, etc. What is needed is to see what weight these concepts have within the whole system, and this in turn requires us to see what constitutes the core and essence of the system. It should become clear now that it is not by way of referring to another system that one recognizes the identity of one. Rather, it is through understanding the identity of one (and that of another) that real comparisons can be made.

Despite the difficulties in doing comparative philosophy between Confucianism and Western ethics, I myself did attempt to do some comparisons, sometimes borrowing concepts from Western philosophies. My reasons are as follows: i) The comparison has already been initiated by Western scholars, e.g. using the concept of "agent-relative approach," and I was only responding to the issues arisen; ii) Some salient features of Confucianism can be made clearer, especially for those foreign to the tradition, by clarifying different meanings of a Western notion, for example, that of universality, and choosing that meaning which most fit for explaining the corresponding notion in Confucianism. That is why I think that such kind of "comparison" is beneficial in that it deepens the understanding of each system, provided that we are not superficially applying one concept in a system to another.

Part Three focuses on the exposition of two Neo-Confucian philosophers: CHENG Ho and CHENG Yi. The thoughts of Neo-Confucianism are considered as inherited from Pre-Qin Confucianism, but developing this philosophy in a more sophisticated way. The relation between the metaphysical/spiritual realm and moral/ethical life is more articulate. Moreover, the discussions on the issue of practice are more refined. Through the study of the above-mentioned philosophers, one may see the unity of theory and practice within the Confucian system.

As said, the task of comparative philosophy requires the deep understanding of the systems being compared. A re-understanding of ancient philosophy within a tradition by means of contemporary concepts and theoretical frameworks involves already the work of interpretation and reconstruction. I have put in considerable effort to this work throughout my research in Confucianism. I hope the comparative studies gathered here have made some positive contributions to an understanding of it.

Acknowledgments

I am indebted to numerous friends and reviewers who have given useful comments and suggestions on various parts of the manuscript. I am most grateful to the late Prof. TONG Liquan (Lik-kuen TONG 唐力權), who encouraged me to participate in my first philosophy conference in the US (the 9th International Congress in Chinese Philosophy) in 1995.

Some articles in this book were previously published as follows:

1. "The Concept of Morality in Confucian Ethics," in *Chinese Philosophy and the Trends of 21st Century Civilization*, K.L. Fang (ed.) (2003), Beijing: Commercial Press, 168–90.
2. "The Moral and Non-Moral Virtues in Confucian Ethics," *Asian Philosophy* (2011), 21:1, 71–82, Taylor & Francis Group. (www.tandfonline.com/10.1080/09552367.2011.540378)
3. "Confucian Ethics: Universalistic or Particularistic?" *The Journal of Chinese Philosophy* (1998), 25. 3: 361–74.
6. "Human Nature in Confucianism: As understood and developed by Contemporary Neo-Confucian Philosphers MOU Zongsan and TANG Junyi," to be published in *Dao Companion to Contemporary Confucian Philosophy*, D. Elstein (ed.), London: Springer.
7. "*Ren*, Empathy and the Agent-Relative Approach in Confucian Ethics," *Asian Philosophy* (2012), 22.2: 133–41. (www.tandfonline.com/10.1080/09552367.2012.692537)
8. "Confucian Ethics and Virtue Ethics," *The Journal of Chinese Philosophy* (2001), 28.3: 285–300.
9. "Confucian Ethics and Virtue Ethics Revisited," in *Confucianism and Virtue Ethics*, S. Angle and M. Slote (eds) (2013), NY: Routledge, 74–9.
10. "Virtues in Aristotelian and Confucian Ethics," *The International Journal of Field-Being* (2006), 3.1: 50–60.
12. "Rethinking the Presupposition of Business Ethics," in *Business Ethics in Theory and Practice: Contributions from Asia and New Zealand* (1999), P. Werhare and A. Singer (eds), Dordrecht: Kluwer Academic Publishers, 177–88.
13. "The Thought of CHENG Hao," in *Berkshire Dictionary of Chinese Biography*, v. II, Kerry Brown (ed.) (2014), Great Barrington, MA: Berkshire Publishing Group, 620–30.
14. "The Thought of CHENG Yi," in *The Internet Encyclopedia of Philosophy* (2009).
15. "The Morally Bad in the Philosophy of Cheng Brothers," *Journal of Chinese Philosophy* (2009), 36.1: 141–56.

16. "The Status of *Li* in the Cheng Brothers' Philosophy," *Dao: A Journal of Comparative Philosophy* (2003), 3.1: 109–19.
17. "The Thesis of 'Single-Rootedness' in the Thought of CHENG Hao," in *Dao Companions to Chinese Philosophy Series: Neo-Confucianism* (2010), J. Makeham (ed.), London: Springer, 89–104.
18. "The 'Confucian Heritage Culture' Learner's Phenomenon," *Asian Psychologist* (2002), 3.1: 7882.
19. "Confucianism and Contemporary Education Phenomena," in *Indigenous Culture, Education and Globalization* (2016), Pak-sheung Ng and Jun Xing (eds), London: Springer, 227–44.

Appendix: "Can the Two-level Moral Thinking Reconcile the Rivalry of Contextualism and Principled Ethics?" *Humanities* (2006), v. 30, 477–508, Chungli: National Central University.

Part One

The Characteristics of Confucian Ethics

1

The Concept of Morality in Confucian Ethics

The condition of morality—Mackie's account and Lukes' criticism

Steven Lukes in his paper "Taking Morality Seriously"[1] discusses the importance of morality and concludes that it is "rooted in every possible form of social life and inseparable therefore from every attainable social ideal." His discussion is based on a demarcation of two senses of "morality," which is made by John Mackie, and the conclusion mentioned above refers to the "narrow sense" of morality. According to Mackie, the broad sense of morality is "a general, all-inclusive theory of conduct: the morality to which someone subscribed would be whatever body of principles he allowed ultimately to guide or determine his choices of action."[2] As a contrast, morality in the narrow sense is "a system of a particular sort of constraints on conduct—ones whose central task is to protect the interests of persons other than the agent and which present themselves to an agent as checks on his natural inclinations or spontaneous tendencies to act."[3] The narrow sense of morality thus conceived has a distinct domain, namely, a domain of principles of justice, and of rights and obligations. Since it purports to protect vital interests and well-being of individuals, including their freedom, it plays an indispensable role in human life.

Mackie then places the point of morality in the narrow sense (which we shall, following Lukes, henceforth call morality-n) on the Humean perception of the inclination of human beings and their situations: human beings are largely selfish and the resources are scarce. Morality-n is a device for preventing evils generated from such inclination and situation by providing principles of constraint on action. In Mackie's view, scarcity and selfishness can be regarded as two conditions of morality-n. Lukes criticizes Mackie's thesis by pointing out that scarcity is a more complex notion than what Mackie suggests. Mackie presents scarcity as a matter of nature's "scanty provision" for men's wants and of "limited resources." Lukes argues that the niggardliness of nature and men's wants are only two variables among many other social, organizational and cultural factors which determine scarcity. Moreover, they are themselves determined by those factors. The crucial point is, Lukes thinks that the task of overcoming all of them is unrealizable.

As for the selfishness of human beings which Mackie considers as another condition of morality-n, Lukes points out that it presupposes rather than explains the conflicts of interests among individuals. This is because Lukes thinks that what counts as selfishness depends on how the "self" and its "interest" are understood. More importantly, Lukes argues that what an agent's natural inclinations are and whether the following of them would result in harming the interests of others will depend on what sort of a person he is and in what sort of society he and they live. It follows that the pursuit of self-interest does not necessarily result in conflicts of interests. The notion of "selfishness" is generally thought as the source of conflicting interests is due to the (mis)understanding of it.

If Lukes' argument is sound, then the two conditions suggested by Mackie, which seems commonly (if not universally) owned by human beings and their societies turn out to be only contingent factors, such as a particular sort of agent, a particular type of society and its social relations, hence the need of morality-n loses a substantial ground and morality-n becomes dispensable. Mackie's account of the conditions of morality-n, according to Lukes, is a view reflecting its author not taking morality seriously. This consequence results from considering the conditions in question in too narrow a way. Lukes suggests that the roots of interest conflicts lie deeper than scarcity and selfishness. For example, the diversity of human ends as well as the conflicting conceptions of the good, that in turn define the interests of individuals, generate the conflict of interest, thus rendering morality-n necessary. Another set of conditions for morality-n can be: lack of rationality, information, and understanding. In this chapter, I will not go into the details of the arguments made by Lukes, instead, I attempt to examine what constitute the condition for morality in Confucian ethics, and whether they are only contingent or contrarily are necessary in all conceivable societies.

Morality-n in Confucian Ethics

Xunzi (荀子) and *Liji* (*Book of Rites* 禮記)

In the last section, it has been shown that the concept of morality-n which is proposed by Mackie and endorsed by Lukes, is a system of constraints on conduct, the function of which is to protect individuals' interests from being harmed by other people. Here we may tentatively adopt this conception for our present discussion. If we try to find a concept which is parallel if not equivalent, to morality-n in Confucian ethics, then the notion of *li* (禮)is a suitable candidate. The notion of *li* signifies several meanings, each of which is emphasized and elaborated by different schools of thought or different philosophers even within one school. Among all these thoughts, Xunzi's interpretation is close to Mackie's. He believes that all men have desires which, if unrestrained, will lead to mutual conflict and confusion. For him the function of *li* is to prevent conflict between men. Therefore, *li* can be regarded as being originated from his widely known doctrine of man's nature (*xing* 性), i.e., the nature of man is evil.

> Now man, by his nature, at birth loves profit, and if he follows this tendency, strife and rapacity come about, whereas courtesy and yielding disappear. Man at birth is envious and hateful, and if he follows these tendencies, injury and destruction result, whereas loyalty and faithfulness disappear. At birth he possesses the desires of the ear and eyes, and likes sound and women, and because he follows these tendencies, impurity and disorder result, whereas the rules of proper conduct (*li* 禮), standards of justice ([*y*]*i*), and finish and orderliness disappear. Therefore to

> give rein to man's original nature and to follow man's feelings, means inevitable strife and rapacity, together with violations of etiquette and confusion in the proper way of doing things, and a reversion to a state of violence. Therefore the civilizing influence of teachers and laws, and the guidance of the proper conduct (*li*) and standards of justice ([*y*]*i*) are absolutely necessary. Thereupon courtesy results, culture is developed, and good government is the consequence.[4]
>
> When do the rules of proper conduct (*li*) arise? The answer is that man at birth has desires. When these desires are not satisfied, he cannot remain without seeking their satisfaction. When this seeking for satisfaction is without measure or limit, there can only be contention. When there is contention there will be disorder; when there is disorder, everything will be destroyed. The early kings hated this disorder, and so they established the rules of proper conduct (*li*) and standards of justice ([*y*]*i*) so as to set limits to this confusion, to satisfy men's desires, and give opportunity for this satisfaction, in order that desires should not be stretched to the breaking point by things, nor things be used up by desires; that both these two should mutually support one another and so continue to exist. This is how the *li* originated.[5]

In translating the above passage, Derk Bodde detects that there are several meanings of *li* and *yi* and carefully chooses the present translation, which is in accord with Xunzi's original meaning. He differentiates the two meanings of *yi:*

> 義, a word which we have generally translated as "righteousness," often in conjunction with the quality of human-heartedness (*jen* [*ren*]). As used by Hsun Tzu [Xunzi] in conjunction with the "rules of proper conduct" (*li*), however, it seems to lose its sense of "righteousness" as practised by the individual, and to become more general and impersonal, a thing possessed by society as a whole. Thus the *li* are the accumulated traditional mores as applied by society to the individual. Likewise [*y*]*i* seems to be the code of what is just and proper, as held by society rather than the individual, and hence is no longer a personal virtue, as is *jen* [*ren*]. As such, we translate it when used in conjunction with *li*, as "standards of justice."[6]

Translating *li* as "rules of proper conduct" and *yi* as "standards of justice" does not merely express Xunzi's usage of these two words, but also reveals the resemblance of their meanings with morality-n in Mackie's sense.

In Xunzi, the purpose, function, and point of *li* resemble those of morality-n, then it is natural to think that the evil nature of man claimed by Xunzi also resembles the selfishness of human beings which constitutes one of the conditions of morality-n. As mentioned in the last section, both Mackie and Lukes agree that whether the pursuit of one's self-interest would harm others' depends on what sort of a person he is and in what sort of society he and the others live. Therefore, selfishness is only a contingent factor and if the importance of morality-n relies on it, then it will result in overlooking the latter. Now the question is, whether Xunzi's account of morality-n also falls under Lukes' criticism. This is closely related to the question whether men's desire in Xunzi's philosophy is a source that will inevitably generate conflicts of interest. Xunzi admits that anyone can be trained to be a sage. This is what the famous claim "The man in the street can become a Yu" asserts. Being a sage means never doing anything which results in harming others for the sake of his own interest. In training to be a sage, one has to learn *li* and *yi* with his mind. However, the human mind, as Xunzi sees it, only possesses the faculty of intelligence, therefore it can only learn to acquire the rules of *li* and *yi* from the world outside. The mind neither creates nor spontaneously attains them from within. Therefore, there is no transcendental ground for a man to become a sage, and there is no ground for a man to have an altruistic desire (in its strict sense). Hence we, as human beings, unexceptionally need these rules to restrain and guide our conduct. There is no room in Xunzi's philosophy for the sort of person in Lukes' possible world whose desires will not only be unharmful to others but also always taking others' interests into consideration. The nature of men thus conceived makes the morality-n necessary.

The meaning of *li* in Xunzi's philosophy is inherited and broadened by *Liji*. In *Liji* one of the functions of *li* is to maintain the social gradations that are necessary if there is to be no conflict in human society.

> The *li* are that whereby are determined (the observances toward) close and far relatives, points which may cause suspicion or doubt are settled, similarity and difference are differentiated, and right and wrong are made clear.[7]
>
> Of all things by which the people live, the *li* are the greatest. Without them, there would be no means of regulating the services rendered to the spirits of Heaven and Earth; there would be no means of distinguishing the positions of ruler and subject, superior and inferior, old and young; and no means of keeping separate the relations between man and woman, father and son, elder and younger brothers, and of conducting the intercourse between contracting families in a marriage, and the frequency (of the reciprocities between friends) or their infrequency.[8]

Apart from the function mentioned in the above two passages, *li* in Xunzi's philosophy has another function: *li* is to provide appropriate expression of joy and grief, and to prevent any excess that may interfere with social order or harm the individual. In other words, *li* is used to regulate and refine human feelings.

> As a general principle, *li* in treating birth provides refinement for expressions of joy, and in sending off the dead it provides refinement for expression of grief. In presenting sacrificial offerings *li* refine the feelings of reverence, and in marshaling troops they refine the feelings of awe-inspiring majesty.[9]
>
> Man's emotions, will, and intelligence, when proceeding according to the *li*, will be orderly. If they do not proceed according to the *li*, they become wrong and confused, careless, and negligent. Food and drink, clothing, dwelling places and movements, if in accordance with the *li*, will be proper and harmonious. If not in accordance with the *li*, they will meet with ruin and calamity. A person's appearance, his bearing, his advancing and retiring when he hastens or walks slowly, if according to the *li*, are refined. If not according to the *li*, he will be haughty, intractable, prejudiced and rude. Hence man without the *li* cannot exist; affairs without the *li* cannot be completed; government without the *li* cannot be peaceful.[10]

As mentioned, *li* is also used to regulate human feelings to prevent them from any excess. The norm of human feelings lies in the mean of them.

> *Li* trims what is too long, stretches out what is too short, eliminates excess, remedies deficiency, and extends cultivated forms that express love and respect so that they increase and complete the beauty of conduct according to one's duty. Thus, elegant adornment and gross ugliness, the sounds of music and the sobs of crying, contented happiness and grief-stricken distress are all opposites, yet *li* use them all, substituting and changing them as the occasion requires. Elegant adornment, music, and happiness are what sustain tranquillity and serve auspicious occasions. Hence, their utilization of elegant adornment does not go so far as to be sensuous or seductive, nor gross ugliness so far as to produce emaciation or self-neglect. Their use of music and happiness does not go so far as to be wayward and abandoned or indolent and rude, nor do weeping and sorrow go so far as to produce despondency or injury to life. Such is the middle course of *li.*[11]

Li provides the refined expression of human feelings, nevertheless, it should not merely be focused on the form of the expression, neither merely on the feeling itself; there should be a balance between these two.

> All the *Li* begins with coarsensess, is brought to fulfillment with forms, and ends with pleasure and beauty. *Li* reaches its highest perfection when both feeling and form are fully reached. In the next order of *li*, feeling and form in turn prevails. In the lowest order of *li*, all reverts to feeling through returning to the conditions of Primordial Unity.[12]

This function of *li* also develops in *Liji*. In *Liji*, one of the purposes of *li* is to seek for the harmony within one's self, which is considered as a preliminary condition of the harmony of the society.

> What are human feelings? Happiness, anger, grief, fear, love, hatred, and desire. Men are able to act with these seven feelings without learning ... Fighting and mutual destruction are understood as men's disaster. It is the purpose of the sage to harmonize the seven feelings, to promote the ten obligations, to teach people trustworthiness and maintain the good relationships, to commend courtesy and diminish rapacity. How can they be realized in the lack of *li*?[13]

Li is not only able to harmonize the diverse feelings, it can also unify them in a refined form of expression. Following on to the above passage, *Liji* said:

> Drinking, eating and sexual pleasure: these are the things men greatly desire. Death, poverty and suffering: these are what they greatly dislike. Thus the feelings of like and dislike are the great (motivating) principles of men's minds. But men keep them hidden in their minds, where they cannot be fathomed or measured. When good and evil are both hidden in their minds, and there is no visible

> manifestation of them, if we wish to have one thing whereby to comprehend them all, what else is there except *li*?[14]

It may be concluded that the second function of *li*—regulating and refining human feelings—in Xunzi as well as in *Liji*, constitutes the necessity of *li* for human beings. That is because no one's feelings are at birth in accordance with the mean, expressing themselves in a refined form. This fact, combined with the doctrine mentioned above that *li* is the rules one has to learn from the outside world, renders the morality-n a necessary condition for a harmonious self and society.

Mencius

From the above conclusion, it naturally leads to a view that since the necessity of morality-n is a theoretical consequence of the doctrine of the evil nature of man, a contrary doctrine of human nature such as Mencius' may undermine the need of morality. I would like to argue here that that is a simplistic and mistaken view. First of all, it should be clarified that Mencius, although well-known for his doctrine of good nature of men, admits that human beings also possess the same desires as those possessed by animals. He agrees that as a matter of fact, all men love tasteful food, beautiful color, musical sound, and fragrant objects.

> Mencius said, "The relation of mouth to tastes, eye to beauty, ear to sounds, nose to fragrance, four limbs to comfort, belongs to our nature; but some of the decreed for us is in them, and the gentleman does not choose to say 'nature' . . ."
>
> *Mencius*, 7B24

In this regard, Mencius' conception is not far from Xunzi's doctrine. Furthermore he, like Xunzi, also thinks that to follow these desires without any restraints will lead to an uncontrollable situation. Mencius said,

> Such an organ as ear or eye, since it does not think, is misled by other things. Being a thing in contact with a thing, it is simply pulled by it . . .
>
> *Mencius*, 6A15

Therefore, *li*, as a set of rules of conduct for restraining human desires, is needed for maintaining an ordered society. In the following passage, Mencius explicitly claims that *li* is more important than the satisfaction of human desires.

> A man from *ren* asked Wuluzi, "Which is more important, *li* or food?"
>
> "*Li*," replied Wuluzi.
>
> "Which is more important, *li* or sex?"
>
> "*Li*."
>
> "Suppose you would starve to death if you insisted on the observance of *li*, but would manage to get something to eat if you did not. Would you still insist on their observance? Again, suppose you would not get a wife if you insisted on the

observance of the *li* of claiming the bride in her home, but would get one if you did not. Would you still insist on its observance?"

Wuluzi was unable to answer. The following day he went to Tsou and gave an account of the discussion to Mencius.

"What difficulty is there," said Mencius, "in answering this? If you bring the tips to the same level without measuring the difference in the bases, you can make a piece of wood an inch long reach a greater height than a tall building. In saying that gold is heavier than feather, surely one is not referring to the amount of gold in a clasp and a whole cartload of feathers? If you compare a case where food is important with a case where *li* is inconsequential, then the greater importance of food is not the only absurd conclusion you can draw. Similarly with sex. Go and reply to the questioner in this way, 'Suppose you would manage to get something to eat if you took the food from your elder brother by twisting his arm, but would not get it if you did not. Would you twist his arm? Again, suppose you would get a wife if you climbed over the wall of your neighbour on the east side and dragged away the daughter of the house by force, but would not if you did not. Would you drag her away by force?'"

Mencius, 6B1

Several conclusions may be drawn from the arguments of Mencius in this passage. First, in normal situations *li* should be observed to restrain one's inborn desires. Second, in some extreme cases, the importance of *li* is outweighed by the satisfaction of one's needs.[15] Third, whether *li* should be overridden is determined by *yi*.[16] We may focus on the first conclusion here.

Since all men have desires and they need *li* to set a limit to these desires, it follows that Mencius consents the morality-n in Mackie's sense is necessary for human beings. However, it remains a question that even granted that it is the case for ordinary people, whether it also holds for a sage, who can always overcome his or her own desires. This question arises from Mencius' philosophy but not from Xunzi's because only the former allows the possibility of the sort of person who does not solely pursue his or her own interests, but also others'. For such a person, it seems that *li* as a set of external rules is not necessary. I am going to examine this inference in the next section.

Another sense of *li*: Confucius and Mencius

When we say that a sage may not need external rules for regulating his or her desires and for constraining his or her act from harming the others, what sort of people have we in mind? Is a sage someone whose act always conforms to *li*? If this is the case, then we still need *li* to set a standard. The crucial consideration is who constitutes *li*. Either the sage or someone other than the sage (for example, former kings) constitutes *li*. If the latter is the case, then even a sage needs *li* to follow. It follows that only those who constitute *li* (no matter it is called a sage or the former kings) do not need the rules because the ability which can constitute *li* can also guide their action. In Mencius' philosophy this ability is the moral heart-mind (i.e., the *xin* of *ren-yi* 仁義之心). According to Mencius, the *xin* is the ground for *li* and also the ground for determining good and evil. He conceives a sage as someone who acts from (the *xin* of) *ren-yi* rather than acts to conform with *ren-yi*, let alone *li*.[17] Mencius asserts that the transcendental ground for being a sage is possessed by everyone and this means that there is a real possibility for everyone to become a sage (this presents one aspect of his doctrine of good nature of humans). Now the question is whether *li* can be replaced by *ren-yi* in Mencius' system. Although the general rules of *li* can find justifications from *ren-yi*, and even the breach of a particular rule in some special situation can only be justified by appealing to the heart-mind of *ren-yi*,[18] nevertheless, *li* has its own meaning and function in Mencius' philosophy.

As discussed above, for Mencius everyone has a real potential to be a sage and it seems odd that a sage constitutes the rules of proper conduct for him or herself to follow. However, for ordinary people, although also possessing the ability of constituting the rules and differentiating right and wrong, sometimes may be due to not having fully developed the said ability thus not being able to activate it from time to time. Sometimes even if they make the judgments by the heart-mind, they still do the wrong act because of the lack of necessary knowledge. In Confucian philosophy, a sage is only an ideal which is for ordinary people to aim at. Before one becomes a sage, he or she needs assistance for achieving that aim. *Li* can serve as such assistance because as a set of objective rules it provides clear criteria and principles for the oughts and ought-nots for different roles and relationships in different situations. In the following passage, Mencius makes analogies to show that in the areas of skill, criteria are necessary for the rightness even for the experts in those areas and this applies also to the practice of *ren*. Therefore, someone who knows the way of Yao and Shun also needs policies which manifest *ren* to run a benevolent government.

> Mencius said, "Even if you had the keen eyes of Lilou and the skill of Kungshuzi, you could not draw squares or circles without a carpenter's square or a pair of compasses; even if you had the acute ears of Shikuang, you could not adjust the pitch of the five notes correctly without the six pipes; even if you knew the way of Yao and Shun, you could not rule the empire equitably except through benevolent policies. Now there are some who, despite their mind and reputation of *ren*, succeed neither in benefiting the people and in setting an example for posterity. This is because they do not practise the way of the Former Kings. Hence it is said, 'Goodness alone is not sufficient for government; the law unaided cannot make itself effective.' The *Odes* say, 'Do not swerve to one side, do not overlook anything; follow established rules in everything you do.' No one ever erred through following the example of the Former Kings.
>
> The sage, having taxed his eyes to their utmost capacity, went on to invent the compasses and the square, the level and the plumb-line, which can be used endlessly for the production of squares and circles, planes and straight lines, and, having taxed his ears to their utmost capacity, he went on to invent the six pipes which can be used endlessly for setting the pitch of the five notes, and 'having taxed his heart to its utmost capacity, he went on to practise government that tolerated no suffering, thus putting the whole Empire under the shelter of his mind of *ren*' . . ."
>
> *Mencius*, 4A1[19]

In the above passage, Mencius holds that *ren* alone cannot bring about perfection, it needs a proper way of manifestation, which is *li*. This idea is inherited from Confucius.

> Zilu asked about the complete man (*cheng ren* 成人).
>
> The master said, "A man as wise as Zheng Wuzhong, as free from desire as Meng Kungzhuo, as courageous as Zhengzi of Pien and as accomplished as Ranqiu, who is further refined by *li* and music, may be considered a complete man."
>
> *Analects*, 14.12

> The Master said, "What is within the reach of a man's understanding but beyond the power of his *ren* to keep is something he will lose even if he acquires it. A man may be wise enough to attain it and having enough *ren* to keep it, but if he does not rule over them with dignity, then the common people will not be reverent. A man may be wise enough to attain it, having enough *ren* to keep it and may govern the people with dignity, but if he does not set them to work in accordance with *li*, he is still short of perfection."
>
> *Analects*, 15.33

> The Master said, "Unless a man has the spirit of *li*, in being respectful he will wear himself out, in being careful he will become timid, in having courage he will become unruly, and in being forthright he will become intolerant . . ."
>
> *Analects*, 8.2

Unless *li* is understood as the manifestation of *ren*, the importance of *li*, which is declared in the above passages and adopted by Mencius, is unintelligible. In other words, *li* is an objectification of the moral mind. *Li* in this sense is not external and thus can be separated from *ren*, rather, *li* and *ren* should be conceived as two aspects of one substance.

Two senses of *li* so far have been discussed: in the first sense *li* is a set of criteria of proper conduct and restraints of desires, in this sense *li* represents external and objective rules; on the other hand, *li* in the second sense is a manifestation of the moral mind hence it represents objectified (but not objective) principles. The first sense of *li* is a device for ordinary people who are not aware of their moral autonomy and activating their moral ability. However, even those who pursue cultivating their moral mind need such rules before they fully become sages. The difference between these two sorts of people is that the latter (let us call them learners or gentlemen (*junzi* 君子), for the sake of simplicity) have more reflections on the spirit of rules while observing them. Apart from this, the gentlemen also seek for ways that can express the moral mind. Hence, they also need the second sense of *li*. However, it is important to note that, for Confucius and Mencius, there are no determined distinctions between these two sorts of people.

In fact, the two senses of *li* only differ in that the first sense provides the rules of conduct either without considering the origin of these rules, or considering the origin as external; whereas the second sense of *li* presupposes that the ability of constituting such rules are rooted in the nature of human beings. The distinction is so delicate that we sometimes cannot identify which sense is used in a particular context.

> Yenyuan asked about *ren*. The master said, "To return the observance of *li* through overcoming the self constitutes *ren*. If for a single day a man could return to the observance of *li* through overcoming himself, then the whole Empire would consider *ren* to be his. However, the practice of *ren* depends on oneself alone, and not the others."
>
> Yenyuan said, "I should like you to list the items."
>
> The master said, "Do not look unless it is in accordance with *li*; do not listen unless it is in accordance with *li*; do not speak unless it is in accordance with *li*, do not move unless it is in accordance with *li*."
>
> *Analects*, 12.1

Li in the above passage looks as if it is signifying external rules for one to observe and it is naturally regarded as being used in the first sense. However, if we understand the thought of Confucius thoroughly, we know that *ren*[20] is the ability of constituting *li* and therefore unless *li* is only understood as objectified principles we cannot explain why it is so important to observe it in achieving *ren*. We can find numerous evidence in the *Analects* and *Mencius* to support the above view.[21]

It may be questioned whether the second sense of *li* deviates from Mackie's sense of morality-n. As shown in the passage just cited, *li*—if we understand it in its second sense—covers an area much broader than the domain of morality-n. It does not merely provide principles of justice, rights, and obligations but applies to everything concerning human behavior. Therefore, the second sense of *li* is closer to morality in the broad sense as described by Mackie. Certainly apart from *li*, there are many other concepts such as *ren*, *yi*, *cheng* (誠), and the like which represent morality in the broad sense.

Conclusion

In the previous sections, we discuss that *li*, when conceived as restraints on actions and desires, as in Xunzi and *Liji*, remains indispensable for an ordered society. This also holds in Mencius' philosophy despite its assertion of good nature of humans. However, there is another sense of *li* in Confucius' and Mencius' philosophy which bears the same (or even more) significance in morality. Its meaning is inseparable from the moral mind, which constitutes the transcendental ground for any autonomous morality, no matter whether it is morality in the narrow sense or in the broad. In this chapter I have taken *li* as an instance to show that in the philosophy of Confucius and Mencius, the importance of its first sense (which belongs to morality-n) relies on that of its second sense (which belongs to morality in the broad sense). However, whether we can generalize the above claim to a conclusion that morality-n has no independent significance exceeds the scope of this chapter. All I can assert here is that granted *li* in the first sense has no independent meaning, morality-n has been taken seriously by Confucians.

2

The Moral and Non-Moral Virtues in Confucian Ethics

Introduction

The question "How should one live?" reflects the central concern in the ethics of Socrates. The answer to this question is not merely related to the concepts of obligation and duty, which constitute the major problems of modern moral philosophy, but it can also be considered from the point of view of self-interest.[1] Although this latter consideration involves a person's well-being, it is not a search for the best way for a particular person to act at any particular time according to his or her personally conceived interests. Rather, as Bernard Williams puts it, "It seems to ask for the conditions of the *good* life—the right life, perhaps, for human beings as such."[2] If we agree with Socrates that an ethical life should include both the pursuit of the well-being and the fulfillment of duties, then the study of ethics should also go beyond the boundary of morality, which focuses on the right or wrong judgments and actions. For Aristotle, a good life is a virtuous life hence virtues ought to constitute a significant part of an ethical life. It looks as if an ethical life is simply a moral life. However, as virtues signify excellence of character or admirable traits by which moral goodness can be achieved on the one hand, and prudential goodness on the other, the practice of virtues is not only for the sake of morality, but also for the reason of prudence.

Similarly, in Confucianism, the ethical concern is not limited to the morally right judgments or actions, but it is also about the good person, good character or good life that one should aspire to. In other words, Confucian ethics is something more than a kind of narrowly defined moral philosophy. This fact is reflected in the wide variety of virtues (signified by *de* 德) commended by Confucians and their different level of meanings. All in all, these virtues can be classified, in terms of their functions, into two categories: one as being beneficial for one to become a morally good person and another as being beneficial for one to become an excellent person. We may term the former as moral virtues and the latter as non-moral.[3] Although there is little doubt concerning the existence of the non-moral realm in Confucianism, yet the relationship between the moral and the non-moral realms has not been carefully examined. Obviously the nature of the existence of the non-moral realm can be clear only if the question whether the non-moral virtues can be defined in terms of, or reduced to, or overridden by moral virtues is resolved. This chapter attempts to scrutinize the relationship mentioned so as to determine the status of prudence within the ethics of Confucianism. As there are definite changes throughout history regarding the relationship in question,[4] I shall limit the scope of this study to the thoughts of Confucius and Mencius.

Virtues and the gentleman (*junzi* 君子)

As early as the time of late western Zhou (1046–771 BC), virtues have been emphasized and used to evaluate a person's behavior, especially in the circle of noblility.[5] They includes filial piety (*xiao* 孝), fraternal duty (*ti* 弟), kindness (*ci* 慈), generosity (*hui* 惠), conscientiousness (*zhong* 忠), empathy (*shu* 恕), moderation (*zhong zheng* 中正), magnanimity (*kuan hong* 寬弘), serenity (*zhuang* 莊), mettle (*gang* 剛), wisdom (*zhi* 知), clearness (*qing* 清), trustworthiness (*xin* 信), *ren* (仁), *yi* (義), courage (*yong* 勇), audacity (*wu* 武), gentleness (*rou* 柔), friendliness (*you* 友), deportment (*duan* 端), harmony (*he* 和), integrity (*cheng* 誠), respect (*gong* 恭), giving precedence (*rang* 讓), thrift (*jian* 儉), stability (*gu* 固), and modesty (*xun* 遜). Among them, *ren*, trustworthiness, conscientiousness, filial piety, *yi*, courage, giving precedence, and wisdom are those which appear most frequently.[6] Some are required by the system of rites, according to one's social status such as that of a prince or a subject. The contribution of Confucius with respect to virtues is to shift the emphases from the external social norms or criteria of behavior to the internal qualities of one's character. Virtues, for him, are admirable traits that are valuable, irrespective of one's social status. Mencius, who inherits and develops from Confucius, tries to establish a transcendental ground for virtues from human nature which is universally possessed by every human being (this will be discussed shortly).

In the *Analects* as well as in the *Mencius*, virtues are usually discussed in the context of being a good person in general. Therefore, it will be more fruitful to study the meaning of virtues in association with the idea of ideal personality or ideal character. The ideal personality in Confucianism is represented by the notion of "gentleman." Traditionally, a gentleman refers to a member of the ruling class. Starting from Confucius, the notion "gentleman" has a moral connotation. When it appears in the *Analects*, for most of the time it refers to someone who possesses morally good qualities. Confucius asserts that although there are many qualities attributed to a gentleman, *yi* is definitely the essential property. The significance of *yi* is emphasized in the following passages.

> The Master said, "The gentleman has *yi* as his basic stuff and by observing *li*[7] puts it into practice, by being modest gives it expression, and by being trustworthy in word brings it to completion. Such is a gentleman indeed!"
>
> *Analects*, 15.18

> . . . The Master said, "For the gentleman it is *yi* that is considered supreme . . ."
>
> *Analects*, 17.24

Yi can serve as a distinctive characteristic especially in comparisons among human beings: a gentleman is only concerned with *yi* whereas a mean person (*xiao ren* 小人) is only concerned with profits.

> The Master said, "The gentleman is versed in what is *yi*. The mean man is versed in what is profitable."
>
> *Analects*, 4.16

Ren is another necessary quality for being a gentleman.

> The Master said, "Wealth and high station are what men desire, but unless I acquired them in the right way I would not abide in them. Poverty and low station are what men dislike, but unless I could remove them in the right way I would not try to take myself away from them.
>
> If the gentleman forsakes *ren*, wherein can he make a name [of gentleman] for himself? The gentleman never deserts *ren*, not even for as long as it takes to eat a meal. If he hurries and stumbles one may be sure that it is in *ren* that he does so."
>
> *Analects*, 4.5

In the context of this passage, *ren* and *yi* share the same meaning and the "right way" (*Dao*道) means the way of *ren* and *yi*. Even though *ren* and *yi* can be understood at different levels and at each level they have different meanings,[8] undoubtedly they are the central moral notions in Confucianism. When *ren* and *yi* are viewed as virtues, they are definitely moral virtues in a sense that the violation of them is immoral.[9] However, morality is necessary, but not sufficient for being a gentleman. A gentleman, after cultivating of himself, should be able to express his essential quality in a proper and refined way (*wen*文). However, *wen* should be regarded as a non-moral virtue.

> The Master said, "When there is a preponderance of native substance over acquired refinement, the result will be churlishness. When there is a preponderance of acquired refinement over native substance, the result will be pedantry. Only a well-balanced admixture of the two will result in gentlemanliness."
>
> *Analects*, 6.18[10]

The "substance" (*zhi* 實) in this passage refers to morality and the "refinement" (*wen*) means the proper way of expression.

> ... Zengzi said, "... There are three things which the gentleman values most in the Way: to stay clear of violence by putting on a serious countenance, to come close to being trusted by setting a proper expression on his face, and to avoid being boorish and unreasonable by speaking in proper tones ..."
>
> *Analects*, 8.4

"*Wen*" hence forms an important part of the teaching of Confucius.[11]

The Master instructs under four headings: *wen*, moral conduct, doing one's best and being trustworthy in what one says.

Analects, 7.25

The formal syllabus of Confucius' teaching is composed of six kinds of arts; in addition to the moral education, they are rites, music, riding, archery, history and mathematics. Besides, it was also necessary for his disciple to learn poetry (*Odes*) (*Analects*, 16.13). These arts lead to the formation of a cultivated person, one who is able to express himself or herself properly. In the following passage, Confucius particularly points out the importance of "*wen*".

The Master said, "The gentleman widely versed in culture (*wen*) but brought back to essentials by *li* can, I suppose, be relied upon not to turn against what he stood for."

Analects, 6.27[12]

The *Analects* 5.15 shows that being "eager to learn" constitutes a significant aspect of "*wen*".

Non-moral virtues other than *wen* also contribute to the effort of becoming a gentleman. Wisdom and courage are two of these.

The Master said, "There are three things constantly on the lips of the gentleman none of which I have succeeded in following: 'A man of *ren* never worries; a man of wisdom is never confused; a man of courage is never afraid.'"

Analects, 14.28

Being free of confusions and fear is important for a good life and wisdom and courage are virtues helpful for this pursuit. It is noteworthy that wisdom and courage are sometimes interpreted as moral virtues by both Confucius and Mencius (*Analects*, 12.4; *Mencius*, 2A2), nevertheless, they themselves have a meaning independent of their moral connotation (*Analects*, 17.23, see the discussion below) and also play a role in the good life.

"Being conscious of his own superiority" (*jin* 矜) and the ability to "come together with other gentlemen" (*qun* 群) are two other non-moral virtues possessed by a gentleman.

The Master said, "The gentleman is conscious of his own superiority without being contentious, and comes together with other gentlemen without forming cliques."

Analects, 15.22

For Confucius, there are goals that a gentleman should aim to achieve, hence the achieved goals constitute part of the qualities of a gentleman.

Confucius said, "There are nine things the gentleman turns his thought to: to seeing clearly when he uses his eyes, to hearing acutely when he uses his ears, to

> looking cordial when it comes to his countenance, to appearing respectful when it comes to his demeanour, to being conscientious when he speaks, to being reverent when he performs his duties, to seeking advice when he is in doubt, to the consequences when he is enraged, and to what is *yi* at the sight of gain."
>
> *Analects*, 16.10

> The Master said of Zi-chan that he had the way of the gentleman on four counts: he was respectful in the manner he conducted himself; he was reverent in the service of his lord; in caring for the common people, he was generous and, in employing their services, he was *yi*.
>
> *Analects*, 5.16

Apparently virtues such as clarity (*ming* 明), respect, conscientiousness, reverence, generosity, and *yi* are possessed by a full-blooded gentleman. Some of them are moral virtues while the others are not.

Having listed the virtues of a gentleman so far, we should examine the relationship between the two kinds of virtues: moral and non-moral. It is clear that, according to Confucius, moral virtues are more important than non-moral virtues, in the sense that the former are the necessary qualities of a gentleman whereas the latter merely play a supplementary role. It also seems that the non-moral qualities are regarded as virtues only if they fulfill the requirement of morality. For example, courage becomes an anti-virtue if an action sprung from it violates *li* or *yi*.

> Zilu said, "Does the gentleman consider courage to be supreme?" The Master said, "For the gentleman it is *yi* that is considered supreme. Possessed of courage but devoid of *yi*, a gentleman will make trouble while a mean man will be a brigand."
>
> *Analects*, 17.23

> The Master said, "Unless a man has the spirit of *li*, in being respectful he will wear himself out, in being careful he will become timid, in having courage he will become unruly, and in being forthright he will become unrelenting."
>
> *Analects*, 8.2

> Yuzi said, "Of the things brought about by *li*, harmony is the most valuable. Of the ways of the Former Kings, this is the most beautiful, and is followed alike in matters great and small, yet this will not always work: to aim always at harmony without regulating it by *li* simply because one knows only about harmony will not, in fact, work."
>
> *Analects*, 1.12

Since the non-moral virtues themselves do not contain a moral dimension, i.e., do not automatically conform to the moral criteria, it is possible that their developments have been led in a wrong direction or by a wrong motivation and therefore become immoral. Immoral acts are definitely not allowed in every ethical system, even from a prudential point of view. Confucianism is no exception. Nevertheless, non-moral virtues are encouraged as long as they are not in conflict with morality. In the case of such conflict, non-moral virtues (leaving aside the question whether or not they are still virtues) have to be overridden by morality. In spite of the overriding status of morality, it is admitted that in Confucianism there is a non-moral realm independent of morality which constitutes a significant part of the ethical life.

The assertion just made is under an assumption that there is a clear distinction between the moral and non-moral virtues, as we have assumed in the previous part of this chapter. The distinction has been mentioned roughly as follows: a virtue is moral if an act which conforms to it is required (obligatory) and its violation is prohibited from a moral point of view; on the other hand, a virtue is non-moral if the observance of it is not obligatory and the non-compliance with it is not contrary to morality. According to this distinction, virtues like *ren*, *yi*, filial piety, fraternal duty, and integrity are moral ones and gentleness, clarity, generosity, harmony, and courage are non-moral. Hence a person is not obliged to possess the virtue of courage, and his/her lack of courage is not immoral.[13] However, the distinction is not as clear-cut as it might seem. For example, when one does not do what one ought to do because of the lack of courage, then this is an immoral character trait. In *Analects* 2.24 where Confucius interprets courage in terms of *yi*, he attributes to the former a moral sense. It follows that whether non-moral virtues can sustain its status as non-moral is subject to the judgment made from a moral point of view. This might lead to a view that the distinction between moral and non-moral virtues is made on a moral criterion. If it is really the case, then non-moral virtue is defined by morality and thus loses its independence. This is a problem I will turn to in the next section.

Ren, *yi* and virtues

> The Master said, "A man of virtue is sure to be the author of memorable sayings, but the author of memorable sayings is not necessarily virtuous. A man of *ren* is sure to possess courage, but a courageous man does not necessarily possess *ren*."
>
> *Analects*, 14.4

> The Master said, ". . . He cannot even be said to be wise. How can he be said to be *ren*?"
>
> *Analects*, 5.19

If we generalize the thought from the above passages, then we may say that a person of *ren* possesses other non-moral virtues such as clarity, trustworthiness, and thrift but a person with these virtues is not necessarily a person of *ren*. Here *ren* is understood as an all-inclusive virtue, and from this understanding it is natural to draw the conclusion that being *ren* implies the possession of non-moral virtues but not vice versa. However, if *ren* remains to be understood as signifying a moral virtue, then it seems true that the value of non-moral virtues consists in morality. This, together with the view reached in the last section that non-moral virtues are defined by morality, undermine the independency of non-moral virtues, which we have assumed in the beginning of this chapter.

As mentioned earlier in this chapter, *ren* and *yi* have been considered two important virtues since the time of late western Zhou. When *ren* is regarded as a virtue per se, it means love people (*ai ren* 愛人) (*Analects*, 12.22; *Mencius*, 4B28, 7A46), of which family love is the most important. For Mencius, family love can be extended to others in general and in this sense it has a moral significance. (*Mencius*, 4A27, 6B3, 7A15, and 7B24) Similarly, when *yi* is used to signify the obligatory relationship between ruler and subject, or the appropriateness of acquisitions judging from the social norms, it expresses a kind of virtue. (*Mencius*, 7A33; *Analects*, 14.12, 16.10, 19.1, 5.16) However, *ren-yi* has another meaning which exceeds the conventional content of a virtue. *Yi* which appeared in the following passage no longer means a virtue per se:

> Mencius said, "A great man need not keep his word nor does he necessarily see his action through to the end. He aims only at *yi*."
>
> *Mencius*, 4B11

Neither does *ren* in the two passages quoted in the beginning of this section. When *ren* and *yi* refer to "inclusive" virtues which give meanings to other virtues, they signify an ability by which one can decide on what one ought to do from an ethical point of view.

Although I have touched on the notions of ethics and morality in the beginning of this chapter, it is important to elaborate on their distinction and relation here. Making an ethical consideration of an action (or a decision, a choice, etc.) presupposes that the action concerned is regarded as making some contribution to the shaping of a good life. Hence when one considers an action from an ethical point of view in the form of a question "what should I do?", one is putting the question in a larger context in which the question "how should one live?" or "what is the good life?" is raised. Morality, which mainly deals with duties and obligations, may constitute part of the good life, but may not the whole of it. Therefore, the practical question "what should I do?" sustains both a moral and a non-moral sense. To follow Williams' usage, hereafter I will use "ethical" as the broad term to stand for the considerations that bear on answering the question "what should I do, all things considered?"; and "moral" as the narrower term to stand for a special system in which duties and obligations are examined.[14]

As the ability of deliberating on what one should do in general from an ethical point of view, *ren* and *yi* can also decide what weight of morality should be given in a particular situation. The following passage may shed some light on this issue:

> Mencius said, "Poverty does not constitute grounds for taking office, but there are times when a man takes office because of poverty. To have someone to look after his parents does not constitute grounds for marriage, but there are times when a man takes a wife for the sake of his parents. A man who takes office because of poverty chooses a low office in preference to a high one, an office with a small salary to one with a large salary. In such a case, what would be a suitable position to choose? That of a gate-keeper or a watchman . . ."
>
> *Mencius*, 5B5

When one considers what kind of job one is to choose, one may deliberate in a non-moral way, i.e., weighing the pros and cons for various non-moral reasons. However, if one starts thinking of the issue by asking the question whether it is good to take office, then one has to introduce the moral dimension because goodness comprises moral goodness and prudential goodness. It is noteworthy that raising the question in such a way is to consider the issue from a perspective which exceeds the empirical level of "what is" (e.g., the benefits that taking office promises). Since there is a maxim that one should not take office because of poverty, if one decides to do so one has to provide reasons for overriding this maxim. In such a case, "*quan*" (權) has been activated.[15] In the above passage, the question "What would be a suitable position to choose?" is no longer seeking a mere prudential decision, nor a mere normative one. This question presumes the admittance of the maxim, yet having been granted a special discretion for that particular situation. Nevertheless, the discretion has an implicit qualification that if a person takes office because of poverty, then he or she should take a low office. Therefore, that one should take the lowly position of a gatekeeper or a watchman is an ethical decision in a sense that it is made under a state that all things, including moral and prudential, have been considered.[16] The "all-inclusive" *ren* and *yi* bring one to think from this ethical perspective and thus do not signify moral virtues any more.

> Mencius said, "When it is permissible both to accept and not to accept, it is an abuse of integrity to accept. When it is permissible both to give and not to give, it is an abuse of generosity to give. When it is permissible both to die and not to die, it is an abuse of valour to die."
>
> *Mencius*, 4B23

From the above passage, we can take "generosity" as an example to illustrate the ethical perspective. If it were permissible both prudentially and morally to give and not to give, and if one is able to see that it may be an abuse of generosity to give, then one is viewing the matter in an ethical way because all things have been considered. Generosity is usually regarded as a non-moral virtue, and it is not a contravention of morality if it is not satisfied. Nevertheless, if it is deemed inappropriate to have the virtue of generosity tarnished then this consideration is neither merely from the moral point of view nor is it simply a point of view of prudence. In the following passage, *yi* means the ability for determining appropriateness from these two points of view.

> The Master said, "In his dealings with the world the gentleman is not invariably for or against anything. He is on the side of what is *yi*."
>
> *Analects*, 4.10

Similar cases can be found in *Mencius* where well-established social norms or rites are queried[17] and Mencius was able to offer solutions by appealing to *ren* and *yi*. Therefore, *ren-yi* should be conceived, apart from moral virtues, as an ability (which is possessed by the heart-mind (*xin*) of *ren-yi* 仁義之心) which helps to deliberate beyond the narrow sense of moral reasoning. We may call the deliberation both with moral and non-moral reasons "ethical reasoning."

As ethical reasoning is concerned with a particular problem in a particular situation, with particular agents, and has a particular choice to face, therefore, general principles are not always applicable. On the other hand, despite the fact that most virtues are qualities or dispositions of character which enable an agent to act appropriately in encountering others with whom he or she has special relations, or to perform suitably according to his or her special position, they are *generally* applicable in particular situations. Nevertheless, there are unusual cases which involve conflicts of actions both of which are prescribed by different virtues, and there are also cases for which the observance of virtues is not the most suitable thing to do. Mencius refers to such a situation when he says, "A great man need not keep his word nor does he necessarily see his action through to the end." (quoted above) In this situation, *yi* is the ultimate ground for all suitable decisions and is hence the ability of ethical reasoning. When Confucius says, "The gentleman has *yi* as his basic stuff . . ."[18] and "For the gentleman it is *yi* that is considered supreme . . ." (quoted above), *yi* is used in this sense. Again, the following passage is intelligible only if *ren-yi* is understood as such an ability.

> Mencius said, "A great man will not observe *li* that is contrary to *li*, nor will he perform *yi* that goes against *yi*."
>
> *Mencius*, 4B6

The first *li* refers to the rites followed by the mass and the second one refers to the spirit of *li*. Similarly, the first *yi* refers to the social norms for a particular role or position and the second one refers to the appropriateness as judged after all things have been considered. Apparently, the first *li* and *yi* signify moral virtues whereas the second ones signify the normative prescriptions that result from the ethical consideration. Similarly, in another passage, Mencius differentiates two kinds of practice of *ren-yi*, ". . . Shun . . . is performing from *ren-yi*, but not conforming to *ren-yi*." (*Mencius*, 4B19) Here "from *ren-yi*" definitely means "from the heart-mind of *ren-yi*," which is rooted in every human being. A gentleman is only the one who activates this ability and does ethical reasoning all the time.

Ren, the sage (*sheng ren* 聖人) and the supererogative requirement

As we have concluded, a gentleman is one who has been cultivated to do ethical reasoning well by the ability of *ren-yi*. In the following passage, Confucius claims that in order to be a gentleman, one has to start with "cultivating oneself with reverence" (*xiu ji yi jing* 修己以敬) and end in "cultivating oneself and thereby bringing peace and security to others (*xiu ji yi an ren* 修己以安人) (including one's fellow men and the people)."

> Zilu asked about the gentleman. The Master said, "He cultivates himself and thereby achieves reverence."
>
> "Is that all?"
>
> "He cultivates himself and thereby brings peace and security to his fellow men."
>
> "He cultivates himself and thereby brings peace and security to the people. Even Yao and Shun would have found the task of bringing peace and security to the people taxing."
>
> *Analects*, 14.42

"To cultivate oneself with reverence" is an embodiment of *ren* in oneself, and "to cultivate oneself and thereby bring peace and security to the people" is the embodiment of *ren* in others. The latter can be regarded as the final stage of the development of *ren* and the achievement of it is not only a gentleman's goal but it also brings him close to being a sage.

> Zikung said, "If there were a man who gave extensively to the common people and brought help to the multitude, what would you think of him? Could he be called *ren*?"
>
> The Master said, "It is no longer a matter of *ren* with such a man. If you must describe him, 'sage' is, perhaps, the right word. Even Yao and Shun would have found it difficult to accomplish as much. Now, on the other hand, a man with *ren* helps others to take their stand in that he himself wishes to take his stand, and gets other there in that he himself wishes to get there. The ability to take as analogy what is near at hand can be called the method of *ren*."
>
> *Analects*, 6.30

It seems that to become a sage is the ultimate aim for every gentleman. Nevertheless, at the time of Confucius, bringing peace and security to the people is a duty which can only be fulfilled by an emperor, and its fulfillment depends on external opportunities and conditions that cannot be controlled by one's own self. Besides, even an emperor may encounter various obstacles in fulfilling this duty. That is why Confucius exclaims that even Yao and Shun found the task taxing. In order to be a sage, apart from those conditions and obstacles in the external world that have to be met or overcome, one has to possess numerous moral and non-moral virtues. For ordinary people who are not in the position of an emperor, to develop the moral heart-mind of *ren-yi* so as to help others "take their stand," etc. is necessary for being a sage. According to Confucius, the cultivation of the moral mind and the transformation of the self, rather than the changing of the world, is of far greater importance for the achievement of human beings. Apart from the above-mentioned moral achievement, a sage should be a person with excellent cultivation in character.

Although the characteristics of a sage represent the ideal for Confucians, becoming a sage is not a moral requirement: failure to achieve this aim is not contrary to morality. To be a sage is better understood as a supererogative requirement, the satisfaction of which signifies both the moral and the prudential perfection, therefore the life of a sage is the best life. Most remarkably, according to Mencius, a sage can manifest himself or herself in various kinds of style. For instance, Boyi (伯夷) was the sage who was unsullied, Yiyin (伊尹) was the sage who accepted responsibility, Liu Xiahui (柳下惠) was the sage who was easy-going, Confucius was the sage whose actions were timely. (*Mencius*, 5B1, 2A9) In dealing with issues on serving the prince, ruling over people, taking and relinquishing office, they made very different decisions. Yet, "All were sages of old." (*Mencius*, 2A2) None of their decisions violates morality, and choosing the most appropriate ones in particular situations is made from a realm exceeding morality. To confer the honor of a sage to these different personalities means that they all fulfilled the requirement of a sage, i.e., they were leading ethically good lives. They had great moral achievements as well as excellent character. The latter is embodied in the non-moral values such as "unsullied" (*qing* 清), "accepting responsibility" (*ren* 任), "easy-going" (*he* 和), and "timely" (*shi* 時). Mencius expresses his preference: "It is my hope and wish to follow the example of Confucius" (as above), perhaps a sage whose actions were timely is the one who employs the heart-mind of *ren-yi* to do the ethical reasoning most tactfully.

The less than full-blooded sage is what is called a complete man (*cheng ren* 成人).

> Zilu asked about the complete man.
>
> The master said, "A man as wise as Zang Wuzhong, as free from desire as Meng Gongzhuo, as courageous as Zhuangzi of Bian and as accomplished as Ran Qiu, who is further refined by *li* and music, may be considered a complete man."
>
> *Analects*, 14.12

A complete man should possess virtues like wisdom, courage, accomplishment and be refined by *li* and music, all of which are non-moral virtues. Only "freedom from desire" can be regarded as a moral virtue. Therefore, it is obvious that even for a complete man, both the moral and the non-moral virtues are important. In the following passage where Confucius is making a remark about himself, art is considered as parallel to moral virtues.

> The Master said, "I set my heart on *Dao*, base myself on virtue, lean upon *ren* for support and take my recreation in the arts."
>
> *Analects*, 7.6

This can be viewed as more evidence that the non-moral virtues are not reducible to, or replaceable by morality.

Conclusion

It has been argued in this chapter that both moral and non-moral virtues are important for living a good life in Confucian ethics. According to Confucianism, a good life is embodied in the life of a gentleman, the complete man, and the sage. Although moral virtues are necessary for being a gentleman, they are not sufficient factors. It has also been shown that *ren-yi* is an essential quality of these characters, yet in some contexts it does not signify a narrow moral meaning. Rather, it means an ability by which ethical reasoning can be carried out. In ethical reasoning, moral as well as prudential reasons would be considered. Therefore, non-moral virtues belong to an independent realm which cannot be reduced to, or replaced by the realm of morality.

3

Confucian Ethics: Universalistic or Particularistic?

Four levels of Confucian ethics

Whether Confucian ethics is universalistic or particularistic has been a controversial topic since Chinese people started to critically review their own traditional culture in the later part of the nineteenth century. Sociologists, anthropologists, philosophers, and even novelists have been involved in this review. Strangely enough, however, its underlying question has never been well discussed: "What is Confucian ethics?" It remains unclear what we refer to when someone makes a thesis about Confucian ethics. Is it a bundle of conventions which Chinese people (in the ancient world as well as here and now) consistently and habitually follow? Is it a set of social norms established and enforced by emperors? Or, does it consist of virtues wedded to various roles? Is it, rather, a system of moral principles entangled with certain metaphysical assertions? Only when we make clear what we mean by Confucian ethics can we attribute to it an adjective such as "universalistic" or "particularistic." Also, answers to the above questions would carry different implications for theses such as "Confucian moral rules suppress human desire and so violate human nature," or "Confucian ethics legitimize class, age, and gender discrimination," or "Confucian ethics gave rise to capitalism in East Asia."

When the question "What is Confucian ethics?" is responded to in a less objectivistic and more functionalist manner, the result shows that its answer depends on our interpretation. In this sense, there are no absolutely right or wrong answers. If we look at the whole problem in this way, then we could agree with Max Weber that capitalism did not arise in China partly because Confucianism did not evoke the feeling of anxiety suffered by the Calvinists and, at the same time, accept that the virtue of being industrious in Confucian ethics has brought about the current prosperity of East Asian countries. However, this does not mean that we can freely assign any meaning to the term "Confucian ethics." Justifications, both historical and theoretical, are needed for any interpretation of Confucian ethics.

For the same reason stated above, it is important to make distinctions within Confucian ethics. Here I suggest it be divided into four levels, which contain the following elements: (1) the moral heart-mind; (2) ethical virtues and moral maxims; (3) institutional moral norms; and (4) customs and etiquette. I am going to examine the characteristics and distinctions of these four levels, and also show the relationships between them all in the remaining part of this section. At the first level, *ren* (仁) is considered as the sole ground and the ultimate authority of moral judgments. *Ren* being used in this level does not signify one of the many virtues, but rather is an ability of transference, which generates empathetic feeling and impartially distinguishes the good from the bad. *Ren* in this sense gives Confucian ethics its autonomous and altruistic nature.[1] Though *ren* is the transcendental ground of morality, it differs from moral principles as found in Western moral theories like utilitarianism. However, *ren* possesses the essential elements of all moral theories: universality and impartiality. To be sure, whether Confucian ethics is a moral theory requires closer scrutiny.[2]

The second level of Confucian ethics contains values and moral rules, which mainly inform the values of ritual propriety throughout history. Virtues and moral rules are necessary in a society to ensure a harmonious order. Different obligations are assigned to different roles, be they the role of a father in a family or that of a sovereign in a state. These obligations and moral rules are considered to be an objectification of *ren*. As they are required by the self and directed to the self, it is clear that their normative and yet unoppressive nature is guaranteed by *ren*, which demands reciprocity as well as autonomy. So, at the second level of Confucian ethics, people are guided to observe the established norms in order to act morally. Moreover, these norms can assist a person in becoming more morally cultivated. All of these represent the positive values of the second level Confucian ethics.

Inevitably any set of moral rules which are objectively established might be followed only for the sake of formality. In such cases, they are abstracted from their essential meaning and so remain a mere form. Lack of awareness of the spiritual meaning in practice means a decrease (if not a total loss) of moral values. In some extreme cases, these rules not only prevent liberation of the self, but suppress human beings (including oneself and other people). Then they become anti-human.

Obligations are not defined by the roles people happen to occupy, but rather are created to suit specific situations. In special cases Confucians even permit obligation to violate social norms set for various roles.[3] It has been indicated very clearly in the *Mencius* that "an action is moral not due to its apparent conformity to *ren* and *yi*, but due to its being motivated by the inner *ren* and *yi*."[4] This concept of morality presupposes a fundamental idea in Confucian ethics, i.e, human beings are capable of creating moral principles for themselves because *ren* is moral creativity in itself.[5] Now we may solve the problem as to whether Confucian ethics is an ethics of roles by answering it in the following way: it *is* an ethics of roles at the second level, but is *not* one at the first level. It is also clear now which level is primary and which one is derivative.[6]

At the second level, Confucians prescribe thousands of virtues and rites (there are three hundred proprieties and three thousand rites).[7] Some are more significant than others in a sense that they are derived from the basic concepts of Confucianism, such as in the relationship between humans and Heaven, the concept of person, and the idea of education.[8] Therefore, it is important to provide justification when one tries to assert that some particular virtues represent Confucian ethics. For instance, those who advocate the cultural explanation for the recent economic development in East Asia need to demonstrate that the virtue of diligence and the maxim "to glorify one's parents by gaining reputation for oneself," both of which stand as motivations for high achievement, are the distinguishing elements contained in Confucian ethics.[9]

As norms and rites prescribe actions in daily life, they are subject to change when the empirical factors alter. If they fail to fit into the contemporary situation, they may become fossilized and lose their original meaning. This does not mean that Confucian ethics is relativistic, since *ren* is the ultimate ground for an action being moral under any circumstance. Consequently, *ren* can serve as a detector for outdated norms and rites, which make people suffer when they are imposed. Similarly, moral conflicts among rules at the second level can also be resolved at the first level by *ren*.[10]

The third level of Confucian ethics can be understood as a kind of institutionalized ethics. Although it also represents itself by social norms, it gains its authoritative status through governing power. Substantial as well as informal punishments by the ruling system make the norms coercive. The second level differs from this one in that it is social, whereas this one is clearly political in nature.

Institutional Confucian ethics have always been condemned by people for its hierarchical, patriarchal, and authoritarian character. However, we have to distinguish two senses of institutional Confucian ethics. One is the realization of Confucian ethical values by a political system, and so it should be viewed as an extended objectification. This has been a Confucian project down through many centuries. Though it is controversial as to whether the extension of ethics into the political realm would undermine the independence of politics, it is less controversial that it would enhance ethical development for individuals as well as society as a whole if the government would manifest moral commitments. Nevertheless, it is a historical fact that a full-blooded Confucian State has never existed in the past two thousand years. The second meaning of institutional Confucian ethics refers to the ruling systems, which make use of ethical norms and ritual proprieties to support their authoritarian government. We can find many suppressive rules in the systems of marriage, family, and education under the name of Confucianism. However, we may test by *ren* whether a rule is only a disguise, just as we have done with the norms at the second level. Ethical rules which combine with institutional commands are effective. Such rules which lose their spiritual meaning are disastrous.

The fourth level is the conventional aspect of ethics. Convention, including customs and etiquette, concerns forms of life which have been developed and followed only half consciously.

Some scholars try to identify the "national character of the Chinese people" with certain qualities, supporting their claims with empirical research on people's inclinations, beliefs, and habits. Furthermore, they conclude that this national character was manufactured by Confucianism. Their assumption (sometimes hidden) is that Confucianism is the most dominant philosophy, therefore every phenomenon can be considered as more or less a result of it.[11] But when we trace the origins of these conventions, we find that some of them sprang from myths and legends. Some were connected with agricultural, geographical, or climatic factors in the environment. Some even arose from a primitive state of mind, which is common to many ethnic groups. Since most of the customs and forms of etiquette are performed without the consciousness of their meaning, it is difficult to decide whether we may properly attribute the term "Confucian" to them. People commit the same error when they try to identify Chinese culture with Confucianism by citing some customs as evidence. I am not refuting any association of this kind, but we have to set up criteria for verification before making any justified conclusion. We should be more cautious, especially when claiming a causal relationship between them.

Although a Confucian might allow that there are times when "common folks apply the principles without knowing them,"[12] he would not consider it as the highest moral achievement. This state is only commendable if it is understood as an effect of moral cultivation for the society as a whole. In this sense, I accept that people who are consciously following the Confucian moral teachings without knowing that those teachings are originated from Confucius or Mencius can be referred to as Confucians, but feel dubious about whether people can be Confucians if they do not even recognize the meaning of their action.[13] What is essential is that Confucianism is not any kind of simple behaviorism. On the contrary, according to it, the value of an action is mainly determined by the meaning which the agent assigns to it. Therefore, in principle we cannot detect a Confucian by his external behavior *alone*. However, I do not maintain that the world of ideas and that of customs are completely separate. As Confucians believe that *Dao* should be realized by human beings in daily life, "Confucian conventions" can be viewed as moral devices which manifest a Confucian spirit. But only when people are aware of their ethical meanings can it fulfill their ethical functions properly. Therefore, we can reaffirm that self-consciousness and subjectivity are emphasized by subjectivist value systems like Confucianism.

Rites and etiquette are both rule systems, often followed only habitually. Rites and etiquette differ from each other in that there is a moral connotation in the former. Etiquette may emerge on aesthetic, prudential, or even expedient bases. On the other hand, rites usually embody certain moral principles. The differential factors just mentioned can be used to distinguish between the fourth and the second level.

Having attempted to make clear the distinctions within Confucian ethics, there remains the problem of how these levels relate to each other. Ideally speaking, a Confucian who fully embraces *ren* should embody it at the level of rites, institutions, and customs, and so reach a perfect situation. The relationship between the first level and the others resembles that between a philosophy and its application. Certainly this situation rarely occurs. For a less than ideal situation, rites and conventions are performed without people being fully aware of their spiritual meaning, so that they simply serve as means for certain purposes under specific conditions. The tie connecting these different levels of Confucian ethics has consequently been loosened. It is an open question in contemporary Chinese society as to what extent Confucian ethics at the first level is applied in daily life through the systems of rites, institution, and customs, just as there is a question as to what extent an idea (or a belief) can influence one's behavior. The problem becomes more complicated when the influential factors are not confined to one school of thought, or even to any spiritual elements.

Generality and universality

If it is agreed that there are different levels within Confucian ethics, we should consider the question of universality in respect to each level. Before entering this discussion, I would like to clarify the key concept of "universality." In normal usage, a rule is considered to be synonymous with a guideline characterized by a high degree of generality. A highly general rule is one which can be applied to a great deal of similar cases and is most probably valid. Normally, the fewer the specific conditions a rule contains, the more situations it can be applied to. For instance, if a Confucian-designed rite contains elements, which refer to a specific society in a certain period, it would probably need a review when the social structure has changed. Similarly, social norms which combine with specific institutional rules might cause alienation to people after a political reform. Customs and etiquette which usually characterize a specific culture are so concrete that they vary from time to time as well as from place to place. So people might conclude that since the Confucian ethical rules at all levels except the first are more or less specific, they therefore can reach only a certain degree of universality. But as we shall see later, this conclusion is wrong due to a confusion between the concepts of universality and generality.

A certain degree of universality surely is not what a universalist aims at. A universal principle is the one which is constantly valid regardless of any spatial-temporal changes. However, universalism is always defeated for its incapability to produce such a universal principle. According to Zygmunt Bauman, moral universalism is a project for modern thinkers.

> It was a characteristic, perhaps the defining, feature of modernity that the aporia was played down as a conflict not-yet-resolved-but-in-principle-resolvable . . .
>
> Modern ethical thought in co-operation with modern legislative practice fought its way through to such a radical solution under the twin banners of *universality* and *foundation* . . .
>
> In other words, the moral thought and practice of modernity was animated by the belief in the possibility of a *non-ambivalent, non-aporetic ethical code.* Perhaps such a code has not been found yet. But it surely waits round the next comer. Or the corner after next.[14]

Nevertheless, from the postmodern view (as Bauman defines it) the works of modern ethical thinkers are wasteful since they can never succeed.

> It is the *disbelief* in such a possibility that is *post*modern . . .
>
> An ethics that is universal and "objectively founded," is a practical impossibility; perhaps also an *oxymoron*, a contradiction in terms.[15]

Apart from the impossibility in practice, Bauman rejects the "universalization of morality" because it will silence the moral impulse and channel moral capacities to "socially designed targets that may, and do, include immoral purposes."[16] Therefore, following Bauman's research and his understanding of the pitfalls of modem universalism, universality is not even an ideal worth aiming for.

> Philosophers defined universality as that feature of ethical prescriptions which compelled every human creature, just for the fact of being a human creature, to recognize it as right and thus to accept it as obligatory.

> If the moral conduct is expressed in rules in universal form, then "the moral selves may be dissolved in the all-embracing 'we'—the moral 'I' being just a singular form of the ethical 'us.' And that within this ethical 'we,' 'I' is exchangeable with 'she or he.'"[17]

The basic idea of morality for Bauman is that everyone is an irreplaceable moral subject, the relations between one and the others are asymmetrical and so irreversible, and moral prescriptions are not-asking-for-reciprocation commands. It follows that every moral event is so unique that general rules can never apply to it appropriately.

> In a moral relationship, I and the Other are not exchangeable, and thus cannot be "added up" to form a plural "we." In a moral relationship, all the "duties" and "rules" that may be conceived are addressed solely to me, bind only me, constitute me and me alone as an "I." When addressed to me, responsibility is moral. It may well lose its moral content completely the moment I try to turn it around to bind the Other.
>
> It is this uniqueness (not "generalizability"), and this non-reversibility of my responsibility, which puts me in the moral relationships.[18]

A general rule is one that will be applied to situations from which all particular features have been abstracted. However, Bauman holds that these particular features are what is most relevant for moral consideration. A moral decision from my stand point would be different from that from others' stand points. Now it is quite clear that the universality that Bauman rejected is one embedded in a sense of "generality." As discussed above, the "general" is contrary to the "specific." Therefore, general ("universal" to a certain degree) rules cannot be applied to any specific moral events.

To a certain extent, I accept the uniqueness of responsibility Bauman maintains. Nevertheless, even if it is agreed that some specific features are relevant for moral consideration, it does not necessarily follow that universality can never be achieved. For instance, according to R.M. Hare, a moral judgment can be universal as well as highly specific. The concept of universality for Hare is that the same judgments are to be made on identical cases.[19] Certainly "no two situations and no two people are ever exactly like each other" in the actual world.[20] Being aware of this, Hare suggests the same moral judgments may be applied to a role-reversed hypothetical situation,[21] where moral judgments are being made the same way in all respects except the roles of the two parties have been reversed. This does not mean that "I" and the "Other" are exchangeable in the sense that Bauman rejects. Universalization consists in putting oneself into other's shoes, which not only requires putting oneself into an other's position and having his or her relationship with other people. In addition, it requires imagining oneself to have the other's personal characteristics, his or her motivational states and preferences.

> It follows from universalizability that if I now say that I ought to do a certain thing to a certain person, I am committed to the view that the very same thing ought to be done to me, were I in exactly his situation, including having the same personal characteristics and in particular the same motivational states.[22]

A moral judgment which has been universalized should be one accepted both in actual and hypothetical situations. Therefore, universality does not require reciprocity (a stipulation that I should do the same thing to others just as the others do to me and vice versa), but asks one to make the same moral judgment were he in the other's situation. "The statement that I ought to do it to him commits me to the view that it ought to be done to me, were I in his situation."[23] This conception of universality and its implications are compatible with Bauman's following claim:

> The moral person and the object of that person's concern cannot be measured by the same yardstick—and this realization is precisely what makes the moral person moral.[24]

It is also agreeable with the view that:

> The readiness to sacrifice for the sake of the other burdens me with the responsibility which is *moral* precisely for my acceptance that the command to sacrifice applies to me and me only, that the sacrifice is not a matter of exchange or reciprocation of services, that the command is not *universalizable* and thus cannot be shrugged off my shoulders so that it falls on someone else's.[25]

However, the command to sacrifice does apply to the other if he has the same moral impulse as I do and so he himself accepts this command. The command therefore is universalizable in a sense that it applies to identical cases.

The meaning of universality which Hare suggests, namely, that same judgments should be made to the identical cases, can be viewed as universality in the strict sense. Universality in this sense, considered as a requirement of moral judgments, not only can be accepted by Bauman because it does not undermine the *moral* feature of responsibilities, but should also be the unique meaning which the universalist can uphold.

Returning to our main theme, we can now assert that Confucian ethics at the first level is *universal* in the strict sense. When the heart-mind of *ren* is activated and the transference takes place, then it would ask one to put oneself into another's shoes and consider the other's interests, desires, and preferences impartially, as if they were one's own. This is a moral requirement, which can be universally applied to any situations regardless of time and space. Moral rules and prescriptions (e.g., the five virtues) which can be justified by *ren* and so can be accepted by the parties involved after the role-reversed test, are also universal in this sense. Because these rules possess universality, they also gain the property of reciprocity. Nevertheless, since moral rules at the second and third levels sometimes cannot be justified by *ren*, in those cases they cannot obtain this universality and so only hold a certain degree of validity. Although they are not universal, they are always expressed in a general form in order to be applied in normal cases. However, there might be special cases in which these rules cannot apply. In such cases, rules would become suppressive when they are implemented coercively. The requirement of reciprocation embedded in rules per se would become unreasonable when they are in conflict with *ren*. Now we can understand more clearly Bauman's reason for rejecting moral rules as a whole when he states in the following passage:

> Were I to look for standards by which my moral responsibility ought to be measured to match my moral impulse, I would not find them in the rules which I may reasonably demand others to follow.[26]

After clarifying the concept of universality and distinguishing different levels of Confucian ethics, now we can maintain a strict sense of universality as a requirement for moral principles, without refuting the autonomy and uniqueness of responsibility emphasized by Bauman. We can also attribute a "universalistic" quality to Confucian ethics without further discourse.[27]

4

The Resolution of Moral Dilemma—From the Confucian Perspective

Introduction

Richard Hare gives a very clear exposition of moral conflict: moral conflict occurs in a particular situation when the actions prescribed by two different moral principles in an ethical system cannot be taken at the same time.[1] This exposition has been widely accepted and used during the discussions of the problem concerning moral conflicts or moral dilemmas. In the recent discussions, the problem whether there is inescapable wrongdoing when a moral dilemma occurs has been raised.[2] This is a more basic problem compared with the problem of how to resolve moral conflicts since the latter presupposes a specific answer to the former, i.e., moral conflicts are resolvable hence there is no inescapable wrongdoing.[3] Although I shall refrain from joining in the debate, I will try to examine the position of Confucianism in this matter.[4]

In this chapter I am going to introduce the characteristic of Confucian virtue system, and some of the misunderstandings about it will be clarified. I will go on to discuss a kind of dilemma that involves moral and non-moral values, which resembles the kind that MacIntyre has excluded from the "genuine moral dilemma." Although the possible conflict between moral and non-moral values does not constitute a moral dilemma as such, the significance of non-moral virtues in Confucian ethics renders the discussion essential. The subsequent section examines how moral dilemma is viewed in Confucian ethics. As "Confucianism" covers a number of schools, each of which developed various theses over centuries, I shall confine this study to the teachings of Confucius and Mencius.

Confucian virtue system

In order to avoid unnecessary confusions, it would be useful to outline the Confucian system of virtues before entering into the main theme. According to Confucianism, there are numerous virtues which constitute a coherent system in which no two virtues are in conflict. Among the various virtues, *ren* seems to be the most important one. It can be achieved if, and only if, other virtues are satisfied. For example,

> The Master said, "... A man of *ren* is sure to possess courage, but a courageous man does not necessarily possess *ren*."
>
> *Analects*, 14.4

> ... He cannot even be said to be wise. How can he be said to be *ren*?
>
> *Analects*, 5.19

> Zizhang asked Confucius about *ren*.
>
> Confucius said, "There are five things and whoever is capable of putting them into practice in the Empire is certainly '*ren*.'"
>
> "May I ask what they are?"
>
> "They are respectfulness, tolerance, trustworthiness in word, quickness and generosity ..."
>
> *Analects*, 17.6

In this sense *ren* signifies a state of moral perfection which rests on the possession of all virtues. Hence, *ren* is not a single virtue, but rather an all-in-one virtue. Therefore, *ren* in this sense should not be considered as a virtue proper.

However, it should be noted that there is another sense of *ren* in which *ren* and other virtues are complementary to each other. In this sense, a morally perfect person should possess a complete set of virtues in which *ren* is only one of its elements. Therefore, if an agent neglects the other virtues, it would cause defects in his or her moral achievement even if he or she possesses *ren*. The following are examples illustrating this sense.

> The Master said, "Yu, have you heard of the six qualities and the six attendant faults?"
>
> "No."
>
> "Be seated and I shall tell you. To love *ren* without loving learning is liable to lead to foolishness. To love cleverness without loving learning is liable to lead to deviation from the right path. To love trustworthiness in word without loving learning is liable to lead to harmful behaviour. To love forthrightness without loving learning is liable to lead to insubordination. To love unbending strength without loving learning is liable to lead to indiscipline."
>
> *Analects*, 17.8

These "six qualities" are six kinds of virtues, each of which contributes significantly to the moral life, but none of them is sufficient in itself.

> The Master said, "What is within the reach of a man's understanding but beyond the power of his *ren* to keep is something he will lose even if he acquires it. A man may be wise enough to attain it and be *ren* enough to keep it, but if he does not rule over them with dignity, then the common people will not be reverent. A man may be wise enough to attain it, be *ren* enough to keep it and may govern the people with dignity, but if he does not set them to work in accordance with *li* (proprieties), he is still short of perfection."
>
> *Analects*, 15.33

This passage shows that *ren*, wisdom, and *li* are necessary in order to achieve perfection. Each of them has its own function according to its specific content.

Apart from *ren*, *li* is another virtue worth mentioning. *Li* signifies the virtue of being considerate and it aims at a state of orderliness. Because of its character, it is frequently confused with rites (which is the form of proprieties) or etiquette (which is called *yi* (儀)). However, *li* as a virtue has a moral connotation and its morality is grounded in human nature. This feature distinguishes *li* from rites and etiquette. This is particularly relevant to our theme here because rites and etiquette are mostly conventional, and they can be overridden by virtues, either *li* or others. In this instance, no dilemmas are involved.

> The Master said, "A ceremonial cap of linen is what is prescribed by the rites. Today black silk is used instead. This is more frugal and I follow the majority. To prostrate oneself before ascending the steps is what is prescribed by the rites. Today one does so after having ascended them. This is casual and, though going against the majority, I follow the practice of bowing before ascending."
>
> *Analects*, 9.3

The former part of this passage shows that the virtue of frugality (*jian* 儉) can override conventional rites, whereas the latter part shows that some rites should be observed if they are justifiable.

From Mencius' point of view, social norms and rites can be overridden by moral judgments in special cases. In such cases, one is free to use one's discretion, but again, there is no moral dilemma.

> Chunyu Kun said, "Is it prescribed by the rites that, in giving and receiving, a man and a woman should not touch each other?"
>
> "It is," said Mencius.
>
> "When one's sister-in-law is drowning, does one stretch out a hand to help her?"
>
> "Not to help a sister-in-law who is drowning is to be a brute. It is prescribed by the rites that, in giving and receiving, a man and a woman should not touch each other, but in stretching out a helping hand to the drowning sister-in-law one is exercising one's discretion."
>
> *Mencius*, 4A17[5]

In the Confucian system of virtues, there is no apparent hierarchy of virtues. Therefore, in cases of conflict of virtues, one cannot choose the "right" virtue by appealing to the hierarchy. *Ren* in one of its senses looks as if it is more important than the other virtues but in this particular sense *ren* does not signify a virtue at all. When *ren* is understood as a virtue of "family love,"[6] for instance, it is not the highest virtue and can be overridden.[7] Same with *yi* (義). Therefore, it is a misconception that *ren* and *yi* are two overriding virtues which are "higher" than the others. Regarding the special status of *yi*, one might cite the following passage as evidence of its high status:

> Mencius said, "A great man need not keep his word nor does he necessarily see his action through to the end. He aims only at being *yi*."
>
> *Mencius*, 4B11

In this passage, it appears that *yi* overrides the virtue of trustworthiness in words, but here *yi* has a denotation other than a sort of virtue to which I would come back later. As a virtue, the weight of *yi* is equal to the other virtues.

> Zizhang said, "One can, perhaps, be satisfied with a gentleman who is ready to lay down his life in the face of dangers, who does not forget what is *yi* at the sight of gain, and who does not forget reverence during a sacrifice nor sorrow while in mourning."
>
> *Analects*, 19.1

> Confucius said, "There are nine things the gentleman turns his thought to: to seeing clearly when he uses his eyes, to hearing acutely when he uses his ears, to looking cordial when it comes to his countenance, to being conscientious when he speaks, to being reverent when he performs his duties, to seeking advice when he is in doubt, to bear in mind the consequences when he is enraged, and to what is *yi* at the sight of gain."
>
> *Analects*, 16.10

In these two passages, *yi* means appropriateness in receiving or gaining benefits.[8] As a virtue, it also means a proper relationship between the prince and subject.

> Mencius said, ". . . The way *ren* pertains to the relation between father and son, *yi* to the relation between prince and subject, the rites to the relation between guest and host, wisdom to the good and wise man, the sage to the way of Heaven, is the Decree, but therein also lies human nature. That is why the gentleman does not describe it as Decree."
>
> *Mencius*, 7B24[9]

From this discussion, it is clear that virtues are specific to the aspects of performance in daily life. Therefore, one virtue cannot be replaced by another.

Pseudo moral dilemmas

MacIntyre distinguishes two kinds of case which obfuscates the discussion of genuine moral dilemmas.[10] The first is that of everyday conflict of duties which can be resolved by skillful management. His example is, "My commitment to attend my friend's concert conflicts with my duty to return my student's papers, duly corrected, by the assigned date."[11] The second kind of case is one in which someone says he could only save one of two persons drowning.[12] MacIntyre claims that there is no dilemma at all. We may call these two cases "pseudo moral dilemmas."

Mencius once discussed an example of conflict of duties which resembles the first kind of case in MacIntyre's classification. In the following passage, Mencius instructs his student Gongduzi on how to respond to such a conflict.[13]

> Mencius said, "[Ask him,] 'Whom do you respect more, your uncle or your younger brother?' He will say, 'My uncle.' 'When your younger brother is impersonating an

> ancestor at a sacrifice, then whom do you respect?' He will say, 'My younger brother.' You ask him, 'What has happened to your respect for your uncle?' He will say, 'It is because of the position my younger brother occupies.'"
>
> *Mencius*, 6A5

To resolve the conflict of duties (if there is any conflict at all), a priority principle which is based on one's position is introduced here (i.e., when one's younger brother is impersonating an ancestor at a sacrifice, one should respect him more than one's uncle). Although one may query the validity of the resolution, in Mencius' view, this case does not represent a moral dilemma.

Apart from the kind of conflict mentioned here, there are always conflicts between non-moral values and moral virtues. Non-moral values include wealth, high station, honor, and ease, etc. which almost every human being desires. However, in Confucian ethics they are overridden by morality.

> The Master said, "Wealth and high station are what men desire but unless I attain them in the right way I would not remain in them. Poverty and low station are what men dislike, but even if I did not acquire them in the right way I would not try to escape from them . . ."
>
> *Analects*, 4.5

> Mencius said, "The way the mouth is disposed towards tastes, the eye towards colours, the ear towards sounds, the nose towards smells, and the four limbs towards ease is human nature, yet therein also lies the Decree. That is why a gentleman does not describe it as nature . . ."
>
> *Mencius*, 7B24

As a human being, one certainly has natural desires for such things as delicious food, beautiful colors, music, etc. but one also has "oughts." In addition, these oughts or morality are inherent in human beings and make them distinguishable from, and superior to, animals. Thus, a gentleman would conceive morality, rather than their desires, as human nature. That is to say, so long as one considers oneself a human being, then one resolves that one's desires should be governed by morality.

> Gongduzi asked, "Though equally human, why are some men greater than others?"
>
> "He who is guided by the interests of the parts of his person that are of greater importance is a great man; he who is guided by the interests of the parts of his person that are of smaller importance is a small (mean) man."
>
> "Though equally human, why are some men guided one way and others guided another way?"
>
> "The organs of hearing and sight are unable to think and can be misled by external things. When one thing acts on another, all it does is to attract it. The organ of the mind can think. But it will find the answer only if it does think; otherwise, it will not find the answer. This is what Heaven has given me . . ."
>
> *Mencius*, 6A15

The "mind" and "think" in this passage signify the moral heart-mind and moral thinking correspondingly. This passage brings out a message that in order to be a great man, one should be guided by one's heart-mind, rather than by one's desires. Among all the various desires, the preservation of life is always conceived as the most basic and important desire. However, from a Confucian viewpoint, even life can be sacrificed if it conflicts with morality.

> Mencius said, "... Life is what I want; *yi* is also what I want. If I cannot have both, I would rather take *yi* than life ... In other words, there are things a man wants more than life and there are also things he loathes more than death. This is an attitude not confined to the moral man but is common to all men. The moral man simply never loses it ..."
>
> *Mencius*, 6A10

Now it can be concluded that there are no moral dilemmas involving non-moral values and morality in the sense that the conflict is irresolvable. Similarly, there are no conflicts of non-moral virtues and moral virtues. Non-moral virtues can be conceived as admirable character traits which can promote non-moral values.

> Confucius said, "... If a man is respectful (恭) he will not be treated with insolence (不侮). If he is tolerant (寬) he will win over the multitude (得眾). If he is trustworthy in word (信) his fellow men will entrust him with responsibility (人任). If he is quick (敏) he will achieve results (有功). If he is generous (惠) he will be good enough to be put in a position over his fellow men (使人)."
>
> *Analects*, 17.6

Insolence, winning over the multitude, entrustment, etc. are non-moral values, and being respectful, tolerant, trustworthy in word, quick, and generous are admirable character traits which would promote those values and are thus virtues commended by Confucians.[14] These virtues are compatible with moral virtues.[15] Furthermore, they would become moral virtues when they have made contributions to one's moral life. In such cases, these non-moral virtues transform themselves from being morally permissible to being morally obligatory. For example, in the former part of the above passage (i.e., Zizhang's query about *ren* which was cited in the previous section), the performance of respectfulness, tolerance, trustworthiness in word, quickness, and generosity would together constitute the greatest moral achievement—*ren*. In such a connection, these virtues are moral ones.[16]

Genuine moral dilemmas

One of the types of moral dilemma which MacIntyre describes is that of someone who, having assumed or been assigned the responsibilities of more than one social role, discovers that to discharge the responsibilities of one will prevent him or her from discharging those of the other. This kind of role conflict (as well as the other types) is considered by MacIntyre as a genuine dilemma since "what is taken to be morally at stake could not be more considerable; which alternative the person chooses determines what wrong they will have done ... and for what therefore he or she will have to acknowledge a guilt appropriately expressed in guilty feeling."[17] A case of this type can be found in *Mencius*:

> Taoying asked, "When Shun was Emperor and Gaoyao was the judge, if the Blind Man killed a man, what was to be done?"
>
> "The only thing to do was to apprehend him."
>
> "In that case, would Shun not try to stop it."
>
> "How could Shun stop it? Gaoyao had authority for what he did."
>
> "Then what would Shun have done?"
>
> "Shun looked upon casting aside the Empire as no more than discarding a worn shoe. He would have secretly carried the old man on his back and fled to the edge of the Sea and lived there happily, never giving a thought to the Empire."
>
> *Mencius*, 7A35[18]

Shun, being the emperor, had the responsibility of apprehending a murderer, whereas in the role of a son, he had the responsibility of serving his father (the Blind Man); in the hypothetical case brought out by Mencius' student, Taoying, Shun had dual responsibilities which he could not fulfill at the same time. Moreover, such a conflict could not have been resolved by any skillful management. In MacIntyre's words, "Now that it has occurred, there is no way to act without someone being gravely wronged. No course of right action appears to be possible."[19] This is the meaning of "inescapable moral wrongdoing." However, from the above passage, we cannot arrive at the conclusion that Confucians admit the existence of inescapable moral wrongdoing. In fact, I am going to argue for a contrary conclusion.

First of all, the way of resolving the conflict which Shun chooses is by abolishing one of the responsibilities, i.e., the responsibility of apprehending a murderer. Since the responsibility just mentioned is derived from the role of an emperor, he can resolve the conflict by abandoning the role together with the responsibility derived from it. Incidentally, in the world as it was, there was a place (which is, in this case, "the edge of the Sea") where one could escape from the law. In such a case, there is no moral dilemma.[20]

Nevertheless, as the resolution in question depends on the possibility of abandoning the role one occupies, it follows that if neither of those roles can be abandoned, then the conflicts cannot be resolved. In fact, there are roles which one cannot abandon, the role of a son and the role of a parent (once one has occupied these roles) are two obvious ones. Still, it remains a problem in the case of conflict, i.e., which one of the two roles should be abandoned. In Shun's case, he chose to abandon the role of an emperor simply because it could be abandoned while the other could not. Among the roles that cannot be abandoned, they can be divided into two kinds: one is that entailed by our being human beings and the other is the role occupied by someone incidentally in the world as it is. The former kind is exemplified by the role of a son and the latter by the role of a citizen.

It is clear by now that when two role responsibilities come into conflict, if one of the roles can be abandoned and the other cannot, then the responsibility derived from the former role has to be overridden by its counterpart, as is shown in Shun's decision. From this discussion, it is natural to think that a genuine dilemma might occur when neither of the roles can be abandoned, notwithstanding that: (1) they are both entailed by human beings as such, or, (2) both roles are of the kind which one occupies incidentally in the world as it is, or, (3) one of the roles belongs to the first kind and the other belongs to the second kind. We might understand Mencius' position on the possibility of moral dilemmas from the following passage:

> Mencius said, "Who are the most important people we should serve? One's parents. What is the most important thing to watch over? One's own character. I have heard of a man who, not allowing his character to be morally corrupted, is able to discharge his duties of serving his parents; but I have not heard of a morally corrupt person who is able to do so . . ."
>
> *Mencius*, 4A19

Here Mencius claims unambiguously that watching over one's character in order not to allow it to go against morality is more important than serving one's parents. This is so because being moral is a necessary condition for one to serve one's parents well. Although serving one's parents is a duty derived from a role which is entailed by one's being a human being, yet being moral is essential for one to be a human being (at least for one to consider oneself as a human being).[21] Therefore, to be a moral self is the most basic and important responsibility if one is a human being. All the other responsibilities derived from the roles should be overridden by it.

At this point one might argue that all the moral virtues are designed and practised for an agent to achieve a higher moral standard, therefore, the "basic" responsibility mentioned above is actually embodied in the possession of every particular moral virtue. Furthermore, the only way of fulfilling the former depends on the latter. In this sense, as it has been asserted earlier, no virtue is higher than the other so far as they all contribute to the moral life. If this reflects the true picture of Confucianism, then for Confucianism there *are* irresolvable moral conflicts.

In order to expose the viewpoint of Confucianism, we have to closely scrutinize the nature and function of moral virtues in Confucian ethics. In our previous discussion, it is assumed that moral responsibilities can be derived from one's role. Truly, we can find strong evidence to support this claim, e.g., the responsibility of serving one's parents well is derived from the role of a son, and respect for one's younger brother because he is impersonating an ancestor. But since these responsibilities which are derived from roles (no matter whether they can or cannot be abandoned) can be overridden, they should be considered as merely prima facie responsibilities.[22] Moral responsibilities, moral virtues, as well as moral principles, even if they are prima facie, are set up for people to fulfil or observe in normal circumstances. The crucial point is that it is not the role or position that decides one's prima facie responsibility, but rather, the heart-mind[23] which determines what should be done when one takes up a certain role. This idea is implicit in Mencius' autonomous philosophy, and expressed explicitly in his claim that *ren* and *yi* are internal.

> "Why do you say," asked Mencius, "that *ren* is internal and *yi* is external?"
>
> "That man there is old and I treat him as an elder. He owes nothing of his elderliness to me, just as in treating him as white because he is white I only do so because of his whiteness which is external to me. That is why I call it external."
>
> "The case of rightness is different from that of whiteness. 'Treating as white' is the same whether one is treating a horse as white or a man as white. But I wonder if you would think that 'treating as old' is the same whether one is treating a horse as old or a man as an elder? Furthermore, is it the one who is old that is *yi*, or is it the one who treats him as an elder who is *yi*?"
>
> *Mencius*, 6A4

In Confucian ethics, there is a basic belief that one can activate one's heart-mind to set up the prima facie responsibility and hence the moral virtue for a certain role, and one can also use one's discretion on some unusual occasion, as shown in the discussion of "ceremonial cap" and "drowning sister-in-law." Similarly one can judge by one's heart-mind which prima facie responsibility should be overridden or, which role should be abandoned, in case of conflict. This is because Confucians think that not only is the moral heart-mind able to establish general moral principles for ordinary practice, it can also make particular judgments for a specific situation. In a specific situation, all conditions are *given*. A situation with conflicting prima facie responsibilities is a special instance of such specific situations. The main concern of moral heart-mind is not whether an act conforms to the requirement of virtues, rather, whether an act is in accordance with morality, the latter of which can only be judged by the moral heart-mind itself.

We have pointed out that *yi* does not signify a kind of virtue in the passage cited in the second section: "A great man need not keep his word nor does he necessarily see his action through to the end. He aims only at *yi*." (*Mencius*, 4B11) It is now appropriate to clarify the meaning of *yi* in this passage since this meaning is relevant to our present discussion. *Yi* in such a context is equivalent to "being obligatory" or "being morally right." Mencius in this passage claims clearly that to be morally right is more important than fulfilling the requirements of moral virtues. *Yi* in this sense is frequently used in the *Analects* as well as in *Mencius*. For example:

> The Master said, "The gentleman has *yi* as his basic stuff and by observing *li* he puts it into practice, by being modest he gives it expression, and by being trustworthy in word he brings it to completion. Such is a gentleman indeed!"
>
> *Analects*, 15.18

> Mencius said, "... *Ren* is man's peaceful abode and *yi* his proper path ..."
>
> *Mencius*, 4A10[24]

Apparently *yi* conceived as a virtue is subordinate to this sense of *yi*. Therefore, in cases of moral conflict, one can resolve the problem by activating one's moral heart-mind so as to make judgments which is *yi* (obligatory). In such a case, although one (even more) of the prima facie responsibilities would not be fulfilled, there should not be any wrongdoing. It is because one judges what should be done, all things considered, in that special occasion, and does it accordingly. Finally, a statement uttered by Confucius may conclude the position of Confucians on this matter: "They sought *ren* and got it. So why should they have any complaints?" (*Analects*, 7.15).

Conclusion

From the above discussion, it is clear that, according to Confucian ethics, all moral dilemmas can be resolved. The resolvability fully depends on the ability of the moral heart-mind which is rooted universally in the human nature. This ability is not separate from the ability of establishing moral principles or moral virtues. Besides, it is the same ability of making moral judgment since to make a moral judgment means to make a morally right decision in a particular situation for a particular person. This may include an act of rule-following or even rule-creating. Every autonomous ethical system must assume such kind of ability, no matter it is called practical reason, moral heart-mind, or anything else.

The assertion that an irresolvable moral dilemma entails an inescapable wrongdoing is usually based on a view of moral realism. From the moral realistic perspective, when an action is prescribed by a moral principle, this prescription reveals a moral truth (viz. the action in question should be done). But in a special situation when it is judged that doing that action is morally wrong, then the corresponding truth cannot be realized. Hence there is a wrongdoing. This view overlooks the fact that the (presumed) moral truth is not universally valid but only so in the normal situations. In the extraordinary situation, if it is judged that the observance of a moral principle is not the right thing to do, then the "truth" should be abandoned in that particular case. Even though the abandonment is inescapable, yet no wrongdoing is involved. This again assumes the ability of judging whether it is right to follow the principle. The way that Confucian ethics attempts to resolve the moral dilemmas is nothing other than judging the conflicting prescriptions by the moral ability mentioned above.

In Western ethics, the way of resolving moral dilemmas proposed by principled ethics is quite different from that by situation ethics. The former can best be represented by utilitarianism. Although utilitarianism can resolve moral dilemmas by the principle of utility, it has to face many challenges in order to maintain a justifiable system.[25] Systems of principled ethics other than utilitarianism have been criticized on grounds that the ethical principles they propose are too abstract to apply in particular situations.[26] On the other hand, situation ethics claims to be able to make particular judgments for particular situations, therefore it avoids moral dilemmas from the very beginning.[27] However, it has not made an explicit claim on this moral ability. Confucian ethics, as we have shown, asserts the significance of general moral principles (or virtues) on the one hand, and also affirms the ability of making particular moral judgments in extraordinary situations such as moral dilemmas on the other. Most remarkably, the ability mentioned comes from the same faculty of establishing moral principles.

5

The Unity of Heaven and Man: A New Interpretation

Tracing back to Mencius

It is beyond debate that "the unity of Heaven and man (*tian ren he yi*天人合一)" is the core concept of Confucianism. However, no statements or words to that effect explicitly appear in *The Analects*. In *Mencius*, the closest meaning to the unity of Heaven and man is "apprehending Heaven" (*zhi tian*知天): "He who has fully activated his heart-mind (*xin*心) apprehends his nature (*xing*性). Apprehending his nature, he apprehends Heaven." (7A1) I do not translate the word "*zhi*" as "know" since I do not consider "*zhi tian*" an act of establishing or attaining knowledge which presumes the dichotomy of the knower and that being known, for reasons that I will explain later. What is the meaning of Heaven in Mencius? It is where the human being's reflecting (*si* 思) heart-mind comes from (6A15).[1] With this reflecting heart-mind, it is possible for one to become a (morally) great man. Man activates his heart-mind so that he can discriminate the good from the bad. Therefore, the heart-mind is the faculty which makes morality possible. Man receives this faculty from Heaven and apprehends Heaven when he has fully activated his heart-mind. This presupposes that the principle of Heaven and that of human beings coincide. From this we may see that Mencius has adopted the traditional view that Heaven has a moral content. For Mencius, these moral elements are represented by *ren, yi, li*, and *zhi* (7A21). Having said this, it is important to note that while it contains a metaphysics of ethics, Confucianism is by no means any sort of metaphysical ethics.

In *Mencius*, 4A12, Mencius clearly says that sincerity (*cheng* 誠) is the way of Heaven and that aiming at sincerity is the way of man. This is evidence that, according to Mencius, Heaven and man meet at some admirable state: sincerity. Although here sincerity is not restricted to a narrow sense of moral virtue (I will come back to this later), at least Mencius' statement shows that it is within human capacity to take a way that is the same as Heaven's. This can be viewed as the ground for the possibility of the unity of Heaven and man.

The exposition in *The Doctrine of the Mean*

A passage in *The Doctrine of the Mean* echoes *Mencius*, 4A12: "Sincerity is the way of Heaven. The attainment of sincerity is the way of man." (ch. 20) Despite the similarity in wordings between the two passages, the first clause "sincerity is the way of Heaven" in *The Doctrine of the Mean* has a different connotation. It means that one possessing sincerity (without making an effort) is nature's way (a natural way).[2] If this is a correct reading, then the second clause should be read as: attaining sincerity with some effort is an ordinary man's way. This understanding is supported by the sentences that immediately follow: "The attainment of sincerity is the way of man. One who possesses sincerity is one who, without an effort, hits what is right, and apprehends, without the exercise of thought; one is the sage who naturally and easily embodies the right way. One who attains to sincerity is one who chooses what is good, and firmly holds it fast." In chapter 21, it is held that if one possesses sincerity without an effort, it follows that sincerity is one's nature. "When we have a clear mind resulting from sincerity, this condition is to be ascribed to nature; when we have sincerity resulting from clear-mindedness, this condition is to be ascribed to cultivation." Having sincerity as one's nature, one can "hit what is right, and apprehend, without the exercise of thought," with the result that one can also have a clear mind. One who attains to sincerity is one who has a clear mind so that one will choose what is good and firmly hold it fast. Remarkably, in spite of the difference between the natural way and the man's way, the assurance of the path of cultivation presupposes that sincerity is accessible by the way of man. Hence, everyone, no matter whether he is the one who possesses sincerity without an effort, i.e., the sage, or the one who attains to sincerity, i.e., an ordinary man, has sincerity as his nature. "But given the sincerity, and there shall be the clear-mindedness; given the clear-mindedness, and there shall be the sincerity." Sincerity is not exclusively possessed by sages but by all men, only that the former have already fully actualized this nature whereas the latter have to make some effort to actualize it.

The meaning of the unity of Heaven and man has been made explicit in chapter 22: when a man fully actualizes his own nature then he would be joining the work of Heaven.

> Only the perfectly sincere person can actualize his own nature. Actualizing his own nature, he can fully actualize the nature of others. Fully actualizing the nature of others, he can fully actualize the nature of things. Being able to fully actualize the nature of things, he can assist Heaven and Earth in their nurture and cultivation. Able to assist in Heaven and Earth's nurture and cultivation, he forms a trinity with Heaven and Earth.

It is clear in this passage that the nature of every kind of thing, no matter whether it is oneself, other people, or things, can be fully actualized through sincerity. Man can assist Heaven and Earth in their nurture and cultivation by fully actualizing his own nature. Ultimately the way of man and the way of Heaven are united.

In chapter 26 it is stated that someone who is high and brilliant can be the coequal of Heaven, and that whoever is large and substantial can be the coequal of Earth. It is entire sincerity that can make man become high and brilliant as well as large and substantial.

So far, we have seen that sincerity is the core notion that makes the unity of Heaven and man possible. But what is the meaning of sincerity? In *The Doctrine of the Mean*, sincerity is not restricted to a moral virtue as it appears in *The Analects*. It has been elevated to a status as the Way (*Dao*) that creates and sustains all things. "Sincerity is just 'self-perfecting' and the Way is just 'self-following'. Sincerity is the beginning and end of all things. Without sincerity there is nothing." (ch. 26) But self-perfecting does not mean that merely perfecting oneself, as sincerity also has a tendency to perfect all things.

"But sincerity is not 'just self-perfecting'; it is the ground for 'perfecting all things'." (ch. 26) This intention of caring for others is obviously inherited from *The Analects*: "The man of *ren*, wishing to perfect himself, seeks also to perfect others; wishing to enlarge himself, he seeks also to enlarge others." (6.30) Therefore sincerity is close to *ren*. "Perfecting oneself is *ren* and perfecting others is wisdom (*zhi*)." (*The Doctrine of the Mean*, ch. 26) Although the sense of *ren* in *The Analects* has broken down into *ren* and wisdom in *The Doctrine of the Mean*, it is certain that sincerity includes both of these two.

The expression "sincerity is the beginning and end of all things. Without sincerity there is nothing" deserves more discussion since it can be interpreted in various ways. First, if sincerity is understood as a moral concept, then what is indicated is a connection between the realm of morality and that of existence. But then it should be made clear how a moral act creates things in the world. Another possible interpretation is that, since "all things" means "all things in the world of values" it is plausible that a moral act can create values. If the first interpretation is adopted, provided that Heaven is responsible for the existence of things, then the expression in question denotes a condition that allows man to do the work of Heaven, namely, the condition of being entirely sincere. Consequently these expressions exhibit the unity of Heaven and man. Yet given the second interpretation, there is no such condition.

From the above-quoted passages, it is still not clear in what way Heaven nurtures and cultivates things. Should this remain unclear, we will not know precisely how man can assist Heaven in nurturing and cultivating things. However, some hints can be found in chapter 26: "The Way of Heaven and Earth can be perfectly expressed in a single clause: 'It is without any doubleness (*bu er* 不二), therefore its production of things is unfathomable.'" Double or two (*er*) symbolizes the dichotomy of true and false, real and illusory, etc. A truth can only be one, without any doubleness. In Chinese "*zhen cheng bu er*" （真誠不二） is a common phrase signifying "sincerity without a fraud." The Way of Heaven and Earth is, unequivocally, sincerity. With sincerity, Heaven and Earth produce things unfathomably. Now we can see that the way of Heaven and Earth and that of man coincide.

What emerges from this discussion is a third interpretation of "sincerity is the beginning and end of all things." If the term for sincerity refers to a common way that Heaven and Earth can produce things, and the way man should treat things, then on the one hand the realm of existence and that of morality remain independent, while on the other hand the unity of these two realms can be achieved through man's effort. This common way is *ren*. *Ren*, as a principle of production, signifies the everlasting creating force with the result of ceaseless production (*sheng sheng bu xi* 生生不息). To quote MOU Zongsan's term, it means "pure creativity."[3] This same meaning can be used in the moral realm. To be moral involves a creative task of expanding endlessly the circle of care. Hence by activating *ren* which is rooted in our nature, man can fully actualize his own nature as well as the nature of things, and can then assist Heaven in its work of cultivation.

We can conclude that in *The Doctrine of the Mean*, Heaven and man can be united through sincerity, the meaning of which can be understood in terms of *ren*. This is one of the ways that makes the unity of Heaven and man intelligible.

Wilber's theory of everything

Ken Wilber, a contemporary transpersonal psychologist and holistic philosopher, has established a theory of integration in order to explain the evolution of Kosmos, which contains not only the physical universe, but also the bios (biosphere), psyche or nous (the noosphere), and theos (the theosphere). The evolution of Kosmos is the transformation of existence from matter to life to mind and to Spirit. Wilber claims that all things are in a spectrum of consciousness, which unfolds itself, actualizes itself and expresses itself in the process of evolution. In the following I shall introduce Wilber's theory of Kosmos very briefly.[4]

Reality is composed of "holons" which is a term referring to an entity that is itself a whole and simultaneously a part of some other whole. For instance, a whole atom is part of a whole molecule, which is part of a whole cell, and the whole cell is also part of a whole organism, and so on. All holons are resting on holons resting on holons. There is no whole that is not simultaneously part of some other whole.

The Kosmos is composed of holons and all holons share certain characteristics. There are four tendencies or drives in every holon. The first one is "agency," by which the holon can maintain its own wholeness, identity, and autonomy in the face of environmental pressure. The second drive is "communion." Since a holon is also a part of something, it has to fit in with its communions as part of other wholes. The third drive is "self-transcendence." Holons have a tendency to move to a higher level. Hence the self-transcending drive produces life out of matter, and mind out of life. The fourth drive is "self-dissolution." Holons tend to dissolve in the reverse direction from that they were built up in. When it breaks down, it decomposes into its subholons.

In the self-transcending process, new holons come into being. Although wholes are composed of their parts, the wholeness is not found in any of their parts. Therefore, a holon cannot be reduced to its subholons. Since self-transcendence is one of the four drives of any holon, self-transcendence is built into the Kosmos. This is a formative drive which organizes Form into increasingly coherent holons.

Holons emerge with hierarchies, which are called "holarchies." All growth processes, from matter to life to mind, occur via orders of increasing holism and wholeness. Wholes are at a higher level of holarchy than their parts because they are more holistic. The higher or deeper dimension provides a principle to unite otherwise isolated parts into a coherent unity. Each emergent holon transcends but includes its predecessor(s). Evolution thus is a process of transcendence and inclusion.

Evolution is a sequence of increasing wholeness. In this sequence if any particular type of holon is destroyed, then all of the higher holons will also be destroyed, but none of the lower holons will be destroyed. That is the meaning of higher and lower organization. In this way, the biosphere is higher than the physiosphere and the noosphere is higher than the biosphere.

The number of levels in any holarchy is referred to as its depth, and the number of holons on any given level is referred to as its span. Evolution produces greater depth and less span. A holon has greater depth than its predecessors, but the population size is smaller.

Each level transcends and includes its predecessor. Spirit transcends all, therefore it includes all. It is at the highest level but also permeates all holons. All beings can be seen as the perfect manifestations of Spirit. In Wilber's words, "the ultimate depth is an ultimate oneness with the All, with the Kosmos."[5] Although all beings are manifestations of Spirit, they are at different levels of growth and transcendence, and therefore their realization of Spirit is not equal. A spectrum of depth is formed in accordance with the degree of realization. The greater the depth of a holon, the greater its degree of consciousness. Therefore, the spectrum of depth is a spectrum of consciousness. Evolution has a general tendency to move in the direction of increasing consciousness. "As depth increases, consciousness increasingly awakens, Spirit increasingly unfolds."[6] The Spirit in human beings has become their self-consciousness and different stages of consciousness present a different worldview. When consciousness fully awakens, it will discover Spirit, the All, and the One.

Wilber's view of the unity of Spirit and human

In Wilber's theory of everything, Spirit is at the highest level of holarchy. Since the process of evolution is endless, there is no final whole at the so-called highest level. The present Spirit will be transcended by the future Spirit. Spirit manifests itself in everything in Kosmos including human beings. There is no Spirit beyond man's consciousness. Spirit manifests itself in a world recognized through a particular worldview of an individual. Spirit is present at every stage, as the process of unfolding itself. "But at each stage Spirit unfolds more of itself, realizes more of itself, and thus moves from slumber in nature to awakening in mind to final realization as Spirit itself. But the Spirit that is *realized* is the same Spirit that was present all along, as the entire process of its own awakening."[7] Hence from the very beginning man and Spirit are one.

The process of development and realization of Spirit is called by Wilber a descending process. Spirit goes out of itself into manifestation, first to produce nature, then mind and self-consciousness. Another way of seeing the relation between Spirit and man is through an ascending process. There is a direction in the evolution of holons which lead to an increasing consciousness. For instance, animals have greater consciousness than plants. Not only the exteriors of holons—atoms, molecules, cells, organ systems, etc.—are in the process of evolution, within the interiors (sensations, images, concepts, rules, etc.), evolution is also taking place. For human beings, as their consciousness increases, their moral response to the world goes from physiocentric to biocentric to egocentric to ethnocentric to worldcentric. Spirit has also gone from subconscious to self-conscious to superconscious in the personal and transpersonal domain. Finally man recognizes himself as Spirit, as Kosmos, as the One. This is another way of seeing the unity of Spirit and man.

CHENG Hao's view on man and things

It seems that Wilber's theory of Kosmos and his view on the unity of Spirit and man have little connection with Confucianism on the same subject. The main reason is that the early Confucians did not have a very clear system of cosmology. However, Neo-Confucians such as CHENG Hao were interested in metaphysics and so discussion about the possible dialogue between him and Wilber is relevant. The goal of the comparison is to borrow some concepts about the Kosmos from Wilber so as to make Cheng Hao's view more intelligible and accessible in a contemporary context. We might also see Confucianism as an instance in Wilber's spectrum of consciousness, which enriches the exposition of his system. However, this latter topic falls outside the scope of this chapter.

I will not introduce the whole philosophy of Cheng Hao here[8] but will only discuss his view related to the unity of Heaven and man. The most well-known expression concerning man and things by Cheng Hao is in *Shi-ren pian* (識仁篇): "He who is of *ren* holistically becomes one substance with all things."[9] A similar expression is found in another place: "A man of *ren* regards Heaven, Earth, and myriad things as one substance, and there is nothing that is not himself."[10] How can a man become one substance with all things? One interpretation is that when a man extends his care from himself to other things having close relation with him, and then to all things, in the way he cares for himself, then he will become one substance with all things. Everything is under his care with the same strength and there will be no distinction between him and things. Cheng Hao illustrates the meaning of *ren* by its opposite *bu ren* and explains the latter by using medical terms. "In medical writings the term *bu ren* is used for paralysis of the hands and feet. This is an excellent description of the point."[11] When the hands and feet are paralysed, they are not able to feel and not conscious of what has happened to them. Contrarily, *ren* is a state in which man can be conscious of anything that happens. A man of *ren* will care for the well-being of all things with the same strength that he cares for himself. This meaning conforms to *The Analects*: "The man of *ren*, wishing to perfect himself, seeks also to perfect others; wishing to enlarge himself, he seeks also to enlarge others." (6.30) According to Cheng Hao, a perfect man of *ren* will regard Heaven and Earth as his own body and all things constitute parts of this body. His love will be equally extended to different things. "When there is perfect *ren*, Heaven and Earth are regarded as one body, and the different things and innumerable forms within Heaven and Earth as the 'four limbs and hundred members.' How can any man regard his 'four limbs and hundred members' without love? The sage is the perfection of *ren*, simply because he alone can actualize this heart-mind."[12] Therefore one can be united with things by activating one's heart-mind of *ren*. This can be regarded as a moral approach to the unity of man and things.

There is another interpretation of "being one substance with all things." Cheng Hao says, "The reason why it is said that the myriad things form one substance is that all have this Principle, simply because they all come from it. 'Change means production and reproduction.' Once things are produced, all possess this Principle complete."[13] All things are one substance since they possess the Principle of Production, which can also be understood as the Principle of *ren*. This idea has been spelt out clearly in the following passage:

> "The supreme virtue of Heaven and Earth is to produce." "From the generative forces of Heaven and Earth the innumerable things are evolved." "The life in us is what is meant by nature." It is most excellent to look into the vital impulses of the innumerable things. This is what "The Originating is at the head of goodness" means, this is also what is meant by *ren*. Man being one thing with Heaven and Earth, why should he belittle himself?[14]

Man and Heaven and Earth, as well as all things are one substance as they all have *ren* as their nature. That is why when one fully actualizes one's own nature one can also actualize the nature of other things. Once things come to existence they possess this Principle [of *ren*] complete. Even though this Principle is possessed by all things only potentially, it provides the ground for the unity of man and things.

Cheng Hao and Wilber

We may interpret Cheng Hao's thought with the theory of Kosmos so as to get a more holistic picture. As illustrated above, according to Wilber, everything shares a certain degree of consciousness. Spirit is pure consciousness and it manifests itself as different things in an endless unfolding process. The everlasting drive of Spirit to unfold itself is embedded in every holon as a tendency of transcendence. This may be viewed as the force of production. If we consider Cheng Hao's thought as a parallel to Wilber's theory, this endless process of the unfolding of Spirit is similar to the everlasting production and reproduction process driven by *ren*. Spirit can be regarded as Heaven in a Confucian sense. Heaven actualizes itself through the principle of *ren*, which can be understood as pure consciousness.

Wilber holds that consciousness is everywhere, and that even Spirit is everywhere. "Consciousness and depth are synonymous. All holons have some degree of depth, however minor, because there is no bottom."[15] Furthermore, "... depth is everywhere, consciousness is everywhere, Spirit is everywhere. And as depth increases, consciousness increasingly awakens, Spirit increasingly unfolds."[16] All things have some degree of consciousness, just as all things have *ren* as their nature. Cheng Hao said, "'All things are complete in myself, and this applies not only to human beings but to things as well; they all act in conformity with this [Principle]."[17] Also, "man and Heaven and Earth are one thing."[18]

What is man's role in the evolution or the unfolding process of Spirit? Wilber said, "We—and all beings as such—are drenched in this meaning, afloat in a current of care and profound value, ultimate significance, intrinsic awareness. We are part and parcel of this immense intelligence, this Spirit-in-action, this God-in-the-making."[19] "And we are invited, I believe, to awaken as this process. The very Spirit in us is invited to become self-conscious, or even, as some would say, superconscious."[20]

For Cheng Hao, man and things equally have *ren* as their nature. The only difference is that man can extend *ren* to other things.

> Man can extend [the Principle] whereas things cannot, because of the *qi* of things is obscure; we should not say that other things do not have [this Principle].[21]
>
> The only difference is that things are incapable of extending it [the Principle in them] to others, whereas man is capable of doing so. But being capable, does this mean that it [Principle] has been increased a little bit? Being incapable, does this mean it has been diminished a little bit? All principles are in existence pervasively.[22]

Where would our superconciouness lead us to? Wilber said, "Depth increases from subconscious to self-conscious to superconscious, on the way to its own shocking recognition, utterly one with the radiant All, and we awaken as that oneness."[23] "And in the highest reaches of evolution, maybe, just maybe, an individual's consciousness does indeed touch infinity—a total embrace of the entire Kosmos—a Kosmic consciousness that is Spirit awakened to its own true nature."[24]

For Wilber, all things, including man, are manifestations of Spirit. By becoming increasingly conscious, man will be united with all things and at the same time with oneness—the Spirit. Cheng Hao, similarly, claims that man has already possessed the Principle, he only needs to nourish it.

> The student need not seek afar, but search what is in his own person and understand the principle of man is only earnestness (*jing* 敬) . . . Therefore, when the reality of the *Dao* and Principle is understood, Heaven and man are one and there is no further distinction between them.[25]

Moreover, Cheng Hao thinks that "initially Heaven and man are not two, so we do not need to urge them to unite."[26]

Cheng Hao thinks that *ren* rooted in man's heart-mind as his nature and *ren* as the Principle of all things are the same, therefore the unity of Heaven and man depends on activating man's heart-mind and actualizing his nature, as well as extending *ren* to other things. That is the real meaning of actualizing the nature of things. In this way, Cheng Hao re-interprets *Mencius*, 7A1 "He who has fully activated his heart-mind apprehends his nature. Apprehending his nature, he apprehends Heaven." He understands this as follows: "Mere heart-mind itself is Heaven. By fully activating his mind one can apprehend his own nature. By fully apprehending his own nature one will apprehend Heaven. (one version is "nature is Heaven"). We should adopt this [relationship] and should not search from outside."[27] "'Exhausted the principles, fully actualized the nature, and thereby attained to the decree.' These three activities are completed simultaneously; there is absolutely no interval between them. 'Exhausting the principles' is not to be taken as a matter of knowledge. If you can really exhaust the principles, nature and the decree are also completed."[28] Since for Cheng Hao, heart-mind is Heaven, therefore by actualizing the heart-mind one can apprehend Heaven, which generates all principles; in this way, exhausting the principles is not a matter of knowledge. Neither are apprehending Heaven and apprehending one's own nature. According to this understanding, I have not translated "*zhi*" as "know" for *Mencius*, 7A1. Knowing something presupposes a knower and those to be known. In this sense knowing Heaven will never lead to the union with Heaven. In the vision of unity of Heaven and man, the subject and object emerge into a whole.

In Wilber's spectrum of consciousness, the awareness of holons in Kosmos evolves from prehension to sensation to impulse to emotion to symbol to reason. In the evolutionary progression of human beings, one's awareness moves from an identity with the material dimension to an identity with the biological dimension to an identity with a mental self. Then the identity switches from egocentric to sociocentric. That means that from a body identity one moves to a role identity, which identifies itself with inter-subjective values and goals. In the next stage, consciousness expands again and identifies with a global perspective. A small step further is to experience identity with all living beings. "Each emergence is a decentering, a transcendence, that finds more of the 'external world' to actually be 'internal,' or part of its very being."[29] At the higher level of consciousness, one would experience the unity of subject and object: "there is no separation between subject and object, between you and the entire natural world 'out there.' Inside and outside—they don't have any meaning anymore."[30]

We have already seen that in *Mencius*, 4A12 as well as in chapter 20 of *The Doctrine of the Mean*, sincerity plays an important role in the unity of Heaven and man. For Cheng Hao, since he also believes that all human beings have *ren* as their own nature, what they need to do in order to become a man of *ren*, and thus to be in union with Heaven, is only to cultivate *ren* with sincerity and earnestness (*jing* 敬). Cheng Hao makes this idea clear in *Shi-ren pian*: "He who is of *ren* becomes one substance with all things. *Yi, li, zhi*, and *xin* are all *ren*. What is necessary is only to understand this principle and preserve *ren* with sincerity and earnestness."[31] "'Being earnest and thereby correcting himself within, being *yi* and thereby ordering the external,' this is *ren* ... If one can be 'earnest and thereby correcting himself within, be *yi* and thereby ordering the external,' he then can be one substance with things."[32] In the same passage he interprets Mencius' "all things are complete in myself" (*Mencius*, 7A4) in the above context: "As Mencius said, 'All things are complete in myself,' and that 'in reflecting myself and seeing sincerity is within me,' and there will be 'great joy' only then. If one reflects oneself and is not yet sincere, then there is still an opposition between two things [i.e., oneself and non-self]. Even though one attempts to be in unity with the non-self, one still does not achieve such unity. How can one gain joy?"[33] An opposition between two things presupposes doubleness or twoness, which, according to *The Doctrine of the Mean* (ch. 26, quoted above), is an obstacle to the production work of Heaven and Earth. Therefore, Heaven and Earth follow the way of sincerity so as to produce things (to exercise the principle of *ren*) while man becomes fully sincere so as to find all things complete in himself and then is in union with all things.

Twoness or duplicity has also been considered by Wilber as something to transcend in order to become close to Spirit. He says, "The *twoness of experience is the fundamental lie*, the primordial untruthfulness, the beginning of ignorance and deception, the beginning of the battered self, the beginning of samsara, the beginning of the lie lodged in the heart of infinity."[34] Although Spirit needs dualities to manifest itself in the world, man can see through these dualities to their Source, which is the Suchness of reality. "These dualisms—between subject and object, inside and outside, Left and Right—will still arise, and are *supposed* to arise. Those dualities are the very mechanism of manifestation … But we are supposed to see through them to their Source, their Suchness."[35] This Suchness of reality is Spirit. Surprisingly enough, like those stated in *Mencius*, *The Doctrine of the Mean*, and Cheng Hao, Wilber thinks that man does not need to make much effort to be united with Spirit, he only needs to be true and sincere. "And precisely because this is the simplest thing in the world, it is the hardest. This effortless effort requires great perseverance, great practice, great sincerity, great truthfulness."[36]

Conclusion

The clause in *Mencius*, 7A4 "All things are complete in myself" certainly can be interpreted without any metaphysical implications, yet it also allows interpretations which show a metaphysical dimension in Mencius' philosophy. These two ways of interpretation also apply to the statement that "sincerity is the beginning and end of all things" in *The Doctrine of the Mean*. However, in *The Doctrine of the Mean*, more evidence that supports a metaphysical interpretation can be found. Cheng Hao undoubtedly explains these early texts in a metaphysical context. If we are convinced by Cheng Hao, then we can conclude that the idea of "the unity of Heaven and man" occurred as early as the time of Mencius, though implicitly. Such an interpretation enhances the intelligibility of the passage: "He who has fully activated his mind apprehends his nature. Apprehending his nature, he apprehends Heaven." (*Mencius*, 7A1).

In this chapter, Wilber's theory of Kosmos and that of spectrum of consciousness have been introduced. I am not arbitrarily selecting some "similarities" between the thoughts of Wilber and Cheng Hao, but am thinking that the latter may be understood more fully if its view on cosmology has been made explicit and systematic. A theory like Wilber's demonstrates such a system of cosmology that can serve this purpose.

6

Human Nature in Confucianism: As Understood and Developed by Contemporary Neo-Confucian Philosophers MOU Zongsan and TANG Junyi

Introduction

The thesis of "human nature (性 *xing*) is good" is the ground of Confucian ethics since it is upheld by Mencius (372–289 BCE). However, it has been controversial from Gaozi (告子) of the same time to DAI Zhen (戴震) (1724–1777) of the Qing Dynasty. Many contemporary Chinese philosophers have also joined the debates. Unsurprisingly, the core figures of Contemporary Neo-Confucianism, MOU Zongsan (牟宗三) and TANG Junyi (唐君毅), have devoted themselves to the task of the articulation and argumentation of defending this thesis, based on their profound philosophy knowledge from both the Chinese and Western traditions. In this chapter, I am going to study the exposition of Mou and Tang on supporting the thesis of human nature is good.

The explication of Mou on Mencius' thesis of "human nature is good"

The thesis of "human nature is good" in Mencius' thought serves as the utmost important theoretical ground for an autonomous ethical system like Confucian ethics, according to Mou. Therefore, it can be considered as one of the fundamental doctrines of Confucianism. In his last monograph *On Perfect Good* (圓善論 *Yuanshan Lun*),[1] Mou uses a whole chapter to elaborate this fundamental doctrine and places it at the beginning of the book so as to establish a solid base for the later discussion of perfect good and perfect-round teaching (圓教 *yuanjiao*). First of all, Mou analyses the views and arguments made in Mencius 6A, where the theme of human nature was mainly discussed. The theses include:

A. Human nature is necessarily good.
   In 6A1 and 6A2, Mencius takes the metaphor of *qi* willow and the metaphor of whirling water to illustrate that human nature is necessarily good. Also, the

passage in 6A6: "As far as what is genuinely in him is concerned, a man is capable of being good, that is what I mean by good" signifies the meaning of good human nature.[2]

B. *Ren-yi* (仁義) are internal.
Mencius argues against Gaozi's view of "*ren* is internal whereas *yi* is external." (6A4) Also, by commenting on the dialogues between MENG Jizi (孟季子) and Guangduzi, Mencius explains his stance on "*ren-yi* are internal." (6A5)

C. The heart-mind (心 *xin*) and the Principle (理 *Li*) are universal.
Mencius in 6A7 claims that the commonality of heart-mind for every human being is the Principle and *yi*.

D. The heart-mind of *ren-yi* is universally possessed by human beings.
By the metaphor of Ox Mountain, Mencius indicates that every human being possesses the heart-mind of *ren-yi*. (6A8) He also takes the metaphor of fish and bear's palm to explain that humans possess values which override the satisfaction of desires, in such cases humans can activate their heart-mind and choose *yi* even though it requires them to sacrifice their own lives. The heart-mind and the human nature are universally possessed by human beings. (6A10)

E. Sensory organs and the heart-mind are distinct in that the former is conditioned whereas the latter is unconditioned. (6A15) Mencius asserts the autonomy of heart-mind by claiming that the heart-mind would get the answer once it reflects (思 *si*).

F. The heart-mind is inborn. It is decreed by Heaven. (6A15)

G. It is important to cultivate the heart-mind: "The sole concern of learning is to go after the strayed heart-mind." (6A11)

Apart from Book 6A, Mencius makes explication of the thesis mentioned also in Book 2 and Book 4. In 2A6, he uses the famous hypothetical episode "all of a sudden, seeing a young child on the verge of falling into a well" to demonstrate the unconditional activation of the original heart-mind. He also reveals that *ren, yi, li* (禮 propriety), *zhi* (智 wisdom) are the content of original (human) nature which are universally possessed by human beings. In 4B19 Mencius remarkably differentiates autonomous from heteronomous morality by two contrary paths: "to act from (the heart-mind of) *ren-yi*" and "to act conforming to *ren-yi*." In 7A1, he brings about the relationship between the heart-mind, the human nature, and the Heaven (天 *Tian*). All of these doctrines amount to a comprehensive ethical system which has become the origin of a tradition of autonomous morality based on the heart-mind in Confucianism.

Mou Zongsan explains and elaborates Mencius' thesis of human nature is good by borrowing the strict sense of freedom of will and autonomy of morality in Kant's philosophy. He further argues that Mencius' system is superior to Kant's in the sense that the freedom of will in the former is not merely a postulate as it is in the latter. A system of moral metaphysics, according to Mou, is the ultimate resolution for justifying the thesis of human nature is good. It can also solve the problem of perfect good and render Confucianism a perfect-round teaching. In this chapter, I will confine myself to the problem of human nature is good, with the following foci:

i. How to justify that human nature is good?
ii. How to justify that the heart-mind of *ren-yi* is universally possessed by human beings?

Mou's justification of human nature is good

As mentioned, Mencius has expressed his clear and strong position on human nature in Book 6 and other passages. The metaphor of *qi* willow and the metaphor of whirling water are brought out by Gaozi, hence Mencius' explanation of his own view is restricted to the given metaphors. On the other side, Gaozi's view of what human nature is is very clear. Gaozi further makes it clearer by claiming that "inborn is what is meant by the nature" (生之謂性 *sheng zhi wei xing*), which can be considered as a guiding principle for understanding human nature: human nature is neutral in a sense that it is neither good nor bad, and it can be good or bad, furthermore, in reality it happens to be good and happens to be bad. Mencius' response to this principle was based on the meaning of "inborn is what is meant by the nature" that he perceives then argues against it by *Reductio ad Absurdum*. Mou has made detailed analysis on the debate between Mencius and Gaozi over "inborn is what is meant by the nature." In a chapter on the philosophy of CHENG Hao (程顥 1032–1085) in *Onto-cosmological State of Original Heart-Mind and Human Nature* (心體與性體 *Xinti yu Xingti*),[3] Mou discusses Cheng's special interpretation of "inborn is what is meant by the nature" by differentiating it from Gaozi's meaning in a whole separate section. He examines the reasoning of Mencius and uncovers the fallacy hidden. Mou emphasizes that it is important to be aware of the validity of logical reasoning and admits that it is not easy to analyse as well as to articulate the fallacy. He says that the reasoning is apparently erroneous, which is not then recognized by Gaozi. People of a later period might have felt something wrong in the argument but cannot identify the problem and some are unable to detect the problem due to the obedient attitude towards an authoritative figure like Mencius. Mou concludes that it is a question of wisdom to grasp the truth but a question of being well-trained in thinking to articulate it correctly.[4]

From Mou's perspective, "inborn is what is meant by the nature" is a description of the empirical human nature understood as natural features of human beings' natural life. This empirical sense of human nature is completely different from the transcendental sense advocated by Mencius, who although he has not made his own view clear in the passages where the metaphor of *qi* willow, the metaphor of whirling water and "inborn is what is meant by the nature" are discussed, presents his stand sharp and accurate in 6A6, 2A6, 6A10 and 6A7. The "good" in "human nature is good" means "capable of being good," as stated in 6A6, and "capable of being good" is read by Mou as "capable of observing the categorical imperative generated from the heart-mind." To be more precise, the heart-mind itself refers to the capability to generate categorical imperatives which human beings are willing to observe, provided that there are no obstacles from the desires or environment. It should be noted that the relationship between the original heart-mind and the original nature is as follows: the original heart-mind is the actualization of the original nature, and the original nature is the transcendental ground of the original heart-mind. If the meaning of good human nature stated above is adopted, then "human nature is good" is analytically true. Therefore, for Mou, human nature is necessarily good.[5] Mou further argues that the necessarily good human nature refers to the rationality which is necessarily possessed by human beings as rational beings: it is "the reality of all rational beings as per rational beings."[6] It seems that the explanations made by Mencius can only be viewed as a kind of conceptual analysis, but not a proof.[7] Now the problem is, how to justify that human beings are rational beings who are capable of being good? In other words, do we have reason for claiming that in reality human beings are capable of being good?

In 2A6, Mencius uses the episode "all of a sudden, seeing a young child on the verge of falling into a well" to demonstrate that for all human beings, the heart-mind of *cheyin* (惻隱之心 compassion) would emerge without aiming at the satisfaction of personal desires. Mencius lists out some probable desires like "wanting to get in the good graces of parents," or "wishing to win the praise of the fellow villagers or friends," or "avoiding the cry of the child." Even though these possibilities are not exhaustive, they are instances of hypothetical imperatives, which do not constitute autonomous morality. The heart-mind of *cheyin* does not emerge from any conditional factors therefore it can provide the moral meaning to the action it generates. In short, it is the heart-mind that makes morality possible. In this sense the heart-mind as well as the human nature is the transcendental ground for morality. No action not sprung from the heart-mind is a moral action. This is what "to act from *ren-yi* yet not [merely for the sake of] conforming to *ren-yi*" means. A moral act is an act sprung from the heart-mind of *ren-yi* but not one observing the norms concerning *ren-yi*. Mencius says, "The heart of *cheyin* is the germ of *ren*" (2A6) and again says more directly, "The heart of *cheyin* is *ren*." Since the heart of *cheyin* is the germ of *ren* or the emergence of *ren*, and the heart-mind of *ren* is the capability that makes an action a moral one, therefore *cheyin* should not be understood as a kind of emotion or emotional response. It is neither a sympathetic feeling in psychological sense. As a psychological feeling, it will be governed by psychological law and in this sense it is conditioned by environmental situation or personal desires and is in no way free (unconditional). When Mencius describes the emergence of heart-mind of *cheyin*, he has already excluded that it is caused by the mental state of disliking the cry of the child. For this reason, *cheyin* is not a feeling or an emotion as such. Mou coins a name for this special feeling, if it must be considered as a feeling at all, an "original feeling" (本情 *ben qing*) to signify that it comes from the "original heart-mind" (本心 *ben xin*).

> The mind of love (愛 *ai*), reverence (敬 *jing*) and shame (羞惡 *xiu wu*) is the concrete manifestation of the original heart-mind. Even though it can be thought as feeling, it is an original feeling under the thesis of "the original heart-mind is human nature as well as the Principle (理 *Li*)." All of them belong to the realm of "above form" (形而上 *xing er shang*), not the feeling in the form of vital energy as in the realm of "below form" (形而下 *xing er xia*).[8]

The heart-mind of *ren-yi* emerges from the internal nature of *ren-yi*. When an action performed is from the former, then we can doubtless confirm that the latter exists. But, how to justify that the feeling that one experiences is the original feeling but not the psychological feeling or emotional response? One step backward, how to justify that one possesses the original heart-mind that can make categorical imperatives? One more step backward, how to justify that one possesses the capability of distinguishing the good from the bad (the good human nature)?

I. From discursive understanding (*jiewu* 解悟) to experiential confirmation (*ti zheng* 體證)[9]

The heart-mind and human nature advocated by Mencius are not merely internal moral principles, they also refer to the inner capability: because of this human nature, one can make categorical imperatives. This capability would be actualized through the original heart-mind. The original heart-mind would manifest itself at the right timing. If the human nature is not an abstract and static principle but containing a motivating force to actualize the principles, moreover, if the original heart-mind is not an empirical mind which is merely contingently observing the principles, then necessarily the heart-mind will manifest and the human nature will actualize. Mou says,

> All rational beings possess this heart-mind. Since the heart-mind and the human nature are the same, how is it possible for the human nature without the capability to actualize? How is it possible for the heart-mind with no motivating force? How is it possible for the original capability with no manifestation, and can we possibly not act as motivated by the awareness of *liangzhi* (良知 enlightened mind)[10]?[11]

It seems that something existing is stipulated by defining concepts like the heart-mind, the human nature, etc. Nevertheless, if one is aware of the original heart-mind at the very moment it emerges, then one will affirm that the original heart-mind and the original human nature substantially exist in the real world. It should be noticed that although the heart-mind has to emerge in the empirical realm, yet itself is transcendental.[12] When one confirms that the heart-mind exists in reality, one only needs to cultivate it by continuing practice. Here there are two senses of cultivation: one refers to the time before the confirmation, to cultivate means to build up good conditions for the emergence of heart-mind, e.g., by reducing one's desires; another refers to the very moment when the heart-mind emerges, then to cultivate means to experience it mindfully and repeatedly, and let the heart-mind stay in this pure unconditional state. Mou indicates that the reality of heart-mind is able to be recognized by supervision at the immediate moment. Moreover, since it can emerge at the immediate moment and can be retained and cultivated, then there is platform for (moral) practice.[13]

The discursive understanding of the Principle, human nature, and the heart-mind is the intellectual base for the experiential confirmation of the heart-mind.[14] On the other hand, the experiential confirmation of the heart-mind is the validation of the above-mentioned understanding in reality. The problem of heart-mind and human nature can neither be resolved by conceptual analysis, nor does it constitute a system of objective knowledge. One needs to justify the heart-mind and the human nature through practice: firstly, to establish the discursive understanding of the substantial existence of them, then validate it as the situation arises; lastly, to transform the discursive understanding to experiential confirmation. This is a real justification of "human nature is good". Mou says,

> Since the words in Mencius are nothing but to inspire people to discover their true life and point out to them the same heart-mind possessed by all humans. From reading through Mencius' words to directing them to one's own mind, **one has to be conscientiously aware of one's own original heart-mind and to render it emerge and activated**. At the same time one also needs to experientially examine oneself if the flow is really from the original heart-mind, and if it is functioning smoothly without even a tiny piece of obstacle caused by personal desires.[15]

From the proper reading of Mencius to directing the understanding to one's own mind, is an approach from discursive understanding to experiential realization (*tiwu* 體悟). It is remarkable that by "being conscientiously aware of one's own original heart-mind and rendering it emerge and activated," Mou reveals that the emergence of heart-mind does not passively depend on waiting for its timely activation in response to some specific occasion. One can actively use one's mind to validate the truth obtained by discursive understanding so as to render the heart-mind emerge, and finally reach the state of "apprehension by the mind through contemplation" (*moshi xintong* 默識心通). Nevertheless, contemplation sometimes can be merely towards knowledge and nothing to do with morality. Mou emphasizes that the contemplation has to be combined with apprehension by the mind, that is, the approach should be from discursively understanding of the literary meaning to moral practice by which the doctrines in Mencius are validated. Then through awareness and experiential self-examination, the heart-mind will really present its ceaselessly pure functioning. Apparently, Mou's way of justifying the reality of the heart-mind is by moral practice and awareness in order to render it emerge. Therefore, an act of creating (moral actions) is equal to an act of justifying.[16]

II. Confirmation by transcending reflection (going against the flow *nijue tizheng* 逆覺體證)

"Apprehension by the mind through contemplation" is close to Mou's special terminology: "confirmation by going against the flow." "Going against the flow" (hereafter signified by "transcending reflection") is an approach to seek enlightenment which is in contrast with "going with the flow" (*shunqu* 順取) (hereafter signified by "empirical apprehension") (to obtain moral knowledge). Mou elaborates these two approaches: "The practice of 'going with the flow' ["empirical apprehension"] follows the things that [incidentally] fall before our eyes to exhaustively understand their principles, and then uses these principles to determine what moral practice to adopt; that is, it uses knowledge to determine morality."[17] As opposed to the approach of empirical apprehension which conflates knowledge with morality, the approach of "transcending reflection," in Mou's words, treats morality as morality.[18] It is not approaching morality with an epistemic attitude, rather, the moral practice adopted by this approach is to reflect so as to confirm the reality of the heart-mind, the reality of human nature and the reality of Principle by transcending the empirical world.[19]

In explaining the meaning of "cultivating" in WANG Yangming's (王陽明 1472–1529) "cultivating *liangzhi*" (*zhi liangzhi* 致良知), Mou says, "The meaning of this 'cultivating' contains the sense of awareness. Cultivating starts with awareness. Awareness is also called 'transcending reflection', that means to transcend from its emergence and consciously be aware of it, not letting it slide away."[20] He thinks that *liangzhi* always emerges at any time unexpectedly, one should be vigilant all the time so that one can be consciously aware of it when it emerges. He asserts, "Therefore the sense of 'affirmation' and 'confirmation' is already embedded in 'transcending reflection,' so that it is called 'confirmation by transcending reflection.'"[21] If one can affirm the *liangzhi* through "confirmation by transcending reflection," then one can consciously render *liangzhi* emerge. Therefore if "confirmation by transcending reflection" is used as a way of justifying the emergence of *liangzhi*, then this justification itself promotes the emergence of *liangzhi*. "If *liangzhi* and the enlightened awareness (*mingjue* 明覺) is truly affirmed through the confirmation by transcending reflection, then itself is the conqueror of the personal desires and material nature (*qizhi* 氣質), itself possesses an irresistible strength to emerge."[22] Hence, the confirmation by transcending reflection as a way for justifying *liangzhi*, expands one's *liangzhi* in that one transforms from being unaware to being aware and the emergence of *liangzhi* changes from being contingently to necessarily. Mou further elaborates,

> And, the awareness (*jiao* 覺) of the transcending reflection is also not a way of placing the *liangzhi* and the enlightened awareness just there, then using from outside another rootless awareness to bring the awareness of it. This awareness of the transcending reflection is merely the vibration from the emergence of *liangzhi* and the enlightened awareness, and through this vibration it reflects[23] itself. Therefore the awareness of the transcending reflection is the self-reflection of *liangzhi* and the enlightened awareness. It is *liangzhi* itself bringing awareness to itself. The ground of this is *liangzhi* and the enlightened awareness itself. It is presented in the duality of subject and object, but in reality it is through its own vibration to achieve self-recognition of itself. Hence ultimately the duality of subject and object will dissolve into one: it is only a genuinely full presentation of itself (not sliding away).[24]

Liangzhi itself is aware of itself and through its own vibration to recognize itself, Mou says that by so doing the duality of subject and object dissolves into one. In this dissolution the sequence of time is also eliminated. It is not the case that it vibrates first then reflects itself, because being aware of *liangzhi* means *liangzhi* presents in our mind, hence to emerge is to present. Since the mind where *liangzhi* presents is not a cognitive mind and presenting is not forming a subject-object relationship, therefore presenting is as same as emerging in that it is a self-awareness without the duality of subject and object. To be aware of it is to justify

> it. It is notably that the justification in question is necessarily a way of excluding the duality of subject and object. Justification in general is to justify a claim by a certain reason, but for inner experience (e.g., the feeling of unease) it should ultimately be self-justified.
>
> The essence of *liangzhi* is self-awareness. Through transcending reflection one would be awakened from one's obscure material desires. Then the freedom of will is activated and the state of self-determined is achieved. Yet sometimes *liangzhi* only emerges in germs, one should consciously cultivate and expand them and not slide away from it. At those times one is to recognize *liangzhi* itself by awareness, "this awareness is not a heterogeneous thing external to the original heart-mind, but it is the original heart-mind holding itself upright and being aware of itself."[25] This is the above-mentioned self-recognition without the duality of subject and object. Since it recognizes the original heart-mind therefore it constitutes the justification.

We can summarize the above discussion as follows: Speaking from the passive side, one should affirm *liangzhi* without sliding away when *liangzhi* emerges. Since the emergence and the affirmation do not take the dualistic form of subject and object, therefore both of them arise simultaneously. We may say that the emergence itself is the justification. We do not need a meta-sense of justification. Speaking from the active side, one can achieve "the apprehension by mind through contemplation" in moral creation, and keep it in virtuous action, then render *liangzhi* emerge. Therefore *liangzhi* is justified through moral creation. It is impossible for someone who has not been aware of *liangzhi* to justify it.

Mou's justification of "all humans possess good human nature"

Mencius says, "The heart-mind of *cheyin* is possessed by all human beings." Also, "Those who do not possess the heart-mind of *cheyin* are not human beings." Granted that we do not treat this claim (all human beings possess the original heart-mind, of which the heart-mind of *cheyin* is one) as a truism about human beings but a truth about reality, then we face a problem of how to justify it. The justification required here is different from the justification of possessing the original heart-mind by oneself, because the confirmation by transcending reflection needed for the latter cannot lead to the affirmation that the original heart-mind is also possessed by other people. Regarding the justification in question, Mou uses the concept of the Way (*Dao, Tiandao*) in the discussion of Cheng Hao's view on "inborn is what is meant by the nature."[26]

Cheng Hao says, "It is production which Heaven regards as its Way."[27] Mou explains that the production mentioned refers to the capability of creation.[28] Humans and things are endowed from the Way of Creation to form their nature, this is also what is meant by "what is endowed from Heaven is nature"[29] and "the functioning changes of the *Dao* of *Qian* fulfill each one's nature and life."[30] Humans are endowed from the Way of Creation so as to possess *ren* as their nature, which represents the innate capability of moral creation. This is, in Mou's words, "'The inborn is what is meant by the nature' in the sense of vertical formation [of human nature] in the cosmo-ontological mode of vertical formation [of nature]."[31] Since the original nature of humans and the Way are all the same as the Principle of Creation, it makes "He or She who has fully activated his or her heart-mind apprehends his or her human nature. Apprehending his or her human nature, he or she apprehends Heaven" (*Mencius*, 7A1) intelligible.

> "Full activation" in the phrase "fully activates the heart-mind" means "full manifestation." The heart-mind fully activated is the original heart-mind of *ren, yi, li*, and *zhi*. Mencius's advocate of human nature is good was made by the approach of "apprehending human nature through the heart-mind of *ren, yi, li* and *zhi*." This is the real nature of human which differs in value from the nature of dogs and horses, it is also the nature of moral creativity. If you can fully manifest your original heart-mind of *ren, yi, li* and *zhi*, you can apprehend your real nature of moral creativity. In this sentence "full activation" has a **stronger** sense than "apprehension," which **is achieved through "full activation**." This can also be regarded as "**practical apprehension**," which has the same meaning of "**confirmation**." If you have confirmed your real nature in this way, then you get to apprehend the Heaven as Heaven. This sense of apprehension is also understood as **confirmation**, which means **confirming through practice.**[32]

"What is endowed from Heaven is nature" does not only apply to humans, things are also endowed with Heaven as their nature when they come into their individual existence. Cheng Hao said, "'Change means production and reproduction.' Once things are produced, all possess this Principle complete. Human can extend [the Principle] whereas things cannot, because of the *qi* (vital force) of things is obscure; we should not say that other things do not have [this Principle]."[33] According to Mou, the Principle of Creation manifests in things only as the principle of formation. It can only potentially exist as their nature, but without the function of realization and emergence.[34] However, being a human, he or she has the Principle of Creation as his or her human nature. From this perspective, "all humans possess good human nature" is guaranteed by the Way.

Having said that the Way guarantees the universality of good human nature, yet the latter is not stipulated by the former. Otherwise, the morality based on it would become heterogeneous.

> If it is stipulated by some outer force, then morality has no independently substantial meaning, i.e. it is only heterogeneous but not autonomous morality. But it is a negation of morality and is self-contradictory if it is not autonomous. Therefore morality cannot be heterogeneous and is necessarily autonomous. Hence 'morality is autonomous' is an analytical proposition.[35]

On the contrary, Mou maintains that the content of the Heavenly Way is verified by the moral creativity of humans. Since "what is endowed from Heaven is nature," thus the Heaven that endows humans with the capability of moral creation to form their nature must itself be the origin of moral creativity. Mou calls it creativity itself, the same as the Way of Creation.

> Contrarily, we can infer from the innumerable things to assert a transcendental substance (God or Heavenly Way) that produces or creates them, this is completely **determined** by human's moral heart-mind and the true nature of human's moral creativity. In other words, Heaven has such kind of meaning, i.e. the meaning of creating innumerable things, is completely **verified** by our real nature of moral creativity. Apart from this, we definitely cannot have another way to verify that it has such meaning. Therefore we can apprehend our nature if we fully activate our heart-mind, and we can apprehend the Heaven as Heaven if we can fully activate our heart-mind and apprehend our nature.[36]

Therefore, the only way of justification of the Heavenly Way depends on one's confirmation of one's own heart-mind and nature. But confirmation is by no means in a cognitive way, but is "an affirmation of practical reason."[37] LU Xiangshan (1139–1193) says,"Mencius says one who has fully activated his or her heart-mind apprehends one's human nature, apprehending one's human nature, one apprehends Heaven, the heart-mind is the one and only one heart-mind. The heart-mind of somebody, that of my friends, that of the sages or virtuous persons of the thousand years in the past, and that of a sage or virtuous person of the thousand years ahead, are the same as such." If one can confirm one's own heart-mind which is equipped with the capability of moral creation, then one can derive from this that other people also possess this heart-mind. It is because the heart-mind is the Principle and the Way of Creation and this Principle and Way does not only bestow the capability to me as my nature, rather, it should also bestow it to other people as their nature. Cheng Hao says, "Mere heart-mind itself is Heaven. By fully activating his or her heart-mind one can apprehend his or her own nature. By fully apprehending his or her own nature one will apprehend Heaven. (one version is "nature is Heaven"). We should adopt this [relationship] and should not search from outside."[38] "Mere heart-mind itself is Heaven" reveals that there are no restrictions to the heart-mind: he or she who has fully activated his or her heart-mind will necessarily apprehend his or her human nature, he or she who has fully actualized his or her nature will fully actualize other people's. He or she who has fully actualized other people's nature will fully actualize the nature of things. He or she who has fully actualized the nature of things can assist the Heaven and Earth in the task of cultivation. He or she who has assisted the Heaven and Earth in the task of cultivation can join the Heaven and Earth. From the full activation of heart-mind to the apprehension of the Heaven to joining the Heaven and Earth, one has gone through the full actualization of human nature and things without boundary. In the horizon of unity of human and the Heaven, oneself, other people, things and the Heaven all become one. Other people's good nature is fully actualized simultaneously with the full actualization of one's own. There is no more distinction between the self and the other. The problem of justification turns from the cognitive requirement to the achievement of horizon from practice and its (theoretical) significance is also eliminated by dissolving the duality of subject and object.

The justification of other's mind by TANG Junyi

How can one know there are other people existing besides oneself? Also, how can one know there are other minds existing besides one's own? Moreover, how can one know that other mind is as same as one's own, which is an infinite mind? In his last two big volumes of monograph *Life-Existences and Horizons of the Mind* (*Shengming Cunzai yu Xinling Jingjie*),[39] TANG Junyi places these questions at different horizons and examines them respectively. The answers differ in accord with the feature and mode of existence of other minds shown in the particular expansion and transcendence of the horizon. Therefore, there is no single answer to the question concerning other minds, the answer only reflects the horizon that the replier posits. For example, in the horizon of "unconnected independent individual units," I and other person are merely facing to and looking at one another and each thinks that he or she is a unique individual.[40] One more example, in the horizon of subjective perception, we recognize the existence of other minds through our perception of the bodily activities of these minds.[41] Tang says,

> I can substantially perceive my consciously self-reflective mind and the existence of its feeling towards other people. Can I also substantially perceive the same mind and the existence of the feelings of others? Philosophers always think that this is impossible. From what I mentioned in the section 2 of the horizon of subjective perception: humans by perception can definitely substantially perceive the existence of other people and things, and humans have self-reflective mind, also, they necessarily have rational thinking to infer from the same body movement by me and others to other people is the perceiver as well. They can intuit that the origin of the same kind of bodily behavior performed by other people and I is that both belong to the "same kind." I have further indicated in the horizon of abstract entity that this self-reflective mind can transform to a purely reflective mind. This capable self-reflective mind itself is merely a pure spirit (*lingming* 靈明) initially without any forms and images. However, we can substantially perceive its existence and know its existence. Can we also substantially perceive the existence of this mind of other people and know its existence? This is a true problem not been tackled in the previous sections that is always neglected by people.[42]

If one confines oneself to a particular horizon and does not make transference (*gantong* 感通)[43] in any directions of forward or backward, left or right, upward or downward, then the existence of other minds can never be sufficiently justified.

Tang maintains that it is of utmost importance to affirm the existence of other minds in the horizon of moral practice. It is because if this is not affirmed, then the objective real world also cannot be affirmed and this would undermine the moral world.

> If we could not substantially perceive and know that other people have a mind, then we could not substantially perceive and know that the feeling in other people's mind is not generated from perceptive activity but is generated from this ideal sense of reflection. The moral feeling of other people is such kind of feeling. Now it is asked, can we have substantial perception towards other people's moral feeling?

> If there were no substantial perception, then our feelings responding to other people's moral feelings such as gratitude, admiration, etc. would have no substantial perception as the ground. These feelings then also could not serve as real moral feeling. One also could not truly have those virtues like gratitude and admiration and this would undermine the moral world. Therefore this substantial perception has to be a real possibility.[44]

Tang admits that how can this be a real possibility and how should this real possibility be understood are extremely difficult questions.[45] Tang holds that the affirmation of the existence of other minds is not obtained from imagination or reasoning, rather, it is through my perception caused by other people's behavior and I find that this behavior is as same as mine. Then I can infer by reason and intuit by analogy that other people are also sensory beings. Moreover, my transference towards other people's behavior helps me to form the behavior of moral feeling. On the other hand, other people also have transference towards my behavior so as to help forming the moral behavior. In the mutual transference and mutually assisting behavior, we can more affirm the reality of other people's mind and will feel that the objective world is more real.[46] However, Tang points out that this feeling of reality is not the same with everyone. If I and other people are lack of transference and mutually assisting moral behavior, then I do not merely lack the affirmation of reality of other people's mind, but will also lack the affirmation of the reality of the world formed with objective things mutually known by me and others.

> We may say, the more we are in the interpersonal or collective community where people mutually rely on the moral minds, meaning that they mutually commit moral behavior towards other people, the more we can affirm the reality of mind and personality corresponding to other people's behavior, and the more we can affirm the objective real world shared by people. Here, the stronger one feels the objective reality of this world, then the more this world appears to the person as a solid and real and not an illusory world.[47]

The feeling of the reality of the objective world is not the same for everyone, it is because the affirmation of other people's mind is not the same. As mentioned, the affirmation of other people's mind is based on transference, if one keeps on increasingly assisting people, then one can keep on expanding the feeling of assisting. Furthermore, the horizon concerning assisting people will keep on elevating. This increasing, expanding and elevating are without limit. When one and other people are in the unlimited living horizon of mind, one can detect that other people are subjects of unlimited meaning. Tang says,

> The events of assisting other people and the people being assisted can be unlimitedly increased, the feeling of assisting others can also unlimitedly expand, the living horizon to which the events of assisting others belong can also unlimitedly elevate from lower to upper according to the sequence. People can mutually perceive the virtues presented in the feelings and respond to each other

> with virtues, and connect to each other with gratitude, ... they can see that their own moral minds are automatically growing subjects and are also subjects with unlimited meanings. When people encounter with each other in a situation that each of them is a subject with unlimited meanings, then each of them is simultaneously a subject who possesses an independent personality. They will have unlimited goals in various living horizons and each of them has formed by his or her own a goal of moral personality.[48]

When one encounters with others with moral personality, he or she will see the others' moral mind and moral personality, and form the value world of truth, good and beauty where moral minds and moral personality are interrelated.

Tang's discussion on human nature is good

Since his early writings,[49] Tang advocates that the capacity of transference is possessed by humans which constitutes their nature. Although such capacity is also possessed by things, only humans can consciously seek for more and better transference to an extent that they are able to abandon the mechanical control of their own past habits or external forces. We can see that this distinctive feature of human nature provides humans the possibility of being free from the control of other things. The emphasis on the possibility of expansion of transference conforms to the classical Confucian view that albeit humans possess good human nature, they need to strive for the growth and development of it. Tang also adopts the Confucian view that the ultimate goal for the cultivation of human nature is "unity of Heaven and Humans." Tang says that the reality of humans does not necessarily exhaust the possibilities of humans. This implies that the inborn nature of humans is not determined and fixed upon their birth, rather, it can develop and transform and open up as many possibilities as possible. Contemporary scholars like Roger Ames particularly emphasize the aspects of freedom and creativity of human being as described by Tang. Human being thus characterized was marked by the notion of "human becoming."[50] So human "being" as well as human nature, is not something to be objectively understood, rather, it is humans who define themselves by activities in familial, communal, and cosmic contexts. Nevertheless, it is misleading to take that human nature is completely indeterminate. It is the possibility of growth, cultivation, and refinement that constitutes the salient feature of the human nature and this possibility lies in the capacity of transference and the self-consciousness of expanding this capacity. Therefore, human nature for Tang is the capacity of transference.

Ames concludes that Tang's understanding of human nature in terms of growing and living in the process of person-making is not "so new" since this idea can be found in Confucian classics.[51] However, in *Life-Existences and Horizons of the Mind* Tang presents a novel interpretation towards the thesis of human nature is good. He thinks that humans are born in this world, "initially as a mere naked life sprung from the void, representing the inborn emptiness and purity, which is the flow of goodness."[52] Since human lives are the manifestation of the flow of goodness, therefore human nature is also good. The original nature of this life existence is only "a life with spiritual awareness," or "the spiritual awareness of life." This spiritual awareness of life does not make any distinctions between I and non-I, moreover, I also can make transference with non-I through this awareness.

It seems that for Tang, only if that humans possess the capacity of transference is affirmed, can human nature is good be justified. Hence, the capacity of transference is crucial for the thesis. However, how to confirm that in reality humans' mind possess this capacity? If this question is treated as a query concerning the truth of life existence or mind itself, then Tang would respond that the answer is depending on the horizon on which the life existence or mind are situated.

> We cannot single out the world and ask the truth or the reality of it. Nor can we single out the life existence or the mind itself and ask the truth or the reality of our own selves. Again, we cannot single out this activity or function and ask after all how many activities or function really exist in the world or in the self. We can only ask: corresponding to what kind of life existence and mind, what kind of real manifestation of the world exists. And what kind of activities will be presented through the transference [with the world] by the mind and life existence. These activities are affecting the world and this life existence and the mind itself or my own self … From the perspectives that the life existence and the mind have transference with each other, and that the world always responds to the transference, every world or horizon is not outside the life existence and the mind. Since the horizon and the world rely on the life existence and the mind, the life existence and the mind are called the real life existence and the mind. Moreover, its existence also exists in this horizon or world. The transference also only exists in this life existence and the mind, and in this horizon or world.[53]

The transference can serve as the activities of the real existence of the human mind because humans can consciously act as the subject of the transference. Also because of this, the world that they view and the activities that they accomplish are unfolding in accord with the aspects and depth of the transference of the subject. Therefore, the subject who can transfer exists in the horizon that he or she reflects and this horizon has to include the world where the subject locates. For instance, for matter which is unable to transfer, this world is a pure material world which is unable to transfer (or making no transference).[54]

On the horizon of moral practice, humans make transference with the existence of moral subject and moral mind, therefore the "human nature is good" is real for the subjects who commit moral practice. But if one only singles out a world and wants to justify "human nature is good," then the good human nature is treated as something outside the life existence and the mind. Such kind of treating good human nature is criticized by Tang as "not an ultimate view."

> Here if someone insists to single out every life existence and the mind, and views from the horizon which has no transference, then this horizon with no transference is outside the immediate transference. It can also be said that it is beyond this life

existence and the mind. If someone singles out a world or horizon and says that no life existence and the mind with whom he or she can transfer, then it can be said that this life existence and the mind are beyond this world or horizon.[55]

Therefore, the problem of human nature is good cannot be regarded as a problem about objective world which can be justified by external evidence. From the perspective of Tang, one has to transcend one's own mind from the horizon of moral practice to that of "interconnectedness of everything in existence" and view from the inner, then one can see the reality of the answer.

Viewing from the horizon of "interconnectedness of everything in existence," from the very beginning that the life existence comes to exist, it does not cling on anything, including the arbitrary distinctions which it later on makes. Humans become clinging on different distinctions, such as distinctions between the I and non-I, objective things and the self, etc. The state of no clinging is good. Therefore, the meanings of goodness are of several folds, which are closely related:

A. The original state of life existence where no distinctions and no fix clingings are made;
B. Humans can be aware that the present existence of their lives and other existence in the world are embedded by a Principle of "no clinging and self-transcending." This Principle or "Dao" is the goodness of original nature that makes living (*sheng* 生) possible. Through this Principle, or Dao, or goodness, or nature, one can transcend from within the self already shaped in this world, and also transcend from the world already shaped, then one can affirm the inner value of one's own life existence as well as the others. Furthermore, one will aim at realizing the full meaning of this Principle, Dao, and goodness.
C. There is metaphysical origin of the spiritual awareness of life which enables the ceaseless growth and development and flow of the spiritual awareness. This metaphysical origin can be named Tian, God, or Tathagatagarbha. Humans are endowed with the nature of creativity from this metaphysical origin. This origin can be understood as the flow of goodness and humans come to exist in this world with the original goodness (capacity of creativity) as their nature. So human nature is good in this sense.
D. Even though humans are endowed with the capacity of creativity from the metaphysical origin, one needs to issue the decree and prescribe to oneself things one is obliged to do. The content of the metaphysical origin depends on the specific content of the self-decree and self-prescription. In this sense the goodness of human nature is not just given but should be accomplished by self-awareness.
E. The ultimate goal of cultivating the human nature is to unite with Heaven, or Dao, which is the metaphysical origin of human nature. At this highest stage of cultivation, the contents of human nature and that of Dao are the same. There is no Dao existing beyond human nature and vice versa. Human nature is just as good as Dao in their capacity of ceaseless creation.

Conclusion

From the above discussion and clarification, we can see that both Mou Zongsan and Tang Junyi do not view the justifications of human nature is good and the universality of good nature as an epistemic question, rather, they think that it is a matter concerning real life existence and mind. One has to transcend oneself to the horizon where the duality of subject and object is resolved and where no distinctions are clung on through practice (not only limited to a narrow sense of moral practice), the justification can then be confirmed. Therefore if the question is misplaced and one wants to verify the answer by empirical facts or logical reasoning, then the criteria in that field (e.g., field of empirical knowledge) will never be satisfied and one will then feel frustrated. But if one can transcend from this field then one can immediately see the infinite horizon beyond knowledge.

Part Two

Confucian Ethics in Western Discourse

7

Ren, Empathy, and the Agent-Relative Approach in Confucian Ethics

Preface

The recent debate[1] on whether Confucian ethics should be viewed as a type of virtue ethics inevitably touches on the issue of the meaning of virtues such as *ren* (仁), *yi* (義), and *li* (禮). However, the argument would be over-simplified to claim that since Confucianism puts significant weight on virtues then it is virtue ethics. The conclusion would mainly depend on how we understand the key concepts such as *ren*, *yi*, and the roles they play in the ethical life of humans. Some scholars interpret *ren* as benevolence, yet others interpret it as empathy. In this chapter I will make a scrutiny of these concepts and their implications. My primary aim is to discern the characteristics of Confucian ethics, rather than to classify it into some categories that are largely constructs of contemporary philosophy.

According to Michael Slote, one of the characteristics of virtue ethics is that it takes an agent-relative approach.[2] Confucian ethics is commonly believed to take such an approach.[3] In this chapter I will challenge this perspective and also discuss the validity of this approach as a distinctive feature of virtue ethics.

Benevolence and empathy

The notions of *ren*, *yi*, *li*, and *zhi* (智 wisdom) are essential elements in Confucian ethics. Many people regard them as virtues. Though they do in fact have that connotation, I have repeatedly argued that their basic meaning refers to an ethical capability[4]: a capability that makes ethical judgment possible. This meaning of *ren*, *yi*, *li*, and *zhi* renders them the possibility of overriding all other virtues (including those bearing the same names as these). Here, I will not repeat my prior discussion of the notions of *ren*, *yi*, *li*, and *zhi*, but will only address some relevant questions related to the present theme.

Van Norden discerns that for Confucius, the broad sense of *ren* refers to "the summation of human virtues" while its narrow sense refers to a specific virtue, which is "loving others." Van Norden points out that for Mencius, the meaning of *ren* typically goes beyond this narrow sense to refer to "the emotion characteristic of benevolence"

(Van Norden's English translation of *ren*) as indicated by *ceyin* (惻隱).[5] Sometimes *ceyin* is translated as "compassion" or "sympathy" in English. Van Norden summarizes the meaning of Mencius' benevolence as follows: "to be benevolent is to be pained by the suffering of others and to take joy in the happiness of others." Therefore benevolence involves an emotional response (such as sympathy) to the perception of a property (such as the suffering of another person).[6]

Slote distinguishes empathy from sympathy. The former "involves having the feelings of another aroused in ourselves, as when we see another person in pain."[7] However, the latter means that even though we feel sorry for others who are in pain, we do not necessarily have their feeling of pain per se. Slote gives an example to illustrate how sympathy can take place in the absence of empathy: when someone is being humiliated, one may sympathize with him or her (feel bad for him or her) without feeling humiliated oneself.[8] In this example, it shows that when one feels bad for the person being humiliated but without feeling his or her pain (of being humiliated), the former feeling is a response to what happens as one observes and cognitively understands it (e.g., assimilates it to his or her past experience). The observer also evaluates it from his or her own value system and reaches a conclusion that it should not have happened, thus the happening provokes bad feeling in the observer. However, since the observer does not feel the pain of others, even though he or she gets the bad feeling towards the situation, it remains external to him or her. On the contrary, to feel empathetic towards others, one has to feel the latter's pain. To feel other's pain, one needs to put oneself in other's shoes and imagine oneself undergoes the same experience and has an internal response to it.

Another example of sympathy I can think of is when one encounters a situation where a person does not have the feeling of suffering, such as a mentally disabled person or a vegetative patient, yet others might grieve for him or her. So the observer's pain is not aroused by the patient's. This is a better case to understand how sympathy is based on the projection of our own perception on others externally. In any case, it is clear that Van Norden's notion of "sympathy" is in fact equivalent to Slote's "empathy."

Since Van Norden merely understands *ren* as a virtue in the *Analects* (no matter in its broad or narrow sense), he contends that Confucius does not perceive *ren* as encompassing empathy as Mencius does. Actually, the saying "Wanting to establish himself, he establishes others; wanting to reach there himself, he helps others reach there" in the *Analects*, 6.28 explicitly reveals "transference (with others)" (*gantong* 感通) as a characteristic of *ren*[9]: the person with *ren* (仁) should be able to appreciate, or transfer into oneself, other's aspirations, desires, ideals, and preferences, and then try his or her best to help them achieve their goals.[10] That is even more constructive than "not doing unto others as you would not have them do unto you" and has no conditional implication as does the moral maxim "do unto others as you would have them do unto you," the well-known "Golden Rule" of the West. Mencius' *ceyin* is actually based on "transference" and because of this it can be regarded as the sprout of *ren*.

Empathy, as understood by Slote, is an object of study of psychology. He agrees with the thesis of recent psychologists such as C.D. Batson and Martin Hoffman[11] that empathy plays a crucial enabling role in the development of caring for others.[12] He points out that even the contemporary rationalist ethicists like Thomas Nagel and John

McDowell have never claimed that morally good actions can occur in the absence of empathy. Slote contends that empathy is important to moral motivation such as the motive of caring for others. Empathy may even influence moral judgment, or be referred to when justifying moral claims.[13] However, so far as we confine our understanding of empathy as a kind of sentiment, it cannot be a proper ground of morality, no matter how much effect it may have on morality.

The Contemporary Neo-Confucian thinker MOU Zongsan (牟宗三) explains the notion of *ren* in a most illuminating way: "*ren* takes transference as its substance, and the nourishment of things as its function."[14] Transference is the direct manifestation of the heart-mind of *ren*. By the transference with others, one can break the barrier separating oneself and the others, hence makes selfless moral judgments possible. "Transference" seems to be synonymous with "empathy," but actually it is not. Empathy is an object of study of psychology, the study of which entails inductive (or hypothetical-deductive) method. It is possessed by human beings only as a contingent fact rather than universally. Slote cites Martin Hoffman's study and concludes that children's moral motivation and propensity for empathy can be developed by the method of "inductive discipline."[15] I will not go into the details here, but just want to point out that Hoffman's study focuses only on the phenomenon (of empathy), which presupposes the capacity for empathy as a universal nature of human beings. This presupposition is not an empirical statement and thus cannot be established by empirical method. The Confucian method for identifying this innate capability (of transference) is called "confirmation by going against the flow" (*nijuetizheng* 逆覺體証, coined by Mou Zongsan).[16] In the illustrious Mencian incident of "a man were, all of a sudden, to see a child on the verge of falling into a well,"[17] the emergence of the feeling *ceyin* excludes not only the factor of interest, but also the psychological factor—"nor yet because he disliked the cry of the child." "Interest" here may include all personal goals. If the emergence of the feeling *ceyin* can be explained by means of some psychological factors, it can also be governed and predicted by psychological laws. Whether *ceyin* is determined by personal goals or by psychological factors, it is then not unconditional and hence not absolutely free. The distinction between transference and empathy is that the latter is empirically conditioned but the former not. Apparently only the capability of transference (heart-mind of *ren*) can be the ground of morality. In *Mencius* 1A7 the example of King Xuan of Qi exchanging a goat for an ox reveals the King's empathy towards the ox and Mencius seizes the opportunity to point out the capability of transference behind his empathetic feelings.[18] Transference subjects neither to the contingency of occasions nor to senses and sensations. Only if one is experientially aware of this capability of transference and exercises it in the interaction with others, would the heart-mind of *ren* be realized.

In *Mencius* 7B1 it states that "the man of *ren*, beginning with whom they love (care for), proceed to whom they do not love (care for)." From the above passage, it is clear that *ren* is not the same as loving kindliness (i.e., what we usually term "benevolence"), but is the capability based on transference to extend loving kindliness to everyone. *Ceyin* is the feeling that directly emerges from the heart-mind of *ren*. Since the heart-mind of *ren* is also known as the original heart-mind, so *ceyin*, which emerges from this original heart-mind, may also be called the "original feeling" (*benqing* 本情) (Mou

Zongsan's terminology[19]). Thus *ceyin* can be viewed as the manifestation of the heart-mind and is sometimes called "the heart-mind of *ceyin*." Although it is commonly conceived as a kind of feeling, its essential meaning is close to the moral heart-mind. The original feeling distinguishes itself from ordinary feeling by not being determined by empirical factors, even though it appears in empirical situations. In actual situation, apart from the agent who makes the moral judgment, one is not able to distinguish between *ceyin* and empathy by merely observing from outside, because it can only be affirmed by the agent's inner personal reflection.[20]

In *The Ethics of Care and Empathy*, Slote has discussed how empathy is relevant to morality.[21] In Confucian ethics, no moral principles are regarded as the basis of judgment of right and wrong, and no specific acts or choices are always right (or wrong). If and only if a person is in a selfless state, i.e., bringing his or her heart-mind of *ren* to bear on making judgment that his or her choice would be the best. This view can be illustrated by Mencius' discussion on ancient sages.[22] While Boyi (伯夷), Yiyin (伊尹), Liu Xiahui (柳下惠), and Confucius were all ancient sages, their attitudes towards and ways dealing with the same kind of issue were very much different.[23]

In his recent article, Slote comments on Van Norden's manuscript and points out that since Mencius' ethics centers on *ren* and other sentiments, his philosophy should more naturally be classified as a form of sentimentalism (Hume-like sentimentalism).[24] However, in the light of the aforementioned distinction between transference and empathy, Mencius' ethics is not a kind of sentimentalism. Moreover, if "benevolence" refers to the feeling of empathy, then it is not a suitable translation for "*ren*" in Confucius' and Mencius' philosophy.[25]

The agent-relative characteristic of virtue

One of the characteristics of virtue ethics is the focus on the virtuous person and the inner traits, dispositions, and motives that qualify him or her as being virtuous. Compared with principled ethics, virtue ethics emphasizes the individual, therefore Slote characterizes it as an agent-focused approach. A radical form of agent-focused virtue ethics is one which evaluates the moral or ethical status of an act entirely as derivative from independent and fundamental aretaic (as opposed to deontic) ethical characterizations of motives, character traits, or individuals. Slote calls it the agent-based approach to virtue ethics.[26] That means an act is right just because the virtuous individuals would perform it. However, in an ethical theory, if the virtuous person judges an act to be virtuous by certain moral principles or concepts, then he or she will have deviated from the agent-based approach. The approach he or she adopts may at most be called agent-prior since characters and motives of the agent are not regarded as fundamental.

In Confucianism, the act of *ren* and *yi* is undoubtedly a virtuous act, but Mencius clearly claims that an act being virtuous does not lie in its observing the standards of some virtues such as (the virtue of) *ren* and *yi*, but rather in its acting from *ren* and *yi*.[27] Here the *ren* and *yi* in "acting from *ren* and *yi*" should be understood as the heart-mind of *ren* and *yi*. It looks as if Confucianism is taking the agent-based approach. However, the heart-mind of *ren* and *yi* is neither defined by virtuous persons nor by moral principles; rather, the heart-mind of *ren* and *yi* motivates a virtuous person to act. Given this understanding, virtuous persons are not defined by possessing the heart-mind of *ren* and *yi*, because the heart-mind of *ren* and *yi* is (originally) possessed by all humans; only that the virtuous persons do not lose it. Therefore, in a loose sense, Confucian ethics is "agent-based" in that a moral act is entirely accounted for by the moral character of the agent. Nevertheless, "virtuous persons" are not a class of human beings which distinguish themselves in possessing a special kind of capability (or character). Therefore, strictly speaking, Confucian ethics is an ethics based on the heart-mind of *ren* and *yi*. The heart-mind of *ren* and *yi* is not a fixed (psychological) state, but rather a capability that can be cultivated to develop ceaselessly. A sage is one who can bring the heart-mind of *ren* and *yi* into full play and exercise it at all times. Yet ordinary people need not imitate the behavior of sages, or imagine how the sages would make a moral decision in a specific situation (as mentioned above, widely divergent choices could be made among the sages). In making moral decisions, what one needs to do is to try to remove obstacles that impede the exercise of the heart-mind of *ren* and *yi*, and through transference, of others' aspirations and needs in the given situation, and then make a (close to) selfless judgment, which would be the best possible one to make.

Another concept related to the "agent-focused" approach is the "agent-relative" approach. One of the differences between virtue ethics and principled ethics such as utilitarianism, is that it is not a thesis of the former that everyone should be treated equally regardless of their relationship with the agent, but instead it asserts that we should differentiate our obligations towards people who are related to us differently; by the same token, we should differentiate our love for people accordingly (which is called graded love). Many people deemed that this mode of agent-relative ethics, in which the relatedness with the agent counts, is that upheld by Confucianism. Van Norden claims that graded love is the characteristic of Confucian ethics. "Graded love is the doctrine that one has agent-relative obligations toward, and should have greater emotional concern for, those who are bound to one by special relationships, such as those between ruler and minister, father and son, husband and wife, elder and younger brother, and between friends."[28] Van Norden also sees *ren* as exactly this graded love.[29]

From Mencius' criticism of Mozi, it is clear that the former objects to the latter's advocacy of universal love. However we cannot infer from this and conclude that the connotation of *ren* is graded love. For Confucianism, graded love is merely the beginning of *ren*,[30] whereas the ultimate goal of *ren* is to eliminate the boundaries between oneself and others. This highest state of *ren* is illustrated in the "World of Great Harmony": "Thus men did not love only their parents, nor treat only their own sons as their children."[31] Mencius also says: "He [a gentleman] is affectionate to his kin, and treats the people with *ren*. He treats the people with *ren*, and is also kind to creatures."[32] That means one should treat one's kin with affection and treat all people with *ren*. "People" here are objects of governance who have no personal relationships with the ruler. So they can be regarded as strangers other than one's kin. This means that one should go beyond affection derived from kinship and establish a relationship with people that is based on selfless sentiment in order to realize the ideal of "Wanting to establish himself, he establishes others; wanting to reach there himself, he helps others reach there."[33]

Confucianism asserts that love is graded. For instance, Mencius thinks that love towards parents and kin is a natural inclination arising from the blood relationship, which should not be distorted by displacing "graded love" with "universal love." However, although love towards parents comes from blood relationship, it could also be the first step in extending love from oneself to others, and hence has moral significance. Treating parents with filial piety has already gone beyond mere natural inclination, and can be considered as the conscious realization of moral value. The intent to pay a debt of gratitude can be regarded as the spirit of filial piety. Love among kin of course differs between close and distant relationship. The system of propriety (*li*) established in the Zhou Dynasty illustrates the spirit of "the decreasing measures of the love owed to relatives, and the increase in honor that is owed to the worthy."[34] WANG Guowei 柳下惠), (1877–1927) said, "The propriety and regulations system in the Zhou Dynasty is actually established for the sake of morality."[35] Paying a debt of gratitude is a moral value, and its realization definitely rests on certain relationship between some people, that is, "the givers" and "the receivers." Parents are the greatest givers for their children because they give them life. Teachers and students, elder brothers and younger brothers, husbands and wives, all have similar relationships. What is called "from close to far" means treating people differently according to different giving-and-receiving conditions in interpersonal relationships. The moral value of paying a debt of gratitude admittedly can be regarded as an "agent-relative" obligation, but if it is interpreted as the embodiment of a general rule (principle) in a concrete situation, then the agent-relative obligation has no significant difference from the moral requirement in principled ethics. For example, "keeping the promise" which is one of the important moral principles in principled ethics, should be and only needs to be carried out between "the person who makes the promise" and "the person whom one makes the promise to." Nevertheless, this principle is usually not considered as an agent-relative principle. It is noteworthy that rule-utilitarianism also admits that people having different relationships should have different moral obligations is a maxim consistent with the principle of utility.

Using the *Analects*, 13.18 as an example, Van Norden asserts that the love Confucius promotes is graded love.[36] Granted that "uprightness" is a virtue, it is realized by rendering the maxim "parent and son or daughter shielding each other" overriding "parent and son or daughter testifying against each other." However, "uprightness" as well as "parent and son or daughter shielding each other" are not absolutely overriding but both should submit to *yi*.[37] Mencius does not think that if one's parent makes mistakes, he or she should be lightly forgiven by all means. "Not to complain about a major wrong committed by one's parent" violates the spirit of filial piety.[38] In *Xiaojing* (*Classic of Filial Piety* 孝經), the greatest filial piety is thought to be "to establish one's self and to practice *Dao* (道)." Xunzi (荀子) also claims that "one should follow *yi* and not to follow the father" (ch. 29). Therefore, judging from the position of Confucianism mentioned above, it is clear that if we merely focus on the special judgments or acts (commonly regarded as partial) relating to kinship, then we would have overlooked *yi* as the ultimate ground of morality in Confucian tradition.

Even though Mencius acknowledges that graded love is a natural inclination in humans, he would never agree that *ren* is graded. The case of "a man were, all of a sudden, to see a child on the verge of falling into a well" is a good illustration of the selfless heart-mind of *ren*. An attempt by Van Norden is to explicate *ren* using WANG Yangming's (王陽明) notion of "forming one body with Heaven, Earth and the myriad things,"[39] which indeed has captured the essence of *ren*. Even though this notion of *ren* is not explicitly articulated by Confucius and Mencius, it could actually be derived from the latter's idea.[40] At the state where a person forms one body with Heaven, Earth and myriad things, there would no longer be distinction between oneself and others, or between close and distant relationships. That is the highest state of *ren*. While this highest state is still to be attained, the needs of some specific situations call for the realization of some virtues such as filial piety, fraternal duty, and trust. These virtues, while can be viewed as graded love or agent-relative obligations, can as well be regarded as the partial manifestation of *ren*. They certainly are with restrictions (for being concrete entails having temporal-spatial or relational attributes, which constitute restrictions to the universal and infinite *ren*), yet they can also be viewed as the concretization of *ren* and hence have their ethical significance. Confucius says, "let the prince be a prince, the minister be a minister, the father be a father and the son a son,"[41] and Mencius says, "between father and son, there should be affection; between prince and minister, there should be *yi*; between husband and wife, there should be attention to their separate functions; between old and young, there should be a proper order; and between friends, there should be faithfulness."[42] For them, obligations are differential according to status and relationship in a situation, and are thus agent-relative. Essentially, they are the embodiment of *ren* in different situations, or different modes of *ren*. From this perspective, the mode of *ren* should fit the roles, statuses, and relationships, but it is absolutely not the roles or relationships that determine how people should act. Mencius has made this clear in his argument against Gaozi's (告子) statement: "*ren* is internal whereas *yi* is external."[43]

Conclusion

In this chapter, I have discussed the role of empathy in making ethical judgment and the difference between empathy and transference in Confucian ethics. I also argued that *ren* understood as the capability of transference can be the ground of ethical judgment whereas empathy cannot. As a virtue, *ren* can be understood as "benevolence," which performs a significant function in daily life. However, its ethical significance is determined by the heart-mind of *ren*. In the sense of virtue, *ren* (benevolence) is manifested as graded love and derives agent-relative obligations. From this perspective, Confucian ethics matches one of the characteristics of virtue ethics. Nevertheless, since the highest state of *ren* entails impartiality and selflessness, Confucian ethics, which regards the realization of the heart-mind of *ren* and *yi* as its ultimate goal, is not an agent-relative virtue ethics.

8

Confucian Ethics and Virtue Ethics

Introduction

In recent years there have been criticisms of theories of ethics by anti-theorists.[1] According to them, there are weaknesses of ethical theories, regardless of their individual substantive content, which need investigation. Of the theories under review, the main ones are Kantian moral philosophy, utilitarianism, and contractarianism. There are neither formal nor informal alliances among anti-theorists, nor are there common grounds for their refutation of ethical theories. Nevertheless, universality and impartiality are generally understood by anti-theorists as the two significant characteristics possessed by theories that have undesirable implications.[2] Since a moral theory consists of a (set of) highly abstract universal principle(s) from which concrete moral judgments are deduced, anti-theorists question whether the individual characteristics of moral agents as well as the particularity of situations in which moral judgments are made can be given proper weight in such theories. Anti-theorists not only object to the view that making judgment is a kind of deductive activity,[3] they also point out that impartiality implies abstraction from particular individuals and relationships, and therefore, an impartial moral principle does not pay adequate attention to particular properties of a concrete situation. Besides, impartiality does not allow the moral motivation of agents to be aroused by the special care for someone with whom he or she has a special relation, a consideration which anti-theorists find acceptable. Apart from the above-mentioned features of moral principles, the following natures and presuppositions of ethical theories also constitute reasons for rejecting them: reductionism, nonexistence of unresolvable moral conflicts, provision of decision procedure for attaining objectively right judgments, admission of moral specialists, etc., all of these are either false or undesirable from the anti-theorists' point of view.[4] In a previous paper,[5] I have examined most of these objections and attempted to find out the possibility of an ethical theory which can escape from them. In another paper,[6] I have scrutinized Confucian ethics so as to see whether it belongs to the kind of theories that anti-theorists reject. By analysing the concept of *ren* and other essential ideas in Confucian ethics, my conclusion is that while admitting universality, impartiality, and normativeness as properties possessed by Confucian ethics, it does not share the demerits which anti-theorists raise. Thus, Confucian ethics can be viewed as belonging to a completely different category of ethical theory, if it is a theory at all. With this conclusion in mind, one might naturally think that Confucian ethics belongs to an alternative camp, i.e., virtue ethics. Nevertheless, whether such is the case needs an independent investigation, which is the task of this chapter. While trying not to repeat the arguments, I would utilize some of the conclusions reached to deal with the present issue.

Two distinctive features of virtue ethics

It seems that it is not wise to give a single definition of virtue ethics since, like anti-theorists, there are different emphases among virtue ethicists.[7] However, we need at least some sort of characterization in order to set a domain for our discussion, reserving at the same time some room for others. Here I am going to borrow a characterization made by Michael Slote,[8] not only because it is more specific compared to others, but also because the issues he brings out in his book have a certain relevance to ours. The following are two distinctive features spelt out by Slote.

> The idea of a virtue ethics is commonly regarded as involving two distinctive or essential elements. A virtue ethics in the fullest sense must treat aretaic notions (like "good" or "excellent") rather than deontic notions (like "morally wrong," "ought," "right," and "obligation") as primary, and it must put a greater emphasis on the ethical assessment of agents and their (inner) motives and character traits than it puts on the evaluation of acts and choices.[9]

Slote points out that the fundamental aretaic notions that virtue ethicists employ for making evaluations are not specifically moral (i.e., not specifically morally good or morally excellent), but are "broader aretaic notions of a good or admirable character trait, an excellence of character, or, more briefly, a virtue."[10] Thus, the notion of admirable would be used to replace "morally good" and other deontic notions. Similarly, "deplorable" would be used for expressing the opposite of admirability and notions like blameworthy which have moral connotation would also be replaced.[11] The aretaic notions are broader in that they give evaluative significance to the well-being of the self and to the well-being of others. The recognition of the well-being of the self and the equal weight given to it as to that of others lets virtue ethics avoid the self-other asymmetry (a problem that we shall deal with) that occurred in Kantianism and common-sense morality. Furthermore, as non-moral goodness is allowed to count in ethical evaluation, "our virtue ethics will cover a great deal of the ground covered by our common-sense thinking."[12] For Kantianism and common-sense morality, only other people's well-being is relevant to ethical evaluation, Slote thinks that this makes the sense of ethics too narrow.

> Roughly speaking, only what concerns people other than the agent or trait possessor counts intuitively as a moral virtue or as morally good, but by our common lights both other-benefiting and self-benefiting traits and actions can be admirable or (instances of) virtues. And clearly it is a part of the business of ethics—though perhaps not of morality proper—to describe and evaluate such (largely) self-regarding traits as prudence, fortitude, heedlessness, circumspection, and injudiciousness.[13]

Apparently we may conceive two kinds of ethics. In a narrower sense, ethics is equal to "morality proper" whereas in a broader sense, ethics comprises "morality proper" and prudence. It is the latter sense of ethics that Slote recommends. Since the functions of an ethical system and the criteria of its validity depend on the conception of ethics as such, the issue in question cannot be reduced to a problem of terminology. If, for certain reasons, we choose to adopt the broader sense of ethics, then we need to revise the key concepts we are accustomed to use in a narrower sense (from now on the broader and the narrower senses just mentioned would be signified by "ethics" and "morality," correspondingly[14]) and examine the implications and problems derived from them. At this early stage of our discussion, I will use the concept of ethics so as to investigate whether Confucian ethics belongs to virtue ethics.

Ethical notions in Confucian ethics

As mentioned above, one of the distinctive features of virtue ethics is that it treats aretaic notions rather than deontic notions as primary. So I am going to determine whether Confucian ethics belongs to virtue ethics by examining whether the three essential ethical notions in Confucian ethics—*ren*, *yi*, and *li*—are deontic notions and also whether they are treated as primary. If this is the case, in what sense are they so treated?

Let us start with *ren* first, since it is the most significant one among the three. Primarily, the meaning of *ren* denotes the ability of transference (*gongtong* 感通) from which an empathetic feeling toward others arises.[15] Confucius once criticizes his student Zaiwo when the latter declares that he is able to enjoy eating rice and wearing finery in the three-year mourning period. His appearances show that he is feeling at ease. Confucius thinks that being at ease when one should suffer with sorrow in a certain situation shows that one is lack of *ren*.[16] By transference from *ren*, one would feel sorrow to see others in pain. In this sense, *ren* can also be understood as "awareness."[17] Mencius asserts, "No man is devoid of a heart-mind sensitive to the suffering of others." (*Mencius*, 2A6) He further claims that "the feeling of *ceyin* (惻隱) is the germ of *ren*" and "the feeling of *ceyin* pertains to *ren*." (*Mencius*, 6A5) Mencius elaborates on this meaning in the following passage:

> Mencius said, "For every man there are things he cannot bear. To extend this to what he can bear is *ren*. For every man there are things he is not willing to do. To extend this to what he is willing to do is *yi*. If a man can extend to the full his nature aversion to harming others, then there will be an over-abundance of *ren*. If a man can extend his dislike for boring holes and climbing over walls, then there will be an overabundance of *yi*. If a man can extend his unwillingness to suffer the actual humiliation of being addressed as 'thou' and 'thee,' then wherever he goes he will not do anything that is not *yi*."
>
> *Mencius*, 7B31

It is clear that *ren* is a capacity by which one can transcend from one's own self to others, and thus one would care for others' well-being as well as one's own. Therefore, the primary meaning of *ren* signifies the transcendental ground of a moral act. Obviously, *ren* itself is not a deontic notion, nor is it an objective principle by which right and wrong can be differentiated. Strangely enough, *ren* in this meaning is not an aretaic notion either, because it is not equivalent to goodness or excellence but is an ability (of transference) possessed by human beings that makes moral goodness possible. Therefore, *ren* itself is not a virtue but a moral heart-mind (to be elaborated shortly) without which no virtues can be qualified as a (moral) virtue. Nonetheless, there is a second meaning of *ren*: it signifies one of the virtues commended by Confucians. As a virtue, *ren* also has two senses, each of which implies a different moral status. In one of its senses, *ren* can be achieved if and only if other virtues are satisfied. So the relation between *ren* and other virtues is a relation of subordination (the latter is subordinated to the former). For example,

> A man with *ren* is sure to possess courage, but a courageous man does not necessarily possess *ren*.
>
> *Analects*, 14.4

> . . . He cannot even be said to be wise. How can he be said to be *ren*?
>
> *Analects*, 5.19

> Zizhang asked Confucius about *ren*. Confucius said, "There are five things and whoever is capable of putting them into practice in the Empire is certainly '*ren*.'" "May I ask what they are?" "They are respectfulness, tolerance, trustworthiness in word, quickness and generosity."
>
> *Analects*, 17.6

The other sense is that *ren* is as valuable as the other virtues, therefore, *ren* and the other virtues are complimentary with each other. Negligence of any of these virtues would cause defects or imperfection in the agent or in his or her moral achievement. This can be viewed as a relation of coordination. The following are examples showing this kind of relation:

> . . . To love *ren* without loving learning is liable to lead to foolishness . . .
>
> *Analects*, 17.8

> The Master said, "What is within the reach of a man's understanding but beyond the power of his *ren* to keep is something he will lose even if he acquires it. A man may be wise enough to attain it and having enough *ren* to keep it, but if he does not rule over them with dignity, then the common people will not be reverent. A man may be wise enough to attain it, having enough *ren* to keep it and may govern the people with dignity, but if he does not set them to work in accordance with *li*, he is still short of perfection."
>
> *Analects*, 15.33

Yi resembles *ren* in that it also has two meanings, and that the two meanings are similar to that of *ren*. In the first meaning, *yi* signifies the capacity of human beings to discern appropriateness[18] in any situation. According to Confucian thinkers, it is not the properties of events, nor the relationship among people concerned, that determine the appropriateness of an action; but it is the agent who activates his or her impartial moral heart-mind who can decide how to act appropriately. This is what the well-known claim made by Mencius that both *ren* and *yi* are inherent means.[19] It can be seen that both *ren* and *yi* in their first meanings refer to the subjective condition of a moral agent and they differ only in the aspects on which they individually focus.[20] *Ren* and *yi* may even be understood as two dimensions of moral heart-mind.[21] That is why these two notions are always expressed simultaneously.

The second meaning of *yi* denotes the traits or behavior which are appropriately performed by the ability mentioned in its first meaning. When *yi* signifies a virtue, its importance is only next to *ren*. But when *ren* is understood as a virtue, particularly as the virtue in its first sense, *ren* consists of *yi*.

> Mencius said, "Slight is the difference between man and the brutes. The common man loses this distinguishing feature, while the gentleman retains it. Shun understood the way of things and had a keen insight into human relationships. He acts from *ren* and *yi*, yet does not act in conformity with *ren* and *yi*."
>
> *Mencius*, 4B19

In the last sentence, the first and the second *ren* and *yi* have different meanings: the former is used in their first meaning (the moral heart-mind), whereas the latter is used in their second meaning (kinds of virtue). For Mencius, it is the moral heart-mind from which an act springs, rather than the conformity of the act to virtues determines its being a moral act. It is true for both *ren* and *yi* that their first meanings are primary whereas their second meanings are derivative. They are primary in that the ability which these two notions signify make the corresponding virtues possible. This is not only an analytic truth, but for Confucians, it is also a practical fact: only when one is always motivated by the heart-mind of *ren* (or *yi*) can one possess the virtue of *ren* (or *yi*). Now with the above understanding of the meanings and the senses of *ren* and *yi*, let us return to the problem of whether in Confucian ethics, the essential ethical notions are treated as primary. Although when they are conceived as virtues, *ren* and *yi* are derivative, what they are derived from are not deontic notions but notions of human abilities. In other words, the second meanings of *ren* and *yi* are derived from their first meanings. But this does not imply that they are derived from the deontic notions. However, since deontic notions are also derived from the same abilities just mentioned, we need to further study this problem.

In the *Analects*, Confucius claims, "It is only those who possess *ren* that are capable of liking and disliking others." (*Analects*, 4.3) This means that the necessary condition for one to be right in liking and disliking others is the virtue of *ren* one possesses. Moreover, as mentioned above, one's being morally right does not depend on his or her acting in accordance with moral rules and social norms, but depends on his or her observing the judgments based on *yi*. Mencius particularly emphasizes this point. For instance, he says that a great man need not keep his word, nor does he necessarily see his action through to the end, if he holds *yi*.[22] This shows that though observing moral rules would lead to right actions in normal situations, yet in some special occasions, it is moral for one to do an action which deviates from moral rules. Mencius' claim also shows that it is the morally great man who embraces and activates the capacity of differentiating right from wrong and determines what is right. It is not the case that he is a moral man because what he is always doing is the right act. Evidence of this kind can be found everywhere in *Mencius*.[23] Therefore it can be concluded that deontic notions like right and wrong are derived from virtues like *ren* and *yi*.

Like *ren* and *yi*, there is more than one meaning of *li* and those meanings are used without attentive distinctions. *Li* is a notion that differs from *ren* and *yi* in that it possesses a weaker sense of human abilities[24] but a stronger sense of norm. The first meaning of *li* denotes one of the virtues the importance of which is just less than that of *ren* and *yi*. As a virtue, *li* signifies the intention of being considerate in attainment. It also represents a sense of orderliness, which the moral heart-mind intends to pursue. Therefore *li* can be viewed as an objectification of moral heart-mind in a specific direction. From a Confucian point of view, the observance of *li* is a path to *ren*.

> Yanyuan asked about *ren*. The master said, "To return to the observance of *li* through overcoming the self constitutes *ren*."
>
> *Analects*, 12.1

Once we overcome our self-interested desires, our moral heart-mind would activate and seek to objectify itself by observing *li*.

When the moral heart-mind is objectified and endowed with a certain specificity, it gives *li* substantive content. For example, the moral maxims which Confucius introduces in the same passage cited above: "Do not look unless it is in accordance with *li*; do not listen unless it is in accordance with *li*; do not speak unless it is in accordance with *li*; do not move unless it is in accordance with *li*" (*Analects*, 12.1) are prescriptions directed to one's various aspects of behavior. Although the contents of *li* mentioned in this passage have not been spelt out, it is understood that for each respect, there are specific rites to follow. Only rites with specific aspects can play a normative role in the empirical world. Such ritual propriety or moral maxims like respectfulness and reverence can be conceived as instances of the second meaning of *li*.

Since maxims or propriety refer to specific situations and roles, people sometimes wrongly think that it is the situations or roles that determine the maxims or propriety. But as I have clarified elsewhere, "obligations are not defined by the roles people happened to occupy but rather, obligations are created to suit specific situations."[25] It is the emphasis on the decisional ability of moral heart-mind rather than on the external conditions that makes Confucian ethics an autonomous ethical system.

There are several functions of maxims and propriety, the details of which shall not be explored here. Of those functions, the main ones are: 1. providing criteria for the right act in normal situations on the one hand, and setting restraints on people from exceedingly following the urges of their desires on the other; 2. enhancing people's awareness of the moral heart-mind and the cultivation of moral life. However, as we have seen, *ren* and *yi* as the moral heart-mind itself are the ultimate ground for *li*, since *li* is only an embodiment of the moral heart-mind. The exclamation from Confucius—"What is the value for one who performs propriety without *ren*?" (*Analects*, 3.3)—fully expresses this view.[26] Similarly, *li* as a virtue provides a moral connotation to maxims and propriety. Maxims and propriety should not be observed as a formality, but should be practiced with awareness of their spiritual meanings.

> Mencius said, "A great man will not observe *li* that is contrary to the spirit of *li*, nor will he perform *yi* that goes against the spirit of *yi*."
>
> *Mencius*, 4B6

Since the virtue of *li* represents the criteria for the right act, performance that conforms to other virtues but in a way deviates from *li* would cause undesirable outcomes and thus is far from being virtuous.

> The Master said, "Unless a man has the spirit of *li*, in being respectful he will wear himself out, in being careful he will become timid, in having courage he will become unruly, and in being forthright he will become intolerant . . ."
>
> *Analects*, 8.92

Since maxims and propriety such as respectfulness, carefulness, and courage represent some sort of rules which right and wrong are based on, and since their moral meanings are derived from the virtue of *li*, apparently deontic notions like right and wrong can be conceived as derivative or secondary.

By now it should be clear that the essential ethical notions such as *ren*, *yi* and *li*, when considered as virtues are treated as primary, while the deontic notions are derived from them. Still, we cannot conclude that Confucian ethics belongs to virtue ethics, so let us move to the second feature of virtue ethics.

Ethical assessment in Confucian thought

According to Slote, another distinctive feature of virtue ethics is that it places a greater emphasis on ethical assessment of agents and their motives and character traits than it places on the evaluation of acts and choices. In this section I am going to show that Confucian ethics does possess this feature.

First there is the fact that cultivation of the heart-mind has been the central concern for Confucians. There are innumerable Confucian teachings on various ways of achieving such an aim. This is based on a fundamental belief that only a human being possesses a moral heart-mind and that it is its cultivation that makes human beings different from beasts. Since the human mind can be extended infinitely, self-cultivation is a lifelong effort for an agent who devotes himself or herself to it. The ultimate state of achievement, as Confucius describes it, is "to follow one's desires without any deviation from the norm." (*Analects*, 2.4) An agent can reach a certain stage toward this state during his or her lifetime and his or her ethical achievement can thus be assessed by judging which stage he or she is at. Having used the term "stage" in the above description, it should be noted that this term is used in a somewhat metaphorical sense.

It does not mean that there are distinctive and clear conceptions of each level of ethical achievement. On the contrary, the way in which one represents oneself is quite unique for each person, and the development of these stages is not linear. Moreover, the stage which one is at would be reflected in various aspects, therefore we cannot judge it by an individual act one performs or a single choice one makes at a particular time or on a special occasion, but we have to assess the agent as a whole person.

As emphasized repeatedly in the last section, it is not certain kinds of behavior that Confucian thinkers aim at conforming to, but it is the performance motivated by the moral heart-mind that they think valuable. Apparently the object of ethical assessment is the motives of an agent rather than the acts or choices he or she makes. Paradoxically, the motive of an agent is something which can hardly be assessed externally. Therefore, a morally good act cannot be judged by other people, this implausibility also applies to a morally good person. In other words, although the assessment of an agent is more important than that of an act, yet practically no objective results can be arrived at. Nevertheless, one can always assess oneself through self-reflection, and then elevate oneself accordingly by purifying one's mind and strengthening one's will. Confucians think that this is the function of making such an assessment. Even though in moral education, ethical assessment of students is useful for giving instructions which suit a particular individual, yet the assessment is supposed to be made by students themselves.

However, if any evaluation of an agent has to be made (e.g., when an exemplar has to be set up for others to follow), then such an evaluation can only be made by judging the agent externally. But we have to bear in mind that an evaluation made externally is not a kind of ethical assessment in its essential sense. It might be regarded as a partial evaluation. For Confucians, an agent's moral achievement can be evaluated partially by his or her performance because they think that moral mind can, and, should be objectified. The virtues possessed by an agent reflect the effect of his or her objectification of the moral heart-mind. Surely, as shown above, it is possible for one to behave in conformity with rites and propriety yet detached from their spirits, but such kinds of behavior cannot be qualified as virtues. That is why virtues of an agent demonstrated externally can only be a partial reflection of the objectification mentioned. As a partial reflection, for example, we can find that a cultivated person appears to be reverent, since one of the descriptions of a gentleman is "one who cultivates oneself and thereby achieves reverence." (*Analects*, 14.42) It follows that a person with reverence is probably, though not necessarily, a gentleman. Besides, Mencius also believes that one's ethical quality is manifested in one's body.

> ... That which a gentleman follows as his nature, that is to say, *ren*, *yi*, *li* and *zhi* (wisdom), is rooted in his heart-mind, and manifests itself in his face, giving it a sleek appearance. It also shows in his back and extends to his limbs, rendering their message intelligible without words.
>
> *Mencius*, 7A21

But it should be noted that only an agent cultivated to a certain degree (like a "gentleman" or a "sage") is able to manifest his or her moral mind fully. Nevertheless, a thorough manifestation of the moral mind is as important as the cultivation of it.

Thus, while Confucian education aims at cultivating the moral mind, it also stresses the transformation of self. The former objective can mainly be achieved by way of self-reflection, whereas the latter depends on living a virtuous life. This is why a gentleman—a person who possesses all the essential virtues—has been treated as a central theme in the early Confucian texts like the *Analects* and *Mencius*. Self-transformation consists in a change of oneself, from selfishly-minded to being considerate, from beneficial oriented to righteous oriented, from insensitive to empathetic, and so on and so forth. Apart from this, self-transformation also aims at seeking the balance of character, i.e., making adjustments to one's original personality if one is too timid, over-confident, too bold, too conservative, too compassionate, or too radical, etc. All of these show that Confucians put greater emphasis on the ethical assessment of one's character traits. In the ethical assessment, acts and choices are relevant only if they can be evaluated from a moral point of view. Therefore, an assessment of acts and choices is meaningful only if it is made within the context of the evaluation of an agent as a whole, with reference to his or her moral motive.

From the discussion in the last two sections, it seems that Confucian ethics possesses the two distinctive features of virtue ethics, hence it can be concluded that it belongs to virtue ethics. But one should be cautious to note that there might be a gap between the meanings of the key concept of "virtue" in the philosophy of Confucianism and that in virtue ethics. If this is the case, it would affect the whole conclusion. Therefore, we need further analysis.

Virtues and admirability

According to Slote, the idea that equal weight should be given to the well-being of the self and to that of others underlies the whole concept of virtue ethics. He also maintains that common-sense and Kantian morality have not given sufficient weight to the interests or well-being of moral agents, "and thus, in an important sense, [they] slight, devalue, or downgrade such agents."[27] Apart from this, the unequal emphasis on the well-being of the self as compared to that of others also brings about a serious theoretical consequence which Slote labels "self-other asymmetry." Self-other asymmetry shows itself in an agent-sacrificing permission which allows an individual to deny himself or herself the very things he or she most wants, or causes himself or herself unnecessary pain or damage. On the contrary, it does not allow an individual to treat others in such a way.

> Consider, then, what our ordinary moral thinking seems to allow and to forbid with regard to our treatment of other people. Negligently to hurt another person seems, intuitively, to be morally wrong in a way or to a degree that it does not seem wrong through negligence to hurt oneself . . . Similarly, if one could easily prevent pain to another person, it is typically thought wrong not to do so, but not to avoid similar pain to oneself seems crazy or irrational, not morally wrong. And so given the agent-sacrificing common-sense permissions we have described, we may now also speak of an agent-sacrificing (or other-favoring) self-other asymmetry that

> attaches to what is commonsensically permissible. Various ways [in which] one may permissibly act against one's own interests or well-being are ways one is commonsensically not allowed to act against the interests or well-being of others.[28]

Slote thinks that self-other asymmetry is not acceptable for an ethical system because it causes "odd and even paradoxical consequences."[29]

> Given that we are thinking critically and theoretically about ethics, we may well wish to avoid asymmetry whenever other things are equal . . .[30]

While ethical systems such as common-sense morality and Kantianism are undermined by the self-other asymmetry, a certain kind of commonsensical approach to virtue ethics can escape this problem. In such a kind of virtue ethics, the understanding of virtues is that "it allows both facts about the well-being of others and facts about the well-being of the agent to support claims about the goodness of some trait possessed by the agent, claims, that is, about the trait's status as a virtue."[31] To illustrate this notion of virtue in another way, we can say that "traits of character can qualify as virtues through what they enable their possessors to do for themselves as well as through what they enable their possessors to do for others."[32] In Slote's account, it is obvious that character traits that are either other-benefiting or self-benefiting can both qualify as virtues. The notion of virtue understood as such is an aretaic notion rather than a moral notion. Apparently, whether common-sense virtue ethics can be free of the problem of self-other asymmetry depends significantly on what is to be or what exemplifies a virtue. It also follows that only those ethical systems which are based on the broader aretaic notions can escape the problem of asymmetry. Slote uses the term "admirable character traits" to signify the aretaic notion of virtue to distinguish it from the moral notion. So we shall use "admirable" to describe traits which are instances of such kind of virtue.

Now there are two problems we have to solve before we can decide what the nature of Confucian ethics is. Firstly, does Confucian ethics contain aretaic notions of virtue and, what are their status? Secondly, does it encounter the difficulty of self-other asymmetry? In a previous paper,[33] I have examined most of the important Confucian virtues and found that both in the area of interpersonal interaction, and in the area of the moral cultivation of an agent, virtues always play an important role, but mainly in one's moral improvement. The well-being of or benefits to the self and that of the other can enter into one's moral life only if they contribute to the matter of improvement mentioned. This means that they do not have any independent significance in moral considerations. In this perspective, virtues are valuable because of their moral values. In this sense, the notion of virtue in Confucian ethics is obviously a moral concept.

However, if as in the quote above, virtue is (loosely) conceived as a character trait which enables their possessors to do something for themselves as well as for others, then, the moral concept of virtue can fit in well with this description. This is so because while benefit cannot be part of the moral consideration, moral achievement is something which an agent aims at and that he or she does for himself or herself as well as for others. Even under moral considerations, one does not necessarily sacrifice one's own interest for others nor is one permitted to deny one's well-being unjustifiably. Moreover, sometimes the benefit of others has to be sacrificed for the sake of morality. It can be easily seen that from the moral point of view, benefit itself, whether it belongs to the self or to others, would not be the object of moral consideration, unless it has a moral implication. Sometimes, by acting for the benefit of others one may add significantly to one's moral achievement, and if moral achievement constitutes part of the (and may be the highest) achievement of human life, then doing for the self and doing for others are **two in one**. In a broad sense of well-being of which moral achievement occupies a large part, it is meaningless to make a differentiation between self and others.[34] Since the distinction of aretaic and moral notions is based on such a differentiation, it seems that there is no point to attribute either of these notions to qualify Confucian ethics.

On the other hand, there **is** a distinction, even if not always an opposed relationship, between the self and the others. It occurs in the non-moral realm where one's well-being is of great importance. In Confucian thought, non-moral values[35] are admitted as aims for an individual to pursue.[36] So character traits which are beneficial for those aims are admirable, and thus regarded as virtues. For example, Confucians think that apart from moral cultivation, to realize one's potential and to develop one's personality are essential for the development of a whole person. In this respect, being wise, free from desire, courageous, and accomplished are admirable as they are necessary components for a "complete man."

> Zilu asked about the complete man.
>
> The master said, "A man as wise as Zhang Wuzhong, as free from desire as Meng Gongzhuo, as courageous as Zhuangzi of Bian and as accomplished as Ran Qiu, who is further refined by *li* and music, may be considered a complete man."
>
> *Analects*, 14.10

In the following passage, it is clear that certain non-moral values are adopted by the Confucians, and that the virtues which lead to those values are worth-promoting.

> . . . If a man is respectful he will not be treated with insolence. If he is tolerant he will win the multitude. If he is trustworthy in word his fellow men will entrust him with responsibility. If he is quick he will achieve results. If he is generous he will be good enough to be put in a position over his fellow men.
>
> *Analects*, 17.6

Obviously, insolence, multitude, entrustment, etc., are non-moral values, and respectful, tolerant, trustworthy, quick, and generous are admirable character traits which are self-benefiting.

It is noteworthy that as far as non-moral values are concerned, Confucians do not hold that one has to fulfill the other's satisfaction **prior to** one's own. Even in moral consideration, the teaching of "helping others to take their stand in so far as he himself wishes to take his stand, and gets others there in so far as he himself wishes to get there" (*Analects*, 6.30) does not suggest that one should let one's benefits be overridden by others' benefits. Confucian ethics is altruistic in a sense that it takes the well-being of others into consideration when making moral judgments. On the other hand, when one's well-being is being pursued, a time which does not necessarily involve morality, the weight of the self and that of others are equal. Apparently, no self-other asymmetry appears here.[37]

Conclusion

From the above discussions, we have seen that Confucian thinkers treat virtues rather than deontic notions as primary, but most of the virtues they commend are specifically moral or have moral implications. In this sense virtue is not a kind of aretaic notion which gives recognition to the well-being of the self and to that of others. However, as it has been shown, Confucian ethics avoids the difficulty of self-other asymmetry. Aretaic notions do exist in Confucian thought, but in the non-moral realm. Therefore, we can view the whole problem in this way: within the moral realm, virtues are specifically moral; beyond this realm, that is, in the non-moral realm, virtues are those admirable character traits that are beneficial to the self as well as to others. In both of these realms, there is no self-other asymmetry. Besides, greater emphasis is put on the assessment of character traits than on that of acts and choices. This is our preliminary conclusion.

One might argue that this preliminary conclusion is too simplistic because it only reveals a truism that one treats traits morally in the moral realm (a realm where things are considered from a moral point of view), and that one treats traits non-morally in a non-moral realm. One might also argue that the crucial stand to define an ethical system is what weight it gives to these two realms. This is a reasonable challenge to which I do not object, but I think more can be discovered. Surely what is moral overrides what is non-moral when a moral point of view is taken. This is true not only for Confucian ethics, but for all moral systems that define morality as something that is overriding. The most important issue here is whether these systems allow the independent existence of another realm beyond that of the moral, and whether they put considerable weight on the non-moral values and suggest people to promote them accordingly. If the importance of these values is recognized, then a number of principles can be established. A branch of study might then develop. We can coin a new name for it, or we may just call it "ethics." Confucian thought does not limit itself to a narrow sense of morality; it extends the domain of discourse and concern to this broader sense of ethics.

9

Confucian Ethics and Virtue Ethics Revisited

Preface

In 2001 I published "Confucian Ethics and Virtue Ethics"[1] which, as its title implies, discusses the relevance of Confucian ethics to virtue ethics. The aim of that article is primarily to explain the characteristics and core concepts of Confucian ethics, rather than to define and categorize the Confucian ethical system.[2] Since then, discussions on virtue ethics as well as on the relationship between Chinese philosophy and virtue ethics have made considerable progress; however, to my disappointment, the understanding and interpretation of Confucian ethics expressed in the discussions were often off the mark. This chapter is an attempt to explain and clarify further some of the biased and inaccurate interpretations. It shares the focus of the previous article, namely, that it is not to compare the system of Confucian ethics with the ethical systems of Kant, Aristotle, and Hume and then to discuss the appropriateness in categorizing Confucian ethics as Humean, Aristotelian, or Kantian virtue ethics;[3] instead, it will concentrate on examining the position of Confucian ethics regarding the features of virtue ethics, so as to reveal its character and significance. What I would like to emphasize is that Confucian ethics should not be limited by (certain types of) "virtue ethics," thereby depriving it of its richer connotation. In "The Moral and Non-Moral Virtues in Confucian Ethics,"[4] I argued that in Confucian ethics, non-moral virtue is independent of moral virtue, so the system of Confucian ethics is not confined to a narrow sense of moral system.[5] As it will be shown below, this discovery is significant to the current issue.

Bryan W. Van Norden joined the debate on whether Confucianism is a kind of virtue ethics in his monograph on the early Chinese philosophy and virtue ethics.[6] Unlike other philosophers of the West, he is aware that Confucianism is "different in many respects from the forms of virtue ethics that have been dominant in the West" even though he thinks that it counts as a form of virtue ethics.[7] In this chapter I will take Van Norden's discussion as an example to illustrate the central problems of the whole issue. In the present discussion, I will restrict the scope of Confucian ethics to the thoughts of Confucius and Mencius.

Flourishing life

Virtue ethics as understood by Van Norden, is an ethical system focusing on "what sort of person one should be, and what way of life one should live."[8] He lists four components of virtue ethics: first, an account of what a "flourishing" human life is like; second, an account of what virtues contribute to the leading of such a life; third, an account of how one acquires those virtues; and fourth, a philosophical anthropology that explains what humans are like, such that they can acquire those virtues so as to flourish in that kind of life.[9] Due to the constraint of length, in this chapter I will focus on the first two elements and only touch on the others when deemed necessary.

"Flourishing," as conceived by Van Norden, is a technical term in virtue ethics. It corresponds to Aristotle's "eudaimonia" in Greek and Aquinas' "beatitude" in Latin. "To flourish is to live a certain kind of life: a life characterized by the ordered exercise of one's capacities as a human."[10] The term "ordered" indicates that some activities are considered to be more valuable compared with some others. In Confucianism, a human's various capacities can definitely be regarded as having differed levels of importance, in relation to the ultimate goal of cultivation, i.e., to become a sage (*cheng sheng* 成聖). This view is manifested in Mencius' discussion on the distinction between the greater body (*da ti* 大體) and the lesser body (*xiao ti* 小體)[11] which highlights the slight difference between humans and beasts.[12] A great person (*da ren* 大人) is one who always acts from his or her greater body and therefore lives a flourishing life. The greater body that Mencius refers to is the original heart-mind (*ben xin* 本心), also known as the heart-mind of *ren-yi* (*renyi zhixin* 仁義之心). At this point, a problem arises: if *ren* and *yi* are understood merely as moral virtues and hence the original heart-mind denotes a moral capacity that enables one to observe these virtues, then, flourishing life which embodies the goal of Confucianism is but a synonym of moral life, and a great person would merely be a moral person. If that were the case, then flourishing life as the core component of virtue ethics would not have taken up such centrality as it does in the system of Confucianism.

For Confucius, a "gentleman" (*junzi* 君子, a person of noble character), striving to achieve the ultimate goal, has a significant status just less than that of a great person. A person is regarded as a gentleman only if he lives up to *ren* and *yi*.[13] In many chapters of the *Analects*, *ren* and *yi* have a moral connotation.[14] Moreover, in the *Analects*, the notion of gentleman is not only explained in terms of *ren* and *yi*, but also involves a moral meaning.[15] Therefore it is natural to think that a gentleman is one who has great accomplishment in the moral realm. As discussed above, if *ren* and *yi* are nothing but moral virtues, then flourishing life is just the same as moral life. If that be the case, these are not what *ren* and *yi* are referred to in Confucianism, and hence Confucianism does not possess the core component of virtue ethics, and thus it is dubious to classify it as virtue ethics.

It is absolutely true that one of the multi-faceted meanings of *ren* and *yi* refers to moral virtues. Van Norden discerns that for Confucius, the broad sense of *ren* refers to "the summation of human virtues" whereas its narrow sense refers to a specific virtue, namely, "loving others." Apparently *ren* is a virtue in any senses. He translates *ren* as "benevolence" with the following connotation: "to be benevolent is to be pained by the suffering of others and to take joy in the happiness of others," which is close to empathy.[16] Van Norden points out that this meaning of benevolence applies to Mencius.[17] In an article entitled "*Ren*, Empathy and the Agent-Relative Approach in Confucian Ethics,"[18] I argued at length that neither "loving others" nor empathy is the primary meaning of *ren*, rather, the capacity of "transference (with others)" (*gantong* 感通) (which differs from empathy) is.[19] I also argued that it is only with the capacity of transference which implies impartial evaluation (*yi*) that moral judgment of the good and the bad is possible.

The problem of "what sort of person one should be, and what way of life one should live" is indeed a central issue for Confucianism, that is why there have been so many discussions on the "sage," the "great man," the "gentleman," and the "*cheng ren*"(成人), etc. Nevertheless, if the ideal personality is merely moral oriented, then flourishing life understood in terms of the ideal person would have to be very narrow. We have argued that *ren* and *yi*, which play a significant role in characterizing the ideal person do not merely refer to moral virtues, as Van Norden sees it. Still, this cannot disprove the conclusion that flourishing life in Confucianism is limited to moral life, since in our discussion so far, *ren* and *yi* in their primary meanings are wedded to morality.

Li as a virtue leading to the flourishing life

Van Norden views *li* as an important virtue, at least for Confucius, that contributes to leading the flourishing life. Although he is aware of the broad coverage of activities where *li* is involved, Van Norden believes that it is useful to think of *li* as "ritual."[20] Ritual, as Van Norden rightly sees, is learned human activity that is regarded as sacred. He also explains that to regard something as sacred is to think that the proper attitude toward it is awe or reverence (*jing* 敬).[21] In this regard, we can consider reverence as the spirit of the activity. For Confucius the importance of ritual does not rest on the form of its performance, but rather on the spirit that the ritual manifests. Apart from reverence which is the common spirit of ritual, specific rituals manifest specific spirits. For example, mourning should manifest the feeling of grief, while making an offering should manifest respectfulness (to a certain object).[22] However, no matter what kind of spirit it manifests, a ritual should be presented from the heart-mind of *ren*. Thus Confucius said: "If a man is without *ren*, then of what use are the rites!"[23] He criticized Zaiwo's objection to the three-year period of mourning as opposed to *ren* since the latter failed to consider the issue from the original heart-mind.[24] Therefore, *li* has a deeper meaning than rituals: the former is grounded on the heart-mind of *ren-yi* whereas the latter is not necessarily so. Only when the connection of rituals and the heart-mind is revealed, the value of *li* which goes beyond the form of rituals can be discovered. *Ren* also provides *li* with a moral meaning. In this regard, the heart-mind of *ren-yi* is the criterion for the adjustment of rituals and their forms will not be arbitrary.[25] Now we can conclude that the difference between ritual and *li* lies in the awareness of *ren* as the latter's ground. *Li* in this sense can be regarded as an expression of the heart-mind of *ren-yi* and since the urge of being expressed is rooted in the heart-mind, therefore *li* is also rooted in the heart-mind. Hence, *li* is considered by Mencius as one of the four elements in human nature.

Mencius also says that "the great man does not perform acts of *li* which are not truly in accord with *li*, nor acts of *yi* which are not truly in accord with *yi*."[26] In the phrase "the acts of *li* which are not truly in accord with *li*," the former "*li*" should be read as social norms or rituals in general and the latter "*li*" as the underlying spirits. If those spirits are essentially in moral sense, then it seems that all rituals are moral-laden. Furthermore, if in the passage quoted above,[27] *ren* merely refers to a moral attribute, then flourishing life (of which *li* is a significant way of expression) is not only inseparable from morality, but is even stipulated by morality. If this is the case, then can Confucian ethics still be classified as virtue ethics?

Non-moral virtues for good life

In "The Moral and Non-Moral Virtue in Confucian Ethics," I argue that in Confucian ethics, there is a domain of non-moral values which is independent of morality and is a constituent of good life. The character traits that can help one to accomplish non-moral values which are called "admirable character traits" by Slote[28] are non-moral virtues. In the *Analects* 14.13, Confucius thinks that "wisdom," "lacking desire," "bravery," and "(mastery of) the arts" are quintessential virtues for the all-rounded person (*cheng ren* 成人). It is remarkable that none of these virtues are embedded with moral meaning and may be considered as non-moral virtues. Confucius goes on mentioning that on top of these non-moral virtues, one should be "cultivated by means of rites and music." The rites and music mentioned here are not necessarily moral-laden. In this passage, subsequent to the above discussion, it is added that "perhaps today we need not ask all this of the all-rounded person. One who, when he sees a chance of gain, stops to think whether to pursue it would be accord to *yi*; when he sees that one is in danger, is ready to lay down his life; when the fulfillment of an old promise is exacted, stands by what he said long ago." This second set of qualifications differs from the first set in that the former is more moral oriented. Therefore we may boldly infer from this passage that non-moral virtues are more important than moral virtues to be an all-rounded person.

It is certain that the virtues that Confucianism advocates include both moral and non-moral virtues. The question is: if the non-moral domain is defined by morality (for example, a non-moral act is, judging from a moral point of view, an act or choice that is neither morally right nor wrong), then the non-moral domain is only "a supplementary set" of the moral domain. Since the non-moral domain is determined by the moral point of view, therefore it loses its independence. We can query whether certain acts or choices should be guided by the moral mind (or moral principles) and are not be able to be guided by non-moral principles. Another question emerges: what (principles) do we adopt when we decide that we "should" take the moral point of view, rather than the non-moral point of view, and vice versa? (This is related to the priority of moral values and non-moral values.) Here, "should" is not used in a moral sense, otherwise it would be question-begging. Therefore, "should" must go beyond both the moral and the non-moral sense. From the text of the *Analects* and *Mencius*, it makes perfect sense to interpret "should" as referring to the appropriateness, "all things, including both the moral and non-moral points of view, considered."[29] This meaning of "should" is signified also by the notion of *ren* (e.g., *Mencius*, 7A46) and *yi* (e.g., *Analects*, 4.10 and *Mencius* 4B11). Remarkably, the ability of making judgment of appropriateness is not a separate ability to making moral judgment, but the former is exactly the same as the latter, namely, the heart-mind of *ren-yi*. The judgment of appropriateness in which moral and non-moral values are considered and weighed against each other, is called ethical judgment.[30] Therefore, the heart-mind of *ren-yi* understood as the ability of making ethical judgment already includes the recognition of non-moral values, and the judgment sprung from it is not limited to the narrow sense of "moral ought." Thus we may call the prescription aiming at appropriateness mentioned "the ethical ought."

The distinction between moral and non-moral virtues is made merely for the sake of discussion. In an actual situation, when one makes an ethical judgment, he or she has already taken both the moral and non-moral values into consideration, and a Confucian would make an ethical judgment by the heart-mind of *ren-yi*. Both moral and non-moral virtues can assist one in accomplishing (moral and non-moral) values. In some extraordinary circumstances, realizing moral values or observing moral principles may result in something contrary to the ethical judgment, and in some other circumstances it may be the case that two different moral values cannot simultaneously be realized (or two different moral principles cannot simultaneously be observed). Then the heart-mind of *ren-yi* can also serve to guide one to choose the value that should be realized or to amend the original moral principle(s) in question. In addition, choices between a moral value and a non-moral one, or between two non-moral values can also be guided by the heart-mind of *ren-yi*.[31] What should be emphasized is that the heart-mind of *ren-yi* is not some ready-made virtues or principles, but rather, an ability of making ethical judgment that is more fundamental than virtues. In this regard, to categorize Confucian ethics as virtue ethics may result from confusion among different meanings and functions of *ren* and *yi*.

Flourishing life within a community

Some people may think that in a Confucian ethical world, every particular act or the way of living in general cannot deviate from morality, so the whole life of humans must be dominated by morality. However, although Confucianism actually endeavors to actualize an ethical perfect state, yet morality is only one aspect of it. Non-moral values, such as harmonious and ordered interpersonal relationship, warm and consonant family life, aesthetic satisfaction, free and unfettered quality of life, broad and sagacious wisdom, and courage facing confusion and obstacles, all play an important role and can be attained by the cultivation of non-moral virtues.

"A flourishing life" in Confucian thought must not be an isolated life,[32] and therefore on the one hand a person should contribute to his or her community in one way or another and people should support each other; on the other hand, a perfect community is also an important factor for the realization of a flourishing life. For Confucius, an ideal society is a World of Great Harmony.[33] A World of Great Harmony is a selfless world in which everyone contributes his or her best to the community and takes what he or she needs, and in which everyone does not merely love his or her own parents and children, but also loves others' parents and children. Because people display this kind of loving care for each other, "the old are properly cared for, the able are suitably employed, and the young can decently grow up."[34] Even the lonely and helpless are taken good care of. Because there is no personal property, theft does not exist. It is noteworthy that in such a world the virtues of *li* and *yi* are not necessary for maintaining social order as everyone voluntarily treats each other selflessly. *Li* and *yi* is only required in a "Society of Small Tranquility" (fairly well-off society) controlled by a single family (with the same family name). A society in which individual or family interest is the paramount focus needs virtues such as *li* and *yi* in order to secure personal interest and to solidify the ruler's power. Since a distinction is made between self and others, as well as the intimate and the distant, consequently people require laws to keep social order, and *li* and *yi* can help in this respect. Moreover, Confucius thinks that because of the emphasis on "self" and "distinction," duplicity and wars emerge. It is thus clear that *li* and *yi* can be viewed as rules enforced upon and are made especially for specific society.

From the above description, we can see that for Confucianism the most accomplished flourishing life is embodied in a selfless society. The ultimate goal of practising moral virtue (such as *ren*) is to achieve selflessness. When everyone is selfless there is no need for virtue. From another perspective, the heart-mind of *ren* is a selfless mind, so activating the heart-mind of *ren* is more effective than blindly following virtue step by step towards realizing a flourishing life. In the "Society of Small Tranquility," even though virtue plays a role in correcting the misfortune and harm brought about by the pursuit of self-interest, a heart-mind of *ren* should be employed to review the abuse and limitation of virtue (and adjust it accordingly) at all times.

Conclusion

This chapter discusses what a flourishing human life is like in Confucianism and what virtues may contribute to the leading of such a life. We can see that the flourishing life that Confucianism constructs is one in which moral and non-moral values are realized. However, virtues that contribute to the realization mentioned are not of the highest significance since their (moral and non-moral) meanings are attributed by the original heart-mind (of *ren-yi*). Because of this, it is dubious to classify Confucian ethics as virtue ethics.

As stated in my preface, the aim of this chapter is not to classify Confucian ethics as any one of the types of Western ethical systems. On the contrary, I attempt to reveal that criteria abstracted from the Western philosophy are not necessarily applicable to the Chinese thought. I also try to characterize the features and meaning of Confucian ethics. I hope that this chapter has achieved this aim.

10

Virtues in Aristotelian and Confucian Ethics

Introduction

One central theme of debates in the field of ethics in the Western world over the past few decades has been related to two ethical systems, namely, principled ethics and virtue ethics. The areas of discussions range from the interpretation of original texts of philosophers, and the historical review of the development and shift of ethical systems from one sort to another, to the identification of the nature of particular ethical thought and the philosophical evaluation of the two systems in question. In recent years, these discussions have extended to the Chinese philosophy and the question "Whether Confucianism is, in one way or another, a kind of virtue ethics?" has aroused great interest in the field. Besides, comparisons between Western and Chinese ethical systems have been made, most of them under the presupposition that they belong to either one of these two contrary systems. In this chapter, I am less ambitious than attempting to make a comprehensive comparison between Aristotelian ethics and Confucian ethics; rather, I am going to investigate several important problems related to the notion of virtue in these two ethical systems, hoping that this will deepen the understanding of both of them and hence reveal the possibility of any comparisons.

The exposition of virtue in Confucianism and Aristotelian ethics

The central question in Aristotle's ethics concerns what the best life for human beings is. The task of ethics, as Aristotle conceives it, is to seek a systematic answer to this question.[1] According to Aristotle, the supreme good for man is nothing other than "activity in accordance with virtue," therefore virtue becomes the main concern of his ethics. As Broadie points out, "... Aristotle's *Ethics* is concerned with virtue and the virtues and would not be what we know as Aristotle's *Ethics* otherwise."[2] However, the contribution that Aristotle has made is not simply his emphasis on virtues to a greater degree than his predecessors such as Homer, who only considers bravery and honor as the two important components of the ideal life of a hero. What makes Aristotle's contribution distinctive is that he gives an account of the traditional virtues in relation to the supreme good and also to human beings as rational beings. In pursuing this task, Aristotle modifies these virtues while providing definitions and detailed expositions.[3]

In ancient Chinese thoughts, *ren*, *li* (propriety), fortitude, trustworthiness, *zhi* (wisdom) and the like are commended by nobility as early as the Chun Qiu period (769–476 BC). They are known as "*de*" (德), which signifies admirable traits as well as inner character. "*De*," with these two aspects of meaning, is generally translated as "virtues." While being aware of the possible distinctions between "*de*" and virtues, I shall hereafter use "virtue" to denote both *de* and the Aristotelian *arete*.[4] In the Chun Qiu period, virtues play an important role in the evaluation of people and their behavior. In one of the passages of *Kuo Yu*, as many as sixteen different virtues are listed and discussed,[5] which are either individual virtues or social virtues. While some of these virtues are supererogative, the breach of some others is nevertheless considered immoral. However, they all represent the norms of that period. The innovative move made by Confucius is to elevate the status of *ren* over that of *li*, which is the most important virtue in the Chun Qiu period. Although *ren* has been regarded as one of the important virtues before Confucius, as seen in *The Analects*, it is elevated to the synthesis of all individual virtues. Above all, the greatest contribution made by Confucius is attributing a transcendental meaning (i.e., the moral heart-mind) to *ren*. By so doing he offers a ground for an autonomous moral system.[6] In this sense, *ren* does not merely represent a social norm governing a certain class at a certain time, but also signifies the ability universally possessed by human beings, which makes (autonomous) morality possible. Besides, though Confucius upholds Chou *li* as a whole, he, like Aristotle, has modified some of the ways of practising the existing *li*. He, and particularly his follower Mencius, also give new interpretations and critical comments to the popular virtues and rites of their time.[7] The justification for these modifications and interpretations is based on *ren*, the meaning of which will be elaborated later.

As mentioned above, unlike their predecessors, Aristotle and Confucius do not take the existing virtues for granted. They both delineate those virtues in relation to their central problems of ethics.[8] Granted this similarity, however, they discuss virtues in quite different ways. In *Nicomachean Ethics* (*NE*) and *Eudemian Ethics* (*EE*), Aristotle investigates virtues by ways of explanation, definition, differentiation, and classification. Therefore it can be regarded as an analysis of different virtues. Confucius, on the other hand, has little interest in the virtues themselves; he always discusses virtues in association with what a gentleman (*junzi* 君子) should perform.[9] Being a gentleman is the primary aim for Confucian learners who are concerned with good character, good performance, and inner transformation.[10] Obviously Confucius and his followers care about a "how" question—how to achieve the ideal of being a gentleman or a sage—more than a "what" question. The answer to the latter is only a partial condition for the solution of the former. This relationship between truth and morality leads us to another discussion in the following sections.

Knowledge and morality

Aristotle divides the soul of human beings into two parts: rational and non-rational. The rational soul has two types of function, both unique to human beings. One of these is rational in a strict sense (i.e., ratiocinative), whereas the other is "listening to reason" (i.e., the reason-responsive part). Corresponding to these two aspects of the rational soul, virtues are also divided into two types: intellectual virtues, and virtues of character or moral virtues. They are, by definition, qualities whereby each of these aspects of the rational soul should function. With regard to moral virtues, courage, temperance, justice, and the like are their instances. However, it should be noted that the prescription in the soul is not only from intellectual virtues, but also from the virtues of character. Since the virtues of character are virtues of the desiderative (*orektikon*)[11] part of the soul, the rational prescriber is not entirely rational in the strict sense but also consists in the desiderative part. As Broadie perceptively points out, the distinction between the two aspects of the rational soul and that between the two types of virtues do not coincide. "Consequently, any strictly distinct and contrasting virtues of mind or intellect would have to do with the latter's ratiocinative and cognitive aspects only. They would not belong to the prescriptive part as a whole, so to speak, and virtues of character do not belong only to the responsive part."[12]

According to Aristotle, human beings as rational beings are to make rational choice (*prohairesis*) if any choice is to be made. In making rational choice, practical wisdom (*phronesis*) plays an important role. Practical wisdom is a kind of virtue, as defined by Aristotle, by which one deliberates well in a practical way (1140 24ff.) An agent can reach a rational decision through deliberation when exercising his or her practical reason. In deliberation, the means to an end are revealed. Hence it seems that for Aristotle, to deliberate is to deliberate only about the means (*ta pros ta tele*) and not about the end. But in asking how to pursue an object O, Broadie argues, is asking how to pursue O so that pursuing it is the best in the situation. Carrying further the previous argument, Broadie says, "The deliberative discovery that there is such a How, or that there is not, is the same as discovering that O is or is not to *be* pursued in this situation. In this way, deliberation yields an answer to the question 'Should I pursue O?'"[13] This means that the deliberation about the means contains that about the end. Moreover, Aristotle holds that though the abilities that one uses for making the end right and making the means right can be referred to different virtues (namely, moral excellence and intelligence respectively), they are qualities comprising practical wisdom. However, no matter whether the end or the means is deliberated, the situation in general and one's position in particular have to be grasped. This introduces the question as to what weight of knowledge, if any, Aristotle puts on deliberation.

In *NE* (1105b 1f.), Aristotle says that knowledge (*episteme*) counts for everything in relation to a craft but has little or no count in the case of virtues. In *EE* VIII, Aristotle rejects the Socratic view that virtues identify with forms of knowledge (1246a). He then proceeds to argue against the Socratic identification of *phronesis* (wisdom) with knowledge, where *phronesis* refers to the practical intelligence that guides a person's conduct (1246b).[14] According to Socrates, knowledge is supreme and vice is a result of the lack of knowledge. On the contrary, Aristotle holds that wisdom is supreme and it is subordinate to virtues of character only. The knowledge one needs for deliberation has to be practical, which is about particulars and contingent details of a specific circumstance. Nevertheless, knowledge of this kind is not acquired by a faculty of cognition; rather, it is from wisdom itself. Nor can theoretical knowledge provide the necessary knowledge for the deliberation. According to the Aristotelian doctrine, theoretical knowledge is about the eternal and necessary, and so it is not in our power to affect anything thus known.[15] On the other hand, with wisdom one can have the knowledge of a particular position and hence at the same time know what to do about it. If one does not know what to do, this only means that he or she does not yet know the facts of his or her position.

In Confucian doctrine, it is held that knowledge of the external world is of little importance for acting and behaving morally. For Confucius, the purpose of extending the scope of knowledge is to select good examples to follow, hence the major, if not the whole, meaning of knowledge lies in assisting one to become a good person.

> The Master said, "... I use my ears widely and follow what is good in what I have heard; I use my eyes widely and retain what I have seen in my mind. This constitutes a lower level of knowledge."
>
> *Analects*, 7.28

As illustrated in this passage, for Confucius pure knowledge with no moral implications has only a secondary status. What Confucius teaches his students is not theoretical knowledge but how to behave properly and to become a gentleman and eventually a sage.[16] Besides, the qualities needed for being a gentleman have almost nothing to do with knowledge.[17] By the same token, the subject matter of learning is the practical knowledge of how to perform appropriately in every respect of life.[18] In *Mencius*, we are told that the goal of education provided by village schools is to teach people the duties proper to sons and younger brothers.[19] Even for Xunzi, a Confucian who particularly emphasizes the importance of learning, the essential purpose of learning does not lie in the acquisition of knowledge of the external world. Its ultimate aim is to become a sage.[20] Even though he holds that a learner should study *The Book of Rites*, *The Book of Music*, *The Book of Odes*, *The Book of History*, and *Spring and Autumn Annals*, he claims that if one becomes a widely learned person but does not exalt *li*, then one will only become an imperfect Confucian. Therefore he says, "Thus, one who exalts ritual principles, though he may never gain a clear understanding of them, will be a model scholar, whereas one who does not exalt them, though he undertakes investigations and makes discriminations, will remain only an undisciplined Confucian."[21]

Zhi (wisdom) has been a virtue since the Chun Qiu period and is commended by Confucius as a contrasting as well as supplementary virtue to *ren*. Though *zhi* means intelligence, the focus of its employment is on the practical rather than theoretical aspect of human life. For Mencius, *zhi* represents one of the four virtues rooted in human nature and manifests itself in the heart-mind (*xin*) of right and wrong. Remarkably the right and wrong lie in the realm of morality. Therefore the virtue of wisdom that Mencius upholds is the ability in human nature which enables human beings to discriminate the morally right from the morally wrong, not only in the observance of general principles but also in making judgments in particular situations. The most noteworthy idea is that the criteria of right and wrong do not depend on the facts of the external world; neither are they defined by or reduced to those facts. Therefore the virtue of wisdom does not refer to the excellence of the faculty of cognition. To this last claim we shall come back later.

It is worth mentioning that there is a commonly accepted division of two sorts of knowledge among the Neo-Confucians, namely, experiential knowledge and knowledge of virtue. Only the latter is deemed relevant to the moral aim. Moreover, even the knowledge of virtue is not a kind of factual knowledge of moral truth, but is merely practical knowledge consisting of hints of cultivating the moral mind, and instructions of acting properly, etc. Since CHENG Yi re-introduces the two notions of *ge wu* (investigating matters) and *zhi zhi* (extending knowledge), all their interpretations echo the traditional view of the significance of knowledge in morality: the significance of knowledge of any kind depends on its contribution to morality.[22]

The moral truth

The answer to the question "Whether an assertion that something is morally good or evil is a moral truth? If so, what kind of truth it is?" is vital to the determination of what mode an ethical system belongs to. It is asserted by some ethicists that there are natural properties in the moral values (i.e., moral values can be defined in terms of natural properties), or, that there are objective reasons for a moral judgment (moral judgments can be, and can only be, justified by facts). No matter in which way they are presented, all of these assertions reflect a belief that making value judgments is equivalent to describing a fact, the truth value of which can be identified. To decide whether both of the Aristotelian and Confucian ethics are of the same mode or not will be fruitful for the understanding of their characteristics, and also helpful for the comparison between them.

In answering what is the supreme good for human beings, Aristotle is thought to employ his famous function argument. For Aristotle, the good life for a human being (the life of *eudaimonia*) consists in an optimal combination of component goods that makes him or her perform his or her function (*ergon*) well. He also holds that *eudaimonia* consists in activities in accordance with virtue (1098a 16–18). It follows that a virtuous act is the act which can bring about component goods to make up the good life. Therefore whether an action is virtuous depends on the component goods it brings about. If these component goods are recognizable, then this leads to a view that there is an objectively right or wrong answer to the question as to whether a specific action can be counted as a virtuous one. It seems evident that in Aristotle's ethics, moral values are composed of natural properties and the correctness of moral judgments is determined by certain facts.

A parallel issue can be found in Confucianism: if a moral action is judged or determined by the fact of observing the rules of *li* or not, which in turn can be characterized by certain recognizable facts, then it can be said that Confucian value judgments are entailed by factual statements. We may take *ren* as an example to facilitate our discussion. There are two remarks characterizing *ren* which are thought to be fundamental: "to love man" and "to return to *li*."[23] Details about "how to love man" and "how to return to *li*" are made explicit in *The Analects*. Apart from these "fundamental" meanings, *ren* has also been defined in terms of psychological feelings or emotions. In whatever ways, provided that an act of *ren* can be identified by certain recognizable criteria or characteristics, value judgments can be defined in terms of natural properties or by factual statements.

Another way of defining moral values that yields the same result is to make them part of the human nature. For example, it is held that Confucianism views filial piety as part of the human nature and the practice of the former is a manifestation of the latter. Besides, it is thought that in Mencius' philosophy, *ren*, *yi*, *li* and *zhi* are four basic virtues rooted in human nature. Moreover, they constitute the essence of human beings. Therefore it is supposed that moral properties are defined by metaphysical assertions. In the beginning of *The Doctrine of the Mean*, the statement "What Heaven confers is called the nature (*xing*). The following of this nature is called the Way (*Dao*)" has also been considered as an evidence of this Confucian idea. Similar views can be found in the doctrines of Neo-Confucians like Cheng Yi and ZHU Xi where they discuss the relationship between human nature and *Li* (Principle 理). All in all, if moral values can be realized by following certain natural dispositions or by embodying certain metaphysical properties, then it is evident that moral judgments are determined by factual statements, no matter whether they are natural or metaphysical.

With regard to Aristotle's function argument, since what is good for human beings is what can fulfill human function, the understanding of what constitutes human function is crucial to the perception of the good. Specifically, since Aristotle conceives that human beings are rational animals, the best life for them is the life of contemplation,[24] and the latter can be described in a value-neutral way.[25] However, such an understanding and the related assertion about human function and, in general, about human nature leads to a view that moral values lie in extra-ethical beliefs.

From the interpretation of the doctrines of Confucianism and Aristotle's ethics given above, it is suggested that there are moral truths, and the task of ethics is to reveal these truths and to use them to justify moral judgments and actions. However, there are other understandings of these doctrines, which will lead to different conclusions.

On one reading of *eudaimonia*, moral values are explained in terms of non-moral values. Suppose that *eudaimonia* is constituted by the activities in accordance with virtue on the one hand, and activities that will bring about optimal combination of component goods fulfilling human function on the other. Under this interpretation, in so far as the assessment of the optimal combination of goods is prior to, and independent of, ethical values, it is the case that what is judged morally good can be externally validated. However, this is just the result of a specific understanding of the conception of *eudaimonia* and Aristotle's function argument. On John McDowell's reading, *eudaimonia* is not something brought about by virtuous actions if all goes well; rather, *eudaimonia* consists in virtuous actions undertaken for their own sake.[26] This appears to be what Aristotle says in *NE* (1095a 18–20) where the conception of *eudaimonia* is a conception of doing well, and "well" is interpreted as "in accordance with virtue." McDowell argues, "Virtuous activity for its own sake is what *eudaimonia* is, not some supposed optimal result of filling one's life with such activity."[27] According to this reading, virtuous behavior has its intrinsic value, which manifests itself in one's own choice.

To interpret *eudaimonia* as doing well is to equate it with virtuous action. Nevertheless, as McDowell sees it, the motivational pull of an agent still lies in an optimal combination of component goods which are independently established. McDowell claims, "There is no suggestion that the distinctive point of doing well is rationally derivative from the motivational pull of goods that are independently recognizable as such."[28] This consequence comes from another conception of *eudaimonia* in which states of character are virtues. Those states of character that Aristotle identifies as virtues are worth cultivating, since a person with those characteristics is likely to secure a life that would come out best (by standards that are independent of a specific ethical outlook).

As mentioned above, it is thought that Aristotle's teleological view of human nature can validate his specific conception of the good life. However, McDowell thinks that there is no strong evidence for the view that Aristotle brings the first principles back into the ethical texts. A more fundamental question is: When Aristotle talks about the *ergon* of a human being, what is it in his mind? McDowell thinks that Aristotle should not be expected to validate his ethical outlook from the first principles, "If he were asked to tell us what it is that it befits a human being to do . . . he would say that these things are the way a virtuous person, or a possessor of practical wisdom, takes them to be."[29] In this view, Aristotle does not mean to offer an external validation for the ethical choice.

In Confucianism, central concepts such as *ren* can be understood in many senses. Each of these senses refers to different levels of thinking in Confucian thought.[30] Apparently *ren* may be conceived as specific ways of behavior commended by Confucians; nevertheless, *ren* should not merely be understood under this definition. In fact, the fundamental meaning of *ren* signifies the ability of transference (*gangtong* 感通) from which the judgment of good and bad from a transpersonal standpoint can be made. Remarkably transference should not be considered as a kind of contingent psychological inclination. It is not caused by empirical factors hence is transcendent. Furthermore, it is universally possessed by every human being and thus can serve as a transcendental ground for morality. The teachings of *ren* at the behavioral level are derived from this meaning and are therefore secondary. For instance, filial piety is only one of the innumerable ways in which *ren* manifests itself. Hence it is *ren* that determines what kinds of action should be taken, and not the other way round. A similar view is expounded by Aristotle, "But for actions expressing virtue to be done temperately or justly [and hence well] it does not suffice that they are themselves in the right state. Rather, the agent must also be in the right state when he does them." (*NE* 1105a 29–31)[31] *Ren* (and even *li*) taken as a virtue should be performed out of the empathetic feeling generated from transference. In this sense, *ren* itself contains the motivational pull, and obviously it does not need, or even allow, any non-ethical, external validation of ethical values.

It is evident that in Mencius' philosophy, both *ren* and y*i* are considered as an ability that makes morality possible. Mencius argues that though *yi* is generally understood as acting appropriately, the criteria of appropriateness are not dependent on either the natural properties of the situation or facts about the relationships among individuals or events.[32]

Similarly, it is not human nature or the metaphysical being such as Heaven (*Tian*) that defines or determines ethical values. On one reading, *ren* (and *yi* as well) determines the moral good and since *ren* characterizes human nature, it may be thought that ethical judgments are derived from metaphysical assertions. But in the assertion concerning human nature, *ren* does not signify particular moral principles or criteria of values; rather, *ren* should be understood in its fundamental meaning described above. With this understanding, *ren* itself is the ability to determine values and the moral good. Even in the above-quoted passage in *The Doctrine of the Mean*, *Tian* is shown to be an origin of human nature and yet this does not render the ethical values dependent. It has been argued convincingly by the Contemporary Neo-Confucian philosopher MOU Zongsan that a distinct tradition of autonomous morality has been established in Confucianism from the Pre-Qin to the Ming dynasty.

Virtuous persons

If one does not adopt Aristotle's function argument as a way of defining virtues, one may still consider the definition in terms of virtuous persons. In this section, I shall examine in what way Aristotle relates virtuous persons to virtues, and what kinds of problems (if any) will arise from it. I shall also discuss what roles virtuous persons play in the ethics of Confucianism.

According to Bernard Williams, the relationship between virtuous persons and virtues in Aristotle's philosophy is as follows: A (fully) virtuous act is what a virtuous person would do, but only if it is done as the virtuous person does such a thing.[33] The problem generated from this formulation is that virtuous acts are rendered dependent on virtuous persons. If it is added to this formulation that a virtuous person is characterized in terms of virtuous acts, i.e., a virtuous person is someone who always chooses virtuous acts for their own sake, then the conceptions of virtuous acts and virtuous persons will be mutually dependent. Williams remarks about this relationship of dependence that "There is no problem just in this, but there will be a problem if it leads to vacuity."[34] Then under what conditions will it constitute a problem? Williams proceeds, "This will be so, if we cannot distinguish one virtue from another, and/or the V [virtuous] agent is left with no determinate content to his thoughts."[35] Therefore, as seen by Williams, one possible way to escape from this vacuity is to give a specific content to the deliberation of a virtuous person. A reading on Aristotle's virtuous persons suggests such a content of deliberation: A virtuous person is one who possesses *phronesis*, by which he or she is able to understand what it is about the situation and the action that makes this particular action in this situation something that would seem to a virtuous person the appropriate thing to do. Since such a virtuous person can be regarded as deliberating in a particular way so as to view this action as appropriate, he can also be thought of as acting for X-reasons where type X is tied to the virtue in question. The X-reasons that are linked with particular virtues are reflected in the "thick" ethical concepts such as "inconsiderate," "disloyal" and the like. Thus a virtuous person is one who always applies these concepts appropriately. When understanding virtuous acts in this way, it is presupposed that "A person with a particular V [virtuous] disposition will have a specific repertoire of considerations that operate for or against courses of action."[36] Although virtuous acts and virtuous persons are still mutually dependent under this way of understanding, these two concepts are not vacuous since different virtues can be distinguished.

If we adopt X-reasons as the specific content of deliberation for a virtuous person who has special disposition to see the relevance of an act to the particular situation, then the content of this disposition is vital for the understanding of a virtuous person. In addition, whether this kind of disposition can be identified independently from the result of deliberations is also important. However, if the disposition in question is to be explained in terms of *phronesis* that is essentially connected to virtues of character, then it seems that Aristotle faces a dilemma. One horn of the dilemma is that *phronesis* is admitted as an ability of applying the "thick" ethical concepts and hence the application is conceived of as involving a truth to which right or wrong can be assigned. The other horn is that *phronesis* is considered as an outcome of habits and the virtues judged by it merely reflect the specific thought of a person under certain upbringings. If we go for the latter, then "being virtuous" becomes arbitrary and contingent. On the other hand, if we go for the former, then it means we accept a definitive set of "thick" ethical concepts, which represents the best achievable human understanding of the ethical, to which Williams objects. However, according to Williams, Aristotle thinks that the virtuous life defined by these concepts is the most satisfying life accessible to a human being.[37] This understanding is supposed to be derived from Aristotle's first principles which I have touched on earlier and I shall not proceed further here with this discussion.

For a Confucian learner, the primary aim is to become a virtuous person, firstly a gentleman and finally a sage. Being a sage is the final stage of the process of ethical cultivation. Therefore a sage is the most honorable and respectable figure who possesses the highest moral status. However, there are only a few agents in history who are commonly agreed to be a sage. Confucius has been indisputably known as a sage by his followers since his time, though he modestly thinks himself not qualified for such a title.[38] Yao, Shun and King Wen are commended by Confucius as sages. Mencius adds Tang, Yu, Gao Yao, Yi Yin, Lai Zhu, Tai Kung Wang, and Sanyi Sheng to the list.[39] Mencius is considered as a sage only second to Confucius. To be a gentleman, according to Confucius, one has to start with "cultivating oneself with reverence" and end in "cultivating oneself and thereby bringing peace and security to others" (including one's fellows and the people).[40] The achievement of the latter is close to the goal of a sage. Nevertheless, since at his time bringing peace and security to the people is a duty which can only be fulfilled by an emperor, the fulfillment of this depends on those external opportunities and conditions that cannot be controlled by the agent. Besides, even an emperor may encounter various obstacles in fulfilling this duty. Confucius has made an exclamation on this that even Yao and Shun find this task taxing. However, for one who devotes oneself to the Confucian ideal, one should do one's best and ignore the external factors. What constitutes the quality of a sage and is also under the control of an agent is to act in accordance with *ren*. One who embodies *ren* will "help others to take their stand in that he himself wishes to take his stand, and get others there in that he himself wishes to get there."[41] A sage is an agent who embodies *ren* and at the same time applies it to public affairs with great effect, e.g., "to give extensively to the common people and bring help to the multitude."[42] Confucius claims that even Yao and Shun would have found it difficult to accomplish as much.[43]

Granted that a sage is the highest model for Confucian learners, should the learners do as what the sage did? "Does the actual performance of the sage define the concrete contents of virtues?" As a matter of fact, when Confucius makes commendation of those sages by showing the appropriateness or the benevolence of their performance, he means to produce examples for his students to follow. Nevertheless, it is not the concrete actions that he wants his students to imitate; rather, he would like them to grasp the spirit embodied in such actions. The spirit constitutes the essential meanings of the virtues. The actual performance of a sage and the concrete contents of the virtue shown by a particular action merely reveal one of the ways of realizing the virtue. In this sense, virtues are not defined by the actual performance of virtuous persons.

Two questions about the account given above might be raised. First, how to choose the right one among the many possible ways of realizing virtues? Second, is it the case that only a virtuous person possesses the special ability of choosing rightly? The first question presupposes there is a right answer to an ought-question.[44] However, if the rightness of a choice or an action is based on some universal criteria or principles, then it is not the virtue itself but those principles by which the action is determined. Confucius does bring about *Dao* for human beings—the Way one should act in accordance with. Therefore it seems that *Dao* is theoretically prior to virtues. On the other hand, Confucius has once spelt out some principles for the gentleman to follow which are explained in terms of virtues.[45] I have discussed this issue at length[46] and the conclusion is: though sometimes the principles seem to be more primary than virtues (at one level of their meanings)[47] since the latter can be adjusted, amended or even dismissed if they violate the former, both the principles and the virtues are derivative. They are both the products of the moral heart-mind which possesses, as mentioned above, the fundamental ability of distinguishing good from evil. It is noteworthy that the ability mentioned is not cognitive in the sense that the exercising of it will result in the grasping of the objective right and wrong. Rather, it is the ability to decide in a non-abstract way the good and the bad in a particular situation. Nor is such a kind of decision an application of universal principles, it is only a kind of ability by which one "sees" the appropriate action to be taken in that situation even without any principles at all. Therefore the ability in question resembles that of creation.[48] This is the answer to the first question.

As discussed above, it is clear that according to Confucianism there is no objective right or wrong.[49] What should one do in a particular situation?[50] Is the realization of a specific virtue good in that situation? What specific action should be prescribed by a particular virtue? How to judge which one is to be overridden in case of conflict of virtues? All of these questions cannot be answered through the conception of the particular virtue itself. Nor can they be answered by any substantive principles since these principles have the same problems as virtues. In Confucian ethical thought, it is believed that the ability of deciding a particular action and adopting the general principles and virtues originates from the same faculty, i.e., the moral heart-mind. As such, Confucianism is not threatened by the dilemma described above. It admits the ability of applying the "thick" ethical concepts but does not accept that there are general moral truths. This results from the fact that Confucian ethics builds its whole thesis on subjectivity, from which an autonomous ethical system is developed.

Apparently for Confucianism, virtues are not defined in terms of virtuous persons. These two concepts are independent of each other: a virtuous person may do something that violates a particular virtue, and a virtue can still be a virtue even if no one can fully realize it. Nevertheless, as argued above, neither of them have a determinate content that clearly presents to the agent whether certain actions are allowed or forbidden. In this sense they are vacuous concepts, but this does not prevent the agent from making ethical decisions. On the other hand, virtues do have definite contents in that different virtues can be distinguished.

Although in the sense just introduced, virtues cannot be explained in terms of virtuous persons, it can be so explained in another sense. Since a virtuous person is someone who makes the decision of doing a particular act as a virtuous act, it may be said that it is this person who defines the good as well as that virtuous act because he decides the relevancy of the act to the virtue concerned. However, it should be noted that the relationship thus formed between the act and the virtue is not a conceptual relationship, but the relationship between an agent and his or her action. Therefore the definition in question is an act of choice rather than a conceptual act.

As regards the second question, the reply can be given on the basis of the Confucian doctrine that the same moral heart-mind is possessed by every human being. A virtuous person is one who has been aware of this ability[51] and has been cultivating it throughout his or her life so that he or she can exercise it when needed. When Confucians hold that setting the performance of sages as examples is important for the cultivation of an agent, it is mainly because these examples show that there are real possibilities for human beings to exercise the moral heart-mind and act on its decision.

According to Confucian thought, a sage may present himself or herself in a specific mode that constitutes his or her character. The character of a particular sage may be different from, and sometimes even contrary to, that of the other. Mencius claims, "The conduct of sages is not always the same. Some live in retirement, others enter the world; some withdraw, others stay on; but it all comes to keeping their integrity intact."[52] "Keeping their integrity intact" means acting in accordance with *yi* which are universal to everyone. Realizing *yi* in a specific way lies in choosing a specific virtue, and a certain set of chosen virtues forms the character of the agent or the sage. Mencius has classified different characters of the former sages by describing their performance into "the sage who was unsullied," "the sage who accepted responsibility," and "the sage who was easy-going."[53] Then he proceeds to praise Confucius for being a sage of timeliness and concludes that "he was the one who gathered together all that was good [in the sages]." It is because Confucius, in contrast with the others who all held to a fixed and immovable rule for determining their acceptance or resignation of office, "would hasten his departure or delay it, would remain in a state, or would take office, all according to circumstances."[54] Admitting the difference in modes and characters among sages can be viewed as evidence supporting the assertion that virtues cannot be defined in terms of virtuous persons. The commendation of timeliness reveals that there are no fixed principles one should observe in a particular situation and no virtues is appropriate on every occasion.

Conclusion

We have discussed so far the problems of the relation between knowledge and virtue, the existence of the moral truth, and the possibility of defining virtues in terms of virtuous persons in Aristotelian and Confucian ethics. The understandings as well as the possible solutions of these problems rely on what readings of the text we are going to take. However, this will not lead to a relativist conclusion, since I believe that evidence of some specific readings is stronger than the others. I hope the above discussion has given strong evidence and sound arguments to support specific views concerning the above problems. Certainly these views do not represent or constitute the whole ethical doctrines of the two schools of thought; rather, they only serve as a fundamental ground for further study and comparison.

11

Aristotle's Practical Wisdom and Mencius' *Xin*

Introduction

The question "What should one do?" is central to almost all ethical systems. This question may be focused on an individual act, as when one considers "How should I act in order to be right?" It may also indicate a general concern for one's whole life: "What is a good life to live?" No matter what the focus of an ethical system is, the ability of discerning the right or the good possessed by every human being is affirmed by autonomous ethics. In Aristotle's ethics, this ability is the practical wisdom (*phronesis*) by which a rational choice (*prohairesis*) is reached.[1] Practical wisdom, as articulated by Aristotle, is the virtue by which one deliberates well: that is, by which one reasons well in a practical way:

> Now it is thought to be the mark of a man of practical wisdom to be able to deliberate well about what is good and expedient for himself . . ., about what sorts of thing conduce to the good life in general."
>
> 1140a 25–30[2]

> It follows that in the general sense also the man who is capable of deliberating has practical wisdom.
>
> 1140a 25–30

Put it in another way, through the process of deliberation (*bouleusis*), a rational choice is formed. With practical wisdom, a virtuous person is able to "see" what one should perform in a particular circumstance. Therefore, in order to understand how practical wisdom works to arrive at a good rational choice, it is necessary to grasp the process through which the question "What should I do?" can be answered in a rational way. On the other hand, in Confucian ethics, some philosophers argue that it is not a rule-following system,[3] nor is it a sort of principled ethics advocating a (or a set of) principle(s) from which particular judgments can be deduced. The judgment of good or bad is primarily made by the heart-mind (for Mencius, it is called *xin*). Therefore, how *xin* operates in reaching a moral judgment is a significant issue. In this chapter, without presuming any similarities (or contrasts) between these two ethical systems at the outset, I first examine the role practical wisdom plays in making a rational choice as well as its nature and exercising process, then proceed, in the context of Confucian ethics, to discover how *xin* works. I will start by explaining the function and aim of deliberation. Then I will further show that when a rational choice is made, deliberation does not only provide a reason for the corresponding act but also contributes to the motivational force of it. Practical wisdom, as a virtue for good deliberation, does not give guidance in an abstract way by providing a general principle, rather, it is an ability to read the specific situation and decide a particular act for such situation. When I move on later, I will discuss that *xin* in Mencius plays a role in making moral decision similar to practical wisdom in that by activating it, one can see what is good in a particular situation. Nonetheless, I will argue that there are some significant differences between these two abilities in question. Furthermore, I will explicate how, if possible, the concept of *xin* can escape from the challenges made against practical wisdom. By so doing, the nature of *xin* and that of moral reasoning in Confucian ethics will be more lucid. In the end of the chapter, I will introduce the concept of "moral creation" to characterize the activity of moral decision in Confucianism, which is a novel interpretation made by MOU Zongsan. Interpreting the system of Confucian ethics in this way, I hope that it will in turn shed light on the understanding of practical wisdom in particular, and Aristotle's ethics in general.

It is understood that apart from practical wisdom, the concepts of "the supreme good," "virtues of character," "*ergon*," "*eudaimonia*," and the "virtuous person" are also manifestations of the entirety of Aristotle's ethics. However, I will not discuss these concepts individually here but will only refer to them when they are related to the issue in question. Furthermore, constrained by the scope of this chapter, I will confine the discussion of *xin* to Mencius's doctrine, though after his time, there has been a richer and fuller development of this concept.

The function of deliberation

"We deliberate not about ends but about means." (1112b 12–15[4])[5] From this citation, it seems that Aristotle asserts that we deliberate only about means. Through deliberation we choose a means X for an end Y.[6] When it is said that in the deliberation X is chosen, it presupposes that there are different options. Moreover, it also implies that the deliberation can explain and justify (rationally) why X is chosen among the available options; i.e., X is a rational choice. Therefore, deliberation reveals the dual aspects of a rational choice: practical as well as rational.

The above citation shows that an act of choosing is possible through deliberation, even though the premise that human beings aim at the supreme good (that is, the ultimate end, the "Grand End" termed by Sarah Broadie[7])[8] is assumed. It is because apart from the supreme good, there are also other goods which contribute to the supreme good. Besides, when a specific end is pursued, one has to choose a means that contributes to that end. Among the candidates of the means to be chosen, we have to examine and compare their qualities, hoping that certain connections with the pursued end will be revealed. These connections would pertain to the effectiveness and appropriateness of the means in achieving the end in the specific instance. Since the implicit connections mentioned are not clear logically or empirically, an agent needs to do some deliberation. Hence, the agent's lack of complete and immediate knowledge of all the possible connections between means and end leaves room for choosing.

A rational choice is practical in a sense that it is chosen either as a means to the supreme good, or to other ends that contribute to the supreme good. It is practical also in another sense: the means chosen through deliberation is immediately practicable, therefore it is the starting point of action.[9]

Sometimes the question "Why are you doing it?" may seek for information about the psychological state of the agent. But if we attempt to answer this question in terms of deliberation, we will discover the formal structure of a rational choice, by which the action can thus be justified. The agent will have to give reasons to explain why the action he or she chooses is appropriate. "When the agent offers his or her reason for doing X—reason in the sense of a *logos* which makes clear the nature of something—he also, and mainly, offers it as a reason in another sense; i.e., as a piece of information that should justify his doing of X."[10] Therefore, one justifies one's choice or action by the rationale that the choice is arrived at by good deliberation; that is, the choice is rational in the sense that it is the right means to a certain end.

The motivational force of practical reason

In some ethical doctrines, it is asserted that reason or thought alone cannot produce action, therefore other elements are called for to explain the emergence of action.[11] Even though the thought or judgment is evaluative, it would still have no bearing on practice; that is to say, value judgments do not imply any actions to be taken. In the terminology of modern ethics, value judgment is not prescriptive at all.[12] Anyway, this is not Aristotle's position. Although Aristotle divides the soul of human beings into different parts, each of which serves different functions, these parts unify to produce a rational choice.[13] Hence when a rational choice is made, it does not only show that the agent accepts it as a right means to a certain end; it also reflects that the agent is ready to accept the result of deliberation and to convert it into a desire to do the corresponding act. Hence, the following can be conceived as two conditions of a good rational choice for choosing to do A: (1) the thought that A is right or good to do is true; and (2) there is a general orectic readiness of accepting the correct reason.[14] To Aristotle, Broadie points out, reason contributes to motivation not by providing the drive, but by giving the drive direction.[15] Therefore, although we cannot claim that in Aristotle's account reason produces action directly, it does contribute to the motivational force of an action.[16] This argument provides another meaning that practical wisdom is practical in nature.

Practical argument in deliberation

When facing a practical problem "What am I to do?", an agent will exercise his practical reason to decide how to convert a particular situation into another where he can realize his objective by taking certain action. It seems that in deliberation an agent is searching the conclusion from the premises. But here two points need attention: (1) the conclusion of the practical argument is a prescription of an act, not a factual statement about the act of the agent. This differentiates practical arguments from theoretical ones, of which the scientifically explanatory argument is an example; and (2) if the reasons constitute the premises and the choice is the conclusion, then the argument shows a mere causal relation between reasons and the choice. However, this deviates from people's ordinary way of finding a good decision on action. For ordinary people, it is unusual to infer the choice from a set of reasons. Broadie thought that this is even an absurd way.[17] Besides, in this argument the desire to realize the objective O in circumstance C appears as a major premise but that might not concern every person. Hence the argument presented in this form can be communicated only to those who have the same kind of concern.

Although the primary objective of making a practical argument is to answer the question "How to realize O in C?", there is another function of practical argument, namely, the justificatory function. For the purpose of telling others that the choice is rational, the choice should be regarded as the premises. In this form of practical argument, the premises also serve as a cause that produces the fact stated in the conclusion.

The ultimate end and deliberation

In order to scrutinize closely the role of deliberation in Aristotle's ethics, the view concerning the "Grand End" of human beings should be studied. The "Grand End" view is attributed to Aristotle in which it is believed that there is an ultimate end pursued by all human beings, though what constitutes this end is subject to different interpretations by later commentators. Under this view, deliberation focuses on the End that "the agent's values and priorities are all subsumed or represented, either in terms of some interminably complex state of affairs to be brought about or in terms of some action to be done providentially designed to take care of all of them."[18] Broadie argues against this view in many respects that I will not elaborate here. I will discuss only those relevant to deliberation and related issues.

First, if the Grand End view is adopted in understanding deliberation, then we will find that there is no room for the agent to choose one means preferable over another. This is because all the means, if they are means to this End, would have the same value. If we prefer one means to another, this presupposes that this preferred one has some value not represented in the End. But in the agent's Grand picture of good, no such extra value exists. Therefore, the agent can consider only the factual question whether, by doing A under the circumstances, he or she will realize E; and if there are options of viable means, he or she can only choose and consider the one that would be most effective. If this is the case, then the "How?" question is purely causal.

Besides, if the agent has a clear picture of the end, in which he or she gets the right values and priorities, then he or she cannot ask himself or herself whether attaining it is the best thing he or she could do, or whether, in attaining it, he or she would attain the best. For these inquiries presuppose a belief that contradicts the Grand End view. However, in real life these questions are possible. A rational agent's deliberated end must be narrow and focused, only then can the choice grounded on it be logically identified.[19] The deliberation is not purely causal, but an evaluation of various values is involved. Then the "How?" question means "What way is there for me to pursue and attain O in this situation so that the pursuit and attainment would be acceptable in terms of all else that matters?"[20]

Apart from the Grand End, concrete details of the circumstance also contribute to the determinate content of deliberation. Broadie remarks, "The formal good is not the object which he has in view when deliberating, but shows up, rather, in the way in which he decides to pursue that object. He decides to pursue it only on condition that in so doing he is pursuing what is here and now best to pursue."[21] Therefore the "How?" question can be framed as "How am I to pursue O so that in so doing I pursue what is the best under these circumstances?" It is important to note that, for Aristotle, what the best is might differ in different situations.

The end in deliberation

In the citation at the beginning of section II (1112b 12–15), it is clear that deliberation is not about ends but about means. It seems that by deliberation the question "Should I pursue the end O?" cannot be answered. But by saying this Aristotle does not necessarily mean that the practical agent cannot ask whether O is now worth pursuing. The passage can be interpreted as meaning that the practical agent does not ask whether he or she should pursue the formal end; or that the specific end O presents itself as one worth pursuing without one's having had to find this out through deliberation. In this connection, Broadie argues, asking how to pursue O is asking how to pursue it so that pursuing it is the best in the situation. "The deliberative discovery that there is such a How, or that there is not, is the same as discovering that O is or is not to be pursued in this situation. In this way, deliberation yields an answer to the question 'Should I pursue O?'"[22] David Wiggins also thinks that deliberation is not only a search for means, but is as well a search for the best specification of ends.[23]

> Practical wisdom on the other hand is concerned with things human and things about which it is possible to deliberate; for we say this is above all the work of the man of practical wisdom, to deliberate well... The man who is without qualification good at deliberating is the man who is capable of aiming in accordance with calculation at the best for man of things attainable by action. Nor is practical wisdom concerned with universals only—it must also recognize particulars. That is why some who do not know, and especially those who have experience, are more practical than others who know.
>
> 1141b 8–18[24]

On the reading of the above passage, Wiggins makes a remark that "practical wisdom in its deliberative manifestations is concerned with both the attainment of particular formed objectives and questions of general policy—what specific objectives to form."[25] According to Broadie, another reason for Aristotle's insistence that deliberation is about how to, not whether to, pursue O is that the latter question might be asked in a way in which O is abstracted from the particularities of the situation, which Aristotle tries to avoid. Contrarily, the "How to?" question presupposes that the answer is to be sought in a particular situation.

Good deliberation

In 1140a 25–30[26] cited above, Aristotle equates excellence in deliberation with practical wisdom.

> Now it is thought to be the mark of a man of practical wisdom to be able to deliberate well about what is good and expedient for himself, not in some particular respect, e.g. about what sorts of thing conduce to health or to strength, but about what sorts of thing conduce to the good life in general.

From the above passage, it looks as if practical wisdom merely contributes to good deliberation which makes one choose the right means. But sometimes when the focus is on ability to find the means, Aristotle uses "practical wisdom" to refer to the right grasp of the end.

> If, then, it is characteristic of men of practical wisdom to have deliberated well, excellence in deliberation will be correctness with regard to what conduces to the end of which practical wisdom is the true apprehension.
>
> 1142b 33[27]

However, practical wisdom, indispensable for fully developed virtue,[28] does not merely pertain to the intelligence giving rise to good deliberation, but it has also to liaise with moral virtue, which pertains to moral character. Thus, the attributes of practical wisdom are of two categories: moral excellence and intelligence. The former makes the end right, whereas the latter makes right the means. "Again, the work of man is achieved only in accordance with practical wisdom as well as with moral virtue; for virtue makes us aim at the right mark, and practical wisdom makes us take the right means." (1144a 7–9[29])

Saying that moral virtue makes the end right (1114b 16–21[30]) does not mean that virtues reveal to the agent which end, among those possible, is the right one to aim for. Virtue only ensures that whatever is aimed for is aimed for rightly. Hence the end is re-evaluated over time to make sure that it is worth pursuing under the circumstances. Character makes the evaluation right. Although Aristotle divides the contributions of moral excellence and intelligence between end and means, virtue is also involved in selecting the means to O.[31] Because the worthiness of O as an end is evaluated under certain conditions (and with the results implied by pursuing it through certain means), whether O is worth pursuing given the cost is inseparable from what kind of means is selected.

As O is subject to change or adjustment, then the initial wish for O is seen only as a provisional affirmation of O as the pursued end. For Aristotle, practical deliberation contains two elements: a wish for O, and an intelligent grasp of the particulars. The question is how to convert the wish into rational choice with the factual awareness of these particulars. It seems that we need some specific ethical principles, including principles of value priority, to guide the conversion. According to Broadie, Aristotle does not tell us anything about general principles of priority mediating the move from factual picture to practical decision.[32] It is thought that if no such principles operate here, then there would be a logical gap. But what Aristotle maintains is: there are rare cases when one knows the facts of a circumstance, yet does not know what to do. For Aristotle, we are not sufficiently aware of the facts of a practical situation until we know what to do in it. Therefore, there is neither a logical gap nor a cognitive gap that requires bridging with general principles.

There are three connected elements involved in a deliberated response: desiderative disposition, reading ability, and appropriate response.[33] Desiderative disposition is both innate and culturally acquired. It refers to an interest in a certain type of object, and it can be regarded as a cognitive disposition to read situations in relevant ways; that is, to read in ways that present the situations as containing or not containing that object. Reading ability is the ability to recognize a particular as an instance of a universal which is already present in the agent's desiderative vocabulary. An appropriate response is one to a situation perceived as instantiating one such universal or another. "Practical intelligence," as Broadie sees it, is "the quality that takes us human agents beyond the several deliverances of whatever special sensitivities (grounded in our standing or pre-existent concerns) we bring to a situation ... This intellectual disposition is activated by the general moral disposition which it in turn makes effective in a determinate way: the disposition, namely, of desiring the formal *best*, which in any given case receives a specified content, but different contents from case to case."[34] Hence, an appropriate (or right) response depends on intelligence as interpreted above, and this operation of intelligence can be taken as definitive of deliberation.

If a moral disposition is expressed in inappropriate occasions or in ways that fail to accommodate the agent's other concerns, then it is not a virtue at all. "The astuteness of wisdom is therefore the ability to read the facts in such a way that a general disposition to do what is best, all things considered, will issue a response that does justice to *all* that one cares about."[35] One reads the situation correctly or truly only if one knows what is really right to do in it, and knowing what is right to do in it is the same as knowing what a virtuous person would know.

The nature of *xin* in Mencius' philosophy

Passage 7A21 in the *Mencius* clearly spells out the ethical attribute of *xin*.

> That which a gentleman follows as his nature, that is to say, *ren*, *yi*, *li*, and *zhi*, is rooted in his *xin* ...

The expression "*ren*, *yi*, *li*, and *zhi*, is rooted in his *xin*" does not mean that *xin* contains *ren*, *yi*, *li* (propriety), and *zhi* (wisdom) as *virtues*. Nor does it merely mean that *xin* has certain predispositions already directed toward the ethical ideal.[36] According to Mencius, what is rooted in *xin* as the nature of a gentleman is not virtues proper, but is the content of *xin* manifesting itself in various directions. Similarly, the expression "the *xin* of *ren-yi*" (for example, 6A8) does not refer to a certain sort of *xin* that contains the virtues of *ren* and *yi*. "The *xin* of *cheyin* (compassion 惻隱)" also does not contain *cheyin*. Nor does "the *xin* of shame, respect, right and wrong differentiated" contain shame, respect, or right and wrong differentiated. *Ren*, *yi*, *cheyin* and the like used in this context are to characterize the essential content of *xin*. Equivocally *ren-yi* (the *xin* of *ren-yi*) and the *xin* are the same. By activating the *xin*, one makes moral judgment, therefore the *xin* is the transcendental ground of morality. So does *ren-yi*. This is the primary meaning of *ren-yi*. The virtue of *ren-yi* only represents its derivative meaning.

Mencius thinks that every human being (and not only gentlemen) has this *xin* (6A6; 6A7; 6A10). Also,

> This is an attitude not confined to the moral man but common to all men.
>
> 6A11

6A15 says that it is a distinctive ability of *xin* to reflect (*si* 思).[37]

> The organs of hearing and sight are unable to reflect and can be misled by external things. When one thing acts on another, all it does is to attract it. The organ of *xin* can reflect. It will get it if it reflects; otherwise, it will not get it.

Also,

> *Ren*, *yi*, *li* and *zhi* do not give me a lustre from the outside, they are in me originally. Only one did not reflect.
>
> 6A6

Mencius holds that as a matter of fact, human beings want to satisfy the desires of the sense organs; however, sense organs themselves are unable to judge where to stop in pursuing the satisfaction of desires. In this respect sense organs are led by external objects which are interconnected and hence are conditioned. Therefore, the question of "ought" does not arise. In the above passage, it is asserted that *xin* is distinct from sense organs in that it can reflect. Here reflection does not mean a way of cognitive thinking, but by reflection value judgment is made. So, by reflection one can seek the answer of what one should do.[38]

Reflection and deliberation

In 6A15, in contrast to the senses, Mencius asserts that *xin* can reflect. Furthermore, he claims that if one reflects, one can get the right answer of what one should do, which is represented by *yi*.[39] Here it is natural to assimilate reflection with deliberation.[40]

However, the similarities and differences between these two kinds of seeking activity should be carefully examined.

By reflection one can get *yi*; that is, by activating *xin* with reflection one can definitely arrive at *yi*. Therefore, *xin*, *si*, and *yi* semantically determine the truism stated above. It is logically impossible to get a wrong answer by activating *xin*. Since *yi* is what arrives at when *xin* is activated and *xin* is the ability of getting *yi*, a wrong answer is obtained only when *xin* is not activated. Besides, *xin* is either activated or not activated. In the case of the former, a moral judgment (categorical imperative in the Kantian term) can be made; in the case of the latter, only a prudential judgment (hypothetical imperative) can be reached. If *xin* is not hindered, then it can be activated. However, although something (from inside, e.g., desires, or from outside, e.g., the environment 6A7) might hinder *xin* and affect its activation, *xin* is the ultimate source for overcoming the hindrance.[41] But in Aristotle's ethics, one can arrive at an irrational choice if one deliberates poorly. For example, a deliberation not made by a person with good character might result in the right means to a wrong end. As discussed in the above sections, for Aristotle, rational choice itself is an evidence that the deliberation is good and operated by a person activating his practical wisdom. Yet in Mencius's doctrine, there is no bad reflection as such. Whether a person can arrive at *yi* depends on whether or not he has activated his *xin*. Therefore, it seems that there is a logical gap between deliberation and rational choice in Aristotle, whereas there is none between reflection and *yi* in Mencius. This difference is significant in that it shows that practical wisdom is an empirical virtue, which is not necessarily possessed by human beings. Practical wisdom thus cannot be the ground of morality. On the other side, for Mencius, every human being possesses *xin*. Although it is possible that *xin* is not activated, *xin* as an ability can decide what the good is. Moreover, *xin* also has the motivating force to manifest itself, unless it is hindered otherwise it will be activated to reflect. For Aristotle, he did not confirm that practical wisdom is transcendent, nor that there is transcendental ground for a rational choice to exist.

It is made clear in the previous section that deliberation in Aristotle involves not only means but also ends because the right means consists of a right end. With practical wisdom a person would choose right objectives because of his good character; therefore, it is impossible that a wicked person could deliberate well and achieve a rational choice with a bad objective. Similarly, Mencius does not allow that someone could reflect with *xin* and then arrive at a decision that violates *yi*. Once *xin* is activated, one is directing one's attention to and seeking *yi*.[42] And once he attempts to seek it, he would get it. According to Mencius, *yi* is what is right and appropriate.[43] In making a moral decision, particulars of the circumstance and every possible means will be considered. Both for Aristotle and Mencius, a virtuous person will make a right and appropriate decision. However, as mentioned above, the additional advocacy made by Mencius is that the *xin* of *ren-yi* is not possessed by virtuous persons only, but also by ordinary people (see earlier section on "The nature of *xin* in Mencius' philosophy"). We also see that both systems admit that choice is practical in the sense that one can choose irrationally, though owing to different factors.

As discussed above, deliberation includes the specification of ends that conduce to the ultimate end and the search for means that are effective for realizing the ends.

Reflection only aims at answering what one should do in a particular situation, without emphasizing the means.

The Grand End and *yi*

As we have seen above, both Broadie and Wiggins reject the Grand End view in interpreting Aristotle's rational choice. They show that this view fails to give instruction or justification for what is to be done rationally. This challenge may have the same bearing on Mencius' view of *xin*. It seems that *yi* is the ultimate end that the goodness of any decisions or acts counts on; but in fact, it cannot guide and justify those decisions and acts. Here Mencius faces the challenge of the following important questions: (1) By activating *xin*, how does one reflect to attain *yi*?; (2) How can we justify that the choice we make is the best, all things considered?; and (3) Is *yi* only a void and remote notion and can it help or not help one to decide?

Question (1) can be reduced to question (2) if one does not attempt to go into the details of psychological or mental processes of reasoning. On the other hand, if one is really asking how reflection could lead one to reason, step by step, until one reaches the right decision, then Mencius has given no answer. Unlike solving a mathematic quiz or a logic problem, where we have some efficient rules to follow, making a moral judgment is similar to making a practical choice. There are no definite steps one has to follow to reach a right decision. As discussed in the "Practical argument in deliberation" section, one can never infer a rational choice by an argument that takes objectives as premises. Practical choice, including moral judgment, resembles scientific discovery in the sense that it is not a kind of rule-following game.

Question (2) can be reformulated as follows: What is the formal structure of a good or rational choice? This in turn can be interpreted as: What are the conditions for a choice to be good or rational? If such a question is posed to Aristotle, Broadie perceptively pointed out, the very question assumes that excellence in reasoning and cognition is judged by standards wholly internal to reasoning and cognition:

> The question was "Granted that the rational activity is *good* when grounded in the various qualities acknowledged as virtues, by what right can Aristotle regard this goodness as a goodness of reason as such?" . . . In the light of our detailed study of deliberation and cognate matters, the question loses its force. Such force as it had depended on the assumption that excellence in reasoning and cognition is judged by standards wholly internal to reasoning and cognition. Thus, e.g., good reasoning is logically or inductively sound reasoning, and good cognition is justified true belief.[44]

Apparently, the rationality of a choice or the goodness of a moral decision does not depend merely on the validity of the reasoning, but depends largely on the suitable weighing among various values, which goes beyond the scope of logic and factual knowledge. Good objective, in Aristotle's ethics, springs from good character. By the same token, one should not expect that the goodness of the choice in Mencius lies in sound logical reasoning;[45] therefore, no logical proofs or empirical facts are sufficient to justify the choice in question. This, however, should not be considered as a defect of the ethical system. On the contrary, this leaves room for a choice to be a real practical one.

It is generally agreed that one of the meanings of a normative ethical system is to provide guiding principles for one to act accordingly. For Aristotle, *eudaimonia* understood as the Grand End does not serve as the ultimate reason for every specific choice, hence it cannot give guidance in answering the question "How to achieve O in C?" Nevertheless, one can still seek the answer by: first, identifying the ends that would contribute to the Grand End; secondly, "reading" the specific situation to decide which facts are relevant to the issue; and finally, choosing among those ends some specific ones and deliberating the means to these ends. In the case of Mencius, the notion of *yi* is always used to show the direction one should pay attention to in a specific context. The direction mentioned represents an ethical ideal. Sometimes it is used to characterize the nature of morality; for example, its contrasting nature with self-interest (1A1). Sometimes "*bu yi*" (violating *yi*)[46] is used to criticize someone immoral. It is evident that "*yi*" in this sense is a state of being ethical. Therefore, *yi* thus used is not meant for offering a guideline in making a judgment or performing an act. Rather, it is used to prescribe people to be moral. So, is *yi* regarded as an ultimate end? The answer will be both "yes" and "no." "Yes" in that *yi* is the ultimate end for anyone who dedicates himself to the ethical ideal. "No" because *yi* is not used to guide or justify a decision or an act. Back to the original question: is the notion of *yi* a void concept that cannot help one to decide on ethical matters? To tackle this question, it should be divided into two sub-questions: Is *yi* a void concept?; and, Can *yi* help one to decide what one should do? The first question has a negative answer because there are a number of virtues that manifest a certain aspect of *yi* in a particular situation; for example, *jing* (reverence), *gong* (respect), *cheng* (integrity), and so on. These virtues constitute (at least part of) the content of *yi*. But neither a single one nor a selective set of them can be regarded as equivalent to *yi* because the specific content of *yi* is subject to change from case to case. Mencius comments on Confucius' choice of action: "He (Confucius) was the sort of man who would hasten his departure or delay it, would remain in a state, or would take office, all according to circumstances." (*Mencius*, 5B1) Therefore even though *yi* has no fixed content, it is not a void concept.

If by asking the second question (Can *yi* be of any help in deciding what one should do?), one is seeking a substantial criterion, rule, standard, or guideline for the right decision, then *yi* can offer none. Just as Aristotle's prescription that we should aim for the mean is unhelpful since it does not tell us what to pursue or to avoid in a non-abstract way. But as Broadie argues, the lack of substantial criterion does not constitute a problem for an ethical system.

> Just so, if anyone seeks from the ethical philosopher advice about how to make every decision, the latter is under no obligation to reply to him on this level (in this case, not because it is not his business or he is not trained, but because, as Aristotle has said, no one can give effective guidance of that sort); but he ought to be able to say something informative about the kind of person one should go to for advice—not about all decisions in the abstract, but about this or that particular problem.

> The kind which the philosopher should be able to characterise is, of course, the person of practical wisdom, who is Aristotle's subject in *NE* VI, being the embodiment of the uniquely ethical type of *orthos logos*.[47]

Aristotle has characterized the person of practical wisdom in great detail and hence has fulfilled his requirement as an ethical philosopher. In Mencius' ethics, no substantial rules or priority principles are provided. One has to read the particulars in a specific circumstance to reach the right and appropriate decision, which conforms to *yi*. Reading the particulars involves getting knowledge of the relevant facts, weighing the moral as well as non-moral values, balancing the good against the bad results, and deciding what means can achieve specific ends.[48] Such ability of reading the situation and making a good choice rests in *xin*. Besides, Mencius has discussed the sages in ancient times who exhibited remarkable decisions and performance on ethical issues. Albeit difference in the decisions they made, they were all considered as sages. He has also described their individual characters and made his own comments on them (*Mencius*, 5B1, 2A9, 2A2).

Moral reasoning as a creative activity

Aristotle's practical wisdom comprises excellence in character and intelligence. Intelligence is the ability to read the facts in a situation and issues the best response, all things considered. The term "intelligence" implies a grasp of the truth (1139b15–17[49]; 1141a3–15[50]). At the end of the "Good deliberation" section, it has been discussed that knowing the truth about what to do is the same as knowing what a virtuous person would know. Here practical truth refers only to a rationally grounded choice, and the term "truth" is not used in a strict sense as it is in the theoretical domain. As Broadie puts it, "practical truth is the intellectually particularised response of the virtuous agent."[51] Therefore, we need to grasp practical truth through the virtuous person. One may think that practical truth (or rational choice, or virtuous act) and the virtuous person are mutually dependent. But Bernard Williams argues that this is a problem only if it leads to vacuity.[52] I have discussed that in the Confucian ethical system no determinate content in *yi* by which it clearly presents to the agent that certain actions are allowed while some others are forbidden, nonetheless, no vacuity is found. Moreover, in the ethical system mentioned, the virtuous act and the virtuous person are not mutually dependent.[53]

Remarkably, the act of seeing the appropriate choice in a particular situation resembles a creative activity. Both kinds of act exclude any determinate steps, rules or criteria, yet the evaluation of the result is never arbitrary. Wiggins uses the notion "invention" to signify such kind of moral activity.

> It is the mark of the man of practical wisdom on this account to be able to select from the infinite number of features of a situation those features that bear upon the notion or ideal of existence which it is his standing aim to make real. The conception of human life results in various evaluations of all kinds of things, in various sorts of cares

> and concerns, and in various projects. It does not reside in a set of maxims or precepts, useful though Aristotle would allow these to be at a certain stage in the education of the emotions. In no case will there be a rule to which a man can simply appeal to tell him what to do (except in the special case where an absolute prohibition operates). The man may have no other recourse but to invent the answer to the problem. As often as not, the inventing, like the frequent accommodation he has to effect between the claims of competing values, may count as a modification or innovation or further determination in the evolution of his view of what a good life is.[54]

In fact, Mou Zongsan uses the term "moral creation" to characterize the feature of moral act in Confucian ethics.[55] In Aristotle, practical wisdom involves both good character that determines the good end and intelligence that enables one to deliberate well. Wisdom (practical or not) cannot be attained merely through the training of logic and cognitive ability. Rather, it depends on the cultivation of sensitivity, by which one can detect the particulars relevant to the judgment. Similarly, in Confucian ethics, the *xin* needs to be cultivated to extend one's benevolent concern to the stranger. Moral judgments about what one should do in a particular situation rest on the *xin* of *ren-yi*. Making moral judgments is neither an act of rule-following nor logical inferring. Furthermore, moral decisions are not reached by imitating the great man's action. Therefore, it is considered an act of creation. Besides, moral creation has another meaning: The extension mentioned above represents the expansion of one's awareness. A person does not exist in the agent's world if he or she is out of the scope of the agent's awareness. Therefore, a person can be thought of as being created by the agent who brings about his or her existence (in his or her conscious world) by expanding the agent's awareness. This is another meaning of moral creation.

Conclusion

In the above discussion, I have examined in Aristotle the formal structure of a rational choice and the role of practical wisdom in making moral judgment. I have also shown that, despite the tradition to which Mencius and Aristotle belong respectively, the *xin* in Mencius plays a similar role as practical wisdom. The goodness of the choice resulting from the activation of *xin* cannot, and does not need to, be justified by logic or facts. *Xin* is an ability which defines what is good and decides what is appropriate in a particular situation. The only guarantee of making a good choice, all things considered, depends on whether the *xin* is always activated, and this in turn depends on the continuing effort one puts into purifying all the hindrances so as to maintain the clearness of the *xin*. There are certainly differences between *xin* and practical wisdom; for example, their distinctive ways of manifestation and how they relate to human nature. Among them, a noteworthy one is: *Xin* differs from practical wisdom in that the former is the transcendental ground of morality and not a mere virtue, whereas the latter is an empirical virtue which is close to "*Li yi*" (理義) in Xunzi's system. However, the discussion for this last assertion is out of the scope of this chapter.

12

Rethinking the Presuppositions of Business Ethics: From Aristotelian Approach to Confucian Ethics

Introduction

When we are discussing business ethics or corporate responsibilities, do we refer to certain sets of codes of conduct, or the application of certain moral principles? This discussion relates to the question whether there are differences between corporate morality and individual morality. Is the morality of a corporation merely an extension of that of an individual and hence do we need only to transfer those moral principles and norms established for individuals to business organizations? If that is the case, then perhaps the reformulation required is only a change from "he or she ought" to "it ought." One might argue that the scope of individual morality exceeds significantly that of corporate morality in that the former also takes certain stands on personal desires and emotion, or even the meaning of life, from a moral point of view (certainly there are moral theories which do not deal with such problems), but the latter mainly makes moral judgments on issues concerning rights and interests. Apart from this, another distinction between corporate morality and individual morality is generally made by, among others, business amoralists when they refute that there are moral responsibilities for business organizations. Their argument takes the following form: the concept of conscience or moral motivation, which is the subjective condition for a moral agent, hardly makes sense for an organization, therefore we cannot urge an organization to be moral. Certainly it may be objected that even though an organization may lack conscience, the people in the organization may not. While we are not going to comment on the soundness of this objection here, it should be noted that any attempts of reducing an organization to an agent would minimize the possible distinction of the two kinds of morality in question. On the other hand, the reduction mentioned might not be the only way of rescuing business ethics.

When the relationships between the community and individual, and that between different communities, are involved in the consideration of organizational morality, the ground of morality for an agent (such as Kant's postulates) and his or her moral norms are difficult to transfer directly to organizations. Hence, we need to formulate a set of moral rules that can fit into the business world, whose presuppositions may not be the same as that of individual morality. In this chapter, I attempt to investigate the special presuppositions of corporate morality from the Aristotelian approach and, furthermore, examine whether Confucianism has also provided a suitable ground for establishing corporate morality.

The Aristotelian approach to business ethics

In many Western moral theories such as Kantian ethics, utilitarianism, and the theory of right, moral agents are conceived as isolated individuals. These theories emphasize the responsibilities of the moral agent as an individual to other individuals or communities, but overlook his or her responsibilities as a member of a community. Such theories base the awareness of responsibilities on the moral rationality of human beings, thus the morality derived from it is a kind of "agent-other" morality. In contrast, the latter depends on the understanding of the relationship between an individual and his or her society, country, and times, and the morality derived from it is a kind of "individual-community" morality. Admittedly, in the "agent-other" morality, an agent may place himself or herself in the context of the society and country concerned when setting up his or her specific responsibilities, but for the "individual-community" morality, this concrete context has already been built into its moral thinking. Generally speaking, provided that the two dimensions of morality mentioned are admitted, there should not be any incoherence of responsibilities set up from one dimension and those from the other within the same moral system. Contrarily, they may be complementary to each other. Nevertheless, for organizations such as the business corporation, to explain and justify responsibility from the "individual-community" dimension can avoid difficulties that arise from the "agent-other" dimension.

In contrast to a person, it is more appropriate to constitute moral rules for a business corporation on a "individual-community" ground. On the one hand, ethical presuppositions such as freedom of will, the necessity of treating human beings as ends rather than means, and basic human rights are inseparable from an agent and are not transferrable to an organization (unless it has been reduced to a person). On the other hand, it is more accurate to conceive an organization as a social entity, hence more readily revealing moral responsibilities. Aristotelian ethics is an ethical system, among numerous Western ethical schools, which is closer to "individual-community" moral thinking, therefore it is suitable to constitute business ethics. Though Robert C. Solomon does not spell out the terminology "individual-community" in his book *Ethics and Excellence*[1] and an article entitled "Business and the Humanities: An Aristotelian Approach to Business Ethics"[2] written two years later (1994), he does argue that the Aristotelian approach to business ethics is not only appropriate, but a better one than the others.

The Aristotelian approach to business ethics particularly emphasizes the idea of "community": each individual is "socially constituted and socially situated," members of a community.[3] As a member of a community, his or her interest is for the most part identical to the interest of that community. From the viewpoint of an ethical system that presupposes the subjectivity of the moral agent, every moral agent is a free and independent individual who is situated in a certain historical setting, but his or her moral choice is unique and only needs to be responsible to his or her own conscience. His or her moral judgment is universal and at the same time specific.[4] The specific tempo-spatial factors that are morally relevant are already embodied in the judgment but this does not hinder its universality. On the other hand, an individual understood as socially constituted is a kind of historical as well as cultural product. He or she attains heritage from history and the domain of his or her concerns and discourses, but at the same time is directed by the time in which he or she happens to be situated. It follows that he or she has particular responsibilities to his or her society, yet the horizon of his or her concern is limited by specific environment. This concept of "social individual" should not be rejected by subjective moral philosophy above-mentioned, as long as the former admits the presupposition of free will.

Since a business organization does not possess the conscience and moral motivation sprung from it, as a moral agent does, the question "why be moral" would be better answered by way of the idea of "community": employers are members of the community of a corporation and corporations are members of the community of a society. Solomon points out,

> In business ethics the corporation is one's community, but, of course, the corporation is itself a part of a larger community—as diverse as that may be—without which it would have no identity, serve no purpose, and sell no products.[5]

As all are members of a community, they share the same interests and at the same time, bear responsibilities to the community. The society, which plays the role of a community, makes the operation of a corporation possible by constituting a beneficial environment in which it can manufacture products, hire employees, provide services, and do business. Moreover, an agreeable understanding of concepts of success and reasonable profit can only be reached within a community. Such an understanding is the common ground for moral discussion and formation of ethical codes.

The idea of community is in contrast with a certain sense of individualism that focuses on isolated individuals with their goals and interests. These individuals are alienated from the group. In case of conflicts between individuals in pursuing their own goals, they will fight against others by competition. The basic belief is that one must win in order to achieve one's aim. A society is merely a constitution that provides the battleground. Wars are brutal in that one will either win or die. The most important fact is that while the pursuit of profit is not the only aim, it is the essential one. Therefore, individuals' interests override others' and even the group's interests. From such an individualistic view, the meaning of morality would become instrumental and the justification of being moral would merely rest on reasons such as "morality will promote long-term interest," "morality will protect justice in competition," etc. But after all, to illustrate the society or business world as a battleground, or a Darwinian jungle, as Solomon and other business ethicists argue,[6] is a very inappropriate metaphor.

> But doing business is not a "battle", and business competition, even when the survival of the company is at stake, should not be confused with the mutual destructiveness of war.[7]

The picture of the business world produced by those inappropriate metaphors or inaccurate descriptions affects people's understanding and expectations of business activities. Solomon makes his observation correctly and warns us accordingly,

> How we look at what we do has a lot to do with how we do, and I would argue that much of the infighting within corporations and many of the casualties of corporate competition can be laid at the feet of the malevolent images that we impose on business and on ourselves. The word 'ethics' refers somewhat ambiguously to both a set of theories and reflections about our behavior and to that behavor as such. Needless to say, the one influences the other, and as our theories and reflections try to be true to our actual intentions and activities, our intentions and activities themselves are shaped and given direction by what we think about them, what we think we are doing, what we think we ought to be done, and what we would like to think we are doing. How a person thinks about business—as a ruthless competition for profits or a cooperative enterprise the aim of which is the prosperity of the community—preshapes much of his or her behavior and attitudes toward fellow employees or executives, competitors, customers, and the surrounding community.[8]

Then, how should one think about business? And, which view is closer to reality? Solomon claims that competition is essential to capitalist society, but to understand this as unbridled competition is to undermine ethics and misunderstand the nature of competition as well. Competition presumes a community in which members are cooperative and mutually trusting.[9]

> However competitive a particular industry may be, it always rests on a foundation of shared interests and mutually agreed-upon rules of conduct, and the competition takes place not in a jungle but in a society that it presumably both serves and depends upon. Business life, unlike life in the mythological jungle, is first of all fundamentally *cooperative*. It is only with the bounds of mutually shared concerns that competition is possible.[10]

The business world is not as violently competitive as it appears, nor is it a "dog eat dog" uncivilized battleground. In order to understand the nature of business correctly, we should first study its goals. Individualism, which thinks that an agent is an isolated individual, focuses on the agent's own goals. She or he aims at making profits in his or her business activities. This is the dominating goal in every competition. However, profit itself should not be regarded as the only short-term or long-term goal of business activities. "Profits are a means of building the business and rewarding employees, executives, and investors."[11] Even though profit-making is one of the aims of business, it becomes so only by supplying quality goods and services and by providing jobs, and, at the same time fitting in with the community. This is not to deny the rights of stockholders but "these rights make sense only in a large social context."[12] All in all, atomistic individualism ignores the fact that business activities are social practices and that business organizations are social constructs. Both are only possible in a shared culture with a set of agreed procedures and expectations. There is shared culture within a company, which is itself situated in a larger shared culture. Although the Aristotelian approach emphasizes the meaning of community and criticizes atomistic individualism, it does not overlook the importance and responsibilities of an individual.

> In fact, the contrary is true; it is only within the context of community that individuality is developed and defined, and our all-important sense of individual integrity is dependent upon and not opposed to the community in which integrity gets both its meaning and its chance to prove itself.[13]

Another characteristic of Aristotelian approach lies in the idea of "excellence." The word "excellence" indicates a demand in quality. But there are two interpretations of "doing well": one suggests market value and the other suggests ethical value. Therefore one is doing well or excelling only if one fulfills the demands of the marketplace as well as that of ethics. In regard to the former requirement, producing high-quality products or services usually is rewarded by "success." But this presupposes a particular sense of justice: fairness in rewarding good work. Although the reward usually appears in return in normal circumstances, one should not seek for excellence for the sake of reward. To encourage excellence is not to encourage blindly that which aims at defeating the rival parties.

> Excellence is first of all cooperation and competition. It essentially represents a contribution to the larger whole.[14]

It is important that it is nonsense to talk about excellence disregarding the *telos* of the job. The aim of business, as discussed above, is contributing to a larger whole while acquiring one's personal profit. Therefore, the basic requirement for excellence in business is doing business morally. It follows that ethics is not a constraint in searching for excellence, rather, it is another important factor of success, in addition to the knowledge, skill, brightness, creativity, commitment, and effort.

Community and teleology capture the essence of Aristotelian approach to business. Besides these two ideas, Aristotelian ethics also emphasizes concrete situations in making moral judgments. In business, the relevant concrete situation is the position one is in or the membership one owns. The company one works for and his or her position in that company constitute his or her role and the concrete situation, and the role itself in turn defines his or her duty.

> To work for a company is to accept a set of particular obligations, to assume a prima facie loyalty to one's employer, to adopt a certain standard of excellence and conscientiousness that is largely defined by the job itself.[15]

The emphasis on the concept of position is closely related to the idea of community: the latter provides a ground for business to be moral, whereas the former offers the content of moral judgment a standpoint; both presuppose that moral should be contextual. It follows that the Aristotelian approach rejects making moral judgments by applying abstract moral theory or principles to the specific situation. Duty in the narrow sense is defined by the nature of the job and one's position, but duty in the wide sense has a moral connotation. Since it is supposed that morality is not abstract, then one is not required to bear extra moral duty besides the job itself; rather, one is expected to fulfill the moral duty by doing his or her job morally. However, doing the job morally depends on making moral reflections on the concrete job. Thus the duty identified is based on the consideration of concrete contexts.

As mentioned above, every individual is situated in a community and has his or her specific place in it, and all of these define his or her duties. However, an individual usually possesses a variety of roles and positions, so business is only one among them. From the Aristotelian ethical point of view, all of these roles and memberships constitute the whole of an individual. They are not separated but related to each other, therefore they can be regarded as different facets of a holistic life. Business is one of the activities performed in human life, so business ethics should not be separated from the morality of other kinds. This is the idea of holism in Aristotelian ethics.

The notion of stakeholder, which is getting more and more popular, embodies holism.

> Holism (not wholism) is concern for the whole rather than some of its parts, an emphasis on the big picture rather than the analysis of narrowly circumscribed details such as profits. We have to reject all of those false dichotomies and antagonisms between business and ethics, between profit and doing good, between personal and corporate values and virtues.[16]

From the holistic point of view, the different roles of an individual form a whole, and in business organizations as well, different positions of people form a whole. Even within the business world, corporations, consumers, government, and other parties affected also form a whole. The integral parts of a whole are not alienated, nor are they antagonistic. Therefore, it should not be presupposed there is antagonism between self and others, labor and management, as well as business and government.

> Holism is not itself another philosophy so much as it is simply the insistence that wherever we find antagonism and competing concepts we should expand our vision until we see the whole context. In the case of business and economics, this means that our vision should take in the whole of human nature and society, not just profits, costs, and benefits and the law of supply and demand. Business is not an isolated enterprise, and to insist that it is so is only to support and strengthen the attack on business as an antisocial activity. The Aristotelean approach to business, by contrast, is ultimately nothing other than the recognition of business as an integral part of the larger society.[17]

Since Aristotelian ethics embraces holism and emphasizes contextuality, therefore, the moral judgment of a specific situation is not made by applying the abstract general principles to it. Good judgments, which Aristotelian ethics searches for, can only be achieved by perception and are the product of a good upbringing and a proper education. For example, justice cannot be discovered by any mechanical decision procedures. Rather, to resolve the disputes about justice, one is required to have an "ability to balance and weigh competing concerns and come to a 'fair' conclusion."[18] What is fair, as Solomon points out, is always disputable but nevertheless well or badly made.

Business virtues

The effects of morality at the personal level result, on the one hand, in the cultivation of the moral sense, so as to make one become more sensitive to and more concerned about others' needs and feelings. At the same time, one becomes more aware that one's behavior is closely related to the well-being of others, so one should not simply aim at a personal goal regardless of possible harm to others. On the other hand, morality can assist one to overcome the weakness of will, which is the obstacle of moral practice. It also enables one to transform oneself in making choices from a personal point of view to an impersonal one. Apparently, the morality of an individual is concentrated on strengthening of one's moral will and widening of one's moral horizon. These presuppose the transcendent practical reason of an agent. The cultivation of virtues is one of the ways of enhancing one's moral capacity on the whole, whereas moral judgment is only a form of the expression of practical reason.

It seems that it is not appropriate to use such a framework to illustrate the effects of morality at the organizational level. The discussion of corporate morality cannot stick to the concept of moral will and moral rationality. Corporate morality so far has been brought out through the policies of government or companies. For instance, problems concerning controlling pollution, monitoring of advertising, due process of hiring, as well as laying off employees, are all presented in the form of policy or regulations, through which companies are expected to fulfill their moral responsibilities. However, there is a shortcoming in such a mode of morality, as Solomon conceives it.

> What is missing from much of business ethics is an adequate account of the personal dimension in ethics, the dimension of everyday individual decision making. Accordingly, I want to defend business as a more personally oriented ethics rather than as public policy, 'applied' ethics so conceived is not 'personal' in the sense of 'private' or 'subjective'; it is rather social and institutional self-awareness, a sense of oneself as an intimate (but not inseparable) part of the business world with a keen sense of the virtues and virtues of that world. It is an Aristotelean approach to business ethics.[19]

The Aristotelian approach to business ethics puts a great concern on the character of an individual, rather than the impersonal policies and abstract principles or theories. Good character is the precondition of business ethics, since an individual with such kind of character would expand the self to become a social individual and thus be aware that morality is something that makes business possible. As Aristotle points out, good character can be defined by a set of virtues. It follows that the cultivation of virtues can help to form good character. For example, loyalty, honor, and a sense of shame are some of the essential Aristotelian virtues that all tie into the central notion of integrity. According to Solomon, they are virtues which are the aim of the Aristotelian approach to business ethics to cultivate. He has discussed this point at length and concluded that an approach to business ethics that is constructed by such virtues is more personal as well as more social, compared with the other business ethics otherwise constructed. Finally Solomon also suggests that the flourish of business ethics depends upon the development of civic virtues and not upon the learning of abstract theories.[20]

The Confucian presupposition

The Aristotelian approach to business ethics as explicated by Solomon has shown an alternative to Kantian ethics, utilitarianism, and theory of right, etc. According to this approach, corporate morality is established on a specific understanding of the individual—the agent of a moral activity is not an isolated individual. Such an understanding does not only make ethics possible, but also business. Hence, morality is not merely an "ought" but also a "must" for business. As the morality established on such an understanding particularly emphasizes the concrete situation and the context in which moral judgments are made, it avoids the difficulty of applying abstract principles. While the Aristotelian approach to business ethics specifies the particularity and moral roles of a business organization, it does not reduce the organization to its policy maker or executives. Nevertheless, the approach in question does regard the organization as a moral agent with specific responsibilities, responsibilities that are not (merely) sprung from the moral conscience, but are based on the idea of community. Interestingly enough, the notion of virtue, which is applicable for moral agents, can be transferred to organizations, albeit re-interpreted as "corporate culture" during the transference, whereas policy, which is generally thought to be a specific mode of corporate morality, has been regarded as secondary for its lack of moral spirit and motivation.

The Aristotelian approach introduced by Solomon is doubtless an illuminating way of thinking of business ethics. In particular, it provides a strong justification for the problem of why, and to whom, a business organization should be responsible. Although we need not accept all of the virtues Solomon commends, we may agree that the cultivation of virtue is one of the ways of practicing business morality thus it can be treated as a supplement of moral principles. Moreover, we may be led by Solomon's introduction to think about the possible contribution of Confucian philosophy to business ethics in a similar direction. In recent years, many have discussed the application of Chinese philosophy such as Confucianism to the field of management. Most of them focus on the guiding function of Chinese philosophy on an applied level. In fact, it is worthwhile to investigate whether Confucianism can also provide a foundation for justifying business's being moral, on a "individual-community" dimension. In the remaining part of this chapter, I am going to discuss this briefly.

Confucian ethics puts great emphases on subjectivity. It is a central tenet in Confucianism that the moral conscience of an agent is the subjective ground for morality, and there are rich teachings about self-cultivation. Nevertheless, the "moral subject" in Confucian ethics is not an isolated individual. Confucius clearly declares,

"One cannot associate with birds and beasts. Am I not a member of this human race? Who, then, is there for me to associate with?" (*Analects*, 18.6)

This shows a strong consciousness of community: an agent is part of the community, and most importantly, the inheritor of culture. Therefore, everyone has a special responsibility to his or her society and culture.

In Confucian ethics, "to expand oneself to others" is one of the important directions of moral cultivation.

> A man of *ren* helps others to take their stand in so far as he himself wishes to take his stand, and gets others there in so far as he himself wishes to get there.
>
> *Analects*, 6.30

Beginning with cultivating the self, one will bring peace and security to fellow citizens and humanity in general. The latter task is the ultimate aim for the sage. The self, family, country, and the whole world are arranged in such a hierarchical order that one is obliged to fulfill one's responsibilities accordingly.

> Zilu asked about the gentleman. The master said, "He cultivates himself and thereby achieves reverence."
>
> "Is that all?"
>
> "He cultivates himself and thereby brings peace and security to his fellow men."
>
> "Is that all?"
>
> "He cultivates himself and thereby brings peace and security to the people. Even Yao and Shun would have found the task of bringing peace and security to the people taxing."
>
> *Analects*, 14.42

The possibility of this moral requirement is based on the belief that everyone has his or her "moral germs" which are universal within his or her moral heart-mind (*xin*), and on the view that everyone's desires and needs are more or less the same. Because of the latter view, Confucian thinkers maintain that people can understand each other. This resemblance is not only a consequence of the similar inborn make up of the human race, but also comes from the same culture they all share. In the Confucian world, *li* (propriety) and music are supposed to be the concrete representation of shared culture. It follows that according to Confucianism, shared culture is the objective presupposition which makes morality possible.

As an individual lives in the commonly-shared culture, he or she should have special responsibility to his or her culture. Apparently Confucius himself shows a great commitment to the preservation of culture.

> When under siege in Kuang, the master said, "With King Wen dead, is not culture (*wen*) invested here in me? If Heaven intends culture to be destroyed, those who come after me will not be able to have any part of it. If Heaven does not intend this culture to be destroyed, then what can the men of Kuang do to me?"
>
> *Analects*, 9.5

> [the master said,] "... While the way is to be found in the Empire, I will not change places with him."
>
> *Analects*, 18.6

> ... Zilu commented, "Not to enter public life is to ignore one's duty. Even the proper regulation of old and young cannot be set aside. How, then, can the duty between ruler and subject be set aside? This is to cause confusion in the most important of human relationships simply because one desires to keep unsullied one's character. The gentleman takes office in order to do his duty. As for putting the Way to practice, he knows all along that it is hopeless."
>
> *Analects*, 18.7

For the sake of the mission of preserving and reconstructing culture, Confucius chooses not to be a recluse who aims at purity without the pollution of reality; rather, he would like to be appreciated so that he could actualize his ideal.

On the one hand, Confucians certainly affirm the responsibility that an individual has to his or her community, and even to his or her culture; on the other hand, they also emphasize that the relation among individuals is not antagonistic. This idea is clearly expressed by the well-known idiom "all within the Four Seas are his brothers" (*Analects*, 12.5). It is this idea too that makes the moral requirements of "to help others to take their stand in so far as he himself wishes to take his stand" and "to get there in so far as he himself wishes to get there" possible.

The Confucian solution to the "ultimate question"—Why be moral?—is based on the Confucian's conception of human.[21] According to this conception, human is superior to beasts in that the former is able to differentiate good from bad and then act on those that lead to the good. Following this line of thought, the understanding of the humanistic world in which human activities (including business activities) are carried out would also affect the nature of morality that governs those activities. Moreover, it might even affect the possibility of morality. From the Confucian point of view, a normal society must not be the one in which everyone is merely pursuing his or her own interests.

> [Mencius said,] "... then those above and those below will be trying to profit at the expense of one another and the state will be imperilled. When regicide is committed in a state of ten thousand chariots, it is certain to be by a vassal with a thousand chariots, and when it is committed in a state of a thousand chariots, it is certain to be by a vassal with a hundred chariots. A share of a thousand in ten thousand or a hundred in a thousand is by no means insignificant, yet if profits are put before rightness, there is no satisfaction short of total usurpation."
>
> *Mencius*, 1A1

Only if one does not understand and treat the world from the standpoint of one's own interests, will the world be full of harmony and joy.

> Mencius went to see King Hui of Liang. The King was standing over a pond. "Are such things enjoyed even by a good and wise man?" said he, looking round at his wild geese and deer.

"Only if a man is good and wise," answered Mencius, "is he able to enjoy them. Otherwise he would not, even if he had them.

"The Odes say,

He surveyed and began the Sacred Terrace.
He Surveyed it and measured it;
The people worked at it;
In less than no time they finished it.
He surveyed and began without haste;
The people came in ever increasing numbers.
The King was in the Sacred Park.
The doe lay down;
The doe were sleek;
The white birds glistened.
The King was at the Sacred Pond.
Oh! how full it was of leaping fish!

It was with the labour of the people that King Wen built his terrace and pond, yet so pleased and delighted were they that they named his terrace the 'Sacred Terrace' and his pond the 'Sacred Pond', and rejoiced in his possession of deer, fish and turtles. It was by sharing their enjoyments with the people that men of antiquity were able to enjoy themselves . . ."

Mencius, 1A2

Confucians insist that the ruler (the King) should not suppress his people for his own interests, on the contrary, no matter whether it is music, or money, or women, or any other things that the ruler is fond of, he has to share them with his people.

[Mencius said,] ". . . You may be fond of money, but so long as you share this fondness with the people, how can it interfere with your becoming a true King?"

Mencius, 1B5

Moreover, only in the company of people will the enjoyment be true and great enjoyment.[22] This is true not merely for the governor who holds the highest authority over people, but also for ordinary people. Similarly, in the business world, one is regarded as despicable if he or she always looks for a vantage point solely for the sake of his or her own interests.

[Mencius said,] ". . . In antiquity, the market was for the exchange of what one had for what one lacked. The authorities merely supervised it. There was, however, a despicable fellow who always looked for a vantage point and, going up on it, gazed into the distance to the left and to the right in order to secure for himself all the profit there was in the market. The people all thought him despicable, and, as a result, they taxed him. The taxing of traders began with this despicable fellow."

Mencius, 2B10

From the quotation cited above, we may conclude that Confucian thinkers conceive business activities, like other activities, as cooperative and mutually beneficial. A set of moral requirements, expectations, and duties has been derived from such an understanding. There is no doubt that these moral requirements and duties have their subjective ground, which is the most significant foundation of the Confucian ethical system and which cannot be dealt with here. However, I hope the exposition and discussion made at least has explored the possibility of Confucianism's contribution in the presupposition of corporate morality.

Postscript

The Confucian presuppositions of business ethics mentioned above do not only apply to the ancient times or to the Confucian thinkers. On the contrary, they manifest themselves as some sort of basic belief in the contemporary business world. Let me cite two examples here.

The first one is about a famous merchant in late Ching whose name is Hu Xueyan (胡雪巖). After he had been successful in his trading business, Hu started to run a business in medicine. When he interviewed the applicants for the post of manager, he rejected many of them who promised to earn big money for him. At last he was moved by the speech of one of the applicants. The main point of that speech was that the business of medicine should not be regarded as an ordinary business. Its central concern should not be profit, which might be the aim of other kinds of business. Then Hu hired this man and thereafter the business flourished. The business of medicine was not a charity but was a business in that it produced and sold goods. Its success depended on the truthfulness and honesty in the transactions as well as the quality of the product. This story of Hu reflects a belief of Chinese businessmen that certain kinds of business should be run for the sake of other people's welfare. They do not worry about or aim at the profit it might bring to them; nevertheless, the profit would naturally arrive. In this respect, business for them is merely an activity among others, the aim of which is not necessarily profit-making. Profit is only one of the goals in one's whole life and goals other than that would also be meaningful. This resembles the Aristotelian idea of holiness. It is noteworthy that although in Confucian teaching, righteousness outweighs profit, Hu himself was neither a Confucian scholar nor a conscious follower. He was even not educated, though he might have been influenced by Confucian thought. However, this view is not restricted to Confucianism (as a similar view can be found in ancient Greek thought) or limited to Chinese-minded people. It is in some sense universal. If one wants it to become a guiding principle, then Confucianism is one of the ethical systems that can provide ethical presuppositions for business as we have discussed.

Another example is about a well-known millionaire in Hong Kong. It is alleged that during the war, he shared material for production with his opponents in business while the latter ran out of resources and could not obtain them by any means. This act is unintelligible in the present day business world in which everyone treats his or her opponents as enemies. In the metaphor of war, this means providing weapons to one's rival party. But if one changes one's outlook and adopt the idea of community, one would find that the business world is somewhere anyone can participate if he or she wishes. One might gain what one wants or one might lose. The crucial point is that one should not aim at defeating the opponents while one pursues success. The participants in business are cooperative rather than competitive. This view is in line with Confucian thought. Here we may conclude that either the Aristotelian approach or Confucian ethics can provide presuppositions as well as ethical principles or virtues for business nowadays.

Part Three

The Heritage and Development of Neo-Confucianism: The Thought of Cheng Brothers

13

The Thought of CHENG Hao

Life and work

CHENG Hao (程顥) (1032–1085) was born in Huangpi (黃陂) in what is the present Hubei Province, where his father was a local administrator. Baichun (伯淳) was his courtesy name, but he was better known as Mingdao (明道). Together with his younger brother CHENG Yi (程頤) (1033–1107), he strove to restore the tradition of Confucius and Mencius in the name of "the study of the Way" (*daoxue* 道學), which eventually developed as the main concern in various schools of Neo-Confucian thought. Although the philosophical views of the two brothers are diverse in some respects, they are usually identified together as the "Cheng Brothers" to signify their common contribution to Neo-Confucian thought. A precocious child, he composed poems at ten, and also excelled in learning. At fifteen he came to study under ZHOU Dunyi (周敦頤) (1017–1073). Although Zhou's own system of thought had yet to be completed, Cheng felt inspired and resolved to dedicate his whole life to the search for the Way (*Dao* 道). In 1056, he traveled to the capital Luoyang (洛陽) in preparation for the civil service examination. At this time, he also made the acquaintance of ZHANG Zai (張載) (1020–1077), who was destined to be regarded by posterity as another pillar of the Neo-Confucian school. In the following year Cheng was awarded the *jinshi* degree and made an official of the government. He served in various capacities at various places thereafter, discharging his duties creditably. In 1069, he came to the notice of Shenzong (神宗), the new emperor, who gave him audiences from time to time and opportunities to voice his political views. However, insofar as the emperor gave more weight to the advice of WANG Anshi (王安石) (1021–1086), leader of the reformation campaign whose ideas Cheng Hao adamantly opposed, Cheng was discredited, demoted to lower offices, and eventually dismissed. In 1072, he returned to Luoyang and there, together with his brother Cheng Yi, built a school, and taught until his death.

The main corpus of Cheng Hao's work comprises conversations as recorded by his disciples, collected in the *Surviving Works of the Two Chengs* (*Er Cheng yishu* 二程遺書). He also wrote short essays, poems, and letters. The best-known essays are "Letter on Stabilizing Nature" (Dingxing shu 定性書) and "On Understanding *Ren*" (Shi-ren pian 識仁篇). The citations in this chapter are mainly from *Collected Works of the Two Chengs* (*Er Cheng ji* 二程集; CHENG and CHENG 1981),[1] a collection that contains most of the Cheng Brothers' writings and conversations. It is an amended edition of the *Complete Works of the Two Chengs* (*Er Cheng quanshu* 二程全書),

which includes *Surviving Works* (*Yishu* 遺書), *External Books* (*Waishu* 外書), *Collected Writings* (*Wenji* 文集), *CHENG Yi's Commentary on the Book of Change* (*Zhouyi Cheng shi zhuan* 周易程氏傳), *Interpretation of Classics* (*Jingshuo* 經說), and *Essential Sayings* (*Cuiyan* 粹言). *Surviving Works* consists of sayings by the Cheng Brothers recorded by their disciples. In some of these texts the speaker is clearly indicated, but in others not so. Some indicate that the quoted expression was "spoken by the two masters." For these unassigned sayings it has been a problem to identify the speaker. The Contemporary Neo-Confucian leading philosopher MOU Zongsan (牟宗三) (1909–1995) was the first person to set criteria for distinguishing between sayings by the two brothers.[2]

Although Mou's criteria are not completely convincing for some scholars,[3] they are so far the most reliable. One criterion is the style of expression of the two brothers: Cheng Hao liked to express ideas in a "sudden and perfect" (*yuandun* 圓頓) way, whereas Cheng Yi did so in an analytical way. *Yuan* signifies a state of perfection and completeness. It also means an all-inclusive state, in that superficially contrary descriptions are included, since it is believed that the duality in conceptual thinking does not apply to the situation being described. *Dun* refers to a kind of transformation without a gradual process. In Buddhism, sudden awakening is contrasted to gradual awakening. Cheng Hao liked to use a "sudden and perfect" way to describe visions that he experienced when he thought that these visions were not the product of logical reasoning. Because of this special way of expression, ZHU Xi (朱熹) (1130–1200) found Cheng Hao's sayings nebulous (*hunlun* 渾淪)[4].

In his brother's words, the path that led Cheng Hao to find the Way was by "browsing through various schools of thought, looking deeply into Daoism and Buddhism for many decades, coming back to the Six Classics and finally attaining it."[5] Cheng Hao inherited and developed the thought of classical Confucianism rather than drawing on preceding Neo-Confucian thinkers such as ZHOU Dunyi, SHAO Yong (邵雍) (1011–1077), or ZHANG Zai.

Ontology

Heaven and Principle

For Cheng Hao, Heaven (*Tian* 天) is a transcendent entity. It has multiple names: the Way (*Dao* 道), the Changes (*Yi* 易), the Spirit (*Sheng* 神), each signifies a specific aspect of the Heaven. The notion Changes is to illustrate the ceaselessly-producing nature of Heaven, the function of which is called the Spirit, as a description of its unpredictable creativity which renders innumerable things' existence. Whereas the Spirit represents the function (*yong* 用), the Changes and the Way refers to the substance. The Way denotes the Principle (*Li* 理) it contains, which is also called the Heavenly Principle (*Tian Li* 天理).

The Principle is one, which includes many. Within this Principle, hundreds of principles are implicitly there to be employed where particular issues arise. The particular principles can be considered as different forms of the Principle, which is everlasting without changes no matter what situation comes up. The Principle is the law of creation, equivalent to creativity. However, it is not only a static law providing governance and guidance to innumerable things, rather, the law has creative/productive power which makes their existence possible. Therefore the Principle can be viewed as the principle of production and the Way as the way of production. The Principle refers to both the law based on which things are formed and the creating activity by which things come into existence. The literal meaning of the Changes is precisely a description of the activity of "production and reproduction" (*shen shen* 生生). This meaning has a long tradition which can be traced back to the "Great Appendix" in the *Book of Change*: "Production and reproduction is what is meant by the Changes." Cheng Hao makes a remark to this text: "It is production which Heaven regards as its Way."[6] The Spirit shows the unlimited and unfathomable function of the activity of creation. Every thing shares the Principle and thus has the potential of "production and reproduction." In sum, no matter which name it bears, Heaven is the transcendent Being which is completely embodied in its activity, and the activity is the manifestation of the Being. Therefore as Being (the creativity itself), it can be understood through activity (act of creation) and vice versa.

Heaven and innumerable things

Heaven no doubt belongs to the realm of "above form" (*xing er shang* 形而上), which is contrary to "below form" (*xing er xia* 形而下) (realm of phenomenon) where instruments (*qi* 器) (innumerable things) emerge. Nevertheless, these two realms are in no way separate. It is because the Heaven or the Way is nothing but its manifestation through the instruments. Also, when the instruments are fully actualized, they embody the Way. Cheng Hao claims: "Outside the Way there are no things and outside things there is no Way, so that between heaven and earth there is no direction to go which is not the Way."[7] He also says that the Way is the instruments and the instruments are the Way.[8]

The Way and vital energy (*qi* 氣)

The relationship between the Way and vital energy is analogous to that between the Way and the instruments. Vital energy, which is divided into *yin* (陰) and *yang* (陽), belongs to the realm of below form. All phenomena are formed by the operation of *yin* and *yang* hence the former can be understood in terms of the latter. To quote an example from Cheng Hao, "The coldness of winter and the heat of summer are respectively *yin* and *yang*. That by which they (*yin* and *yang*) are moved and transformed is Spirit."[9] It is noteworthy that Cheng Hao distinguishes with clarity *yin* and *yang* from their operations. Apparently he thinks that only the above form can be the explanatory and operational ground for the below form. Yet he emphasizes that "outside vital energy there is no Spirit and outside Spirit there is no vital energy."[10] Spirit is present in the vital energy, no matter it is clear or turbid. This means that the Way may manifest itself in any forms. Cheng Hao thinks that since the Way should not be confined to a certain form, therefore he objects the view that the source of the innumerable things locates only in the "clear, void, one and great" which are commonly considered as positive.[11] The Way, for him, "becomes one substance with things without exception."[12]

Philosophy of human nature (*ren xing* 人性)

It is out of the question that Cheng Hao endorses what was advocated by Mencius, that "human nature is good." However, he particularly focuses on the origin of human nature. In Mencius, it is claimed that the greater body, by which human is capable of discerning good and evil, is decreed by Heaven (*Mencius*, 6A1). The greater body refers to the heart-mind, the actualization of human nature. Following this line of thinking, the passage that "by fully activating one's heart-mind one can apprehend one's own nature, by fully apprehending one's own nature one will apprehend Heaven" (*Mencius*, 7A1) is deemed intelligible. Even though the capacity of discerning good and evil is decreed by Heaven, it is by no means that goodness is decided by it. Therefore, Confucian ethics is not a kind of metaphysical ethics.

Cheng Hao holds that the origin of human nature is Heaven and both human nature and Heaven share the common quality of creativity. I have mentioned that every thing shares the Principle of Creation, so does human. Therefore human is endowed with the power of production and reproduction as his or her nature. Although things and human share the common nature, i.e., the creativity by which they come into existence, they individually have different characteristics. Hence on the one hand all innumerable things are the same and on the other they differ from each other.

Apart from attributing human nature a specific content, Cheng Hao also gives "good" his own interpretation. He says, "It is production which Heaven regards as its Way, and what succeeds this productive Principle is goodness. Goodness has the implication 'Originating' (*yuan* 元). 'The Originating is at the head of goodness.'"[13] This means that the productive power is the origin of goodness. Human nature, which possesses this productive power, also possesses the origin of goodness. Therefore the attribute "good" in the assertion "human nature is good" has a totally different meaning from that appearing in a moral judgment. The former indicates an inborn capacity of human beings which is considered as the ground of making moral judgment. The actualization of human nature means the succession of the original good, which is also considered good. This is how Cheng Hao interprets the passage in the "Great Appendix": "That which succeeds is goodness; that in which it is completed is the nature."

Cheng Hao has quoted the saying of Gaozi (告子) (Mencius' contemporary) that "inborn is what is meant by the nature," nevertheless, he and Gaozi do not hold the same view. It is true that both agree on the view that every being possesses the inborn qualities of life to come to exist, but for Gaozi these qualities are composed of natural dispositions, desires, and abilities that make one species different from another, whereas for Cheng Hao the inborn quality refers to the productive power which is commonly shared by all kinds of things. Cheng Hao maintains that since the innumerable things share the same productive power, all things are the same. Based on this reason, he further claims that human and the things can become one.

As mentioned, the innumerable things and humans obtain the ceaselessly productive power from Heaven as their nature. Since they completely possess this productive power once they are formed, in order to become one with Heaven they are complete within themselves without the need of attaining anything outside. Cheng Hao interprets Mencius' saying that "the innumerable things are all complete in myself" (*Mencius*,

7A4) as mentioned above and adds that "this is so not only of human but of all things."[14] Having said that, in the phenomenal world, things differ from each other in kind, and also from human. Cheng Hao explains this differentiation in terms of vital energy with which things are endowed when they become an individual being. The vital energy obtained by things is impure or obscure. Although like human, the innumerable things obtain the Way of Principle when they come into existence, they only possess it ontologically, meaning that the Way (of production) exists within things themselves merely as potential. Only human is endowed with the vital energy that allows him or her to actualize his or her own nature as well as to extend it to actualize others' nature. Therefore, only human can nurture his or her nature and cultivate the nature of things, and also because of this capacity they can form a trinity with Heaven and Earth.

The innumerable things receive the Principle from Heaven, but the Principle endowed only manifests as the structure of their existence. In the case of human, the Principle endowed constitutes the human nature of ceaseless productive power. Since the Principle is one and the same, therefore as human we can get in touch with the Principle by watching the manifestation of productive power in living things, for instance, the activity of grass growing. Cheng Hao exclaims that "It is most excellent to look into the vital impulses of the innumerable things."[15] It is because from the vital impulses he can take a glimpse of the Changes.

Heart-mind (*Xin* 心) and the theory of cultivation

Human is endowed with the Principle thus can extend his or her nature to the nature of things. Adopting Mencius' conception of heart-mind, Cheng Hao also takes the heart-mind as the faculty of extension mentioned above. Mencius says, "by fully activating one's heart-mind one can apprehend one's own nature, by fully apprehending one's own nature one will apprehend Heaven" (*Mencius*, 7A1). According to Mencius, through "extending from whom one loves to whom one doesn't" (*Mencius*, 7B1) one will exhaust one's heart-mind then apprehend Heaven. Cheng Hao makes a further claim that "the heart-mind alone is Heaven."[16] What he emphasizes is that the heart-mind and the Heaven are originally one, since they both have creativity (the ceaselessly productive power) as their virtue. Therefore one only needs to actualize/restore this virtue which is inherent in one's own heart-mind.

The virtue of creativity inherent in the heart-mind is called "*ren*" (仁), sometimes translated as "benevolence" since one of its meanings is the capacity of loving people without discrimination. *Ren* presents in the transference of feeling (*gantong* 感通) with other people, which makes this universal love possible. Whereas love is empirical, the capacity of transference is transcendent since it is not conditioned by empirical factors. By activating *ren*, one will regard others' interest as one's own and will "help others to stand while wishing to stand oneself and help others to arrive while wishing to arrive oneself" (*The Analects*, 6.30). The creativity of *ren* presents in the ceaseless extension of care and love. Ultimately, one who fully activates *ren* will treat oneself and the innumerable things as one substance, "so that nothing is not Oneself."[17] Cheng Hao likes to take "the numbness in the hands and feet" as a metaphor to illustrate the unconnected condition of one and the others. He says the sage, who achieves *ren* to perfection, would regard heaven and earth as one body and the innumerable things as four limbs and other organs, such a person would love the innumerable things as his or her own limbs. When the limbs are "unfeeling" then this situation would be described as paralysis. By the same token, if one does not feel the suffering of others, then it would be said that his or her heart-mind is paralytic and *ren* within it is not activated.

As mentioned, the heart-mind possesses the virtue of Heaven, i.e., creativity as its own virtue. Therefore all one needs for actualizing the virtue of Heaven is to activate one's heart-mind. Activating one's heart-mind means actualizing one's nature. Once one's nature is actualized then one can actualize the nature of others as well as that of innumerable things. When the nature of others and things are actualized, then one can assist Heaven in transforming and nurturing things. On the contrary, if the heart-mind has not been fully activated, then one cannot apprehend the nature of things and that of Heaven. Cheng Hao says, "Exhausting the Principle, actualizing the nature and reaching the decree [of Heaven], these three events can altogether be completed at one time. Definitely there is no priority. Exhausting the Principle should not be regarded as a cognitive act. If the Principle is really exhausted, then the nature and the decree are also completed."[18] If exhausting the Principle is not a cognitive act, then the accomplishment of knowledge, even about the principles of innumerable things, is not essential to the apprehension of the Principle. Once the heart-mind is actualized, the Principle is exhausted. This idea is well-developed from *Mencius*, 7A1.

Cheng Hao maintains that merely through sincerity (*cheng* 诚) one can activate one's heart-mind. He says, "By perfect sincerity one can take part in (*zan* 赞) the cultivation of Heaven and Earth."[19] According to him, this is possible since perfect sincerity is the cultivation of Heaven and Earth which is manifesting ceaseless creativity. This view can be traced back to Mencius that sincerity is the way of Heaven and that aiming at sincerity is the way of man (*Mencius*, 4A12). Also in the *Doctrine of the Mean*, it is claimed that "The Way of Heaven and Earth can be perfectly expressed in a single clause: 'It is without any doubleness (*bu er* 不二), therefore its production of things is unfathomable.'" (ch. 26) Double or two (*er* 二) symbolizes the dichotomy of true and false, real and illusory, etc. Only if the dualistic way of thinking is abolished, the ultimate truth that constitutes the ground for all existence can be revealed. Hence the Way of production is, unequivocally, sincerity. In the *Doctrine of the Mean* it is held that through perfect sincerity one can actualize the nature of oneself, that of other people and things. It is clear that Cheng Hao combines these two sources and concludes that by actualizing the heart-mind through sincerity one can realize the virtue of Heaven. In sum, the ceaseless creative power, *ren*, and sincerity are but one virtue in the human's heart-mind as well as in Heaven. Therefore, through the actualization of this virtue, human and Heaven are united. For practice in daily lives, once one understands Heaven and the Principle, one merely needs to preserve *ren* by sincerity and composure (*jing* 敬). Cheng Hao maintains that there is no need to be on one's guard nor to conduct deep inquiries. He argues, "If the mind relaxes we must be on guard; but if not, what is there to guard against? Inquiry is necessary only because there are principles which have not yet been grasped; if they have been constantly preserved they will be clear of themselves, and what need is there to inquire?"[20] Precisely, for Cheng Hao, it is because human and the Principle are originally one and both have *ren* as their content, therefore understanding the Principle means understanding human nature which can be actualized by the heart-mind through sincerity.

The highest achievement of cultivation

In Confucianism the ultimate goal of cultivation for an individual is to become a sage, a person who has achieved the highest state in the moral realm. To achieve the highest moral accomplishment, the sage has been cultivating his or her heart-mind so as to unlimitedly extend the circle of care and concern and eventually treat others and things equally as treating oneself. For Cheng Hao, apart from devoting himself or herself to the moral pursuit, a sage also aims at uniting with Heaven. As mentioned above, human and Heaven are originally one since both share the common nature and virtue of the power of production. However, if human and Heaven are but one, there is no need to speak of the union of Heaven and human. By the same token, it is odd to speak of forming a trinity with Heaven and Earth or uniting with others and things. When Cheng Hao claims that "outside the Way there are no things and outside the things there is no Way" and "the Way is instruments and instruments are the Way," what kind of expressions are they? Obviously they are neither empirical statements of fact nor a metaphysical belief. The former demands one way or another for verification or confirmation. The latter is commonly regarded as something speculative without a convincing ground. Rather, the expressions in question can be considered as a description of a vision which can only be achieved by a sage. A sage can achieve this kind of vision since as a sage he or she completely embodies the Way. Therefore he or she can apprehend the Way by activating his or her heart-mind, furthermore he or she will find that the Way manifests itself in his or her heart-mind and in any forms of instruments without confinement. It seems that the above explanation commits the fallacy of begging the question: the metaphysical claim is accounted for in terms of a sage and a sage is characterized in terms of the content in the metaphysical claim. If this is the case, then the metaphysical claim and the description about the sage are mutually dependent. This problem is analogous to that arising from the conceptual relationship between virtuous acts and virtuous persons. If a virtuous person is characterized in terms of virtuous acts, i.e., a virtuous person is someone who always chooses virtuous acts for their own sake, and a virtuous act is what a virtuous person would do, then the conceptions of virtuous acts and virtuous persons will be mutually dependent. Bernard Williams comments on this relationship of dependence that "there is no problem just in this, but there will be a problem if it leads to vacuity."[21] Under what conditions will it constitute a problem? Williams proceeds, "This will be so, if we cannot distinguish one virtue from another, and/or the V [virtuous] agent is left with no determinate content to his thoughts."[22] In the present case, being a sage can be identified without depending on the metaphysical claim. Because after some practice one can completely apprehend one's heart-mind, thus knows vividly whether one treats others as oneself. This merely depends on personal reflection which usually well applies to inner experience. Thus from the perspective of a sage, when he or she sees that himself or herself and others are one, then he or she would also find that the Way and the instruments are one. The theses of this oneness apprehended by a sage is called by Cheng Hao "one-rootedness" (*yiben* 一本).

A problem remains that if Heaven and human are originally one, then why is cultivation needed anyway? According to Cheng Hao, human is endowed with vital energy which might hinder the actualization of his or her nature, therefore, human needs to make effort in order to resume the unity with Heaven. Through activating *ren*, sincerity, and the productive power, one is taking the path towards the aim.

The duality of good and bad

A.C. Graham, in his book *Two Chinese Philosophers: Ch'eng Ming-tao and Ch'eng Yi-ch'uan*[23] discusses the issue of "monism or dualism" in Cheng Hao's thought. He singles out the contrariness of good and evil in one chapter and argues that Cheng Hao admits the bad, like the good, is a necessary part of the Way. Graham points out that Neo-Confucians in general and Cheng Hao in particular, make no distinction between descriptive and normative principles[24]: since bad is a necessary part in the world of existence, it is equally so in the moral world. Graham thinks that it is a conceptual contradiction to prescribe that human ought to do good and at the same time to regard bad as a necessary component of the natural harmony. He guesses the solution for a modern European is to distinguish between the two senses of the principle.

In fact, Cheng Hao has distinguished between these two senses. As mentioned above, the Way decree human with the Principle as his or her nature. In the ontological sense of the principle, i.e., the Principle (it is not proper to regard it as descriptive since the truth it refers to is not an empirical fact), as it possesses the power of production, which is the origin of good (that which succeeds is goodness) therefore human nature is good. Nevertheless, when an individual comes to existence, he or she is also endowed with vital energy, which might lead to the bad. Even though the bad is not originated from the Principle, the process of coming into existence is also under the governance of the Principle. This is what is meant by Cheng Hao's saying "there are good and bad events, all are heavenly Principle."[25] However, as far as the normative sense of Principle is concerned, one ought to activate one's heart-mind and thus actualize one's nature. This is the way of observing the Principle. But since one is endowed with vital energy which might hinder one from actualizing one's own nature, therefore one needs to cultivate one's heart-mind to resume the Principle. It is in this sense he speaks of good or bad acts in a normative sense.

Although in Cheng Hao's thought, it is admitted that the Principle has to manifest itself through vital energy, where the bad originates, it does not mean that human is "born with good and bad as two contrasting things present in his or her nature from the very beginning."[26] Therefore, underlying the dualistic view of good and bad, for Cheng Hao it is the original goodness which is the ultimate ground for the contrasting attributes. He uses a water parable to illustrate this: water is originally clean and it becomes muddy only if it is polluted. The cleanliness and the muddiness are not two contrasting attributes in the nature of water. The water inevitably becomes muddy once it starts to flow, in this sense the nature of water also includes the possibility of being polluted. However, it does not follow from this that it could not be purified to obtain clean water. For the present issue, we have seen that the two principles, namely, the ontological principle and the normative principle are one. The former accounts for the origin of good and bad while the latter governs the good and the bad. Yet the fact that the principles are but one would not render Cheng Hao's ethics a metaphysical ethics. This is so because the recognition of the latter does not depend on that of the former, rather, it is through the heart-mind that both principles are apprehended. Therefore, contrary to Graham's view, firstly, the two principles have not been mixed up; secondly, there is no contradiction between these two principles.

The significance of Cheng Hao's thought

Cheng Hao is the first one who focuses on the heart-mind and *ren* among the Neo-Confucians in the Song Dynasty (960–1279 CE). He is also the first one who emphasizes the unity of heart-mind, human nature, and Heaven which is based on the single-rootedness doctrine. Although his theses are inherited from the Confucian classics including the *Analects*, *Mencius*, the *Book of Change* and the *Doctrine of the Mean*, of which his interpretation and elaboration offer learners a new insight and perspective in understanding Confucianism. For example, the notion of Heaven has existed very early in the history of Chinese thoughts and in pre-Qin Confucianism, Cheng Hao claims that he has picked up the notion of Principle by himself and developed it to refer to the ontological Being as well as activity. His thesis is so influential that the thoughts of various schools of Neo-Confucianism are commonly called "the study of Principle" (*lixue* 理学). Therefore, his contribution to Confucianism is regarded as going beyond restoration, as re-vitalization and re-construction of Confucianism.

Cheng Hao and his brother Cheng Yi have shared the same interest in traditional Confucianism in theory and moral cultivation in practice. However, there are wide disagreements between the views of the two brothers. Cheng Hao gives significant role to the heart-mind in ontology and in moral philosophy. His thought is further developed by LU Xiangshan (陸象山) (1139–1193) and WANG Yangming (王陽明) (1472–1529), and has evolved into the tradition of the study of mind (*xinxue* 心學). This tradition becomes the rival school of the study of Principle (in a narrow sense) which is founded by Cheng Yi.

14

The Thought of CHENG Yi

Life and work

CHENG Yi (程頤) (1033–1107), a native of Henan, was born into a family of distinguished officials. He used Zhengshu (正叔) as courtesy name, but was much better known as Yichuan, the river in his home country. Cheng Yi grew up in Huangpi, where his father served as a local administrator. At fourteen, he was sent along with his elder brother CHENG Hao (程灝) (1032–1085) to study under the tutelage of ZHOU Dunyi (周敦頤) (1017–1073), the Song Dynasty's founding father of Neo-Confucianism. Driven by a strong sense of duty and concern for the nation, at the early age of eighteen, he memorialized to the emperor, offering a penetrating analysis of the current political crisis as well as the hardships of the common people. In 1056, led by his father, he and his brother traveled to Luoyang, the capital, and enrolled in the imperial academy. There they made the friendship of ZHANG Zai (張載) (1020–1077), who also eventually became a paragon of Neo-Confucianism.

With an excellent essay, Cheng Yi won the commendation of HU Yuan (胡瑗) (993–1056), the influential educator, and he gained celebrity status in the academia. Young scholars came to study with him from regions far and wide. In 1072, when Cheng Hao was dismissed from his government office, Cheng Yi organized a school with him and started his lifelong career as a private tutor. Time and again he turned down offers of appointment in officialdom. Nonetheless, he maintained throughout his life a concern for state affairs and was forthright in his strictures against certain government policies, particularly those from the reform campaign of WANG Anshi (王安石) (1021–1086). In 1085, as the reformers were ousted, Cheng Yi was invited by the emperor to give political lectures regularly. He did that for twenty months, until political attacks put an end to his office.

At the age of sixty, Cheng Yi drafted a book on the *Yizhuan* (*Commentary on the Book of Changes*) and laid plans for its revision and publication in ten years. In 1049, he finished the revision, complete with a foreword. He then turned to annotate the *Analects*, the *Mencius*, the *Liji* (*The Book of Rites*) and the *Chunqiu (Spring and Autumn Annals)*. In the following year he began working on the *Chunqiu Zhuan* (*Commentary on Spring and Autumn Annals*). In 1102, however, as the reformers regained control, he was impeached on charges of "evil speech." As a result, he was prohibited from teaching and his books banned and destroyed. In 1109 he suffered a stroke. Sensing the imminent end of his life, he ignored the restriction on teaching and delivered lectures on his book *Yizhuan*. He died in September of that year.

Apart from the book mentioned above, Cheng Yi left behind essays, poems and letters. These are collected in *The Works of the Two Chengs* (*Er Cheng Ji* 二程集), which also carries his conversations as recorded by his disciples. *The Works of the Two Chengs* is an amended version of *Complete Works of the Two Chengs* (the earliest version was published in the Ming Dynasty), which includes *Literary Remains* (*Yishu*), *Additional Works* (*Waishu*), *Explanation of Classics* (*Jingshuo*), *Collections of Literary Works* (*Wenyi*), *Commentary on the Book of Change* (*Zhouyi Zhuan*), and *Selected Writings* (*Cuiyan*). *Reflections on Things at Hand* (*Jinsi lu*) which was compiled by ZHU Xi (朱熹) (1130–1200) and LU Zuqian (呂祖謙) (1137–1181) also collected many of Cheng Yi's conversations.

Ontology

The concept of *Li* (the Principle 理) is central to Cheng Yi's ontology. Although not created by the Cheng Brothers, it attains a core status in Neo-Confucianism through their advocacy. Thus, Neo-Confucianism is also called the study of *Li* (*li xue* 理學). The many facets of *Li* are translatable in English as "principle," "pattern," "reason," or "law." Sometimes it is used by the Chengs as synonymous with *Dao* (道), which means the Way. When so used, it referred to the way one should follow from the moral point of view. Understood as such, *Li* plays an action-guiding role similar to that of moral laws. Apart from the moral sense, *Li* also signifies the ultimate ground for all existence. This does not mean that *Li* creates all things, but rather that *Li* plays some explanatory role in making them the particular sorts of things they are. Therefore *Li* provides a principle for every existence. While Cheng Yi is aware that different things have different principles to account for their particular existence, he definitely thinks that these innumerable principles amount to one principle. This latter principle is the ultimate transcendental ground of all existence which is later signified by Zhu Xi as *Taiji* (太極). While the ultimate principle possesses the highest universality, the principle for a certain existence represents the specific manifestation of this ultimate principle. Therefore the latter can be understood as a particularization of the former.

Apparently, for Cheng Yi, *Li* is both the principle for nature and that for morality. The former governs natural matters; the latter, human affairs. To illustrate this with Cheng's example, *Li* is the principle by which fire is hot and water is cold, it is also the principle that regulates the relation between father and son, requiring that the father be paternal and the son be filial.

As the principle of morality, *Li* is ontologically prior to human affairs. It manifests itself in an individual affair in a particular situation. Through one's awareness, pre-existent external *Li* develops into an internal principle within the human heart-mind (*xin* 心). On the other hand, as the principle of nature, *Li* is also ontologically prior to the multitude of things. It manifests itself in the vital force (*qi* 氣) of *yin-yang* (陰陽). The relationship between *Li* and *yin-yang* is sometimes misconstrued as one of identity or coextensivity, but Cheng Yi's description of the relationship between the two clearly indicates otherwise: for him, *Li* is not the same thing as *yin-yang*, but is rather *what brings about* the alternation or oscillation between *yin* and *yang*. Although *Li* and *qi* belong to two different realms, namely, the realm "above form" (*xing er shang* 形而上) and the realm "below form" (*xing er xia* 形而下), they cannot exist apart from one another. He stated in no uncertain terms that, apart from *yin-yang*, there is no *Dao*.

In summary, no matter whether as the principle of nature or that of morality, *Li* serves as an expositional principle which accounts for what is and what should be, from an ontological perspective. Therefore, as MOU Zongsan argues, for Cheng Yi, *Li* does not represent an ever producing force or activity, as his brother Cheng Hao perceives, but merely an ontological ground for existence in the realm of nature as well as morality.

Philosophy of human nature, mind, and emotion

Human nature and human feeling

The attribute of human nature (*xing* 性) has been a topic of controversy ever since Mencius championed the view that human nature is good (*xing shan* 性善). The goodness of human nature in this sense is called the "original good," which signifies the capacity of being compassionate and distinguishing between the good and the bad. Cheng Yi basically adopted Mencius' view on this issue and further provided an ontological ground for it. He claimed that human nature and *Dao* are one thus human nature is equivalent to *Li*. Human nature is good since *Dao* and *Li* are absolute good, from which moral goodness is generated. In this way Cheng Yi elevated the claim that human nature is good to the level of an ontological claim, which was not so explicit in Mencius.

According to Cheng Yi, all actions performed from human nature are morally good. Presenting itself in different situations, human nature shows the different aspects of *Li*, namely, *ren*, *yi*, *li* (propriety 禮), *zhi* (wisdom 智), and trustworthiness (*xin* 信). These five aspects of *Li* also denote five aspects of human nature. Human beings are able to love since *ren* is inherent in their nature. When the heart-mind of compassion is generated from *ren*, love will arise. Nevertheless, love belongs to the realm of feeling (*qing* 情) and therefore it is not human nature. (Neo-Confucians tended to regard human feelings as *responses* of human nature to external things.) Cheng Yi argues that we can be aware of the principle of *ren* inherent in us by the presentation of the heart-mind of compassion. Conscientiousness (*zhong* 忠) and empathy (*shu* 恕) are only feelings and by the same token, they are not human nature. Because of *ren*, human beings are able to love, to be conscientious and be empathetic. Nevertheless, to love, in Cheng Yi's words, is only the function (*yong* 用) of *ren* and to be empathetic is only its application.

As a moral principle inherent in human nature, *ren* signifies impartiality. When one is practicing *ren*, one acts impartially, among other things. *Ren* cannot present itself but must be embodied by a person. Since love is but a feeling therefore it can be right or wrong. It may be said that *ren* is the principle to which love should conform. In contrast to Cheng Hao's understanding that *ren* represents an ever producing and reproducing force, *ren* for Cheng Yi is only a static moral principle.

Ren, understood as a moral principle which has the same ontological status as *Li* or *Dao*, is substance (*ti* 體) while feelings of compassion or love are function. Another function of *ren* consists in filial piety (*xiao* 孝) and fraternal duty (*ti* 弟). These have been regarded by Chinese people as cardinal virtues since the time of the early Zhou Dynasty. It was claimed in the *Analects* that filial piety and fraternal duty are the roots of *ren*. However, Cheng Yi gave a reinterpretation by asserting that filial piety and fraternal duty are the roots of **practicing** *ren*. Again, this showed that for Cheng Yi, *ren* is a principle, and filial piety and fraternal duty are only one of the ways of actualizing it. When one applies *ren* to the relationship of parents and children, one will act as filial, and to the relationship between siblings, one will act conforming to fraternal duty. Moreover, Cheng Yi considered the filial piety and fraternal duty the starting point of practicing *ren*.

Having said that *ren* is substance whereas love, filial piety, and fraternal duty are its functions, it should be noticed that according to Cheng Yi, the substance cannot activate itself and reveal its function. The application of *ren* mentioned above merely signifies that the mind and feeling of a person should conform to *ren* in dealing with various relationships or situations. This is what the word "static" used in the previous paragraph means. Thus understood, *ren* as an aspect of human nature deviates from Mencius' perception, as well as the perception in *The Doctrine of the Mean* (*Zhong Yong*) and the *Commentary of the Book of Change*, as Mou Zongsan points out. Mou also argues that the three sources mentioned have formed a tradition of understanding *Dao* both as a substance and as an activity. Not surprisingly Cheng Yi's view on human nature and *Li* is quite different from his brother Cheng Hao's.

By the same token, other aspects in human nature such as *yi*, *li*, *zhi*, and trustworthiness are mere principles of different human affairs. One should seek in conformity with these principles in dealing with issues in ordinary life.

Mind

The duality of *Li* and *qi* in Cheng Yi's ontology also finds expression in his ethics, resulting in the tripartite division of human nature, human mind, and human feeling. In Cheng Yi's ethics, the mind of a human being does not always conform to his nature, therefore a human sometimes commits morally bad acts. This is due to the fact that human nature belongs to the realm of *Li* and the mind and feelings belong to the realm of *qi*. In so far as the human mind is possessed by desires which demand satisfaction, it is regarded as dangerous. Although ontologically speaking *Li* and *qi* are not separable as mentioned above, desires and *Li* are contradictory to each other. Cheng Yi stressed that only when desires are removed, can *Li* be restored. When the desires are removed and *Li* is restored, Cheng maintained, the mind will conform to *Li*, and it will transform from a human mind (*ren xin* 人心) to a mind of *Dao* (*dao xin* 道心). Therefore human beings should cultivate the human mind in order to facilitate the above transformation. For Cheng Hao, however, *Li* is already inherent in one's heart-mind, and one only needs to activate one's heart-mind for it to be in union with *Li*. The mind does not need to seek conformity with *Li* to become one, as Cheng Yi suggests. It is evident that the conception of the mind in Cheng Yi's ethics also differs from that in Mencius' thought.

Mencius considers the heart-mind as the manifestation of human nature, and if the former is fully activated, the latter will be fully actualized. For Mencius, the two are identical. Yet for Cheng Yi, *Li* is identical with human nature but lies outside the mind. The difference of the two views of the relationship between the mind and *Li* later developed into two schools in Neo-Confucianism: the study of *Li* (*li xue*) and the study of *xin* (*xin xue* 心學). The former was initiated by Cheng Yi and developed by Zhu Xi and the latter was initiated by Cheng Hao and inherited by LU Xiangshan (陸象山) (1139–1193) and WANG Yangming (王陽明) (1472–1529).

The source of evil

According to Cheng Yi, every being comes into existence through the endowment of *qi*. A person's endowment contains various qualities of *qi*, some good and some bad. These qualities of *qi* are described in terms of their being "soft" or "hard," "weak" or "strong," and so forth. Since the human mind belongs to the realm of *qi*, it is liable to be affected by the quality of *qi*, and evil (*e* 惡) will arise from the endowment of unbalanced and impure allotments of *qi*.

Qi is broadly used to account for one's innate physical and mental characteristics. Apart from *qi*, the native endowment (*cai* 才) would also cause evil. Compared to *qi*, *cai* is more specific and refers to a person's capacity for both moral and non-moral pursuits. *Cai* is often translated as "talent." It influences a person's moral disposition as well as his personality. Zhang Zai coined a term, "material nature" (*qizhi zhi xing* 氣質之性), to describe this natural endowment. Although Cheng Yi has adopted the concept of material nature, A.C. Graham notes that the term has not appeared in the works of the Cheng Brothers except once as a variant for *xingzhi zhi xing* (性質之性). Nevertheless, this variant has superseded the original reading in many texts. Cheng Yi thinks that native endowment would incline some people to be good and others to be bad from early childhood. He uses an analogy to water in order to illustrate this idea: some water flows all the way to the sea without becoming dirty, but some flows only a short distance and becomes extremely turbid. Yet the water is the same. Similarly, the native endowment of *qi* could be clear or muddy. However, Cheng Yi emphasizes that although the native endowment is a constraint for ordinary people to transform, they still have a power to override this endowment, as long as they are not self-destructive (*zibao* 自暴) or in self-denial (*ziqi* 自棄). Cheng Yi admits that the tendency to be self-destructive or in self-denial is also caused by the native endowment. However, since such people possess the same type of human nature as any others, they can free themselves from being self-destructive or being in self-denial. Consequently Cheng Yi urges us to make great efforts to remove the deviant aspects of *qi* which cause the bad native endowment and to nurture one's *qi* to restore its normal state. Once *qi* is adjusted, no native endowment will go wrong.

As mentioned in the previous section, Cheng Yi maintains that human desires are also the origin of selfishness, which leads to evil acts. The desires which give rise to moral badness need not be a self-indulgent kind, but since they are by nature partial, therefore one will err if one is activated by the desire. Any intention with the slightest partiality will obscure one's original nature, even the "flood-like *qi*" described by Mencius (*Mencius*, 2A2) will collapse. The ultimate aim of moral practice is then to achieve sagehood where one will do the obligatory things naturally without any partial intention.

The Cheng Brothers write, "It lacks completeness to talk about human nature without referring to *qi* and it lacks illumination to talk about *qi* without referring to human nature." Cheng Yi's emphasis on the influence of *qi* on the natural moral dispositions well reflects this saying. He puts considerable weight on the endowment of *qi*; nevertheless, the latter is by no means playing a deterministic role in moral behavior.

Moral cultivation

Living with composure

For Cheng Yi, to live with composure (*ju jing* 居敬) is one of the most important ways for cultivating the mind in order to conform with *Li*. *Jing* appeared in the *Analects* as a virtue, which A.C. Graham summarizes as "the attitude one assumes towards parents, ruler, spirits; it includes both the emotion of reverence and a state of self-possession, attentiveness, concentration." It is often translated as "reverence" or "respect." In the *Analects*, respect is a norm which requires one to collect oneself and be attentive to a person or thing. Respect necessarily takes a direct object. Cheng Yi interprets *jing* as the unity of the mind, and Graham proposed "composure" as the translation. As Graham puts it, for Cheng Yi, composure means "making unity the ruler of the mind" (*zhu yi* 主一). What is meant by unity is to be without distraction. In Cheng Yi's own words, if the mind goes neither east nor west, then it will remain in equilibrium. When one is free from distraction, one can avoid being distressed by confused thoughts. Cheng Yi says that unity is called sincerity (*cheng* 誠). To preserve sincerity one does not need to pull it in from outside. Composure and sincerity come from within. One only needs to make unity the ruling consideration, then sincerity will be preserved. If one cultivates oneself according to this way, eventually *Li* will of itself become plain. Understood as such, composure is a means for nourishing the mind. Cheng Yi clearly expresses that there is no better way than being composed for a human being to enter into *Dao*.

Cheng Yi urges the learner to cultivate himself by "being composed and thereby correcting himself within." Furthermore, he indicates that merely by controlling one's countenance and regulating one's thought, composure will come spontaneously. It is evident that controlling one's countenance and regulating one's thought is an empirical way of correcting oneself within. Such a way matches the understanding of the mind as an empirical mind which belongs to *qi*. Mou Zongsan points out that this way of cultivating the empirically composed mind is quite different from Mencius' way of moral cultivation. For the latter, the cultivation aims at the awareness of the moral heart-mind, a substance identical with Heaven. Since the mind and *Li* are not identical in Cheng Yi's philosophy, they are still two entities even though one has been cultivating one's mind for a long time, and what one can hope to achieve is merely always to be in conformity with *Li*.

Investigating matters

To achieve the ultimate goal of apprehending *Li*, Cheng Yi says, one should extend one's knowledge (*zhi zhi* 致知) by investigating matters (*ge wu* 格物). The conception of extending knowledge by investigating matters originates from the *Great Learning* (*Da Xue* 大學), where eight steps of practicing moral cultivation by the governor who wants to promote morality throughout the kingdom were illustrated. Cheng Yi expounds the idea in "the extension of knowledge lies in the investigation of things" in the *Great Learning* by interpreting the key words in "the investigation of matters." The word "investigation" (*ge*) means "arrive at" and "matters" (*wu*) means events. He maintains that in all events there are principles (*li*) and to arrive at their principles is *ge wu*. No matter whether the events are those that exist in the world or within human nature, it is necessary to investigate their principles to their utmost. That means one should, for instance, investigate the principle by which fire is hot and that by which water is cold, also that embodied in the relations between ruler and minister, father and son, and the like. Thus understood, the investigation of things is also understood as exhausting the principles (*qiong li* 窮理). Cheng Yi emphasizes that these principles are not outside of, but already within human nature.

Since for every event there is a particular principle, Cheng Yi proposes that one should investigate each event in order to comprehend its principle. He also suggests that it is profitable to investigate one event after another day after day, as after sufficient practice the interrelations among the principles will be evident. Cheng Yi points out that there are various ways to exhaust the principles, for instances, by studying books and explaining the moral principles in them; discussing prominent figures, past and present, to distinguish what is right and wrong in their actions; experiencing practical affairs and dealing with them appropriately.

Cheng Yi rejects the idea that one should exhaust all the events in the world in order to exhaust the principles. This might appear to conflict with the proposition that one should investigate each event, yet the proposal can be understood as "one should investigate each event that one happens to encounter." Cheng Yi claims that if the principle is exhausted in one event, for the rest one can infer by analogy. This is possibly due to the fact that innumerable principles amount to one.

From the above exposition of Cheng Yi's view on the investigations of matters, the following implication can be made. Firstly, the knowledge obtained by investigating matters is not empirical knowledge. Cheng Yi is well aware of the distinction between the knowledge by observation and the knowledge of morals as initially proposed by Zhang Zai. The former is about the relations among different matters and therefore is gained by observing matters in the external world. On the other hand, the latter cannot be gained by observation. Since Cheng Yi says that the *li* exhausted by investigating matters is within human nature, it cannot be obtained by observation, and thus is not any kind of empirical knowledge.

This may be confusing, but if we compare Cheng Yi's kind of knowledge to scientific knowledge, things may become clearer. It is important to distinguish between the *means* one uses to get knowledge, and the *constituents* of that knowledge. One uses observation as a *means* to better understand the nature of external things. But the knowledge one gains is not observational by nature. It is not the sort of knowledge scientists have in mind when they say, "objects with mass are drawn toward one another." It differs in at least two respects: first, the content of one's knowledge is something we can draw from ourselves, as people who have the same *li* in our nature; second, the knowledge we gain does not rest on the authority of observations. We *know* it without having to put our trust in external observations, since the knowledge is drawn from inside ourselves. We only need external observation in order to liberate this internal knowledge. So we need it as a means, but no more.

Secondly, according to Cheng Yi, investigating matters literally means arriving at an event, it implies that the investigation is undertaken in the outside world where the mind will be in contact with the event. Only through the concrete contact with the event, the act of knowing is concretely carried out and the principles can be exhausted.

Thirdly, Cheng Yi believes that through the investigation of matters the knowledge obtained is the knowledge of morals. When one is in contact with an event, one will naturally apprehend the particulars of the event and the knowledge by observation will thus form. Nevertheless, in order to gain the knowledge of morals one should not stick to those concrete particulars but has to go beyond to apprehend the transcendental principle which accounts for the nature and morals. Thus the concrete events are only necessary means to the knowledge of morals, they themselves are not constituents of the knowledge in question, as Mou Zongsan argues.

The relation between composure and extension of knowledge

According to Cheng Yi, the learning of an exemplary person (*junzi* 君子) lies in self-reflection. Self-reflection in turn lies in the extension of knowledge. Also only by self-reflection can one transform the knowledge by observation to the knowledge of morals. This is possible only if the mind is cultivated by the maintenance of composure. With composure in place the mind can apprehend the transcendental principles of events. Cheng Yi has made a remark on this idea: "It is impossible to extend the knowledge without composure." This also explains the role composure plays in obtaining the knowledge of morals by investigating matters.

Contrariwise, once knowledge of morals is obtained, this can stabilize the composed mind and regulate concrete events to be in conformity with *Li*. Cheng Yi describes this gradual stabilization of the mind by accumulating moral knowledge as "collecting righteousness (*ji yi* 集義)."

Self-reflection for Cheng Yi is cultivating the mind with composure. However, as mentioned above, the mind cannot be identical with *Li*; it can only conform to it since they belong to two different realms. Since the knowledge obtained by the composed mind comprises the transcendental principles, the knowing in question is a kind of contemplative act. Notwithstanding that, this act still represents a subject-object mode of knowing. On the contrary, the meaning of self-reflection for Mencius reveals a different dimension. The knowledge of morals gained by self-reflection is not any principles which the mind should follow. The knowing is an awareness of the moral mind itself through which its identification with the human nature and also with *li* is revealed. Therefore the object of knowing is not the principles out there (inherent in the human nature though) but the knowing mind itself. The awareness thus is a self-awareness. The reflection understood as such is not the cognition per se, it is rather the activation of the mind. In the act of activation, the dichotomy of the knowing and the known diminishes. Moreover, when the mind is activated, human nature is actualized and *li* will manifest itself. Hence, the mind is aware of itself also being a substance, from which *li* is created. Here Cheng Yi draws upon the distinction between a thing's substance, understood as its essential and inactive state, and the active state in which it behaves in characteristic ways. Anticipating that his account of the mind will be misread as suggesting that the mind has two parts—an active and inactive part—Cheng Yi clarifies that he understands the two parts to be, in fact, two aspects of one and the same thing.

The influence of Cheng Yi

The distinctive and influential ideas in Cheng Yi's thought can be summarized as follows:

1. There exists a transcendental principle (*Li*) of nature and morality, which accounts for the existence of concrete things and also the norms to which they adhere.
2. This principle can be apprehended by inferring from concrete things (embodied as *qi*) to the transcendental *Li*.
3. This principle is static, not active or in motion.
4. Human nature is identical with *Li*, but this should be distinguished from the human mind, which belongs to the realm of *qi*.
5. *Ren* belongs to human nature and love belongs to the realm of feeling.
6. Moral cultivation is achieved gradually, through composure and the cumulative extension of knowledge.

Cheng Yi had tremendous impact on the course of Confucian philosophy after his time. His influence is most manifest, however, in the thought of the great Neo-Confucian synthesizer Zhu Xi, who adopted and further developed the views outlined above.

15

Morally Bad in the Philosophy of the Cheng Brothers

Introduction

The problem of "the morally bad" (*e* 惡)[1] has been a central issue for Confucianism ever since Mencius (孟子) claims that "human nature is good" (*xing shan* 性善). Xunzi (荀子) takes an opposing position and attributes moral badness to human nature, attempting to account for the phenomena of mutual conflict and confusion among human beings by their innate tendencies and desires.[2] However, those who find Mencius' view more appealing have to face a particular challenge: If the human nature is good, why the morally bad exists? Furthermore, Mencius considers the "heart-mind" (*xin* 心) is a transcendental ground for morality which makes moral goodness possible; he has to deny justifiably the factors which cause moral badness function dominantly. This challenge is particularly urgent for Neo-Confucians, since some of their metaphysical assertions provide support for the transcendental ground mentioned above, therefore it seems that it is more difficult to explain the existence of the morally bad. This fact though makes it particularly interesting to explore the ways that Neo-Confucians have taken to address this problem. In this chapter I shall focus on examining the Cheng Brothers' (程氏兄弟)[3] approach to tackling this issue.

The badness of an event or state of affairs

An event or state of affairs can be described as good or bad as a function of whether it accords with or deviates from the values adopted within a given value system. Mingdao (明道) thinks that the existence of good as well as bad is supported by "Heavenly Principle" (*Tian Li* 天理). It claims:

> There are good and bad events; all are Heavenly Principle. Within Heavenly Principle some things must be excellent and some bad; for "it is inherent in the essence of things that they are unequal."[4] When looking into this, we must not allow ourselves to enter into what is bad or allow things to be rolled into one.[5]

This does not mean that Heavenly Principle is split into good and bad, but merely that Heavenly Principle admits and allows that there are good events and states of affairs and bad ones. The duality of good and bad, just like other contrary qualities, is conceptually as well as factually accepted as a necessary part of Heavenly Principle. From a *metaphysical* point of view, both good and bad should be recognized equally.

> The sage is heaven and earth. Within heaven and earth, what thing is lacking? How should heaven and earth ever have the intention of discriminating between good and bad? Everything is contained between heaven above and earth below; it is only that things must be handled in accordance with *Dao* (the Way 道). If the sage kept near to the good and far from the bad, the things with which he had nothing to do would be many; how could he be heaven and earth? Therefore, the aim of the sage is merely "to make the elderly contented, be faithful to his friends, and nourish the young."[6,7]
>
> Of the principles of heaven and earth and the innumerable things, none stands alone; all must have opposites. All are as they are naturally; it is not that they have been [purposely] arranged. Each time I think of them at midnight, "before I know it, my hands begin to dance them out and my feet step in time to them."[8,9]
>
> All the innumerable things have their contraries; there is an alternation of *yin* and *yang*, of good and bad. *Yin* diminishes when *yang* grows; bad is reduced when good increases. This principle, how far can it be extended? Human beings just need to understand this.[10]

The ideas expressed in these passages conform to the long tradition of Chinese philosophy, which holds that both sides of various complementary opposites are necessary components of the cosmos. Nevertheless, in the context of the morally good and bad, we as human beings have an obligation to make contributions to the good and oppose what is bad. This is reflected in the last sentence of the first quotation, which says that "when looking into this, we must not allow ourselves to enter into what is bad or allow things to be rolled into one." The message here is very clear. First, even though it is a metaphysical truth that the bad is necessary for the formation and operation of the cosmos, human beings nevertheless can and must make and follow normative prescriptions. In short, the necessary existence of the bad does not imply that it is normatively justified to accept bad states of affairs or commit morally bad actions. Second, since human beings can participate in the formation of what is morally good and bad, they have the capacity to understand what is good and what is bad. Moreover, there is a presupposition that human beings can choose to be good or bad, which is necessary for any ethical doctrine.

The badness discussed above is a quality of a state or an event, the existence of which has metaphysical support.[11] It is primarily descriptive of empirical facts and does not imply any ethical value. In the next section, I will examine the ethical sense of the morally bad.

The ethical sense of the morally bad

Good and bad have an ethical meaning when they are attributed to human behavior or action. The Cheng Brothers' primary concern is morally bad acts. Despite what they say about the equal metaphysical standing of good and bad, such behavior can and should be corrected.

> The worst kind of behavior is a morally bad action; even so, all that is required is correction. The worst state of affairs is chaos; even so, all that is required is good order. Who is incapable of becoming a gentleman provided that he is not "self-destructive" (*zibao* 自暴) or "self-denying" (*ziqi* 自棄)?[12]

The notions of someone being "self-destructive" or "self-denying" first appeared in *Mencius*,[13] in the context of his analysis of the pursuit of moral improvement. For Mencius, a person who attacks *li* (propriety 禮) and *yi* (righteousness 義) is self-destructive, and in this sense he is doing violence to his own nature. On the other hand, a person who says "I do not think I am capable of abiding by *ren* (仁) or of following *yi*" is in self-denial, and in this sense he is throwing himself away. As shown in the last passage, the Cheng Brothers believe that anyone could become a gentleman unless he was self-destructive or in self-denial. Yichuan (伊川) uses the notions of self-destructiveness and self-denial to characterize the "most stupid" (*xia yu* 下愚) kind of person, one who is incapable of transforming himself.

> [Someone asked], "Man's nature is originally good. Why is it that some people cannot change?"
>
> [Cheng Yi replied], "In terms of their nature, all men are good. In terms of their 'native endowments' (*cai* 才), there are the most stupid who do not change. The most stupid are of two kinds, those who do violence to their own nature and those who throw themselves away.[14] If only one manages himself with goodness, he can always change. Even the most beclouded and most stupid can gradually polish themselves and advance. Only those who do violence to their own nature refuse to change because they do not believe in it [i.e., the goodness of their original nature], and only those who throw themselves away cut themselves off from it because they do not want to do anything. Even if a sage should live among them, he could not influence them to enter [the path of moral improvement]. These are what Chungni (仲尼) [Confucius] called 'the most stupid.'"[15]

Confucius says, "Only the most intelligent and the most stupid do not change."[16] Yichuan interprets "the most stupid" as those who were self-destructive or in self-denial. And so, the fact that some people do not change is not due to any of their inborn qualities, but only because they "cut themselves off from goodness." Hence, even the most stupid person is responsible for his failure to become a gentleman and also for his morally bad actions.

The source of the morally bad

According to the Cheng Brothers, a "mean person" (*xiao ren* 小人) or a "small-minded man" (*xiao zhang fu* 小丈夫) does not do what is morally bad because he is born to be mean; such people are not bad by nature. "Mean or small-minded men should not be regarded as [inherently] mean. They are not originally morally bad."[17] This view is based on Mencius' earlier discussions of the "mean person" and the "small-minded man." For Mencius, a mean person is one who is guided only by the interests of the lesser parts of his person, such as the organs of hearing and sight;[18] a small-minded man is one who "when his advice is rejected by the prince, takes offence and shows resentment all over his face, and, when he leaves, travels all day before he will put up for the night."[19] Apparently it is only the limitation of the person's mode of thinking and reacting that constitutes his mean-ness; the bad actions performed by such people are not rooted in their original nature.

The native endowment (*cai*)

It is a popular view that different people possess different innate capacities and that it is because of these differences that some become good and some become bad. As it is observed by Gongduzi (公都子) in Mencius' time, "Xiang could have Yao as prince, and Shun could have the Blind Man as father, and Qi, Viscount of Wei, and Prince Bi Gan could have Zhou as nephew as well as sovereign."[20] This innate capacity is called *cai* (often translated "talent"). *Cai* concerns the level of a person's natural abilities and tendencies and is determined by the particular quality of *qi* (氣) with which that person is endowed at birth.[21] *Cai* influences not only a person's moral disposition, but also his personality. ZHANG Zai (張載) (1020–1077)[22] describes this natural endowment as one's "material nature" (*qizhi zhi xing* 氣質之性), and the Cheng Brothers follow Zhang in using this conception.[23] "Things have their material nature after they take on physical form."[24] The Cheng Brothers admit that this endowment can be good or bad, which inclines some people to be good and others to be bad from early childhood: "According to [Heavenly] Principle, there are both good and bad endowments of *qi* … Because of their different endowments of *qi*, some people become good from childhood and others become bad."[25] The Chengs[26] then use a water analogy to illustrate this idea:

> Water [as such] is the same in all cases. Some water flows onward to the sea without becoming dirty. What human effort is needed here? Some flows only a short distance before growing turbid. Some travels a long distance before growing turbid. Some becomes extremely turbid; some only slightly so.[27]

Yichuan points out that endowment of *qi* would also influence one's intelligence.

> *Cai* is [one's] endowment of *qi*, and there is clear and muddy *qi*. Those endowed with clear *qi* become wise; those endowed with the muddy *qi* become foolish.[28]
>
> "Some understand when they are born; some understand after learning";[29] it is due to *cai*.[30]

From the above passages, it seems that one's inclination to become a good or bad person as well as one's intelligence is influenced by *cai*, which is part of one's inborn nature. Nevertheless, like the "most stupid," one still can change as long as one is not self-destructive or in self-denial. One may go on to ask whether the "most stupid" person's being self-destructive or in self-denial are states actually caused by *cai*. In answering this question, the Cheng Brothers emphasize that even though the tendency to be self-destructive or in self-denial is caused by *cai*, such people still have the power to change. In fact, one is able to free oneself from being self-destructive or being in self-denial.

> [Someone asked], "Is it true that what causes one to be self-destructive or in self-denial is *cai*?"
>
> [Cheng Yi replied,] "Certainly it is, but it cannot be said that such a person cannot change. The nature is common to all; how could such a person be incapable of change? Because he is self-destructive and in self-denial, he is not willing to learn, and therefore he cannot change. Provided that he is willing to learn, it is still possible for him to change."[31]

In another passage, Yichuan, expanding upon a line from the *Mencius*, explicitly rejects the idea that the morally bad can be attributed to one's *cai*. It is not the *cai* that causes people's hearts to become ensnared.

> [Cheng Yi said,] "'If one follows one's *qing* (*nai ruo qi qing* 乃若其情), then one is able to be good. If one does what is bad, this is not the fault of one's *cai*.'[32] This says that if a person's heart sinks and becomes ensnared, this is not the business of *cai*. *Cai* is like timber. If it is bent, then it is suitable for making a wheel. If it is straight, then it is suitable for making a beam. If the wheel or the beam is destroyed, how could this be the business of *cai*? Doesn't another passage [in the *Mencius*] talk about how every human being has the four heart-minds?"
>
> Someone asked, "Since a person's *cai* can be excellent or bad, how can you say that it is not the fault of *cai*?"
>
> [Cheng Yi] replied, "When we say that a person's *cai* can be excellent or bad we are speaking from the perspective of viewing all of the people in the world. When we are talking about a particular person's *cai*, then we say things like 'in good years the young men are lazy, while in bad years they are violent.'[33] How could a person's endowment of *cai* determine such things from the start?"[34]

It is generally thought that talent is determined by one's *cai* and cannot quickly or easily be changed by experience or learning. Nevertheless, this is the case only for those whose capacity is below that of a great worthy. A great worthy can transform himself from foolish to clever, from weak to strong. Therefore, *cai* is not a constraint for a great worthy. As for a sage, his virtue is united with heaven and earth and does not come from the skill he attains; therefore, a sage does not rely upon *cai*. Yichuan thinks that only ordinary people who have not yet transformed their limited physical bodies need to utilize *cai* in order to attain certain objectives.

> [Someone asked,] "There are people who can recite ten thousand words [from memory] each day, or whose skill is extraordinary and sublime. Can such things be learned?"

> [Cheng Yi replied,] "No, they cannot. For the most part, the *cai* with which one is endowed can only be improved a little bit, even though one applies great effort. Such effort though cannot make the dull [suddenly] become sharp; it can only help them [gradually] advance in understanding. Nevertheless, after a long period of accumulating learning, people can transform their material nature and then the foolish can certainly become clever, the weak can certainly become strong. Those who are [at the stage of] great worthies and below can be evaluated in terms of *cai*; those above the [stage of a] great worthy cannot be evaluated in terms of *cai*. A sage is one whose virtue is united with heaven and earth and whose clarity is united with the sun and the moon. An ordinary person has a body only six feet tall; how much skill can he possibly possess? One who [is concerned with] having a body needs to rely upon *cai*. As for a sage, who has forgotten his own body, how can he be evaluated in terms of *cai*?"[35]

To sum up, I have argued that since the moral badness that springs from *cai* can be changed, such moral badness is not in any way fundamental to one's nature; *cai* influences but does not determine the level of one's moral achievement.

Qi

In various ways, both *cai* and *qi* refer to the native endowment of human beings; the former is more specific and refers to a person's capacity for both moral and non-moral pursuits, whereas the latter is more general and is used more broadly to account for one's innate physical and personal characteristics. Every being comes to exist by getting a form through an endowment of *qi*. The Cheng Brothers say, "Everything with a form is *qi*; what is without form is just *Dao*."[36] The goodness or badness of one's *cai* is determined by the quality of one's *qi*. There are both deviant and correct varieties of *qi*. "That which is received from heaven is nature. One's endowment of *qi* is called *cai*. The goodness or badness of one's *cai* is caused by whether one's *qi* is deviant or correct."[37] A given person's material endowment normally contains various qualities of *qi*, some good and some bad.[38] These different qualities of *qi* are described in terms of their being "soft" or "hard," "weak" or "strong," and the like, according to Yichuan.[39] Impure and unbalanced allotments of *qi* influence one's tendency of becoming a bad person;[40] therefore, one should work to remove the deviant aspects of *qi* within one's endowment.[41] Provided that one adjusts one's *qi*, then no *cai* is bad (*bu shan* 不善).

> The master said, "Those received from Heaven is called *xing*, those endowed from *qi* is called *cai*. There are good or bad in *cai*, just like there are normal or deviant in the endowment of *qi*. No *xing* is *bu shan*. If one can nurture one's *qi* to restore the normal state, then also no *cai* is *bu shan*."[42]

The body and desire

For some schools of thought, like Daoism and Buddhism, the body is regarded as one of the sources of moral deviance. The Cheng Brothers also regard the body as a possible source for what is morally bad. "In the final analysis, every human being who has a body will tend to be selfish. It is understandable that it is difficult to unite with *Dao*."[43] Since human beings have bodies, they have desires to satisfy. But the Cheng Brothers thinks that it is not the body, per se, but rather desires that are the origin of selfishness, which leads to what is morally bad.

> It is only because human beings are selfish that intentions arise from their bodies; this is why they can come to regard principle as small and beneath them. Let go of the body and consider it as one of the innumerable things, then there is great pleasure in every one of them, no matter whether they are big or small.[44]
>
> Once the "mind" has a desire, then it will depart from *Dao*.[45]
>
> In every human heart-mind there is awareness. If it is clouded by human desire, then the heavenly virtue will be lost.[46]

The desire that leads to what is morally bad need not be of a self-indulgent kind; any distinct and particular intentional aim constitutes a desire.[47] And so, whenever one has the slightest partial intention, one cannot be *ren*.

> "For three months there would be nothing in [Yan] Hui's heart-mind contrary to *ren*."[48] This was simply because he had not the slightest partial intention. If one has the slightest partial intention, he is not *ren*.[49]
>
> When one is activated by Heaven, he will be free from error, but when he is activated by human desire, he will err.[50]

Apparently for the Cheng Brothers, it is partiality that causes moral badness and any desire is by its very nature partial. Therefore, moral badness arises when one's original nature is covered over and obscured by the partial mind. When Mingdao interpreted the passage concerning the "flood-like *qi*" (*haoran zhi qi* 浩然之氣) in the *Mencius*, he says:

> The flood-like *qi* is my own *qi*; if it is nourished and no obstacle is placed in its path, then it will fill up the space between heaven and earth. Once it is covered by the partial heart-mind, then it will immediately collapse and become exceedingly small.[51]

Yichuan focuses on the partial intention that will make the "flood-like *qi*" collapse.

> "It is a *qi* that is matched with *yi* and *Dao*."[52] *Qi* must be subordinated to *yi* and completely in accord with *Dao*. It will collapse as soon as the slightest partial intention is attached to it.[53]
>
> Once one is attached to a single partial intention, then it [the flood-like *qi*] will collapse; this is how the flood-like *qi* will be found lacking.[54]

The partiality is not necessarily generated from a selfish mind; the deliberateness of doing what should be done reflects that the partial mind is operating.

> People say that we must practice with effort. Such a statement, however, is superficial. If a person really knows that a thing should be done, when he sees anything that should be done, he does not need to wait for his attention to be aroused. As soon as he deliberately arouses his attention, that means he has a partial mind. How can such a spirit last long?[55]

However, in the moral practice one may start with arousing his intention deliberately and when he achieves sagehood, he will do the obligatory things naturally.

Since the selfish desire or partial intention causes moral badness, one of the most important ways to practice moral self-cultivation is to restrain one's desire.

> Mencius said, "There is no better way to nurture the heart-mind than by reducing the number of one's desires."[56] If the desires are few, then the heart-mind will have integrity.[57]
>
> [Mencius said,] "There is no better way to nurture the heart-mind than by reducing the number of one's desires."[58] Where there are no desires there is no confusion.[59]

I have shown above that according to the Cheng Brothers the sources of moral badness lie in the native endowment of *qi*, the body, and the inherent desires of human beings. They are not completely separated. As mentioned above, the native endowment is determined by *qi*, by which the body is formed. When the intention of human beings arises from the body is formed, they will become selfish. If all of these sources are inborn and cannot be changed, then human beings are destined to be bad. In the next section I am going to scrutinize the status of moral badness in the Cheng Brothers' philosophy.

The origin of the morally bad

As we have seen, morally bad behavior arises from the makeup and psychological constitution of human beings; the idea of a varying physical endowment also explains why some people tend to be good and some tend to be bad. If this account is correct, then it seems that morally good action is purely contingent; it appears to be simply a function of whether one is fortunate or unfortunate in terms of the allotment of *qi* that one receives.

Mencius initiates the discussion concerning the ground of morality in terms of "human nature" (*xing* 性). His teaching that "human nature is good" seeks to establish that there is a ground in human nature that makes morality possible. Kwong-loi Shun's analysis of *Mencius* has revealed that when *xing shan* is understood in terms of *ke yi wei shan* (可以為善), it is understood as making a claim that people are *capable of becoming good*.

> Thus, in saying that human beings *ke yi* become good, Mencius was saying that human beings have a constitution comprising certain emotional predispositions

> that already point in the direction of goodness and by virtue of which people are capable of becoming good; this, according to Mencius, is what he meant by *xing shan*.[60]

We might ask whether these "emotional predispositions that already point in the direction of goodness and by virtue of which people are capable of becoming good" can be construed as a transcendental ground of morality. Here "transcendental" has two connotations. The first is that it makes something possible. The second is that it is not empirical. Only if the origin of good is not empirical can it be universally valid for every human being. Furthermore, only if the origin of good is transcendent will moral badness avoid being on a par with the good, in which case there is always a possibility that the bad might win and no clear reason to choose one over the other.

Shun believes that according to Mencius the constitution of human beings has an asymmetrical relation to goodness and badness. The Cheng Brothers explicitly advocate this kind of asymmetry: "In the endowment of *qi* that men receive at birth there will in principle be both good and bad, but this does not mean that we are born with good and bad as two contrasting things present in our nature from the first."[61] This claim is made in the context of discussing *xing*. The Cheng Brothers are upholding Mencius' doctrine of *xing shan*. For example:

> No *xing* is morally bad; it is only the *cai* that can have moral badness.[62]

"Good and bad are not two contrasting things present in our nature from the first" implies that moral badness does not originally exist in the *xing*. When we talk about the *xing* in itself, we can only describe it as morally good.[63] A water analogy again is used to illustrate this view: Water is originally and fundamentally clean; it becomes dirty only when it has been polluted.

> Water [as such] is the same in all cases. Some water flows onward to the sea without becoming dirty. What human effort is needed here? Some flows only a short distance before growing turbid. Some travels a long distance before growing turbid. Some becomes extremely turbid; some only slightly so. Although the dirty water is different from the clean, it must still be recognized as water. This being so, it is necessary that man should accept the duty of cleansing and regulating it. The water will be cleaned quickly if his efforts are prompt and bold, slowly if they are careless. But when it is cleaned, it is still only the original water; it is not that clean water has been fetched to replace the dirty, or that the dirty has been taken away and put on one side. The cleanness of the water corresponds to the goodness of *xing*. Hence, it is not that good and bad are two contrasting things within *xing* that emerge independently.[64]

When the water is clean, it does not possess any special quality that renders it clean. The cleanness of the water is realized in the water itself, without anything being added to it. Therefore, when we say that the water is clean, it only indicates the purity of the water. In this sense, although "the water is clean" is not analytically true, "pure water is clean" is. If we can take this as an analogy, then goodness[65] is not something added to *xing* to render the latter good; it is already embodied in the *xing* that human beings received at birth. Obviously what is morally bad is not original in the sense that it constitutes part of the *xing*. Yichuan's point is that to speak of *xing shan* is to talk about the original and fundamental character of *xing*. "When we say that the *xing* of human beings is good, we are talking about the original and fundamental character of *xing*."[66] In contrast, the doctrine of "human nature is bad" (*xing e* 性惡) abandons the foundation of morality. According to Yichuan, "Xunzi is most deviant and impure. By merely asserting that *xing* is bad, he had already lost the great foundation"[67]

As I have noted in the previous sections, there are many sources for the badness that is born with human beings. Yet human beings are capable of transforming these inborn qualities or endowments and performing good acts. Therefore, the forces of badness and goodness are not symmetrical.

> Di asked, "Confucius and Mencius talked about *xing* differently. What about this?"
>
> [Cheng Yi] replied, "When Mencius talked about the goodness of *xing*, he was talking about the original and fundamental nature. When Confucius said that 'by nature we are close to one another'[68] he was saying that the endowments [of *qi*] that people received are not far away from each other. All human *xing* is good; what makes it good can be seen in the four sprouts of man's 'essential qualities' (*qing* 情). That is why Mencius said, 'How can that [i.e, badness] be a man's genuine *qing*?'[69] Those who cannot follow *qing* and violate *Tian Li* will finally become bad. And so, Mencius said, 'If one follows one's *qing* (*nai ruo qi qing*), then one is able to be good'[70] *Ruo* means 'to follow.'"
>
> [Di] posed a further question, "Does *cai* come from *qi*?"
>
> [Cheng Yi replied,] "If the *qi* is pure, the *cai* is good; if impure, it is bad. Those who are endowed from birth with completely pure *cai* become sages; those with completely impure *qi* become fools. The men Han Yu wrote about and Gongduzi asked about are examples of this. But this applies only to the sages, who understand from birth. As for those who understand by learning, they are not endowed with either perfectly pure or impure *cai*, and yet all may arrive at the good and return to the roots of *xing*. 'Yao and Shun had it by nature'[71] refers to those who know from birth. 'Tang and Wu returned to it'[72] refers to those who attain knowledge by learning. When Confucius said that 'Only the perfectly wise and the most foolish do not change,'[73] he did not mean that change is impossible. There are only two reasons why people do not change: self-destructiveness and self-denial."
>
> [Di] posed a further question, "What is *cai* like?"
>
> Answer: "It is like timber. To pursue the analogy, whether wood is crooked or straight is its *xing*; whether it is suitable for making a wheel or shaft, a beam, a rafter, is its *cai*. Nowadays when people say *cai* they refer to excellence of *cai*. The *cai* is a man's resources; if he cultivates it in accordance with *xing*, even a completely bad man is capable of becoming good."[74]

Some of the views concerning the relationship between *cai* and *qi* that appear in this long passage have been discussed above. The most notable idea is expressed in the last sentence: "if he cultivates it in accordance with *xing*, even a completely bad man is capable of becoming good." If, in principle, badness can be overcome by a positive force, then the bad is not on a par with goodness. The above passage is followed by another discussion of original goodness.

> [Di] posed a further question, "What is *xing* like?"
>
> [Cheng Yi answered,] "*Xing* is principle. What is referred to as "principle" is *xing*. If we trace the principles of the world back to their source, they always prove to be good. Before joy and anger, sorrow and pleasure are emitted, where is the bad? If they are emitted in due order and measure, in no circumstances shall we do what is bad. Whenever we talk about good and bad, we always say good prior to bad; whenever we talk about fortunate and unfortunate, we always say fortunate prior to unfortunate; whenever we talk about right and wrong, we always say right prior to wrong."[75]

Since the bad is not an original or fundamental part of human nature, the battle between good and bad can be settled by exercising the commanding force of the heart-mind.[76]

> If the heart-mind does not act as a master, nothing can be done . . . Some people always seem to have two persons in their chest. When they want to do good, it seems that there is bad in the way; when they want to do something bad, it seems that there is the heart-mind of shame. In fact, there are no such two persons; it is only the sensation of inner conflict.[77]
>
> It should be taught that if one cultivates one's good heart-mind, then the bad will diminish on its own.[78]

Conclusion

We have seen that for the Cheng Brothers what is morally bad comes from *qi*, *cai*, body, desires, and so on. Yet none of these is deterministic in a sense that it necessarily produces moral badness. Furthermore, neither brother accepts the view that there is original badness inherent in human beings. Even though they grant metaphysical parity to the dual qualities of good and bad manifested in the things in the world, they insist that this metaphysical assertion should not influence the ethical pursuit of human beings. As human beings, people have the responsibility to act on the original good that is rooted in their *xing*. Only in this way can they contribute to the realization of "Heavenly Principles" in the world.

From the analysis presented in this chapter we can see that the Cheng Brothers' views concerning the source and significance of what is morally bad did not stray too far from Mencius' position. In fact, they always elaborate the view in question along the line of Mencius' original position. Although there is no novelty in this respect, the Cheng Brothers put forth tremendous effort to reconcile and synthesize the thought of Confucius, Mencius, and texts like *The Doctrine of the Mean* (*Zhong Yong* 中庸) and

The Commentaries on the Book of Change (*Yizhuan* 易傳). From their work we can grasp the common beliefs in the tradition of early Confucianism. The Cheng Brothers also draw many comparisons and contrasts with their philosophy and the views of other early Chinese schools of thought, as well as with schools and traditions from later periods. Last but not least, the Cheng Brothers develop their own distinctive metaphysical system, which goes beyond anything one finds in early Confucianism.

16

The Status of *Li* in the Cheng Brothers' Philosophy

Introduction

The notion of *li* (禮) appears in ancient Chinese texts, such as *The Book of Odes* (*Shi Jing* 詩經) and *The Book of History* (*Shu Jing* 書經) before Confucius. Its original meaning relates to religious ceremonial and burial rituals. As the humanistic spirit emerges in the early Zhou (周) period, *li* also undergoes a humanistic turn. Its meaning is enriched to include the order and roles of administrative systems and the propriety of human behavior and rituals. Seven out of the nine words referring to "*li*" appearing in *Shi Jing* have nothing to do with ceremony. In the Chun Qiu (春秋) period (770–476 BC), *li* has a status similar to that of social and ethical norms. One will be condemned if he or she violates a rule of propriety. Comments of historical facts made in *Zuo Zhuan* (左傳) and *Guo Yu* (國語) reflect that *li* is the supreme criterion of behavior.[1]

Though *li* is as important as law, it is observed by people of that period only for the sake of formality; they have little awareness of its spiritual meaning. Besides, *li* is prescriptive to people even when it leads to inhuman consequences. One of the contributions of Confucius is to provide these acts of propriety and rituals with a moral ground by introducing the idea of *ren* (仁) and *yi* (義). Thus from Confucius onwards, *li* has a vivid moral connotation. The meaning of the practice of *li* is not limited to rule-following, but is also revealed as a significant means for one's moral development (*Analects*, 12.1).[2] In order to make the moral implication of *li* explicit, Confucius finds it necessary to reinterpret some of the conventional rituals. There are cases in which Confucius amends and even alters certain unreasonable proprieties, although, on the whole, he upholds Zhou *li* (周禮). While regarding *li* as an objectification of one's moral heart-mind and as an essential means of its cultivation, Mencius is more critical in reviewing the rules established long ago.

Having the critical attitude of both Confucius and Mencius towards the rules of propriety notwithstanding, Xunzi (荀子) reaffirms the importance of *li* for its political and social function. Schwartz observes that "it is clear from the outset that the word *li* is used in its very broad extension embracing all the status and roles of familial and political order as well as all the prescriptions of behavior embedded in these institutions."[3] This political aspect mentioned by Schwartz is exactly that which Xunzi emphasizes. In the Han (漢) Dynasty, *li* is utilized by rulers as a governing strategy and as a consequence it became more institutionalized than ever before. Since then, *li* has played a great role in maintaining social hierarchy.[4] The fact that Confucianism has been institutionalized and the importance of *li* has grown since Han gives people an impression that *li* becomes the central, if not the only, concern of Confucianism. *Li* then serves as a criterion by which right and wrong, good and bad, gentlemen or small men are differentiated.

The Song (宋) Dynasty is a time when Neo-Confucianism emerges on the one hand, and *li* seems to have become most authoritative and rigid on the other. It is, therefore, interesting to study the significance of *li* in Neo-Confucian thought. Besides, as Kai-wing Chow observes, "The strong interest that neo-Confucianism has received in American scholarship notwithstanding, ritual, a major concern in neo-Confucian ethics, remains understudied."[5] In this chapter, I start research in this area with the Cheng Brothers. Although it is generally agreed that there are considerable differences between CHENG Hao's (程灝) (Mingdao 明道) and CHENG Yi's (程頤) (Yichuan 伊川) philosophies, I presume that there is no great discrepancy between their views on *li*. Therefore, I will not discuss their views separately.[6] On the other hand, as the notion of *li* denotes several different meanings, I will examine them individually, no matter whether these meanings appear under the name *li* or otherwise.

Li as propriety

Li as propriety[7] is something that can be changed, according to the Chengs' view, when it is found outdated and loses its original meaning. Therefore one shall not stick to the ancient rules of propriety without examination:

> Do not stick completely to ancient rules when performing *li*. One shall notice that the contemporary situation has changed to such an extent that one has to deviate from the ancient rules. Just like our face, it is no more the same as our ancestors', therefore it might not be appropriate to use ancient artifacts completely. Were the former sages to live in the present world, they would make some adjustments.[8]

In their view, when one understands the original meaning of *li*, then one can change the rules accordingly: "Learners of *li* who want to understand propriety deeply should try to grasp the intentions of former kings. Having grasped their intentions, they can choose either to follow or to revise it."[9] Then what were the former kings' intentions in instituting *li*? In other words, what was the ground for instituting *li* for the sages or the former kings? The Chengs' answer is that *li* is based on human feelings (*qing* 情): "The sages institute *li* on the basis of human feelings, and regulate the events by *yi*."[10] In their view, "The setting of *li* depends on human feelings. The appropriateness of human feelings is *yi*" (MD).[11]

According to Cheng *yi*,

> The essence of *li* originates from the feelings of people and the sage only states the rules accordingly. The instrument of *li* originates from people's convention and the sage only regulates as well as decorates some of it accordingly. Suppose the former sages live in the present world, they must regulate and decorate the existing

clothing and instruments accordingly. That which makes the saying that "the essence of *li* should be valued and its function should be practical" intelligible lies also in the reflection and adjustment made by the king of that time.

YC[12]

Therefore, *li* does not permit rules that repress human feelings. It only sets constraint on human desires. For this, we can refer to the *Analects* where Confucius points out that to overcome the desire of one's self and return to *li* is *ren* (*Analects*, 12.1). The Chengs go one step further and claim that when one is used to overcoming his or her desire and acting according to *ren*, he or she does not need *li* to guide his or her act, for by then what he or she does is spontaneously in accordance with *li*. The Chengs state, "Look at, listen to, speak, and do nothing which is contrary to *li*. If one puts efforts [on overcoming one's desire] constantly, there will be an accumulative effect. Where is *li*?"[13] Here *li* as external norms has only an auxiliary function for one's moral enhancement. We shall see later that *li* in the above sense is derivative.

Li, according to the Chengs' view, originates from the need of human feelings. As seen in the passage previously cited, the appropriateness of human feelings consists in *yi*. Therefore *yi* constitutes the value of *li*. In their view, "All *li* has to have *yi*. *Li* is valuable because *yi* is valued. If the essense of *li* is lost and only its details remain, then the serving of *li* becomes the work of the masters of ceremonies" (YC).[14] It is clear that the value of *li* lies in *yi*.

Li as virtues

Li is usually used by Confucius and Mencius as the whole set of rules of propriety which consist of norms like sincerity (*cheng* 誠), trustworthiness (*xin* 信), respect (*gong* 恭), modesty (*rang* 讓), conscientious (*zhong* 忠), empathy (*shu* 恕), serenity (*zhuang* 莊), reverence (*jing* 敬), and thrift (*jian* 儉). The norms mentioned above are also considered virtues when one manifests the corresponding character traits which help him or her to observe those norms. In this section, I will study *jing*, one of the most important virtues in the Chengs' philosophy.

A.C. Graham carefully distinguishes between two aspects of *jing*. One is used in the *Analects*; it signifies "the attitude one assumes towards parents, ruler, spirits; it includes both the emotion of reverence and a state of self-possession, attentiveness, concentration."[15] It is generally translated as "respect" or "reverence." The other aspect is used by the Chengs, to mean the unity of the mind. While admitting that these two aspects of *jing* are interdependent, Graham thinks that the latter aspect should have a translation other than "reverence." He suggests the word "composure," which I am going to use hereafter.

There is a great deal of discussion of *jing* in CHENG and CHENG (1981). This is understandable because the Chengs think that *jing* is an important and precise way of moral cultivation. For example, it is stated that "sincerity is the way of Heaven; composure is the basis of human affairs [note by the disciple LIU Xuan (劉絢): 'Composure is the function']. When there is composure there is sincerity" (MD);[16]

again, "The most important and precise way [for moral cultivation] is to correct oneself within through composure" (YS);[17] and "There is no better way than being composed for one to enter into *Dao* (the Way). It is implausible to extend knowledge without composure" (YC)[18]

As Graham points out, the Chengs stress a different aspect of *jing* from that shown in the *Analects*. In the latter, *jing* requires one to collect oneself and to be attentive to a person or thing. Therefore, there is always an object which *jing* is directed to. For example:

> The master said of Zichan (子產) that he had the way of the gentleman on four counts: he was respectful in the manner he conducted himself; he was reverent (*jing*) in the service of his lord; in caring for the common people, he was generous and, in employing their services, he was just.
>
> *Analects*, 5.16

> The master said, "In guiding a state of a thousand chariots, approach your duties with reverence and be trustworthy in what you say; avoid excesses in expenditure and love your fellow men; employ the labour of the common people only in the right seasons."
>
> *Analects*, 1.5

Similar meanings can be found elsewhere in the *Analects* (16.10; 13.19).[19] It is clear that in this aspect *jing* serves as a norm and thus can be viewed as an objectification of the moral heart-mind (*xin* 心). As mentioned above, in CHENG and CHENG (1981), *jing* has quite a different meaning. It is interpreted by Yichuan as *zhu yi* (主一),[20] which means, in Graham's words, "making unity the ruler" of the mind:

> The human mind is bound to interact with the innumerable things; how can one prevent it from thinking about them? If you wish to avoid confusion of thought, the only course is for the mind to have a "ruler." How does one give it a ruler? Simply by composure . . . In general the human mind cannot be put to two uses at once. If it is applied to one matter, others cannot enter it; this is because the matter has become its ruler. Merely by making some matter as its ruler, you can avoid being distressed by confused thoughts; and if you can give it a ruler by composure, you will always be free from such distress. What is meant by composure is making unity the ruler; and what is meant by unity is to be without distraction.
>
> YC[21]

When *jing* is understood as making unity the ruler of the mind, then it is a way for nourishing the heart-mind and hence a means of moral cultivation:

> To correct oneself within through composure has a connotation of moral cultivation. A speech without serenity and composure will arouse the intention of deception; an appearance without serenity and composure will arouse an intention of prejudice.[22]

As a means of moral cultivation, *jing* is fundamentally directed to one's self, rather than being a rule to be observed externally. This makes it different from the sense of a norm.

> Question: There is someone who particularly concentrates on correcting himself within through composure, but does not care about ordering the external with *yi*, is he right?
>
> Answer: What is internal will necessarily express externally as it is. It matters if one does not correct himself within; once having corrected himself within, then the external is necessarily ordered.[23]

If one can preserve one's mind with *jing*, then it might be redundant to speak of overcoming one's desire. Thus, "If one is composed then there is no self to overcome. Yet we should be free from the four deviations from the beginning" (YC).[24] Another passage also expresses this concept: "Composure itself is *li*; there is no self to overcome" (YC).[25] "To practice *ren* is to overcome the self and to return to *li*" is generally understood as "if one aims at *ren*, he or she should overcome his or her desires and also act in accordance with *li*." To overcome desires and to return to *li* are two separate, though interdependent ways of achieving *ren*. Overcoming desires is directed to one's inner self and returning to *li* focuses on observing the external rules. Here it appears that in saying "there is no self to overcome," the Chengs are trying to dismiss the necessary effort of overcoming desires. However, the intriguing point is, since the Chengs have interpreted composure as an internal endeavor which already consists in overcoming one's self (correcting oneself within through composure), now by identifying composure as *li*, the Chengs incorporate the external *li* into composure. Therefore, the one actually having been dismissed is "returning to *li*," rather than "overcoming one's desires," which is contrary to the surface meaning of these two passages. It shows that *li*—when regarded as external norms—offers little help in moral cultivation.

Compared with *gong* (respect), composure is a way of nourishing the moral self, whereas respect is an attitude shown when one is in contact with people: "Composure is a matter of nourishing the [moral] self, respect of contact with people" (YC).[26] People who nourish their moral selves at all times will be in full possession of themselves. This in turn enables them to be respectful when they come into contact with other people.

> Question: "When abroad behave as though you were receiving an important guest, when employing the services of the common people behave as though you were officiating at an important sacrifice," but when not abroad and not employing the services of the common people, what one should pay attention to?
>
> Answer: ... if when abroad one is composed to such an extent, it can be imagined how composed one is when not abroad. Besides, what is observable externally comes from what is internal. Employing the services of the common people and going abroad are events. One is not merely composed for a certain event. One is composed at all times ...
>
> YC[27]

As *jing* is a state of the unity of mind, it should not be bound to particular objects. If it is a state of mind not tied to any particular object, it will emerge naturally on any occasion. "Composure is only composure. No words should be added to it. To take 'reverence to one's father' as an example, do we need 'reverence to one's brother' as a supplement?"[28]

As mentioned above, the Chengs give *jing* a meaning other than that used in the *Analects*. In the *Analects*, *jing* is a norm, which a gentleman should observe, whereas in the Chengs' philosophy, *jing* represents a way of moral cultivation. Therefore, one who is composed at all times can be considered as possessing the virtue *jing*. Here we can see that *jing*, like other kinds of *li*, means both a norm and a virtue. The fact that *li* carries these double senses is based on the conviction that a harmonious situation will emerge through the practice of virtues (which have internal roots in human beings), and also that these norms are adopted universally by human beings (because the roots are universally possessed by them). This is why norms (being one of the meanings of *li*) can be regarded as the objectification of virtues, and this is also what "return to *li*" actually means. Here we discover that no matter whether *jing* is understood as a norm or as a virtue, it is deeply connected with the theory of human nature (*xing*性) which has constituted the foundation of Confucianism since Confucius and Mencius. The Chengs think that even though one's human nature has been slightly polluted or damaged, he or she can be treated with *jing* so that his or her human nature will be restored.[29]

Filial piety (*xiao* 孝) and fraternal duty (*ti* 弟)

Filial piety and fraternal duty are considered by early Confucianism as two very important virtues, of which the former has been especially commended by Chinese people throughout the centuries. Both of these virtues have significant familial as well as political functions (see the *Analects*, 1.2). In the *Analects*, Confucius teaches his disciples that one of the ways to fulfill the duty of filial piety is *jing*:

> Ziyou (子游) asked about being filial. The master said, "Nowadays for a man to be filial means no more than that he is able to provide his parents with food. Even hounds and horses are, in some way, provided with food. If a man shows no reverence, where is the difference?"
>
> *Analects*, 2.7

From the discussion in the last section, we find that the Chengs stress the aspect of moral cultivation of *jing* as something that should not be bound to certain objects such as parents or elder brothers. As far as *jing* is understood as a unity of mind, the Chengs believe that one would spontaneously be filial if he is composed. Therefore, filial piety can be regarded as subsuming under *jing* and the practice of the former is reducible to that of the latter. In short, in the Chengs' philosophy, filial piety loses its independent position. This view can be further confirmed by the following passage where the Chengs give a new interpretation of a well-known piece in the *Analects*: "'Filial piety and fraternal duty is the root of *ren*' refers to the root of practising *ren*, not the root of *ren*" (MD).[30]

The word "is" (*wei* 為) in ancient Chinese may mean "be" or "to make it become." In the above passage, the Chengs are correcting the wrong interpretation that has appeared throughout history. This new interpretation can find support from the general usage of the language in pre-Qin time, and therefore it is closer to the linguistic truth. Moreover, the Chengs' saying is more than a clarification of the meaning of a word; it also implies that filial piety and fraternal duty should not carry so much weight as they have. This hidden message is rendered clearer in another similar passage:

> Question: "Filial piety and fraternal duty is the root of *ren*," can one achieve *ren* by way of filial piety and fraternal duty?
>
> Answer: No, it merely means one can practise *ren* by starting from filial piety and fraternal duty. Since filial piety and fraternal duty is one of the duties of ren, it is correct to say that it is the root of practising *ren*, but not so to say that it is the root of *ren*. It is because *ren* is human nature, filial piety and fraternal duty is the function. There are only *ren*, *yi*, *li*, and *zhi* (知) in human nature; when does filial piety and fraternal duty come to exist?
>
> YC[31]

Thus, filial piety and fraternal duty are at most the root of practising *ren*. Moreover, the "root" here only means a starting point. Therefore, though filial piety and fraternal duty originate from human nature, the former itself does not constitute the latter. It is only one of the functions (*yong* 用) of the substance (*ti* 體), viz. *ren*.

From ethical norms to the metaphysical principle

From the above discussion, it is shown that the Brothers Cheng downgrade the status of *li*, by putting much more emphasis on the cultivation of the inner self in moral development than on the effort of governing external behavior (as in the case of re-interpreting the meaning of *jing*), and also by distinguishing between the substance and the function (as in the case of filial piety). However, it must be pointed out that in the following passage, the Chengs seem to elevate *li* to a status as high as the Principle (*Li* 理): "No matter it is looking, listening, speaking, or moving, never do anything not in accordance with the Principle. The Principle is *li*. *Li* is equal to the Principle" (YC).[32]

The Principle or the Principle of Heaven (*tian Li* 天理) is a metaphysical concept in Confucianism. Though Cheng Hao and Cheng Yi interpret the Principle differently (which I will not expound upon here), both of them think that the Principle is the supreme and ultimate reality in the universe. Furthermore, the two brothers hold a common view that to be in harmony with the Principle should be everyone's aim. They also believe that when one is free from one's selfish desire, one would spontaneously preserve the Principle within oneself, and the Principle will be embodied in one. Therefore, moral cultivation is a way for one to become in harmony with the Principle. Thinking along this line, it is not difficult to understand the Chengs' view that ways of moral cultivation that are themselves the effort of overcoming one's self (apart from their own moral purpose) aim at revealing the Principle. For example, although they do not consider *jing* as an attitude to be assumed regarding an object, the Principle can be thought of as a kind of "object" (not in the empirical sense) that the effort of *jing* should be directed to. Note this concept in the following passages:

> What does the Principle of Heaven mean? Integrity is the integrity with regard to it; composure is the composure with regard to it. There is not another integrity, nor another composure.[33]
>
> As far as the Principle is concerned, there is only one Principle ... Therefore composure is the composure with regard to it, *ren* is *ren* with regard to it, and trustworthiness is the trustworthiness with regard to it.[34]

From the above passages, it is now clear that when the Chengs advocate that *li* is equal to the Principle, they are not elevating the status of *li*; rather, they are giving *li* a metaphysical ground, which transcends the empirical norms that *li* signifies. In the same passage, immediately following the statement "*li* is equal to the Principle," it reads: "Anything if not being the Principle, is selfish desire. Even if it is a desire to perform something good, it is still contrary to *li*. Once free from human desires, there will exist the Principle of Heaven."[35] To overcome one's self means being free from human desires. If so, the Principle of Heaven will emerge, and *li*, when interpreted as the external norm (rite), plays only a minor role. This passage conveys a message similar to the one with the exclamation "where is *li*?" The difference of the weight that the Chengs give to the Principle and *li* (in the sense of rite) is apparent in the following passage: "*Li* is the principle, it is also the pattern. The principle is the substance and thus is primary. The pattern is the decoration and thus is derivative" (MD).[36]

In addition to *jing*, there are other virtues that have been given a metaphysical meaning by the two brothers, especially Cheng Hao. Sincerity (*cheng* 誠) is one of these. It possesses a clearer metaphysical status than *jing*. The origin of its metaphysical meaning can be found in the *Mencius*: "Sincerity is the Way of Heaven, and to think how to acquire sincerity is the way of man" (*Mencius*, 4A12), and "Everything is complete here in me. Can there be any greater joy than in plumbing oneself and finding oneself true (*cheng*)?" (*Mencius*, 7A4); and also in the *Doctrine of the Mean* (*Zhongyong* 中庸), "Sincerity is a self-completion." The following passages show the metaphysical meaning of *cheng* in the Chengs' (mainly Cheng Hao) philosophy:

> Sincerity is a union of the internal and external way. If there is no sincerity, nothing will exist.[37]
>
> Sincerity is the way of Heaven; composure is the basis of human action. [Note by the disciple Liu Xuan: "Composure is the function."] When there is composure there is sincerity.
>
> MD[38]

> There is only one root in *Dao*. It is alleged that to speak of the mind containing sincerity is not as good as to speak of sincerity containing the mind, and that to

> contribute to the work of Heaven and Earth by the supreme sincerity is not as good as to be in union with others and things by it. This implies that there are two roots.
>
> MD[39]

> Composure implies continuity. Only by composure and sincerity then we can be in union with things without omitting any one of them. If there is no sincerity, nothing will exist.
>
> MD[40]

It is noteworthy that *cheng* as shown in these passages is not only a way to be in union with *Dao*, but is itself *Dao*. Therefore, the way of Heaven and the way of the human are one. This reflects the relationship between metaphysics and moral philosophy conceived by Neo-Confucianism in general and by the Chengs' philosophy in particular.

Concluding remarks

We have discussed so far that the Cheng Brothers grant to *li* only a peripheral status when it is understood as the rules of propriety. Although *li* in this sense is based on *yi*, the concrete rules are subject to change from time to time. *Li* is empirical, conventional, and has only an auxiliary function for moral development. On the other hand, for virtues such as *jing*, the meaning has shifted from the observance of external rules (conformity to ethical norms) to the moral cultivation of the inner self. In this respect, since the connotation of norms in the concept of *jing* fades out, the possible contribution of *li* in moral enhancement through the practice of *jing* also diminishes. Apart from *jing*, the status of filial piety has been reconsidered by the clarification of the meaning of a dialogue in the *Analects*. Moreover, the metaphysical meaning of another virtue, *cheng*, has been given more weight; therefore, its meaning as a norm is also neglected. It is concluded that the significance of *li* as external rules is replaced either by the way of inner moral cultivation or by the metaphysical reality—the Principle, in the Chengs' philosophy. The relationship between metaphysics and moral philosophy in their philosophy is discussed in "The Thought of CHENG Hao"[41] and "The Thought of CHENG Yi."[42]

17

The Thesis of Single-Rootedness in the Philosophy of CHENG Hao

Heaven and man

The term "single-rooted" appeared in the following passages of CHENG Hao:

> *Dao* is single-rooted. Someone might say, "To embrace sincerity (*cheng* 誠) by the heart-mind is not as good as subsuming the heart-mind within sincerity; to form a trinity with Heaven and Earth (*tiandi* 天地)[1] with perfect sincerity is not as good as uniting with other people and things with perfect sincerity." This is still double-rooted (*er ben* 二本). Knowing not to be double-rooted is the way of earnest respectfulness that leads to peace throughout the entire world.[2]
>
> If it is not single-rooted, how is it possible that "when [the great man] precedes heaven, heaven does not act contrary to him; when he follows after heaven he abides by the seasons of heaven?"[3]

The meaning of single-rootedness can be apprehended through its opposite: double-rootedness:

> Heaven and man originally are not two. There is no need to speak of union.[4]
>
> The cold of winter and heat of summer are the *yin* (陰) and *yang* (陽). That by which they are moved and transform is divine (*shen* 神). "Divine is without confines" and therefore "Change is without a body." If, like some, you conceive a Heaven distinct from man and say that it cannot be subsumed within man, you imply that the divine has confines. This is double-rooted.[5]
>
> "The extension of knowledge lies in the investigation of things." Investigation means "approaching." It is double-rooted to interpret investigation to mean "abiding in things."[6]

The expression "Heaven and man originally are not two" unequivocally means that they are one. Cheng Hao explicitly expresses this thought in the sentence "there is no gap between Heaven and man":

> Now, even if it is understood that "desiring is good," one still needs to have it within oneself in order to talk about sincerity. On this understanding, sincerity is the way

> of uniting inner and outer. However, not to see things as one is merely a product of the mind.[7] Apart from the body there is nothing but *Li* (Principle) and on this basis we can speak of uniting Heaven with man. Yet the unity of Heaven and man has already become a subject on which ignorant people have applied themselves. There is no gap between Heaven and man. If one is not able to embody [sincerity] fully then one cannot nurture and cultivate [things]. To talk about assisting nurture and cultivation is already to talk in a way that is removed from man.[8]

The premise that Heaven and man are one entails that "there is no need to speak of the union" of Heaven and man. By the same token, "to form a trinity with Heaven and Earth with perfect sincerity" and "to unite with others and things with perfect sincerity" presupposes that the individual is separated from Heaven and Earth or from other people and things. Similarly, if sincerity and the heart-mind are one, it is nonsense to say either "to subsume sincerity within the heart-mind" or "to subsume the heart-mind within sincerity." Both expressions presuppose that sincerity and the heart-mind are two separate things. This criticism also applies to the issue of "subsuming Heaven within man."[9] Therefore the ideas behind these criticisms are twofold: individual persons, Heaven and Earth, as well as other people and things, are one; and sincerity and the heart-mind are one.

In what sense are man and Heaven and Earth one? This is intelligible only in the sense that "the way of man and the way of Heaven and Earth are the same." Cheng Ho understands the way of Heaven and Earth—sometimes expressed as the way of Heaven (*Tian Dao* 天道), or just the Way (*Dao*)—not merely as a transcendent and abstract entity, because for him its truthfulness lies in its concrete manifestations. *Dao* manifests itself in every form of existence, but its full manifestation is in sages. In other words, a sage is a person who completely embodies *Dao*. It can be said that a full-blooded sage is *Dao*. Therefore the expression "man and Heaven and Earth are one" is not a description of fact, but rather a description of a vision, an experience which can be achieved only by the way of moral cultivation and practice. Because of this, the expression in question is neither a logical nor an empirical truth which can be justified by conceptual analysis or by empirical examination. Conceptually speaking, sincerity and the heart-mind are two notions with totally different connotations and denotations. To speak empirically, it is legitimate to talk about "containing the heart-mind with sincerity" or "containing sincerity with the heart-mind." Furthermore, striving to become a sincere person is a common goal for Confucian thinkers. Whether the goal is to subsume (sincerity, Heaven, etc.), or to assist (nurturing and cultivating things), or to unite (man and Heaven and Earth), they all presuppose that man and *Dao* are two. However, from Cheng Hao's perspective, they are one. It is remarkable that the perspective Cheng adopts is based on the highest achievement of moral practice. The twoness signifies the empirical fact which can be transcended by human effort. When one reaches the highest achievement, the twoness or duality would be included by the one root: *Dao*. Once one sees this oneness, it is trivial, if not wrong, to talk about assisting Heaven and Earth or uniting man and *Dao*.

Saying that man and *Dao* are one, is a "sudden and perfect" mode of expression. It is perfect because in the vision that it reveals, there are no more differentiations between

Dao and its manifestations, between inner and outer, or between heart-mind and its full actualization. In this perfect state, the duality of "to assist and being assisted," "to subsume and being subsumed," and "to unite and being united" also dissolve. It is sudden because *Dao* and man do not gradually become one. They are one as soon as an individual accomplishes the vision and fully embodies *Dao*. *Dao* and man are in a "sudden and perfect" way one and this state needs to be expressed also in a "sudden and perfect" way. The idea of doing away with words like "assist," "subsume," and "unite" is presented in the passages quoted above, and here are some more sayings in which this idea is embedded: "In saying 'to experience the cultivation of Heaven and Earth,' the word 'experience' still remains. Merely this is the cultivation of Heaven and Earth. There should not be another Heaven and Earth apart from this one."[10] This means that when an agent has really experienced the cultivation of Heaven and Earth, he or she is already identical with the cultivation of Heaven and Earth. This is because Heaven and Earth manifest themselves in their cultivation, which in turn manifests itself in the cultivation of the agent. If there were Heaven and Earth apart from that embodied in the agent, then Heaven and Earth would be abstract entities independent of man, and which man cannot fully grasp. Then there would be a gap between Heaven and man. In Cheng Ho's words: "To talk about assisting nurture and cultivation is already to talk in a way that is removed from man."[11]

> In all cases, accounts of "fully filling" (*chongsai* 充塞) resemble having the frame of a container and then filling it with vital energy. But this is merely an approximate analogy used to describe [the state of filling up]. Vital energy is vital energy, how can it be said to be "fully filling"? Just like "to nurture" is only "to nurture," how can it be said to "assist"? "Assisting" and "fully filling" are altogether other activities.[12]

Cheng Hao takes the expression "full respect leads to the peace of the entire world" as an instance to illustrate the meaning of single-rootedness. How can the full respect by an individual lead to the peace of the entire world? This can make sense only when it is understood as a partial description of the highest vision. Through full respect an individual becomes the full manifestation of *Dao*, under which the entire world is at peace. Now it is obvious that the way of a sage is no different from the way of Heaven and this is what single-rooted means. This meaning is clearly presented in the following passage:

> By perfect sincerity one can take part in (*zan* 贊) the cultivation of Heaven and Earth, and then one can form a trinity with Heaven and Earth. The meaning of *zan* is "take part in." It means "when [the great man] precedes heaven, heaven does not act contrary to him; when he follows after the heaven he abides by the seasons of heaven." *Zan* does not mean helping. There is only one sincerity, how can one speak of helping?[13]

The claim that "there is only one sincerity" means that sincerity is both the way of Heaven and Earth and the way of man. If there is only one way, then with perfect sincerity an agent is already taking the way of Heaven and Earth, and it is more appropriate to say that he or she contributes to the Way rather than helps Heaven and Earth. However, sincerity is usually understood as a state of mind or attitude that enhances an agent's moral cultivation, therefore it is considered a virtue. So in what sense can a human virtue also be shared by Heaven and Earth? One may find the answer in the following passage:

> "Heaven and Earth have fixed positions and Change (*yi* 易) operates between them": this is nothing but respect. Being respectful is therefore unceasing. It is only sincerity and respect that are able to generate things yet omit nothing. Without sincerity there would be nothing. It is said in the *Book of Odes*, "The decree of Heaven, how profound it is and unceasing. Was it not apparent, the purity of King Wen's virtue?" "Purity likewise is unceasing." Being pure never stops.[14]

This passage conveys the message that sincerity and respect[15] are the way of Changes (and of *Dao*) and are also the virtues that render King Wen a great king. The commonality between sincerity in the way of Heaven and in the way of a great person is that both have a characteristic of ceaselessness. By sincerity Heaven produces and reproduces unceasingly. Similarly, by sincerity a person enhances his or her awareness and activates his or her moral creativity. This activity can also be considered an unceasing act of production and reproduction in the moral realm. For Heaven, the unceasing process of production results in the endless nurture and cultivation of people and things, and this is the same for man. Cheng Hao makes this clear by saying that "Heaven and man are unceasing."[16] The connection between Heaven and man as putatively featured in the above-cited ode originally appeared in the *Doctrine of the Mean*, and Cheng Hao here elaborates the idea embedded in it only based on his own understanding. Cheng maintains that Heaven fully manifests itself through sincerity in the activity of production and reproduction and it can be said that there is no Heaven apart from this activity.[17] Therefore Heaven and the way of Heaven (the activity of production) are identical. Furthermore, since the way of Heaven is sincerity, Heaven is identical with sincerity. A perfectly sincere person in his or her unceasing production and reproduction is identical with sincerity itself and thus with Heaven. This is the ontological ground for man and Heaven being one.

The heart-mind and Heaven

Cheng Hao's thesis of single-rootedness not only presents itself in the relationship between Heaven and man, it also does so in the relationship between Heaven and the heart-mind. Since it is the heart-mind that is responsible for the activity of production and reproduction, it is natural to claim that heart-mind and Heaven are one. This is not a novel claim but is one based on an interpretation of *Mencius* 7A1: "He who fully activates his heart-mind apprehends his nature. Apprehending his nature, he apprehends Heaven." Cheng Hao revises Mencius' wording to express his own emphasis: "The heart-mind alone is Heaven. By fully exhausting one's heart-mind one can apprehend one's own nature. By fully apprehending one's own nature one will apprehend Heaven. (One version reads: 'the nature is Heaven'). We should adopt this [relationship] and should not search outside."[18] "'The great man unites his virtue with Heaven and Earth and his brightness with the sun and the moon', they are not outside him."[19] To fully activate an agent's heart-mind already presupposes that the agent who activates, and the heart-mind that is activated, are two separate things. For Cheng Hao, only through sincerity can the agent fully activate his or her own heart-mind, but sincerity is not something outside the heart-mind, since the former is already implicit in the latter. Therefore to fully activate means to become aware of. As related in the previous section, Heaven is sincerity and there is only one sincerity: as once an agent becomes fully aware of his or her implicit sincerity, he or she is identical with Heaven. On this understanding, the agent does not need to "apprehend" Heaven by his or her heart-mind in such a way that Heaven and the heart-mind are two separate things. Again, the claim that Heaven and heart-mind are one is expressed in a "sudden and perfect" way in that the expression is made from the perspective of someone who has accomplished the highest vision:

> The heart-mind possesses virtue from Heaven. If the heart-mind is not fully activated then it is because the virtue from Heaven has not been fully activated, then how can it apprehend the nature and Heaven? When one's own heart-mind has been fully activated then it can also fully activate [the nature of] other people as well as [that of] things and form a trinity with Heaven and Earth and take part in nurturing and cultivating. "To take part in" means to nourish directly.[20]

The speaker of the above passage is not identified. If read in the context of the thesis of single-rootedness, however, it supports Cheng Hao's view that in order to form a trinity with Heaven and Earth, one needs only to activate one's own heart-mind. The underlying reason is "mere heart-mind itself is Heaven."

The following passage shows that the virtue of the heart-mind is no different from the virtue of Heaven and Earth. "Mingdao [Cheng Hao] said, 'The decree of Heaven, how profound and unceasing it is, isn't this conscientiousness (*zhong* 忠)? Heaven and earth change and the wood and grass flourish, isn't this empathy (*shu* 恕)?'"[21] Conscientiousness and empathy are ordinarily considered as virtues of heart-mind, yet here they are used to describe *Dao* and its manifestations. It is quite clear from this that man understands *Dao* through his own virtues, which are innate in the heart-mind. Therefore man does not follow the virtues conferred by Heaven, rather, he sees *Dao* in terms of these virtues.

Dao and the instruments and vital energy

The relationship between *Dao* and vital energy is discussed in the following passage: "'Above form it is *Dao*, below form it is instruments (形而上為道， 形而下為器)'—the emphasis must be stated in this way. *Dao* is also the instruments and the instruments are also *Dao*. So long as *Dao* exists, then matters of present or future, self or others are irrelevant."[22] The sentence "above form it is *Dao*, below form it is instruments" is a modification of a frequently cited sentence from the "Great Appendix" (*xici* 繫辭). A.C. Graham noted that DAI Zhen 戴震 (1723–1777) had discussed the difference between "what is meant by" (*zhi wei* 之謂) and "is called" (*wei zhi* 謂之). Since Cheng Hao clearly states that in the version of the sentence as it appears in the "Great Appendix" "is called" cannot be changed to "what is meant by,"[23] then Graham, after Dai Zhen, comes to the conclusion that, according to Cheng Hao, *Dao* and instruments are the same but are simply called by different names to refer to the stages designated as above form and below form.[24] However, as shown in the passage cited above, Cheng Hao states that *Dao* and instruments are one without analysing the wording of the sentence used in the "Great Appendix." In what sense are *Dao* and instruments the same? It is not from a naturalistic view that all things in nature[25] are *Dao*, nor is it the case that Cheng Hao's thinking is so nebulous that he is somehow incapable of distinguishing between the two. Cheng Hao admits that speaking analytically, *Dao* and instruments are differentiated by "above form" and "below form." He further claims that it has to be said in this way, which meant that it is necessary to make the differentiation. Nevertheless, he says that *Dao* is also instruments and instruments are also *Dao*. This is also a "sudden and perfect" way of expression. *Dao* is nothing but its manifestations in instruments. All instruments, when their natures are fully actualized, embody *Dao*.

This view can also be found in another passage: "Outside *Dao* there are no things and outside things there is no *Dao*, so that between heaven and earth there is no direction to go which is not *Dao*."[26] However, only a person who has achieved perfect vision can see this. Embracing this vision is a "sudden and perfect" experience and it needs to be expressed accordingly to avoid conceptual analysis.

For Cheng Hao the relationship between *Dao* and instruments is analogous to that between *Dao* and vital energy.

> According to the "Great Appendix," "Above form it is called *Dao*, below form it is called instruments." And, it is said, "[The sage, fixing the lines of the hexagrams,] established them according to the way of Heaven, calling them *yin* and *yang*, and according to the way of Earth, calling them soft and hard, and according to the way of man, calling them *ren* and *yi*." And, it is said, "The *yin* and *yang* in alternation are what is meant by *Dao*." The *yin* and *yang* are also below form, but they are called *Dao*; this statement is enough to make it perfectly clear how 'above' and 'below' are to be distinguished. *Dao* has never been anything but these; it is essential for man to be aware of it in silence.[27]

Here, on the one hand, Cheng Hao adopts the view from the "Great Appendix" that *yin* and *yang* are below form, and on the other, claims that they are *Dao*. Unlike his brother Cheng Yi, he does not interpret "the alternation of *yin* and *yang* is what is meant by *Dao*" to mean "that by which the *yin* and *yang* alternate is *Dao*."[28] For Cheng Hao, *Dao* manifests itself in *yin* and *yang*, which are the original form of vital energy. It is perfectly clear for him that although *yin* and *yang* are below form, they represent *Dao* which is above form. Again, to say that *yin* and *yang* are *Dao* is expressed in a "sudden and perfect" way means that from the perspective of perfect vision, *Dao* is nothing other than its activity of producing. Moreover, in a "sudden and perfect" perspective, the distinction of above and below is transcended. Therefore he says, "*Dao* has never been anything but these [i.e., the *yin* and *yang*]." Now it is apparent that the transcendence has presupposed the distinction. In the last sentence Cheng Hao asks people to be aware of it in silence since he is sure that it cannot be grasped by conceptual thinking, through which distinctions are made.

According to the "Great Appendix" the activity of production and reproduction is what is meant by Change. Cheng Hao regards it as the divine function of *Dao* ("The function of production and reproduction is divine.")[29] As discussed above, *Dao* is nothing other than its activity (Change), it is also nothing apart from its function. In this sense *Dao*, Change, and the divine are one, with different names to refer to different aspects.

> "The operations of high Heaven are without sound or smell." Its substance is called Change, its principle is called *Dao*, its function is called divine, and its decree for man is called the nature.[30]
>
> "Production and reproduction are what is meant by Change"; it is this which Heaven regards as its way (*Dao*). It is production which Heaven regards as its way, and what succeeds this productive principle is goodness.[31]

For Cheng Hao, substance, activity, and function are not in a relation of opposition. The substance itself is activity and function. However, this assertion does not spring from a "sudden and perfect" perspective. On the contrary, the following passage is expressed in the "sudden and perfect" way: "Outside vital energy there is no divinity, outside divinity there is no vital energy. If it is said that the pure is divine, then is the impure not divine?"[32]

Elsewhere Cheng Hao used both an analytic and a "sudden and perfect" way to discuss the relationship between the divine and vital energy, and of that between Heaven and man: "The cold of winter and heat of summer are *yin* and *yang*. That by which they are moved and change is divine. 'The divine is without confines' and therefore 'Change is without substance.' If, like some, you conceive of Heaven as distinct from man and say that man cannot embrace it, you imply that the Divine has confines. This is double-rooted."[33] Describing phenomenal change to be a function of the divine is expressed in an analytic way, but to understand that Heaven and man are one requires a "sudden and perfect" perspective. Although Cheng Hao is aware of the different realms to which *yin* and *yang* and the divine belong, he also maintains that Heaven (or *Dao* or the Divine) is not independent of man.

I have shown in this section that the single-rootedness of *Dao* presents itself not merely in the Heaven-man relationship, but also in the *Dao*-vital energy relationship. In the next section I discuss the ground in human nature that makes the union of man with Heaven possible.

Human nature and vital energy

In the passage quoted in the last section, Cheng Hao explains his view on human nature. This same passage provides hints on how it is possible that man and Heaven can be one: "'The operations of high Heaven are without sound or smell.' Its substance is called Change, its principle is called *Dao*, its function is called divine, and its decree for man is called the nature."[34] The classical view that human nature is ordained or decreed by Heaven or *Dao* can be considered as the ground for the possibility of the union of Heaven and man. Furthermore, this ground renders possible "apprehending his nature, he apprehends Heaven." (*Mencius*, 7A1) What has Heaven decreed? It is the unceasing power of production and reproduction:

> "The supreme virtue of Heaven and Earth is to produce." "From the generative forces of Heaven and Earth the myriad things evolve." "Inborn is what is meant by the nature." It is most excellent to look into the vital impulses of the myriad things, this is "the Originating (*yuan* 元) is the leader of goodness," which is what is meant by *ren*. Since man is one thing with Heaven and Earth, why should he belittle himself?[35]

The view that "inborn (*sheng* 生) is what is meant by nature" is attributed to Mencius' contemporary Gaozi 告子 and means what is attained by birth constitutes human nature. This expression admits that all the inborn qualities of life such as desires, natural dispositions, and abilities constitute human nature, therefore the nature is neither good nor bad. In quoting Gaozi's claim, together with the sentences from the "Great Appendix," Cheng Hao is emphasizing the significance of giving life or producing. This leads Graham to translate *sheng* here as "the life in us."[36] Nevertheless, Cheng Hao is not "borrowing" the expression from Gaozi to illustrate the act of giving life but rather is quoting it in its original meaning. He does so because he thinks that being given life implies receiving all the inborn qualities mentioned above. In this sense he endorses Gaozi's view that the myriad things are the same in that they possess inborn qualities to become an individual, although he does not agree with Gaozi that all these qualities are held in common.[37] Inborn qualities make one individual being different from another, or at least one species different from another. However, apart from inborn qualities, the productive power in every single thing is decreed when it is produced. The same productive power is shared by each of the myriad things, and this is the most important reason for claiming that all the myriad things are the same. Being the virtue of Heaven and Earth, this productive power is also the virtue of every existing thing. It is presented in their vital impulse and is the origin of goodness. (I will come back to this later.) Sharing this unceasing productive power with Heaven and Earth, man can then be one with the latter. Furthermore, since the productive power shared by the myriad things is the same, man and the myriad things can (in principle) become one:

> The reason it is said that the myriad things are all one substance (*ti* 體) is that all have this [same] principle—it is simply because it is from there that they come. "Production and reproduction is called Change." Once things are produced, all possess this principle complete.[38]

The myriad things are all one because they completely possess the principle (of production) once they are produced. It also follows that they are complete within themselves and do not need to attain anything outside them to become one with Heaven and Earth: "'The myriad things are all complete within themselves.' This is so not only of man but of all things; it is from here that all have emerged."[39]

In a passage previously cited,[40] Cheng Hao uses Gaozi and the "Great Appendix" to make the point that the myriad things, including man and things, obtain the productive power from Heaven as their nature. Therefore the nature of production is the same for man and things. I have also shown that it is the inborn qualities—vital energy or native endowment—which differentiate man from things. Since the vital energy of things is impure or turbid, they are unable to actualize their own nature, much less extend their nature to actualize the nature of others. Only man can nurture and cultivate things and form the trinity with Heaven and Earth. Following the last sentence of the last passage quoted, we read:

> The only difference is that things are incapable of extending it to others, whereas man is capable of doing so. But does being capable mean that it [principle] has been increased a little bit? Does being incapable mean it has been diminished a little bit? All principles are present, complete and fully disposed.[41]
>
> Man can extend whereas things cannot because the vital energy of things is turbid. But it cannot be said that other things do not have this [principle].[42]

It is clear that for Cheng Hao, man and things possess the complete principle of production or *Dao* once they come to existence, therefore ontologically they have the same nature as each other and also as Heaven. Nevertheless in reality they are different since they are endowed with different inborn qualities. This has potential to hinder their capability to actualize their own nature if this nature is obscured.

> "Production and reproduction is what is meant by the Changes"; it is this which Heaven regards as its *way*. Heaven regards production alone as its *way*. What succeeds this productive principle is goodness. Goodness has the sense of Originating (*yuan* 元). "The Originating is at the leader of goodness." That the myriad things all have the impulses of spring is what is meant by "What succeeds [the way] is goodness; that in which it is completed is the nature." But its completion depends on the myriad things completing their natures of themselves.[43]

Ontologically Heaven has decreed the principle of production as the nature of the myriad things. In this sense, they are all complete within themselves. However, in the final sentence of the above passage it is claimed that they should complete their natures themselves. This means that in order to succeed the productive principle, the myriad things have to actualize the principle which is present within their nature merely as potential. Nevertheless, among the myriad things only man can fulfill this requirement, and therefore goodness can only apply to man.

Good and bad

Good and bad are commonly regarded as two contrasting attributes but in Cheng Hao's thesis they spring from one root. According to Cheng Hao, the principle of Heaven subsumes good as well as bad events: "There are good and bad events; all are heavenly principle. Within the principle of Heaven some things must be good and some bad for it is inherent in the condition of things to be unequal."[44] For Cheng, the duality of good and bad, just like other contrary qualities, is conceptually as well as factually accepted as a necessary part of principle. From a metaphysical point of view, both good and bad should be accepted equally.

> Of the principles of Heaven and Earth and the myriad things, none stands alone; all must have opposites. All are as they are naturally; it is not that they have been [purposely] arranged. Each time I think of them at midnight, "before I know it, my hands begin to dance them out and my feet step in time to them." [*Mencius* 4A.27][45] All the myriad things have their opposites (*dui* 對); there is an alternation of *yin* and *yang*, of good and bad. *Yin* diminishes when *yang* grows; bad is reduced when good increases. This principle, how far can it be extended? Man just needs to understand this.[46]

The ideas expressed in these passages conform to the long tradition of Chinese philosophy, which holds that both sides of various complementary pairs are necessary components of the cosmos. ZHONG Caijun (鍾彩鈞) points out that this view has a tone of naturalism.[47] Nevertheless, the necessary existence of the bad does not imply that it is normatively justified to commit morally bad actions.

When talking about what is morally good and bad, Cheng Hao is upholding Mencius' view that human nature is good, albeit with his own interpretation:

> "Inborn is what is meant by nature." The nature is vital energy, vital energy is the nature: it is what is inborn. In the endowment of vital energy which man receives at birth, there will in principle be both good and bad; but this does not mean that we are born with good and bad as two contrasting things present in our nature from the first. Some are good from infancy, some are bad from infancy; that they are so is due to their endowment of vital energy. The good is of course the nature, but the bad must also be recognized as nature.[48]

As discussed in the previous section, Cheng Hao uses Gaozi's view of "inborn is what is meant by the nature" to maintain that the myriad things are endowed with inborn qualities as well as the principle of production when they are formed with vital energy. Both of these endowments constitute their nature. In other words, the nature, with the principle of production as its content, is embodied in the vital energy of an individual with certain inborn qualities. In this sense, nature and vital energy are inseparable. There is good and bad vital energy that makes some people good from infancy and some bad. While acknowledging that vital energy constitutes part of the nature, he upholds Mencius' claim that "human nature is good" and supports it by the idea embedded in the sentence "what succeeds it is goodness" in the "Great Appendix." In this sentence "it" refers to *Dao*. For Cheng Hao, the unceasing productive power of *Dao* is the good in itself (which is also the origin of the good), and is decreed to man as human nature. When looking from *Dao* to man, it is the decree of Heaven, whereas looking from man to *Dao*, it is an act of succeeding. No matter which way we look, nature is good. The cause of badness is the vital energy. When an individual is formed and his or her nature is mixed with the vital energy, then badness might appear. But, as quoted above, Cheng Hao said the bad should also be recognized as nature. It sounds confusing, if not contradictory, to say that the nature is good and simultaneously that the nature also consists of badness. This is due to the fact that such a claim involves two senses of nature. One refers to the act of following after or succeeding the *Dao* and the other refers to the inborn qualities endowed in an individual when formed. Cheng Hao is aware of this ambiguity:

> "Inborn is what is meant by the nature." Nothing can be said of that which precedes the birth of man, a state of stillness. As soon as we speak of nature it has already ceased to be the nature. Usually when people speak of the nature, they are only talking about "what succeeds it is goodness," for example, the saying of Mencius that the nature is good.[49]

Cheng Hao thinks that it is not proper to speak of the nature before an individual is born. When an individual is born, his or her nature is decreed from the way of Heaven (*Dao*) which exists before his or her birth. Cheng Hao also recognizes that when an individual is born with vital energy, then the nature we speak of is such that it has already mixed with vital energy and has ceased to be the original nature. According to the phrase, "inborn is what is meant by nature," however, even though it has ceased to be the original nature, it should be regarded as nature as well. Therefore the two senses of nature, i.e., that before birth and that after birth, have different implications concerning the good or bad attribution of the nature. The nature before one's birth is good (which is "what succeeds it is goodness" means). After birth, the nature is mixed with vital energy and can be good or bad. However, usually when people speak of the nature, they are only talking about "what succeeds it is goodness." Cheng Hao also adopts this common practice and thus asserts that the nature is good. He uses a water parable to illustrate that "this does not mean that we are born with good and bad as two contrasting things present in our nature from the first": water is originally clean and if it becomes muddy it is only because it has been polluted:

> Whatever happens to it, it is still water. But some flows right to the sea without ever being polluted; this needs no effort to keep it clean. Some is certain to get progressively muddier before it has gone far; some gets muddy only after it has gone a long distance. Some has plenty of mud, some only a little; although the muddy water is different from the clean, it must still be recognized as water. This being so, it is necessary that man should accept the duty of cleansing and regulating it. The water will be cleaned quickly if his efforts are prompt and bold, slowly if they are careless. But when it is cleaned it is still only the original water; it is not that clean water has been fetched to replace the muddy, nor is it that the muddy has been taken away and put on one side. The cleanliness of the water corresponds to the goodness of the nature. Hence it is not that good and bad are two contrasting things within the nature which emerge separately.[50]

When the water is clean, it does not possess a particular quality to render its cleanliness. The cleanliness of the water embodies in the water itself, without anything added to it. Therefore when one says that the water is clean, it only indicates the purity of the water. In this sense although "the water is clean" is not analytically true, "the pure water is clean" is. If we can take this as an analogy, then goodness is not something added to nature to render the latter good, but rather is something already embodied in nature. It can be seen from the above discussion that the goodness which belongs to the original nature has transcended the duality of good and bad (inclinations). In this sense it can be said that good and bad have one root: the unceasing power of production of *Dao*.

Conclusion

It has been revealed that the thesis of single-rootedness of Cheng Hao is presented in the domain of Heaven and man, heart-mind and Heaven, *Dao* and instruments and vital energy, human nature and vital energy, and finally in the good and the bad. Some of these relationships are expressed in a "sudden and perfect" way and some are not. All the surface dualities are integrated in *Dao*, which signifies the unceasing power of production and reproduction, and which manifests itself in man as well as other beings. Taking this thesis as the metaphysical background, Cheng Hao's claims regarding the ways of moral practice and cultivation should be easier to understand.

Part Four

Confucian Ethics and Contemporary Cultural Phenomena

18

Reflections on the "Confucian Heritage Culture" Learner's Phenomenon*

Introduction

In the past decades, the outstanding performance of Asian students, especially in the subject of mathematics, had raised the eyebrows of sociologists, educationalists, and psychologists.[1] The cover story, "The New Whiz Kids" which appeared in *Time Magazine*[2] may have been the first to bring this phenomenon to the notice of the public, as well as sociologists and educationalists. Since then, such a "myth"[3] persisted:

- Hong Kong scored the highest in the 2nd IEA Mathematics Study and Japan was second.[4]
- China came in first in the 1992 IAEP (International Assessment of Education Progress) mathematics study, while Taiwan and Korea were dual second.[5]
- The four Little Dragons (Japan, South Korea, Singapore and Hong Kong) rank as the top four in Third International Mathematics and Science Study held recently. Singapore was way ahead of the others.[6]
- The Chinese team achieved outstanding results (champion[7] in 1990, 1992, 1993, 1995, 1997, 1998, 2000 and 2001; runner-up in 1991 and 1994) in the International Mathematical Olympiads since the 1990s.[8]

In the article "The New Whiz Kids," Brand[9] stated a number of facts that may have been disturbing those who believed in Western superiority to the oriental system in respect of the educational system and saw that the latter relies mostly on drilling and rote learning.[10] The article also deliberately drew a distinction between the Confucian and the Buddhist traditions among various Asian cultures, and argued that "immigrants from Asian countries with the strongest Confucian influence—Japan, Korea, China and Vietnam—perform best. By comparison, ... Laotians and Cambodians, who do somewhat less well, have a gentler, Buddhist approach to life."[11] Thereafter, the CHC (Confucian Heritage Culture) learner's phenomenon has become one of the most researched areas worldwide.

* Co-authored with Ngai-ying Wong.

Attempts to reveal the myth with empirical research

It is generally perceived that the CHC learning environment stresses recitation and memorization, large class with passive learners, teacher-centered, and teacher being authoritative, the setting of which are quite opposite to what is found to be conducive to learning.[12] However, it was repeatedly found that CHC students have stronger preference for deep approaches to learning, which is the opposite to rote learning, than do Western students.[13] Biggs made a clear distinction between rote learning and repetitive learning.[14] Other researches supported the hypothesis that excellent academic performance of the CHC learners may be due to a synthesis of memorizing and understanding uncommonly found in Western students.[15] It was also found that recitation was common among CHC learners to bring about sharp focus and better understanding.[16]

Biggs offered a new perspective on "the teacher as the authority in the classroom" which formerly was often regarded as having a dampening effect on the students.[17] He identified that the relationship between teacher and students was one of "mentor/mentee relationship." Besides, Hess and Azuma did note a mixture of authoritarianism and student-centeredness in the CHC classroom.[18] However, regardless of these new insights, the academic success of the CHC learner is still largely inexplicable.[19] Various empirical research also made similar observations. The CHC teacher was found to bear a moral responsibility of caring for their students and an implicit influence (especially on character cultivation) exists behind the façade of the transmission of knowledge.[20]

Finding the Chinese from cultural origins

Since the notion of Confucian Heritage is repeatedly stressed, some scholars turned their attention to the ideology of Confucianism per se. It is often stated that salient characteristics of learning in the CHC were social-achievement orientation (as opposed to individual-achievement orientation),[21] emphasizing diligence, attribution of success to effort, a competitive spirit, and a strong belief in the maxim "Practice makes perfect."[22] Bond[23] integrated classic studies of Hofstede[24] with the studies of Chinese Culture Connection[25] and Schwartz[26], and identified hierarchy, order, discipline, and a strong achievement orientation as the salient values common to such CHC regions as Hong Kong, Singapore, and Taiwan. CHC was often identified as a collective culture too.[27]

It has been argued that Confucianism is "congruent with the cultural system of traditional China, basically an agrarian state."[28] This agricultural economy tied the vast majority of the population to the land and peasants can only maintain their livelihood on a subsistence level.[29] The factor contributing to outstanding success among CHC students seems to be their orientation towards achievement the origin of which could be traced to the de-emphasis of non-mundane pursuits in their culture, as reflected from a Confucian anecdote. When Confucius was asked about life after death, he replied, "You do not understand even life. How can you understand death?" (*The Analects*, 11.12) Thus, it was perceived that the CHC philosophy of life is to concentrate one's efforts on the secular goals of this life. Moreover, not only are a person's distinction and honor passed on to the next generation, but the degree of his or her success in life is judged by both his or her worldly career and his or her contribution to the welfare of society.[30] These factors are often seen as the origin of the achievement orientation of CHC societies.[31] Since it is thought that the target of one's life can be fully achieved by the continuing efforts of one's descendents, parents always have high expectations of their children in respect of academic success. Retrospectively, children try to repay their parents by working hard in school, aiming at honoring them by obtaining good academic results.[32] However, we also find some results contradictory to this notion in empirical studies. For example, Ray and Jones[33] discovered that Hong Kong students' achievement motivation was lower than that of Australian students.[34]

Vagueness of cultural explanations

Though phrases like "the Asian learner," "the Chinese learner," and "the CHC learner" were used interchangeably, what does CHC really represent? During an international conference,[35] a participant from Singapore objected that Singapore should be classified as a CHC region on the basis that Singapore was a country of multi-cultures. Some also pointed out that Hong Kong, being greatly influenced by Western culture, could neither be classified as CHC. The only truly CHC regions could be China (including Mainland and Taiwan), Japan, and Korea. However, China alone is made up of twenty-eight provinces and fifty-six minority tribes. No doubt Chang asserted that we were all searching the Chinese from the wrong place![36]

We think that one should be cautious when trying to make cultural explanations (especially on attributions to Confucianism herein) in interpreting empirical data (be they quantitative or qualitative).[37] Let us elaborate here.

i. First of all, "institutionalized Confucianism" may greatly differ to the original Confucian political ideal. It was DONG Zhongshu (179?–104? BC) (Han Dynasty: 206 BC–AD 220) who put forth the idea of banning all other schools of thoughts, while upholding alone Confucianism. Since then, Confucianism was given the official political recognition, giving the wrong impression that politics in the past two thousand years in China were dominated by Confucianism. Some Western academics even mistakenly equate Confucianism with traditional Chinese culture.[38] They have overlooked that this was precisely the ruling strategy of these emperors to put Legalism or Daoism in the guise of Confucianism. Emperors' own interests often had the highest priority in respect of the governing of the country. They rationalized their ways by sporadic quotations from Confucius and Mencius. As LAO Siguang points out that "in Han Dynasty, those who called themselves Confucians had already confused Confucianism with Yin-Yang school, the 'five elements' doctrine and even divination according to mystical Confucian beliefs."[39] In fact, the ideal of sages ruling the world with Confucian ethical code has never been actualized in history.[40] Therefore, the influence of Confucianism through political system is not as powerful as people suppose.
ii. Naturally, systems, administrative systems in particular, could be derived from various ideas and as these systems further develop, they may deviate from the

original ideas. However, it is not appropriate to evaluate the original ideas by the outcome of the implemented system, or vice versa. Furthermore, though public examination in ancient China had great influences on curriculum and recruitment of officials, how much Confucian ideas of pedagogy, including the goals of education, learning objectives and methodology, were embedded in design of these examinations still needs further exploration. Before any close scrutiny is made, mixing up the ideas of Confucianism with the ideology of the official systems is obviously an oversimplification.

iii. Apart from the systems, schools of thought also had strong impact on culture as well. However, it is not at all easy to trace the influences of ideas and concepts on the formation of human behavior. People usually link "effects" (phenomena) backward with the "causes" (thought).[41] First of all, how can we ascertain a social behavior is the consequence of a particular school of thought (and not others)? For instance, achievement orientation is also present in schools of thought other than Confucianism.[42] It is an oversimplification to label such phenomena as sole products of Confucianism. Moreover, it is important to distinguish whether certain concepts under investigation are central or peripheral to a school of thought. Furthermore, though every school of thought has its central thesis, it does not mean that it remains unchanged over time. It could evolve in time to address new problems. Obviously, Confucian thoughts in the time of Confucius, Neo-Confucianism of the Song (960–1279) and Ming (1368–1644) Dynasties are quite distinct in terms of their ways of presentation and the areas of emphases they put. Therefore, when we talk of Confucianism, we must make ourselves clear which period of the school of thought we are referring to.

iv. If we turn our attention from the political to the social and behavioral aspects, likewise, it is not easy to identify some behaviors as "Confucian." For instance, though filial piety is an important virtue advocated in Confucianism, nevertheless, such a virtue might also be derived from Buddhism and other religious beliefs (or even Christianity). By the same token, attributing academic success of CHC students solely to Confucianism is questionable. Besides, such social norms and conventions may not necessarily be the product of a conscious prescription. Often, people behave (say, respect their parents) quasi-consciously, if not habitually. These behaviors are affected by environmental factors too. For instance, the status of kinship may experience a tremendous change with the dissolution of big families. More precisely, no evidence is found so far that the greater the role of Confucianism plays in a society, the stronger the achievement orientation of people possess.[43]

v. Even if we accept the belief that pre-modern Chinese society was largely shaped by Confucianism, how can we explain the CHC phenomenon in modern China as Western thoughts deluge the East? How can we account for the case of Mainland China when traditional culture was basically wiped out by Communism; or the case of Taiwan which was ruled by Japan for a long period of time and Hong Kong, being a British colony for over a century? To what extent is Confucian thought still in play and do the remains, however sparingly there still exists, of such thoughts constitute only the superficial part and/or present only as some distorted forms of Confucianism?

vi. As we mentioned above, CHC is also affected by Mohism, Daoism, Buddhism and other traditions. For instance, Chan Buddhism,[44] has great impact on CHC pedagogy.[45] Masters of various traditions like calligraphy, painting, martial arts, Chinese medicine also have unique ways of schooling their disciples; and these ideas of learning and teaching were also responsible for the shaping of CHC pedagogy.[46]

vii. Finally, as it was common to quote from Confucius (and other philosophers), we must be careful in making interpretations. Ancient Chinese words often carry different levels of connotation. Besides the case of "Practice makes perfect" mentioned above,[47] let us state a few more examples:

1. "[I] transmit but do not create" (*The Analects*, 7.1) was quoted to conclude that Confucius did not emphasize creative thinking,[48] however, Confucius was also quoted (*The Analects*, 7.8) to demonstrate that threats to comfort constitute the essence of learning, under which circumstances it may be interpreted as one can transfer what is learned to other areas (which may, in this sense, be interpreted as creating).[49] "[I] do not create" shall be interpreted as "not inventing his own ideas without ground." Moreover, we shall not understand this statement in isolation and consider it as a panacea. Rather, we shall understand it in the context of the life and times of Confucius and his achievement during his life. For a person of such a stature, it is odd to conclude that Confucius "discouraged creativity" or "suppressed innovation."
2. On another occasion, Confucius said "it is a pleasure to learn and practice frequently" (*The Analects*, 1.1) was repeatedly quoted to infer that Confucius advocates drill and practice (and hence learning by rote). However, a more appropriate explanation of the quotation should be "it is a pleasure to frequently put what is learned into practice." Marton also pointed out that Confucius' saying "to know the new by reviewing the old" (*The Analects, 2.1*) should illustrate a kind of repetitive learning from which a further deepening of understanding will be achieved each time.[50]
3. The Chinese word "understanding" has different levels of meanings. For instance, knowledge is regarded as one of the two major obstacles to enlightenment.[51] Awareness is often regarded, especially by the great neo-Confucian ZHU Xi, as a result of "doubt."[52]
4. The Chinese phrase "read a book" also has different levels of meanings and functions. It may mean reading out literally, or reciting, memorizing or memorizing by reciting.[53] For instance, the Pure Land sect of Buddhism has been using name chanting (reciting) of Amitayus (Buddha of longetivity) to implant deeply the vision of Amitayus into the mind of the practitioner.[54]

Conclusion

The exposition on the interrelations of CHC learning phenomenon and Confucianism (as have been quoted as evidence from some sayings of Confucius and Mencius) resembles to a very large extent the cultural explanation on the Far East economic "miracle" which also refers to Confucian ethics as the key. The similarity of the two is not only limited to the object of discussion but also on the methodology employed. Many academics have pointed out that amongst all the cultural explanations on the economic phenomenon, the concept of Confucian ethics is exceptionally ambiguous and vague, and some have gone to the extent of saying such concept was tailor-made merely for the purpose of proving the object of discussion.[55] For example, GU has sharply criticized, "Confucianism discussed today is no longer the pillar of Chinese political and economical system. Confucian ethics does not have a specific and concrete reference. Hence it can be equated at will with such terms as 'familial ethics,' 'achievement motivation,' 'work ethics,' 'relationships orientation,' even 'Chinese style management.' As such, discussing Confucian ethics is not any different from discussing 'the characters of Chinese people.' We can also say that Confucian ethics has lost its uniqueness since Chinese culture has been over-Confucianized and such ethics is used in a general way to describe the Chinese race. In other words, when we look with the eyes of Westerners and observe 'the mysterious China' from a distance, we will be unable to differentiate Confucianism, Daoism and Legalism. In fact, we simply do not bother to note the difference between Confucianism, Daoism, Buddhism and other popular religious beliefs. In a word, we equate 'Confucianism' with 'China' rather offhandedly and disregard the genuine meaning and the difference of their ideas. It may be excusable that Western academics are affected with such a sweeping impression. We ourselves, nevertheless, must review such attitude and see whether the conceptual structure can be fit in the actual situation in a more appropriate fashion . . ."[56] This criticism is also applicable in today's discussion on learning attitude or mode. Some academics who are aware of this problem tried to view "Confucian ethics" or Confucianism from different levels,[57] thereby giving a clearer and more detailed explanation on the characteristics of each level. This approach can give a stricter and more relevant exposition.

Regarding the excellent academic results of CHC students, the "examination culture"[58] which was designed for governance purposes, could have a far greater impact on achievement orientation than Confucianism. Individuals, regardless of their family background, could climb up the social ladder by striving to pass a hierarchy of examinations.[59] So whether CHC students are really brilliant or just skilful in passing examinations could be another issue worthy of more in-depth investigations.[60]

Chang suggested that the "search" for "Chinese" shall not be targeted at the geographical regions or kinship but rather at the "vernacular culture that common people endorse" which includes "the beliefs and values held by ordinary folks who identify themselves as Chinese."[61] This approach no doubt could lead to the possibility of sidetracking an issue only to find another. Yet, Lee[62] did make a brief analysis on the shared beliefs in education (e.g., high regards on education, the educability for all . . .) of CHC. This analysis could probably form the basis of further investigation along this line.

19

Confucianism and Contemporary Education Phenomena†

Introduction

The CHC learner's phenomenon has attracted much attention worldwide. Why do students in CHC regions outperform their Western counterparts? The topic generated a myth and resulted in a fruitful area of research, producing an abundance of intellectual discourse. The scope ranged from students and teachers in the school and university sectors, from those residing in CHC regions, overseas students, and immigrants. Investigations were made on the features of students and teachers in these regions, the practices that might lead to such an excellence and searching for cultural explanations. With such a fruitful discourse, there is a pressing need to look into some fundamental issues, which include:

- What are the underlying cultural traditions of these regions?
- Is there a unified culture commonly embraced by these regions?
- Does there exist causal relationship between cultural spirit and cultural phenomena?
- What are the educational practices of these regions, their strengths and limitations?
- What good practices can inspire us?
- What are the precautions when we decode these studies?

In the sections that follow, we would like to offer our perspectives on the issues listed above.

Current studies on educational phenomena in East Asian regions

East Asia: focus of attention

In the past half a century, the excellent academic performance of the Asian (East Asians, in particular) has caught the attention of psychologists, philosophers, sociologists, and educationalists worldwide. As early as the mid-1980s, results from the Second IEA Mathematics Study (SIMS) showed that Hong Kong students scored the highest, followed by Japan as a close second.[1] At that time, China (here it refers to the Chinese

† Co-authored with Ngai-ying Wong

mainland), the most populous country, did not take part. Before the recent Programme for International Student Assessment (PISA), Chinese mainland participated in the 1992 IAEP mathematics study for the first time. At that event, the Chinese mainland came out first, followed by Taiwan and Korea in second.[2] These records were further reinforced by China's brilliant records in the International Mathematical Olympiads. Since then East Asian regions have continued to outperform their Western counterparts at various international competitions. The fact that the four Little Dragons[3] took the top four positions in the Third International Mathematics and Science Study (TIMSS)[4] (together with the results in subsequent two rounds of PISA) generated a wave of media attention, discussions, research, speculations, and academic discourse.

In the *Time Magazine* cover story, "The New Whiz Kids," in 1987, it was stated that a considerable percentage of students in US best universities were of Asian descent. This may disturb those who believed that the Western educational system was superior to the Asian system with its reliance on drilling and rote learning.[5] In an article in that same issue, a distinction was deliberately drawn between the Confucian and the Buddhist traditions. It was argued that "immigrants from Asian countries with the strongest Confucian influence—Japan, Korea, China and Vietnam—perform best. By comparison, Laotians and Cambodians, who do somewhat less well, have a gentler, Buddhist approach to life."[6]

In a series of studies performed by the Stevenson, Hiebert, and Stigler's group, Confucianism was once again cited and the East-West cultural divide was attributed to effort vs ability.[7] Their books *The Learning Gap*,[8] which basically focus on IAEP and SIMS, and *The Teaching Gap*,[9] which basically focus on the 1995 TIMSS-video study, were two of the most frequently cited publications on the subject.

In another vein, a group of expatriates began to join the teacher education profession in Hong Kong. For instance, John Biggs from Australia took up chair professorship at the Faculty of Education at the University of Hong Kong in 1987. A few others took up various positions in tertiary education in Hong Kong. They were taken by a cultural shock, a "myth"[10] or "paradox"[11] as to why Hong Kong Chinese students could perform so well under such a seemingly conservative educational environment. At the beginning they used the term "Asian learner,"[12] and later the label "Confucian heritage culture" (CHC) was coined.[13] Biggs and Watkins soon published their seminal works *The Chinese learner*[14] and *Teaching the Chinese learner*.[15] Some of the more recent publications on the topic include *Revisiting the Chinese learner*,[16] *International education and the Chinese learner*,[17] and *Learning and development of Asian students*.[18]

These studies were soon supported by psychologists like Bond who joined the Chinese University of Hong Kong earlier in the mid-1970s. His investigation on Chinese values made substantial contributions to the field through a series of publications, including *Beyond the Chinese face*,[19] *Psychology of the Chinese people*,[20] *The handbook of Chinese psychology*,[21] and *The Oxford handbook of Chinese psychology*.[22] Though teaching and learning was not the focus of these books, they provide psychological and sociological perpectives on the discussions about Chinese learners.

All these seminal works soon began to catch the attention of Chinese scholars. A book *Growing Up the Chinese Way*[23] was released in 1996 and in the field of mathematics, Chinese scholars saw the need of publishing a book by Chinese scholars who could introduce the Chinese learner phenomenon to the world, instead of just having non-Chinese discussing this Chinese issue. As a result, two books *How Chinese Learn Mathematics*[24] and *How Chinese Teach Mathematics*[25] were published.

The CHC learner

In fact when these expatriates began their academic inquiries, they did not focus on a particular nation at the start but Asian learners in general. In particular, Watkins, as a cross-cultural psychologist, conducted his Ph.D. study in the Philippines[26] and then proceeded to Asian countries like Malaysia,[27] Nepal,[28] and even other parts of the world.[29] As mentioned above, the term CHC was eventually coined and gave rise to some fundamental issues, which will be discussed in the following sections. Despite problems of the term, for simplicity's sake, in this section we still use CHC loosely to include regions like the Chinese mainland, Taiwan, Hong Kong, Japan, Korea, and possibly Singapore.

CHC is noted for these salient characteristics of learning as follows: social-achievement orientation (as opposed to individual-achievement orientation)[30], emphasizing diligence, attribution of success to effort, a competitive spirit, and a strong belief in the maxim "practice makes perfect."[31] It is often quoted in the TIMSS results that though CHC (Hong Kong in particular) students perform well they lack self-confidence.[32] However, recent discussions have it that test anxiety and self-doubt could be a driving force to achieve better outcomes.[33]

The notion of 'Me Generation' was put forth in one of the studies. In this regards, silence (often in a cross-cultural setting) was taken as a right and strategy among CHC students rather than as being passive in class.[34] This view echoes earlier findings that CHC learners could be seemingly passive yet mentally engaged.[35] Hatano and Inagaki[36] also pointed out that it was the CHC tradition to emphasize *listenership* rather than *speakership* in the West. In other words, it is not only that CHC learners possess a reserved personality of keeping silence in class, but also this is an intentional part of the training and educational goal. Though Ha and Li[37] devoted a whole section on pedagogical implications, more specific teaching strategy is, however, expected. In fact these findings piece together nicely with earlier and other research results that have come up with pedagogical recommendations, which we will discuss in later sections.

Reflection on conceptual methodology

It is always misleading to speak of "cultural impact" or "cultural influence" in a way as if (some) culture causes social behavior. Clarifications of two concepts related to "culture" made at the outset are helpful for the discussion. They are cultural spirit and cultural phenomena.[38]

Cultural spirit

This concept includes thoughts or ideas in religion, metaphysics, and values. These thoughts or ideas arise from "free will" or the "conscious mind," which refers to an autonomous capacity of human beings. Cultural spirit manifests itself through cultural activities. Different values or world views motivate different activities. It is in this way that thoughts or philosophy are able to change the world. It is noteworthy that cultural spirit exists in value-orienting consciousness, which incorporates an inner force to realize itself.

Cultural phenomena

Cultural spirit has to consciously realize itself as cultural phenomena through cultural activities in the empirical world. Therefore, cultural phenomena can be regarded as the products of cultural spirit. Having said this, not all cultural phenomena are the conscious products of cultural spirit. For those cultural activities, empirical factors such as geographic condition, production modes, etc., are also in operation beyond the control of consciousness. These factors will shape the living styles, conventions, and social relations, which are hardly considered as conscious products. However, these living styles, etc., themselves do not form the core of a cultural system. We should examine the cultural spirit behind the phenomena in order to understand the outstanding features of a particular culture.

Ideas and thoughts are the direct manifestation of cultural spirit. Although they are abstract entities, they still have specific contents. Through conscious cultural activities, attitudes towards the way of living emerge; hence a cultural system is formed. In fact cultural system is not as formal as the notion implies. In its broad meaning it includes political, economic, education systems, and the like. For example, political thoughts concerning equality, human rights to freedom, the purpose of a state, etc., contribute to the constitution of a political system. Thoughts about human nature and certain religious beliefs might also affect the formation of the system on a more fundamental level, even though not in an explicit way. Apart from the conscious aspects, as mentioned above, a political system is also influenced by geographic and historical factors. Even within a political system, ideas become more concrete as one goes closer to the operational level, and might even be compromised by the hard facts of reality. For example, the voting system is not deduced merely from the assumption concerning the adopted idea of democracy, but is decided on the power structure of society.

Relationship between cultural spirit and cultural phenomena

In this regard, it is obvious that the relation between cultural spirit and cultural phenomena is not a logical one that the former is neither the sufficient nor the necessary condition of the latter. Take the political system as an example again: An idea of democracy does not entail the emergence of a democratic system and vice versa. The idea of democracy certainly contains the design of a system in which democracy can be realized, but we would be mistaken if we think that the idea itself provides all the conditions for its realization. By the same token, we cannot say that if there is no democratic system in a particular society then the idea of democracy is wrong or that it is disapproved by its people. The existence of a system does imply validity of the idea behind it, but the latter is usually obtained by introspection. At most we might say that the idea has had certain influence on the system, especially on the design of its construction. We should pay more attention to the empirical and contingent factors which affect the system existing in reality. Now it is apparent that, on the one hand, we can never build a logical relationship between our thoughts and an existence in reality. The relationship can only be found between two thoughts. On the other hand, it is legitimate to establish a causal relationship between a thought and an event that occured in history, for example, a thought about human rights to private property and the rise of capitalist economic system in Europe during the eighteenth century. However, to make this relationship convincing, one should provide adequate evidence and, like other empirical assertions, it should be falsifiable.

Theoretically, it is probable that a causal relation can be established between an idea and an event; yet the confirmation, not to speak of the verification, is extremely difficult. Even though some linkage between these two is likely to be established, how much weight of influence can we attribute to the particular factor among the others? There is no commonly agreed measurement. On top of these difficulties, there is another related one. Due to the uniqueness of every historical event, it is deemed impossible to obtain evidence from the past to generalize a causal relationship.

Apart from cultural systems, conventions and collective behavior are also parts of cultural phenomena which are shaped with lesser consciousness. As mentioned earlier, they are influenced by historical, environmental, as well as biological factors. The causal relationship between conventions and the like and these factors is relatively easier to establish. This is because they all belong to the empirical realm.

Confucianism and the learning phenomena

As far as CHC learner phenomena is concerned, the discussion about the relationship between cultural spirit and cultural phenomena contribute to clarify how, if any, belief in Confucianism affects the phenomena in question. We will proceed with the clarifications made in mind.

Chinese culture and Confucianism

It seems that there is general agreements among scholars that Confucianism has played an important role throughout the history of China since the Spring and Autumn Period. Nevertheless, if we do not take this role for granted and start to scrutinize closely, then we may gain a clearer picture. Similar to other schools of thought, Confucianism has claims and doctrines on metaphysics, ethics, political philosophy, and the like. We may divide Confucianism into four levels, which contain the following elements as follows:

i. Metaphysical claims on *Tian Dao* (The Universal Principle) and human nature: In Confucianism it is believed that *Tian Dao* regulates the cosmos as well as human beings and it is the ultimate principle that accounts for the existence of every being. According to Confucianism, every human being has in his or her human nature a capacity for distinguishing the good from the bad. Therefore, human nature is the transcendental ground for morality and in this sense it is good.

ii. Ethical virtues and moral maxims:
From the capacity stated above, virtues and moral maxims are formed to provide guidance for ordinary life. They make moral choice and decision easier for people. In Confucian terms, moral maxims are known as *li* (propriety). Usually obligations demanded by *li* are assigned to people in accordance with their roles in society.

iii. Institutional rules:
Moral maxims can be reinforced by institutional authority like governing power and present themselves as social norms or rules in various sectors. Substantial or informal rewards or punishments by the ruling system make the norms coercive. However, although it has been a great project since Confucius to realize the moral ideal in the political realm, it has never succeeded in the past two thousand years since no ruler endorsed the ideal sincerely. Contrarily, the rulers embraced the political thought of Legalism in the name of Confucianism and implemented many very suppressive and unfair rules in the systems of marriage, family, and education throughout Chinese history.

iv. Customs and etiquette:
Confucius endorsed certain rites and rituals stipulated in early Zhou for their spiritual meanings which conformed to his moral ideal. Nevertheless, in the Spring and Autumn Period people practised them merely for the sake of formality without being aware of their meanings. Confucius tried to bring them to resurrection but was not quite successful. In the post-Confucius period, some of the rites Confucius advocated continued to be performed by people, but others were completely abolished. Even for those that were still in practice, few were performed with their meanings ever being recognized. Essentially, Confucianism is not a school of thought which merely proposes certain behavior for an orderly society. Instead, it values the awareness of the spiritual meaning behind human behavior. In this sense only if certain behavior is performed with the said awareness can it be regarded as possessing a Confucian meaning. Obviously, it is very difficult, if ever possible, to identify whether certain customs and conventions are endowed with Confucian beliefs simply by looking at the external behavior alone. Hence it is always too vague to attribute the term "Confucian" to customs or conventions without verifying their true awareness.

How does Confucianism affect the phenomena?

When it is alleged that Confucianism plays an important role in Chinese history, we should make clear at what level the statement refers to. It is true that Confucianism as a school of philosophy serves as the mainstream in the history of Chinese thought. It provides the metaphysical ground for the values of human beings and also makes humans valuable. Since the innovative discovery in the Spring and Autumn Period and the Warring States, Confucianism had developed further and elaborated its doctrines in the later periods of Chinese history. It is a philosophy which does not only intend to solve the current moral issues in ancient time, but can also tackle problems of humans in general in the contemporary world.

Confucianism on the second level was also important in ancient times. However, as time changed, some maxims could no longer give proper guidance for human behavior. They need to make amendments accordingly to fit contemporary situations. The amendments were made in light of the basic ideas of Confucianism at the first level.

As listed above, institutional Confucianism only existed as a Confucian ideal but has never been established in history. It owes its significance to providing guiding principles for the ruler; yet, in reality it gained power only if the ruler endorsed it. For example, in principle a Confucian ruler can utilize the examination system to select candidates for the government office to serve people, and, thus, realize the ideal of Confucianism. Nevertheless, the rulers had been abusing the system to choose only people who would strengthen their own authority.

Finally, with regard to rites and rituals, the burden of proof is on those who suggest Confucianism as a school of thought that has had an impact on the conventions and customs. Similarly, it is also the case for moral maxims and social norms. However, it is easier to see the link between norms and conventions. As mentioned above, it is hard to single out one particular source which is sufficient to account for the emergence of a custom. For example, the avoidance of openly talking about death among ordinary people might be due to the fear of death which was generated from the description of hell by Daoist religious belief or Buddhism, but it might not be easy to trace it to the Confucius' saying that "how can we know death without knowing life" as directly as one often thinks.

If we want to establish a thesis that a particular phenomenon comes from Confucianism, we should specify on which level of Confucianism and in which aspect we refer to. Then we should provide evidence for that linkage. We should exclude other factors which might cause the phenomenon as well. This will apply to the issue of learning phenomena discussed in previous sections.

How true is the explanation of CHC Learner's phenomena in Confucian terms?

When we assess the explanatory power of the thesis in question, we need to bear in mind the conceptual relationships clarified in previous sections. Besides, we should consider historical and cultural factors. First of all, to what extent are East Asian regions influenced by Confucianism? For instance, though Confucianism earns high regards in Singapore, the government there has always stressed that it is a multi-cultural country. What is more, taking the Chinese, Japanese, and Korean learners as a homogeneous group presents another challenging issue. In fact, Hatano and Inagaki have showed their skepticism on whether we can group the Chinese and Japanese mathematics classrooms as "Asian" at all.[39] Hirabayashi, for another example, commented that "[i]t was historical necessity that many domains of Japanese culture have been influenced by the 'CHC (Confucian Heritage Culture)' which was described in Professor Wong's[40] thesis in the Proceedings of ICMI EARCOME 1 [The first East

Asian ICMI—East Asia Regional Conference on Mathematical Education] in Korea in 1998. However, this is not to say that there are not many other unique traditional features which are proper to our[41] cultural field, even in today's mathematics education."[42] Yuan and Xie[43] have raised similar concerns. Often, we are polarizing the East and West, giving an impression that the East and the West are dichotomized and that all Eastern regions are lumped together without due respect.

The same issues pertain even if we confine our attention to the Chinese situation. China is a huge country and learning environment varies greatly from the coastal to inland regions, and from rural of urban areas;[44] not to mention differences in education among the four regions across the strait. While Hong Kong had been a British colony for a century, education in Taiwan was very much influenced by the US, whereas in the Chinese mainland by the Russians.[45] Furthermore, after the May 4th movement, how "Chinese" is contemporary Chinese education needs further inspection. Though the study of Wang[46] reveals that Chinese students' conceptions of learning are very Confucian, it is possible that high stake examinations (Keju), as a means of government control with little to do with Confucianism, have far more impact on learning and teaching than any schools of thought. If this is the case, then it is the institution (of examination) that affects the learning phenomenon.[47]

Besides variations across geographic regions, there were also discussions on changes across time. Not only did Confucianism itself undergo changes and rejuvenations in history, but Asian societies were transformed with changes as they face new challenges in the wave of globalization. In education, by inspecting the mathematics curriculum around the turn of the millennium, Wong, Han, and Lee[48] revealed that the East-West distinction became blurred, when compared with similar studies performed about 10 years ago. "Western" notions (though many of them also exist in Eastern ideologies) like hands-on experience, constructivism, cooperative learning, lifelong learning, learning to learn, began to creep into the Asian educational contexts.[49] The global flow of human resources has also initiated changes for the CHC educational environment (including beliefs, values, goals, and contexts).[50]

Enhancing teaching and learning in the Confucian cultural context: Pedagogical inspirations drawn from current studies

Inevitably, the outstanding academic performance of the CHC learners has led to the search of their good educational practices, and has served as food for thoughts for improvement in other countries or regions. Although it is common knowledge that "good" (educational) practices that are effective in one place may not be so in another,[51] we often turn to look for practices without pre-determining whether they are good or not.[52]

For example, Biggs has distinguished between repetitive learning and learning by rote.[53] Marton, with the lens of phenomenography, argues that repetition is indispensable as we need repetition with variation in order to have discernment, which is a prerequisite for concept formation.[54] So it is understood that repetition with variation systematically introduced would broaden students' *lived space* which will result in a richer *outcome space*.[55] This is quite in line with the notion of *bianshi* teaching which is widely practiced in the Chinese mainland[56] as well as experimented in Hong Kong.[57] This is precisely the theme of Huang and Leung,[58] claiming to crack the paradox of the Chinese learner. Marton has further developed his pedagogy of variation into *learning study* project, helping schools to enhance their teaching.[59]

Marton's other research outcomes have supported the hypothesis that excellent academic performance of CHC learners may be due to a synthesis of memorizing and understanding, which is not commonly found in Western students.[60] Recent studies on Malaysians have revealed similar results.[61] It was also found that recitation was common among CHC learners to bring about a sharp focus and better understanding.[62] Li and Cutting[63] have even asserted that "CHC learners' use of RL (rote learning) involves far more complex processes than have been so far acknowledged. The researchers suggest a new term 'Active Confucian-Based Memory Strategies' (henceforth ACMS), to distinguish these strategies from passive RL."[64] Other researchers have also revealed that procedural (or instrumental) understanding (which was in fact not regarded as understanding in the earlier days)[65] and conceptual (or relational) understanding are not segregated.[66] Tall[67] has even put forth the notion of *procept*. A group of scholars, including Baroody, Reil, and Johnson[68] have proposed the idea of deep procedures, in which connectedness is the key indicator.[69] Again, by letting the learner experience systematically varied phenomena, the learner could gradually connect them through varied repetitions and practices, resulting in the acquisition of deep procedures.

In simplistic terms, from the perspective of *bianshi* teaching (quite similar for pedagogy of variation—though the learning study should develop into three kinds of variations)[70] after getting accustomed with exercises like 3 + [ ] = 2, 5 + [ ] = 4, the learner is led to proceed and experience more complicated problems like 125 + [ ] = 28, 12.9 + [ ] = 6.7 and even 7 + [ ] = –5. The learner is guided to summarize that if a + x = b, x = b – a. The proof could be introduced here: a + x = b infers to a + x – a = b – a, leading to the above result. The next phrase of variation could be problems like 5 + 2x = 8, or even 3 + 8x + 7 – 3x = 3 – 7. By doing so, not only does the learner proceed from simple to more complicated procedures, but procedures are linked (connectedness) together, generating a deep understanding.

As for teaching, Biggs[71] has offered a new perspective on "the teacher as the authority in the classroom" which was often regarded as having a dampening effect on students. He has identified the relationship between a teacher and students as one of "mentor/mentee relationship." In a recent paper,[72] it is pointed out that the notion of "learned-centeredness" is being abused and "teacher-centric environment can create great thinking and creative thinking".[73] In fact, Hess and Azuma[74] have noted a mixture of authoritarianism and student-centeredness in the CHC classroom. Wong[75] has further suggested the possibility of a *teacher-led yet student-centered*[76] classroom environment, which in fact was borrowed from works of earlier cognitive psychologists like Ausubel.[77] One may note that Ausubel's paper was published in the peak of discovery/enquiry learning. His idea, to a certain extent, was to counteract that trend and argued that teacher's verbal instruction can be meaningful. However, Wong[78] pointed out that in order to have such a *teacher-led yet student-centered* script put into play, attentiveness and compliance to routines were prerequisites.

Extracting from the training of some classical Chinese arts, Wong[79] has identified the route of going from "entering the *way*" to "transcending the *way*"[80] in traditional Chinese way of instruction. The student is first given a model to imitate and practice, gradually, with the initiation of the guru (master). The student is able to come up with his or her own personal style of creative work. The interplay between doubt (arousing the discomfort within the learner) and realization (i.e., the cycle of arousing doubt—rests in realization—arousing another doubt—realization again) serves as a means to "transcending the *way*" after one has entered it. This would offer another clue on how and why repetitive learning can lead to higher order thinking and acquisition of deep procedures.[81]

Piecing up all these, though CHC learners may be seemingly silent in class, yet, with suitable motivation from the teacher, it is possible to have them intellectually engaged and listen to the teacher's lecturing. The teacher designs step by step learning experiences for the students through a systematic introduction of variations, guiding them from "entering the *way*" stage to the "transcending the *way*" stage. Such a teacher-led classroom can still be student-centered if the teacher and student maintain a mentor/mentee relationship, in which the student earns a lot of individual guidance from the teacher after class.[82] Not only that, after soliciting students' feedbacks during the whole process, the teacher revises his or her teaching strategies, which makes this *teacher-led yet student-centered* strategy possible.

All the strategies, including teaching with variations to come up with deep procedural understanding, a teacher-led yet student-centered learning environment, going from "entering the *way*" to "transcending the *way*," could provide useful guidance for other regions worldwide. Whether we could attribute these to Confucianism is a separate issue. Although, as mentioned above, these good practices may not be easily transferrable, just as the Chinese maxim goes, "Those stones from other hills can be used to polish the jade,"[83] it is hopful that by studying these practices, educators in other places can reflects on their own culture, understand themselves better, and build capacity to move forward in their own way. Again, by doing so, it is very likely to not just get the stone from the other hill, but use these stones to polish their own jade, so to speak.

Conclusion

Introduction

As stated in the preface, the central aim of Confucianism is to look for ways of transforming oneself to become a better person. Doctrines about the attributes of human nature, the role of virtues, and the relationship between Heaven and humans serve primarily as the theoretical ground for this aim. In this sense, Confucianism is not (merely) a descriptive set of philosophical theories on the cosmos, on human beings, on morals, and the like. Rather, it is more appropriate to characterize it as a "teaching" (*jiao* 教). To quote the Contemporary Neo-Confucian MOU Zongsan's words, "Teaching is that can adequately inspire the reason of humans and guide humans for purification of life to the fullest extent through practice."[1] Religions and some schools of philosophy which possess this quality can also be viewed as a teaching.[2] Confucianism, specifically speaking, is a teaching of accomplishing morals (*chengdezhijiao* 成德之教). The most important ethical concern for Confucians is the practical question of how to accomplish sagehood.

Ways through which one endeavors so as to perfect oneself are called *gongfu* (工夫). Starting from Confucius, and throughout the different periods of the development of Confucianism, *gongfu* has undergone flourishing discussions. Mou says, "From the establishment of Confucianism by Confucius and Mencius, speaking of substance (*ti* 體) (fundamental principles in moral philosophy) must entail speaking of *gongfu*. This means that substance is confirmed by *gongfu*. Speaking of *gongfu* must presuppose substance, which means that *gongfu* is led by substance."[3] Acknowledging the importance of *gongfu*, expositions about substance and *gongfu* in Confucian ethics have been adequately made in the previous chapters where Confucianism in general and some Confucian thinkers in particular are introduced. However, it would be helpful to understand Confucian ethics thoroughly if *gongfu* is independently discussed.

Gongfu on different levels of Confucian ethics

In the preface, four levels of Confucian ethics have been introduced to avoid confusions in making arguments. Similarly, it is beneficial to examine *gongfu* on each level for the sake of clarity.

1. The level of heart-mind

The practice of *gongfu* on this level aims at fully activating the heart-mind of *ren*. The advocates of "overcoming the self" (*Analects*, 12.1), "cultivating oneself" (*Analects*, 14.42), "extending one's concern to others" (*Analects*, 4.15; 6.30) by Confucius, "reflecting" (*Mencius*, 6A15), "cultivating the flood-like *qi* (*Mencius*, 2A2), "extending *liangzhi*" (*Mencius*, 7A15), "extending from whom one loves to whom one doesn't" (*Mencius*, 7B1), "nurturing the parts of greater importance" (*Mencius*, 6A14), "going after the strayed mind" (*Mencius*, 6A11) by Mencius are descriptions of different paths of *gongfu*, which are unexceptionally presupposing the autonomy of the heart-mind. Therefore one is not required to utilize resources from outside. He or she only needs to rediscover the heart-mind and fully activate it. This tradition of early Confucianism is inherited by Song and Ming Confucians. CHENG Hao is a representative figure among them. For Cheng, the *gongfu* lies in "exhausting the Principle," "actualizing the human nature," and "activating the heart-mind." As elaborated in ch. 13, exhausting the Principle is not a cognitive act, nor the Principle an objective law of nature. Rather, by fully activating the heart-mind, the Principle is exhausted. It is not necessary to obtain knowledge of principles of myriad things in order to fully activate one's heart-mind. Apart from this path, with perfect sincerity one can take part in the cultivation of Heaven and Earth and thus can achieve the state of being united with Heaven (ch. 5, 13).

2. The level of ethical virtues and moral maxims

Numerous ethical virtues, including those moral and non-moral, and moral maxims are commended in the Confucian ethical system. They themselves and the ways of performing them are inevitably "thick" guidance embedded with cultural factors and therefore they are valid only relative to particular times and environments. Nevertheless, the normativity they possess does not borrow from any arbitrary authority of the outer (e.g., political) or inner (e.g., psychological) world. They are generated from the heart-mind and their validity and appropriateness corresponding to the particular context can also be examined by the heart-mind. These virtues and maxims are necessary to shape one's character so that he or she will do a morally good act spontaneously when it is called for. When the heart-mind is activated, one is able to "read" the relevant particulars of the situation and observe the most suitable virtues and maxims in such context.

On this level, therefore, the *gongfu* would be the cultivation of virtues. Take *ren* as an example. On the first level, it is the heart-mind of *ren* that makes the moral decision. More precisely, the emergence of the heart-mind of *ren* defines what is good in the particular situation. However, on the second level, the virtue of *ren* demands one to activate the ability of transference. Then one will choose an act which brings forth the satisfactions of oneself and those of others impartially. In order to activate transference some *gongfu* can be done. Sharpening the sensitivity to perceive others' joy or suffering by putting oneself into others' shoes is one of the relevant practices. Moreover, as Mencius suggests, reducing one's desires would also contribute to cultivating the heart-mind.

3. The level of institutional moral norms

Moral norms as one kind of social norms are employed in the socio-political realm. They possess the authority from the ruling system of the institution or society, therefore, they are empowered with some mechanism that guarantees the observance by the members. Strictly speaking, norms in this realm deviate from the autonomous nature of Confucian ethics, especially if they become coercive. Although norms in this realm have a tendency to fall outside the realm of ethics and become social requirements, some work could be done to prevent them becoming harmful. The work to be done will be twofold: for the ruler, and for the ordinary people being ruled. For the former, they should have trust in the human nature of the people and remind them of their own nature by way of education.[4] In addition, they should cultivate the virtues of the people. The ruler should try his or her best not letting the normative power of morality be replaced by that of the legal system.[5] All in all, they should bring the people, sometimes through following norms, back to the second level and first level. However, this task presupposes the moral cultivation of the ruler himself or herself so that he or she would not take these norms to serve his or her own interests. This is the *gongfu* of the ruler. As regards the ordinary people, the *gongfu* they should undertake is, given sets of moral norms, to reflect on their moral meaning and validity with their heart-mind when they act on them, rather than just follow them.

4. The level of customs and etiquette

Conventions expressed in the form of customs and etiquette are shaped and developed without the complete consciousness of humans. Although they have their own functions in specific times and environments, merely conforming to them has little ethical meaning. Hence, as with moral norms, one should return to the heart-mind of *ren* and *yi*. In this way the agent provides them the ethical status. LAO Siguang has concluded that the contribution of Confucius' thought to the ancient Chinese ethics is the idea of "bring *li* back to *yi*" and "bring *li* back to *ren*."[6] *Li*, no matter whether it reads as moral virtues or as etiquette, has to return to *ren* and *yi* to attain its ethical validity. The *gongfu* that one needs to do on this level is similar to the third level, though the object of reflection is different. Apart from this, one should practice the etiquette, which have ethical meanings sincerely in the daily life so as to reduce the inclination of deviating from them because of weakness of will. Consequently the practice will cultivate a personality helpful for the heart-mind to emerge in an ethical situation. This is among the implications of "overcoming the self and returning to *li*" (*Analects*, 12.1).

Mou Zongsan on *gongfu*

In the development of Confucianism throughout the centuries, theories of *gongfu* have been profusely discussed, particularly in the Song and Ming dynasties. Instances of these theories can be found in the chapters where the Cheng Brothers' thoughts are introduced. It would be illuminating to learn how Mou, as a Contemporary Neo-Confucian philosopher, concludes the most significant ways to sagehood among the diverse paths brought about by his predecessors.

Confirmation by transcending reflection (going against the flow)

The most important *gongfu* in Confucianism is to rediscover the heart-mind of *ren*. Since the heart-mind of *ren* is the transcendental ground of morality (as well as non-morality, ch. 2), one should firstly recognize he or she possesses the heart-mind. Here, to recognize does not mean to know in a cognitive sense. Nor is it meant to provide knowledge of the empirical world. It is only an awareness of the distinctive moral ability endowed in human beings. The way of attaining this awareness is by transcending reflection, rather than through sensations. As the awareness is going against, then transcending, the flow of desires, it leads to the confirmation of the ability of self-determination.

According to Mou, there are two approaches to the confirmation by transcending reflection. One is called "inner confirmation" and the other is called "transcendent confirmation." Inner confirmation refers to the confirmation of the heart-mind in the reality at the moment it emerges.[7] If one is mindful enough, then he or she will discover the self-determining ability in the turbulent daily life. The awareness passes beyond the realm of below form and reaches the realm of above form. Mou describes this move as "heterogeneous." The attention and reflection are not towards the ever-changing feelings and emotions, but to the original heart-mind.[8] "Transcendent confirmation" refers to the confirmation of the heart-mind when one is disentangled from the reality, for example, in a meditation retreat. No matter which approach one takes, in the end when the heart-mind emerges, even though it is one aspect of the heart-mind, he or she can apprehend the whole heart-mind from this particular aspect.

Making the thought sincere and extending *liangzhi* (*chengyi zhizhi* 誠意致知)

Having confirmed the heart-mind in the realm of above form, one should employ it in the empirical world. The *gongfu* for making this possible is "making the thought sincere and extending *liangzhi*," to adopt WANG Yangming's term. Making the thought sincere, as interpreted by Mou, is "to transform purely those unreal and self-deceptive to something real, without a tiny bit of self-deception."[9] For extending *liangzhi*, it refers to the *gongfu* that leads to "avoid the blocking of *liangzhi* by personal desires and extend it to every single event."[10] When one is not self-deceptive, then he or she will confirm *liangzhi* as the transcendental ground of morality, and furthermore, will have trust in its unforbidden power of overcoming the desires. Consequently, *liangzhi* will be in charge at any time.

Transforming the personalities

Every human being possesses particular emotional dispositions, endowments, desires, skills, worries, and complaints, therefore he or she is inevitably influenced by them and cannot always do the right act. Mou maintains that the emotional dispositions and the others themselves are not evil, only when one indulges in them would something evil occur. He says, "The good and the bad are two sides of emotional dispositions, endowments, desires, skills, worries and complaints. Whether they are good or bad all depends on their being indulged or not. If the heart-mind stands mighty, then they can be used appropriately and be transformed to the good side."[11] Understood as such, emotional dispositions, endowments, desires, skills, worries, and complaints should not be abandoned or suppressed. Moreover, Mou proposes that making good use of these endowed personalities would help to promote the beauty of life. However, one should transform the unbalanced or sluggish (slow) personalities so as to render the flow of life smooth. Apparently it is one of the aims of the Confucian practical project since non-moral values contribute essentially to the forming of the perfect personality (ch. 2).

Going with the flow (*suibozhulang* 隨波逐浪)

In *Zongyong* it says, "*Dao* may not be left for an instant. If it could be left, it could not be *Dao*" (Zongyong, ch. 1). This is the Confucian position of the relationship between *Dao* and affairs which can be concluded as "through affairs render the prominent of *Dao*". Similarly, the ethical goodness also cannot leave daily life. Therefore, one important aspect of ethical practice is to make the ethical goodness prominent in ordinary life. Mou elaborates this as follows:

> What is meant by "affairs" are one's daily life involved, based on himself or herself, and the relevant events involved in that daily life. What is meant by "*Dao*" is the moral imperatives, moral law and both the substantial principle and the heavenly principle in the moral sense which becomes prominent through moral practice. Moral practice is done for the sake of one's own affairs. One's own affairs are natural and factual, and colorless. If moral practice is done for the sake of one's own affairs, then the principle of "ought" (*Dao*) goes beyond it, and good and bad, right and wrong become evident. The principle of "ought" guides, completes and stabilizes it. *Dao* also becomes prominent in its acts of guiding, completing and stabilizing the affairs. Undoubtedly *Dao* is human-centered and humanistic, and it is the one that moral practice has to make prominent. . . . Human-center is not centering at humans in reality, but taking the human affairs in reality as the starting point and practice point. The ground is *Dao*. *Dao* in the moral sense is manifesting through moral practice, for sure not leaving human affairs behind. Also, it cannot exist in any other place if human affairs are left behind. Nevertheless, it exists everywhere. Therefore, it "fully embodies in oneself and fully exists in heaven and earth", and through moral practice it becomes prominent. This is the "moral idealistic doctrine" of Confucians.[12]

The above idea can be considered an elaboration of the claim that "it is humans who are capable of broadening *Dao*" (*Analects*, 15.29). Having said this, it should also be admitted that *Dao* is capable of broadening humans as well. It is so when humans extend the *liangzhi* and when *Dao* fully emerges in every single affair, even in one's body, just as Mencius's illustration: "manifests in one's face, giving it a sleek appearance;

shows in one's back and extends to one's limbs, rendering their message intelligible without words" (*Mencius*, 6A21).

Even though *Dao* manifests itself in daily affairs like carrying water or cutting wood, it should be noted that the affairs of carrying water or cutting wood themselves are not *Dao*. Otherwise, *Dao* would decline into something sensible.[13] Therefore, to avoid this declination, one should pay more attention to the confirmation of *Dao* as well as the heart-mind by transcending reflection and extending *liangzhi*. The *gongfu* of going with the flow should be treated as an auxiliary path.

These four modalities of *gongfu* are not exhaustive, either in the tradition of Confucian ethics or those commended by Mou. Nevertheless, it is obvious that they belong to the different levels mentioned above. The first two modalities belong to the heart-mind level where the *gongfu* aims at rediscovering *Dao* (within a human's heart-mind) and fully activating the heart-mind. On the level of moral virtues and maxims, one of the aims of *gongfu* is to transform personalities and virtues and maxims play a significant role. On the level of customs and etiquette, with the *gongfu* of going with the flow, one can offer meanings for the etiquette in such a way that it is seen as a manifestation of *Dao*.

The above-mentioned *gongfu* is ways of practice for personal cultivation. However, for the institutional level, as Mou reflects, *gongfu* can be done in the formation of a political organization viewing from a macro-perspective. He elaborates in MOU (1988) that an objective normative system is necessary for a healthy society where its members can have space to devote themselves to personal practice.

> Hence a political organization is established for the actualization of objective values. It aims at fulfilling people's needs and nurturing them. It is organized in the form of roles and ranks which are finite. Each member in this finite organization is finite. Therefore the power of each member is also finite. The desire for power of the members in this organization can never arbitrarily expand without any limits. As this is finite, something transcending this finite being must be affirmed. What has transcended this finite being is the Principle (*Li* 理), which is the transcendent ideal. This is the root of education and the ground of morality. The transcendent ideal has to be affirmed if we want to speak of objective and independent education and moral academic culture. Both the finite and the transcendence of the finite are accomplished by the normative status of "*li* (禮)". *Li* (禮) implicitly establishes the roles and ranks whereas it explicitly establishes the transcendent ideal.[14]

It can be concluded that the *gongfu* on the institutional level is to affirm the transcendent ideal as the ground of establishment of a political system. In so doing, the limitation to power (for the ruler as well as the ruling ranks) has also been attributed. Moreover, *li* serves as a principle to ensure the execution of all ranks is within the limitation. This is the objective function of *li*, which itself is an objectification of the heart-mind. It should be noted that one of the distinctive features of Contemporary Neo-Confucian thought is the emphasis on the objective function of ruling principles and institutions.

The presupposition of *gongfu* and the limitation of moral achievement

In the above sections, it is shown that substantial weight has been given to *gongfu* in Confucian ethics. This supports the status of Confucianism as being a teaching. However, moral practice presupposes two assertions: 1.) Humans are rational beings, and are sentient beings as well. Therefore their acts are not always good since they could follow desires (or be blocked by other empirical hindrances) and get lost from what they should do. 2.) Humans have an ability to overcome desires and other emotions and can be self-determined. The first assertion is empirically evident whereas the second one is based on metaphysical theses (about the transcendental ground of morals), which can also be empirically confirmed. It would render the discussions of *gongfu* void if either one of the above presuppositions proves to be false. Apparently, both of them are adopted by Confucianism. Mencius has particularly made these explicit in the following passage:

> Mencius said, "The way the mouth is disposed towards tastes, the eyes towards colors, the ear towards sounds, the nose towards smells, and the four limbs towards ease is human nature, yet therein also lies the Decree. That is why the *junzi* does not describe it as nature. The way *ren* pertains to the relation between father and son, *yi* to the relation between prince and subject, *li* to the relation between guest and host, *zhi* to the good and wise man, the sage to the way of Heaven, is the Decree, but therein also lies human nature. That is why the *junzi* does not describe it as Decree."
>
> *Mencius*, 7B24

In the first part of the passage, Mencius holds that the fact that the mouth disposes towards good tastes, the eyes towards beautiful colors, the ear towards musical sounds, the nose towards fragrance, and the body towards comfort signifies the nature of sentient beings and this nature is also shared by animals (hereafter signified as "animal nature"). Although this fact is undeniable, whether one ought to satisfy these dispositions depends on the Decree that he or she obeys. Therefore being a fact itself (is) cannot justify the ought. Given that a *junzi* is a person who strives for transforming himself or herself from being a mere animal, he or she would not adopt this fact as human nature. This echoes the two presuppositions mentioned above.

In the second part of the passage, it is demonstrated that *ren*, *yi*, *li*, *zhi* are obligatory to be realized in various human relationships. However, there are limitations which hinder their full realization. Even though limitations exist from time to time, as a *junzi* he or she should still endeavor to perform them. He or she should not put major weight on the limitations or difficulties, but rather on the ability that generates this obligation. Hence a *junzi* would adopt this ability as nature (hereafter signified as human nature), which distinguishes humans from animals.

We can see that there are two kinds of constraints given to humans, both from the Decree. One is the ethical constraint made upon human desires, the other is in the form of fate. As a *junzi*, on the one hand, he or she is devoted to the ethical project to become a sage and is glad to put the constraint onto his or her own desires. On the other hand, he or she should learn to gladly accept the fate even if during the process it turns out that it is not so pleasant. What he or she can do is to keep on doing what he or she ought to do. Eventually it is not the result but the sincere commitment that counts.

Admittedly humans are sentient beings, and they need ethical constraints to regulate their acts. Nevertheless, for Confucianism, ethical constraints are not dictated by an outside authority (e.g., *Tian*) but by human nature itself. It is clear now in Mencius' thought that the two natures of humans together make ethical obligations possible and necessary. They also make *gongfu* significant. It is not suitable to attribute either optimism or pessimism to Confucianism. This is so not only because it provides a way for one to transcend from being an animal, but most importantly, it offers a choice for one to adopt his or her own nature.[15] It is understandable that sentient beings need *gongfu* to overcome desires, to strengthen the will in order to bring the "ought" to practice, for example, but few recognize that one also needs *gongfu* to become aware of his or her human nature. That is the *gongfu* on the first level which has been elaborated in detail.

Concluding remarks

Mou agrees with the ancient meaning of philosophy and philosopher in terms of *summom bonum* as described by Kant in *Critique of Practical Reason*[16]:

> For to be a teacher of wisdom would mean something more than to be a student, who has not yet progressed far enough to conduct himself, and even less anyone else, to so high an end; it would mean to be *a master of the knowledge of wisdom* [of *summum bonum*], which says more than a modest man would himself presume to claim. Philosophy as well as wisdom itself would always remain an ideal, which objectively is represented completely only in reason and which subjectively is only the goal for the person's unceasing endeavors. No one would be justified in professing to be in possession of it, under the assumed name of philosopher, unless he could show its infallible effect (in self-mastery and the unquestioned interest which he pre-eminently takes in the general good) on his own person as an example. This the ancients required as a condition for deserving that honorable title.[17]

For Mou, this meaning and requirement of a philosopher also applies to the idea of the sage in Chinese philosophy. We can re-write some of the sentences from the above passage as follows: "Sagehood would always remain an ideal, which is only the goal for the person's unceasing endeavors. No one would be justified in professing to be in possession of it, under the assumed name of sage, unless he could show its infallible effect (in self-mastery and the unquestioned interest which he pre-eminently takes in the general good) on his own person as an example. This the ancients required as a condition for deserving that honorable title." When being a sage remains an ideal, the state of sagehood is a vision. No one would be justified in professing to be in possession of it, therefore the endeavors would be unceasing. Yet with unceasing endeavors, once the agent confirms his or her human nature, which makes all the ethical accomplishments possible, then he or she attains the highest wisdom[18] and this in turn fulfills the condition of deserving that honorable title. This is why Confucianism is a teaching in which *gongfu* is the central concern.

Appendix

Can Two Levels of Moral Thinking Reconcile the Rivalry of Principled Ethics and Contextualism? —A Conversation between Winkler and Hare

The impotence of principled ethics

Traditional normative theories—essentially principled ethics—have been challenged for their impotence in providing guidance in a moral decision. The challenge is twofold: Firstly, there is skepticism that one can reach a moral judgment by reasoning deductively from general ethical principles; secondly, these theories are insensitive to and thus do not give due weight to the contextual variabilities in a specific situation. As E. Winkler illustrates, there is doubt about the **applicability** and **relevance** of general ethical theory.[1] The difficulty mentioned is more serious in applied ethics since the domain specificity specially required by applied ethics has been ignored by the traditional normative theories. Winkler points out that special ethics such as biomedical ethics, business ethics, and environmental ethics has been understood as a type of applied ethics which only requires an application of general ethical theories in making moral judgment. This fact leads special ethics in a wrong direction, under which no special principles or methods are needed.

> The basic philosophical conception of applied ethics has been that it is continuous with general ethical theory. Biomedical ethics, as a primary division to applied ethics, is not a special kind of ethics; it does not include any special principles or methods that are specific to the field of medicine and are not derivable from more general considerations. The practical field of medicine is governed by the same general normative principles and rules that hold good in other spheres of human life. If certain values and requirements are central to the practice of medicine, they will be explained and justified from the perspective of general moral theory.[2]

The traditional normative theories to which Winkler and anti-theorists refer, fall into two main categories: utilitarianism (i.e., "classical utilitarianism," to follow Winkler) and Kantianism. In Winkler's view, the mistake utilitarianism makes is based on its commitment to "a particularly uncompromising form of impartiality in ethics" which derives from the idea that equal weight has to be given to every human being.

Hence in making moral judgments it does not take into account the "commonly recognized contextual variabilities," the consideration of which might lead to a violation of such an impartiality.[3] Contrary to utilitarianism, common-sense morality accepts that one has special obligation to those one has special relationship with. Apart from the problem of impartiality, utilitarianism is criticized on the grounds that, in the pursuit of the greatest utility, it does not hesitate to sacrifice justice and human rights.

> Classical utilitarianism simply cannot properly recognize that factors of relationship, both personal and professional, as well as of rights and desert radically restrict or qualify the morally single-minded promotion of everyone's interest. Consequently, utilitarianism is blind to many forms of contextual variability in the weight of morally relevant considerations that commonsense morality embodies.[4]

Deontological theories like Kantianism also have a problem in accommodating the contextual variables in the force and import of moral principles, though in a different way. "Deontological reasons for action are commonly thought to owe their primary status as moral reasons to our nature as persons, not to circumstances or particular relationships."[5] Therefore, in case that there are moral reasons for and against an action, it is impossible to weigh them by the variations of context. Deontologism either fixes the weights of these reasons in a general context-independent way or determines their weights differently in different context by appealing to our intuition. Winkler claims, "Such resort to intuition, however, means abandoning any hope of systematically *explaining* the variable force of moral reasons or of offering any *method* of resolving conflicts about these variations."[6] On the other hand, if the weights are fixed independently of the context, then deontologism is committed to the denial of contextual variability of the kind in question.

Apart from the problem of accommodating contextual variability in making moral decisions, there is another problem for principled ethics: it is dubious that a moral judgment can be attained to guide an action simply by "applying" the principle to the specific situation. An alternative suggestion is that the **interpretation** of the situation should play an important role in the decision procedure.

The criticism of paradigm theory

In his paper "Moral Philosophy and Bioethics: Contextualism versus the Paradigm Theory" Winkler discusses at length the paradigm theory developed by Beauchamp and Childress. This paradigm theory comprises three main principles, namely, those of autonomy, beneficence (including non-maleficence), and justice. Since the aim of the paradigm theory is to tackle ethical problems in biomedical practice, it is domain-specific. The three principles are general and abstract but can nevertheless guide moral practice. As Winkler points out, the aim of the paradigm theory is to bridge the gap between principle and the actual case.

> The paradigm theory promises to bridge the logical chasm between the abstractions of normative theory—principally utilitarianism and Kantianism—and the moral complexities of the world of medical particulars. For on the one hand, its three

> mid-level principles are articulated and explained in relation to medical practice ... The paradigm theory thus appears to provide enough substance to guide practice. On the other hand, it keeps faith with the ideal of comprehensive justification because each of its principles is linked with one or another of our central traditions in normative theory.[7]

However, Winkler criticizes the paradigm theory for a serious limitation in solving moral problems in the field of medicine. First of all, the paradigm theory does not provide an account of what constitutes moral status. Since moral status is a fundamental issue in many areas of bioethical decision making,[8] the omission of such an account makes the theory useless in these areas. Secondly, although the principles in the paradigm theory are domain-specific and thus more specific than the traditional normative theories, they will be applied to different situations with equal force. Attention has not been adequately paid to the contextual variation which might affect the moral force of the principle.

It can be agreed that the problem with the paradigm theory is the same as with the traditional normative theories, though perhaps in a weaker degree. It arises from the nature of generality of principle, and this in turn leads to the problem of the top-down process of application and justification. The latter problem can be viewed as constituting the central issue in the debate between principled ethics and contextualism in ethics in general, as well as in bioethics in particular. The point of issue is summarized by L.W. Sumner and J. Boyle as follows:

> Generalists about bioethics support an essential justificatory or deliberative role for ethical principles or theories. At their most ambitious, they argue that we need to suscribe to the best normative theory in order to do bioethics successfully. Moral justification or deliberation then operates in a "top-down" manner—that is, from general principles to particular cases. One problem with this approach is that generalists have not managed to agree on which normative theory is the best, some defending consequentialism while others affiliate with one or another version of deontology or virtue theory. Another problem is that the rarefied abstractions of any such theory seem to do little real work in resolving the concrete problems of particular patients and institutions.
>
> Particularists have reacted to these problems by advocating a rival "bottom-up" approach. On this way of thinking we begin by working with, and attempting to resolve, particular cases in all of their contextual detail.[9]

In the following section I shall examine whether contextualism, as a rival of principled ethics, is able to provide a vital methodology in respect of guiding and justifying moral decisions.

An examination of contextualism

If the traditional normative theories and the paradigm theory are described as adopting a top-down process, contextualism can suitably be described as bottom-up oriented.

Contextualism holds that "moral problems must be resolved within the interpretive complexities of concrete circumstances, by appeal to relevant historical and cultural traditions, with reference to critical institutional and professional norms and virtues, and by relying primarily on the method of comparative case analysis."[10] Since the decision made does not involve the application of general moral principles, it can avoid the difficulty arising from the gap between principle and specific case. By the same token, since it does not borrow any guidance from principle, it remains a question as what resources to make use of in making moral judgments. Furthermore, without appealing to principles, we have to find some other way to decide whether differences between situations are morally relevant. It seems that while it accuses principled ethics of its inability to guide moral decision, contextualism itself cannot provide any guidance. The method of interpreting and comparing cases itself cannot resolve moral issues. As Sumner and Boyle query, "How can we be confident that our 'resolutions' of these cases are anything more than a reflection of our initial biases?"[11]

Some clarification is needed for answering this question. Firstly, contextualism does not belong to a radical form of anti-theory in which no principles are admitted into the process of moral deliberation. Rather, its bottom-up approach leads to the adoption of principles. What it suggests is, by accumulating agreement around cases we can reason our way "analogically" toward some modest principles.[12] Consequently, the principles and rules thus arrived at are domain sensitive in a sense that "the weight and import of many rules and morally relevant considerations may vary across domains and contexts."[13] Secondly, contextualism merely rejects the deductivist approach of principled ethics and the invariable weight of principles it claims to have. By contrast, contextualism emphasizes the relative importance of inductive method in moral reasoning.[14] However, how to resolve moral issues by employing the inductive method mentioned above remains a problem, as does the introduction of interpretation and comparison of cases.

Universality, specificity and generality

With respect to the rival views of principled ethics and contextualism, Hare thinks that both theories have grasped the truth, but only part of it. For instance, contextualism has hold of an important truth, that one has to judge each situation on its own merit.[15] But if contextualism persists in asserting that in morals one cannot appeal to general principles, then it is mistaken. It is important here to note the distinction between universality and generality made by R.M. Hare. Universality contrasts with particularity, whereas generality contrasts with specificity. According to Hare, it is possible for a moral judgment to be universal and at the same time highly specific. The specificity thus meets the requirement made by contextualism that every detail in the context has to be recognized and accommodated. A specific judgment can be universal if and only if one is ready to apply it to the similar case where the situation is exactly the same except that the roles in it are reversed. This similar case need not be a real one, it may only exist hypothetically. Given this conception of universality, it would be a confusion either to deny that a specific moral judgment can be universal (i.e., it is valid only for the particular situation in which it is made) or to think that a universal judgment has to be very general (and thus neglect the contextual details which might affect the judgment).

> The confusion between universality and generality, which I have been exposing, leads people to think that if one makes a universal judgment about a situation, one must be making a very general judgment about it. This is not so. The judgment can be specific enough to take in any details of the situation that anybody thinks relevant. Only a victim of the confusion I have been exposing will think that a statement cannot at the same time be universal and highly specific.[16]

It can be seen from Winkler's perception of contextualism and criticism of traditional normative theory in the following passage, that he falls victim to the confusion described by Hare.

> Contextualism, by contrast, is sceptical about the very possibility of any complete, universally valid ethical theory that is even remotely adequate to the moral life. This scepticism springs from the sense that whatever appearance of universality is achieved by general normative theory is necessarily purchased at the price of separating thought about morality from the historical and sociological realities, traditions, and practices of particular cultures. The result of this separation is a level of abstraction and ahistoricism that makes traditional ethical theory virtually useless in guiding moral decision making about real problems in specific social settings.[17]

However, the problem as it appears to contextualism is that, granted that it admits a specific moral judgment can be universal in Hare's sense, it remains dubious that whether, and how, it can apply to other similar cases. It is commonly agreed that for a principle to have guiding force, it should have a certain degree of generality. Therefore the skepticism here is about the **generality** of moral principles. The questions concerned are: 1. "Do general moral principles have a role to play in moral decision?" and 2. "Is it the case that we only need to make specific moral judgments by studying the actual case and no generalization should be made, as what situation ethics maintains?" If one gives a positive answer to the latter question, then one has to face the criticism which has been addressed to contextualism in the last section. On the other hand, if one claims that the general moral principles definitely play an important role in making moral decision, one should be able to defend principled ethics against the attack from contextualism.

While Hare admits that we may consider each situation on its merits and make moral judgments upon such consideration, he is aware of the problem of contextualism.

> ... they [the situation ethicists] do not say how we are to judge the merits or situations. In default of some *method* for judging, everybody will be at liberty to say what they feel like saying.[18]

In order to ensure a moral judgment to be non-arbitrary, one has to give some reasons and these reasons have to be universal. Hence, in making a moral judgment for a particular case, one is at the same time endorsing a universal moral principle, though the latter may be a specific one.

> It is hard to see any method for judging situations can get far without giving *reasons* for judging them one way rather than another. And any statement of the reasons is bound to bring in principles—not the very simple general principles that the situation ethicists so dislike, but universal principles all the same. If it is a reason for banning a drug from public sale that it could endanger life, then that is because of a principle that drugs which endanger life ought not to be on public sale. Of course reasons can be much more complicated than that; but they will have to state certain *features* of situations which make it right to do this or that; and these features will always have to be described in universal (though not always highly general) terms.[19]

In short, Hare argues that even though contextualism puts the emphasis on the contextual variability of the situation, the moral judgment so made has to be a universal one, as far as it is qualified as a "moral" judgment. The universality is embodied in the features which the judgment singles out as reasons. However, there must be some method for selecting certain features of the situation from among the others, as the relevant features. Therefore, contextualism, in order to be an acceptable ethical theory, has to offer a method for deciding moral relevance.

As stated above, a principle formulating moral reasons for an act can be as specific as one wants. When a highly specific principle is formed in this way, it is only valid for that particular situation and situations similar in relevant respects. For any other situations which do not contain those features, the principle is inapplicable. Nevertheless, even a principle which is so specific that no similar cases would exist in the actual world is universal. However, this kind of principle would be the object of another criticism made by contextualism: it cannot guide moral decision. It is because in order to apply to other situations in the future, guidelines have to be to some degree general.

> We have, indeed, to look carefully at particular cases; but after we have done that we shall want to learn from these cases principles that we can apply to other cases. Cases differ from one another, no doubt; but that does not mean that we cannot learn from experience. The salient reasons for one decision may also be important for another decision. So, while avoiding oversimplification and too rigid general rules, we can still, and good medical practitioners do, form for ourselves and others general guidelines for the future. These guidelines have to be to some degree general, or they will apply to only one situation, and be useless for preserving the lessons of experience for later situations.[20]

Before affirming that general principles are able to provide guidelines for the future decision, it should be agreed in the first place that we need general principles to guide our acts. Given that we can, and should make specific judgment after considering the situation on its own merits, as contextualism urges, why do we still need general principles? In answering this, Hare gives the following reasons. First, a general principle can help us to cope with moral issues in the world. Moral judgment we made in the past can apply to future cases which have certain salient features in common and thus can serve as a practical guide. In other words, following principles would give us the best chance to act rightly.[21] This is a fact that Hare thinks situation ethics overlooks.

> What is wrong about situation ethics and certain extreme forms of existentialism ... is that they make impossible what is in fact an indispensable help in coping with the world (whether we are speaking of moral decisions or of prudential or technical ones, which in this are similar), namely the formation in ourselves of relatively simple reaction-patterns ... which prepare us to meet new contingencies resembling in their important features contingencies in which we have found ourselves in the past.[22]

Second, Hare points out that we, as human beings with more or less dominant desires and interest, always have a temptation to "cook" our moral thinking so as to make a judgment which suits our own interest. If we have general principles or intuitions firmly built into our characters and motivations, it is easier to overcome such temptation.[23] These are practical and psychological reasons for us to learn general moral principles. Surprisingly, Winkler, being a proponent of contextualism, also conceives contextualism as a kind of socially embedded rule-utilitarianism, which emphasizes the importance of moral rules that guide social interactions and relationships within social contexts.[24]

Although Hare and Winkler have different understanding and evaluation of principled ethics and contextualism, they both admit that general moral principles are indispensable. They also recognize, with different weight, that contextual details should be considered carefully so that we can sort out the morally relevant features and decide whether they would fall under a certain principle. Now the problems remaining seem to be these: "How to reconcile the conflict between these two theories?" and "How do they defend themselves from the attack of their rival theory?"

Two levels of moral thinking

As mentioned above, Hare thinks that contextualism has grasped an obvious truth that two similar situations may be in some important respects different.

> The situations in which we find ourselves are like one another, sometimes, in some important respects, but not like one another in all respects; and the differences may be important too.[25]

Therefore, from the point of view of contextualism, principled ethics cannot recognize these different respects thus should be rejected. But according to Hare, this is a mistaken view in that it ignores another obvious truth that some situations are similar in some morally relevant respects, and also in that it holds that these two truths are incompatible. Hare conceives that this mistake arises from failing to make the distinction between two levels of moral thinking, namely, intuitive level of moral thinking and critical level of moral thinking. Since Hare has expounded these two levels of moral thinking in great detail in his book *Moral Thinking*, I will only summarize his idea briefly here. The intuitive level is the day-to-day level at which most of us do most of our moral thinking. General principles are used at this level to help us solving moral problems. If we have absorbed certain principles and acquired certain virtues, we "will have the corresponding intuitions about right and wrong, good and bad, and will also, unless overcome by temptations, follow the principles and display the virtues in practice."[26] Nevertheless, these principles are neither self-evident nor self-supporting, they are only implanted in us by our upbringing and education. Moreover, there are always cases where these principles are in conflict. In order to resolve moral conflicts and justify our moral principles, we have to turn to the critical level of moral thinking.

At the critical level, we are going to make moral judgments by critical moral reasoning. As Hare puts it, "Critical thinking consists in making a choice under the constraint imposed by the logical properties of the moral concepts and by the non-moral facts",[27] the choice mentioned is a decision of principles. Hare's account of the method of moral reasoning at the critical level "draws heavily on both the utilitarians and Kant and is based on an analysis of moral language and its moral properties."[28] Hare admits that his account on how we have to reason remains a matter for dispute, which we shall not deal with here. His method of moral reasoning at the critical level is that, by employing the principle of utility, we can detect the right one among the conflicting moral judgments in a specific situation; or, we can discover other judgment beyond those conflicting. In the latter case, the new judgment is an improved one in a sense that it is more specific. Furthermore, it can be justified. Apart from resolving moral conflicts, by critical thinking we can also select the best set of prima facie principles which would most likely produce optimific results in the usual cases in the actual world as it is. Optimific results are those which would be chosen if we were able to use critical thinking all the time.

In short, at the critical level, we may form principles (which are universal) as specific as required to deal with any individual cases. And for the reason stated above, we also select principles of a certain generality for use at the intuitive level. At the intuitive level, we only need to pick out some features of a situation as morally relevant. These morally relevant features constitute the essential descriptive content of a general moral principle. That means that when we select a prima facie principle, we at the same time decide the relevant features. Our critical thinking is equipped to do both of these jobs. The prima facie principles thus selected will be justified by the principle of utility and the requirement of universality.

> The critical level of moral thinking is used, not only to settle conflicts between intuitions at the intuitive level, but to select the moral principles and . . . the virtues that we should seek to cultivate in our children and ourselves. On my own account of critical thinking, the selection is done by assessing the acceptance utility of the virtues and principles—that is, by asking what are on the whole the best for society to acknowledge and cultivate . . . If the critical thinking has been well done, and if, therefore, the right virtues and principles have been chosen, the person who has them will be a person of good character, that is, a morally good person.[29]

It seems that the two-level structure of moral thinking introduced by Hare can reconcile the rivalry of principled ethics and contextualism. It can accommodate both the contextual variability emphasized by the latter at the critical level and the general principles employed by the former at the intuitive level. Finally, Hare is able to evaluate contextualist theories by applying the distinction between these two levels.

> It is obvious that a distinction between levels can explain what is right and what is wrong about such a theory. Taken literally, the theory would require us to use critical thinking in all our moral decisions however straightforward. But usually we do not have time for this, nor always the necessary information about the consequences of alternative actions. We are also affected by personal bias, which, in spite of what some of the people I have discussed say, is often a source of wrong decisions.
>
> So the sensible thing to do is to form for ourselves principles and cultivate virtues, which in the general run of straightforward cases will lead us to do the right thing without much thought, and reserve our powers of deep thought for the awkward cases … When we do this critical thinking, we have to consider each situation on its merits and in detail, as the situation ethicists say we should. But it would be absurd and impracticable to do this on every occasion.[30]

The division of labor between general prima facie principles and contextual reasoning in making moral judgment is analogical to that between rule-utilitarianism and act-utilitarianism, with its two-level structure. Therefore it is useful here to quote Hare's discussion of the two kinds of utilitarianism.

> Much of the controversy about act-utilitarianism and rule-utilitarianism has been conducted in terms which ignore the difference between the critical and intuitive levels of moral thinking. Once the levels are distinguished, a form of utilitarianism becomes available which combines the merits of both varieties. The conformity (for the most part) to received opinion which rule-utilitarianism is designed to provide is provided by the prima facie principles used at the intuitive level; but critical moral thinking, which selects these principles and adjudicates between them in cases of conflict, is act-utilitarian in that, in considering cases, actual or hypothetical, it can be completely specific, leaving out no feature of an act that could be alleged to be relevant. But since, although quite specific, it takes no cognizance of individual identities, it is also rule-utilitarian in that version of the rule-utilitarian doctrine which allows its rules to be of unlimited specificity, and which therefore is in effect not distinguishable from act-utilitarianism. The two kinds of utilitarianism, therefore, can coexist at their respective levels: the critical thinker considers cases in an act-utilitarian or specific rule-utilitarian way, and on the basis of these he selects … general prima facie principles for use, in a general rule-utilitarian way, at the intuitive level.[31]

The two kinds of utilitarianism, as Hare conceives them, can coexist and have specific roles to play at different levels. Similarly, principled ethics and contextualism can also coexist as different but complementary ways of moral reasoning. With the distinction of levels of thinking, Hare accommodates the merits of each theory. Furthermore, on Hare's account, it is noticeable that an aspect of a theory which is considered as a merit at one of the two levels, will become a problem if it is still emphasized at another level.

By the two-level moral thinking, the problem of utilitarianism raised by Winkler can be resolved. As mentioned in the first section, utilitarianism is accused of committing the uncompromising form of impartiality in ethics and thus violates the commonly acceptable partial behavior, e.g., a mother should give priority to the needs of her own children over those of other people's children. However, Hare thinks that partial principles can be adopted at the intuitive level and can also be justified by impartial thinking at the critical level. Importantly, impartial critical thinking will also prescribe partial principles to use at the intuitive level.

> If we were concerned impartially for the good of all children, we should want mothers to behave partially toward their own children and have feelings which made them behave in this way. We should want this, because if mothers are like this, children will be better looked after than if mothers tried to feel the same about other people's children as about their own. The same applies to doctors and nurses. Thus, impartial critical thinking will tell us to cultivate partial virtues and principles. But it will also tell us to cultivate impartiality for certain roles and situations. These obviously include that of judges, but also those of anybody who has to distribute benefits and harms fairly, as doctors do when they have to divide scarce resources between their patients.[32]

The two-level structure of moral thinking seems not merely able to reconcile the rivalry of principled ethics and contextualism, it can also solve the conflicting views of top-down and bottom-up approach. I shall discuss this in the next section.

The dynamics of particular judgment and general principle

The dispute of the top-down approach versus the bottom-up approach is partly due to the different weight put on general principles by the theories in question. Most importantly, the debate is over the way by which principles are produced. As I have pointed out above, even a contextualist like Winkler thinks that principles are indispensable. Moreover, Winkler claims that "contextualism's recognition of variable weight for moral considerations can be both principled and critical."[33] Nevertheless, contextualism maintains that the principles should be attained by the bottom-up approach, as contrast with traditional normative theory.

However, the dispute is expressed in a somewhat misleading form. It sounds as if we begin with nothing when we are doing contextual reasoning. As Sumner and Boyle describe, principles follow, not precede, the resolution of particular problems.

> On this way of thinking we begin by working with, and attempting to resolve, particular cases in all of their contextual detail. Once we have managed to settle

> some of these cases, then we can apply these results to other, similar, cases, gradually widening our network until larger patterns begin to form. Some of these patterns we might then codify as rules or guidelines, or even principles, but any such generalizations would follow, not precede, the resolution of particular problems.[34]

In fact, prior to the resolution of particular problems, principles, no matter in which ways they are achieved, have already existed. The denial of the possible contribution of principles in solving moral problems, makes the bottom-up process as well as the principles attained by this process redundant. If contextualism admits a certain degree of significance that principles have in making moral judgments, as it has been shown is the case, then the question is how these principles enter into the process. Here Winkler makes a sensible suggestion: we begin with conventional moral principles and norms unless the moral judgment derived from them is challenged by other principles or by other moral judgment derived from them.

> Contextualism thus begins with conventional morality and the norms and values that currently play justificatory roles in various domains of social life. These moral rules and values are presumed to be reasonable unless they can be shown to be unreasonable. Moral judgment is regarded as sufficiently justified by appeal to other moral beliefs or principles not challenged by the particular issue in question. Accordingly, relevant levels of theoretical reflection are determined by what is actually required to establish a judgment as most reasonable in the circumstances. Ultimately, contextualism tries to bring a case under a rule that can be shown to have, or properly presumed to have, instrumental validity for the social domain that contains the case.[35]

This shows the method of moral reasoning of one kind of contextualism that Winkler favors. In the above quotation, "levels of theoretical reflection" is mentioned. This way of thinking is coherent with Hare's two-level structure. In fact, the conventional morality and the norms and values are prima facie principles, in Hare's terminology. They apply at the intuitive level. Nevertheless in case of challenge or conflict, they have to be reviewed and modified when needed at the critical level. The "instrumental validity" mentioned also resembles the principle of utility which is used to justify and to select prima facie principles at the critical level. This resemblance is shown more clearly in the following passage where Winkler illustrates the instrumental validity more fully.

> The kind of contextualism I favour would seek to explain or justify such differences [variable weight for moral considerations] in instrumental terms; in terms, that is, of the basic purpose of given moral rules, or of their purpose in relation to the primary social functions and values that help to define different domains of social life—such as the family, the criminal justice system, the economic system, the medical system, and so on.[36]

In the same paper, Winkler explicitly discusses the view of two levels of moral thinking.

> By contrast, contextualism agrees with the view that a fundamental pattern of moral reasoning consists of appeals to moral rules that combine instrumental validity at one level with deontological force at another. What contextualism adds to this perception is the idea that the instrumental justification of rules and standards may be domain sensitive. In consequence, the weight and import of many rules and morally relevant considerations may vary across domains and contexts. In so far as governing purposes and values associated with various domains are reasonable, however, these variations will be essentially systematic and explainable. It is these basic theoretical features of contextualism, together with its thoroughly bottom-up and socially embedded orientation to moral problems themselves, that give this approach considerable power and relevance to applied ethics.[37]

It is quite clear that Winkler and Hare have a common view on the two-level thinking structure, even the domain sensitivity which contextualism emphasizes is accepted by and incorporated into Hare's structure. On the other hand, it is agreed that contextualism of this kind is, as Winkler puts it, a socially embedded rule-utilitarianism. The sort of rule-utilitarianism Winkler rejects is the one which focuses on impartial aggregation over individual utilities and leaves no room for contextual variations. But that is a principle used at the intuitive level and thus considered by Hare only as a prima facie principle. According to Hare, there is plenty of room at the critical level for the principle of utility to produce, review, and modify moral rules so as to guarantee their instrumental validity.

Now let us return to the point of issue between the two approaches. Once the distinction between two levels has been made, the issue loses much of its significance even if it cannot be totally dismissed. The bottom-up approach as commended strongly by contextualism involves inductive reasoning such as comparison of relevant cases and generalization of particular judgments. Above all, interpretation of cases and that of principles is most important in this process.

> It is largely from a close comparison of relevant cases that we discover, or invent, more determinate meanings for the often conflicting values and principles that give situated moral problems their basic shape.[38]

As illustrated above, in making moral decision in a particular situation we start with conventional moral principles and norms until we are challenged. Then we will move to critical level of moral thinking. At the critical level, any method, including the comparison of cases, collection of relevant information concerning the individual interest group, analogy of similar cases, etc., will be used. Even in a normal case where no controversy arises, interpretation of the moral issue would come into the process prior to the introduction of any principles. Intuitive thinking does not imply a blind application of principles. However, a reinterpretation is necessary when critical thinking is called for.

At the end of his paper, Winkler sums up the view of contextualism:

> All that contextualism need insist upon is our recognizing that, in confrontation with real moral problems, the deductive construction of moral explanation and

> justification is retrospective. In a far more important, essential, and primary sense, justification is a *process*. It is the process, in all of its interpretive and analogical complexity, of arriving at a considered moral judgment and defending it as a reasonable alternative within the context of the problem.[39]

If this really grasps the important aspects of contextualism, then contextualism is not in conflict with principled ethics, given the roles they play are at the right level as proposed by Hare.

The two levels of moral thinking in practice

As explained above, in Hare's two-level structure, we use general moral principles at the intuitive level to deal with uncontroversial cases. Since they are selected by the principle of utility, then it would be for the best of the society if everybody follows such principles. On the other hand, we should tackle unusual or extraordinary cases by critical reasoning and might arrive at some highly specific but still universal judgments. The distinction of the two levels not only preserves the function of our well-established principles and intuition but also provides the justification for them on the one hand, and reserves the room for their reformation on the other. Therefore this distinction appears fruitful at the level of theory. However, there may be some problems in practice.

The first problem is how to decide that the "extraordinary" case is extraordinary enough to be considered at the level of critical thinking? Hare insists that not only the principles, but also the moral feeling involved should be cultivated in us so that we would not cook the situation for our own interest. This is the positive side of moral feeling. Nevertheless, if the feeling is strong enough to overcome the temptation, it might also result in resistance to reflecting on cases that should be considered as departing from the generally accepted principles. Hare admits that in cases of challenge or conflict, we should bring the case to critical thinking level. But a person with good training and education from his or her upbringing, which has formed a good character, cannot easily be brought to discover that his or her principles are being challenged. He or she may see the alternative views as brought out by someone who lacks moral sense. By taking the issue of euthanasia as an instance, Hare illustrates the dilemma.

> Medical people often say, "Our whole training and our attitudes are directed towards the saving of life; how can you ask us to kill people?" Here it is a question of the attitudes that we think doctors ought to have in general; it is certainly true that unless, in general, a doctor is devoted to the saving of life, he is likely to be a bad doctor. So if a doctor is asked to end a patient's life, or even (though this is not euthanasia strictly speaking) to refrain from saving the life of a patient whom it is far better to let die, he will, if he is a good doctor, feel the greatest reluctance; to do either of these things goes against the grain— the "grain" being his training as a doctor in the saving of life.[40]

Hare argues that despite the reluctance the doctor feels, he or she should overcome it provided he or she is certain that is a right act to do.

> If the advocates of euthanasia or of letting people die in certain cases are right, the doctor ought to overcome this reluctance, provided that he is certain that this is a case in which the patient will be better off dead.[41]

How can the doctor be certain that it is a right thing to end the patient's life? If we ascend to the critical level and appeal to the principle of utility, then we should investigate the case in close detail. Consequently we may reach a conclusion about the right act, which can "serve the interests of all the parties affected by our own action, treating the equal interests of each of them as of equal weight".[42] In doing this, the degree of the suffering of the patient has to outweigh the aversion of the doctor, as well as the unpredictable influence on society as a whole. Hare is aware of the danger of departing from the general principles and warns us:

> But there is a practical danger that, if it is overcome in these particular cases, this will lead to a general change of attitude on the part of doctors and perhaps also of patients; doctors will stop being thought of, and will stop thinking of themselves, as devoted to the saving of life, and will come instead to be thought of as devoted to doing what *they* think is best for the patient or even for people in general, even if it involves killing him, and this development might not be, taken all in all, for the best.[43]

It seems that until we have a strong case where the advantage and disadvantage are very clear, we do not bother to consider it as a special case. This may result in an insensitive response to the current issue.

The second problem is, when should the conclusion of reflections on extraordinary cases contribute to the change of established principles? Hare indicates that extraordinary cases should be dealt with at the critical level. After going into the case in detail, we can decide what ought to be done in these precise circumstances. Then we shall end up with a very specific and sometimes fantastic principle which, Hare claims, will not be used at the intuitive level.

> ... when we are doing the selection, we ought not to pay too much attention to particular cases, actual or hypothetical, which are not at all usual or which are unlikely to recur. For we are selecting our principles as practical guides in the world as it actually is, and not as it would be if it were composed of incidents out of short stories, or out of philosophers' examples. So it makes a difference if, for example, the number of people who die in agony of terminal cancer either is very small, or would be very small if proper care were taken of them. This is the point of the maxim that hard cases make bad law.[44]

Certainly what doctors and ordinary people need is general principles which give guidance in the ordinary cases. If the specific principles generated from the special case cannot be guidance, what kind of general principles do we want for our ordinary life?

Here the consideration for a rule-utilitarian would be: What is the best attitude for doctors to adopt to this kind of question?

> But at any rate we seem to have reached a point in the argument at which we can investigate, with some hope of discovering the answer, what is the best attitude for doctors to adopt to this kind of question. For we can ask what it would be like, in hospitals and in the homes of dying patients, if one attitude or the other were adopted, and which would be the better state of affairs. So the philosophical exercise would have resulted, as all good philosophy should, in returning the problem to the non-philosopher for further investigation, but in a form in which it is better understood, clearer, and therefore easier of solution.[45]

Practically, it is not easy to decide whether the benefit of the new principles outweighs the negative impact to the public. Besides, to shift the problem from philosophical to non-philosophical admits that philosophy lacks the resources to solve this kind of problem. On the contrary, I think that the answer should depend on whether the judgment is a right one, and this is indisputably a philosophical question. If we are certain that the specific principle we formulate for the extraordinary case is right, we should imagine possible similar cases to which this principle can apply (perhaps with slight modification) and then form more general principles accordingly. In addition, moral education should introduce and promote these new principles. As a result, general principles may in turn affect ordinary people's thinking and then make the principles appear not so fantastic. This would decrease the repugnant feeling of the public.

Hare's reason for resisting to accommodate the judgment of extraordinary case at the intuitive level is that they are rare cases.

> If we give weight to cases of precisely that type, we shall be more likely to adopt principles whose general adoption and preservation will lead to the best results, on the whole, for those who are affected by them.[46]

But if we believe that principles at the two levels are not fixed and static, and the relation between these two levels is dialectic in a sense that an important change at one level would ultimately result in an alteration at another, then our giving some weight to the rare case itself would promote the general acceptance of such fantastic judgment. Perhaps, the whole issue seems whether the philosophers are willing to take the leading position of reflection and reformation of old principles, or, to adopt the role of being driven by the majority of the existing society.

Notes

1 The Concept of Morality in Confucian Ethics

1 Lukes (1991).
2 Mackie (1977), 106.
3 Mackie (1977), 106.
4 *Xunzi*, 23. la. The translation is from Derk Bodde, in FUNG (1952), 286–7.
5 *Xunzi*, 19. la. FUNG (1952), 297.
6 See FUNG (1952), 287.
7 *Li Chi* [*Liji*], ch. l. The translation is from Bodde, see FUNG (1952), 339.
8 *Li Chi* [*Liji*], ch. 27. FUNG (1952), 339.
9 *Xunzi*, 19.7b. The translation is from Knoblock, Knoblock (1994), vol. 3, 68.
10 *Xunzi*, 2.2. The translation is from Bodde, Fung (1952), 298.
11 *Xunzi*, 19.5b. The translation is from Knoblock, see Knoblock (1994), vol. 3, 65. This idea can also be found in *Liji*, ch. 28.
12 *Xunzi*, 19.2c. The translation is from Knoblock, see Knoblock (1994), vol. 3, 60, with slight modification.
13 *Liji*, ch. 9. My translation.
14 *Liji*. The translation is from Bodde, see FUNG (1952), 338.
15 Only if *li* is conceived as mores or conventional rules, is it allowed to be outweighed. Besides, only if the satisfaction of needs has moral implications, can it override the conventional rules.
16 Other cases have been discussed by Mencius. See *Mencius*, 4A17 and 5A2. Interestingly, Mackie also holds that morality-n can possibly be overridden, cf. Mackie (1977), 106–7.
17 *Mencius*, 4B19.
18 There is a remarkable discussion in *Mencius*, 4A17.
19 All translations of the *Analects* and *Mencius* in this book are made by D.C. Lau, with slight modifications when needed (cf. D.C. Lau (trans) (1992), *The Analects*, Hong Kong: The Chinese University Press; D.C. Lau (trans) (1984), *Mencius*, v. 1–2, Hong Kong: The Chinese University Press).
20 *Ren* also has several meanings, see ch. 3, "Confucian Ethics: Universalistic or Particularistic."
21 See ch. 8, "Confucian Ethics and Virtue Ethics."

2 The Moral and Non-Moral Virtues in Confucian Ethics

1 Bernard Williams elaborates this view clearly in Williams (1985).
2 Williams (1985), 20.
3 Virtues that are beneficial for one to become an excellent person surely include the moral virtues, here non-moral virtues signify those virtues extra to the moral ones.
4 There are dramatic changes of views concerned particularly in Song Dynasty.

5 For example, in *Yi Zhou Shu* "nine kinds of virtues," "nine kinds of conduct," "nine kinds of thought," "five kinds of cultivation," and many other kinds of "*de*" have been mentioned See HUANG, ZHANG, and TIAN, 1995. Also cf. Shanghai Shifandaxue Guji Zhenglizu (ed.) (1978).
6 CHEN (2002), 269.
7 *li* is usually translated as "propriety," but it contains many more meanings than this (see ch. 3, "Confucian Ethics: Universalistic or Particularistic?") therefore here I also leave it untranslated.
8 See ch. 3, "Confucian Ethics: Universalistic or Particularistic?"
9 For the detailed exposition of the meanings of *ren* and *yi* as virtues, see the next section.
10 Similar meaning appears also in *Analects* 12.8.
11 "*Wen*" has been regarded as an important virtue which can be dated back to *Guoyu*. See *Guoyu*, vol. 3.
12 Also see the *Analects*, 9.11; 12.8; 1.6.
13 The question whether one ought to be responsible for one's own character is asked by Williams, see Williams (1985), 38. Confucianism would give a positive answer to this question since it is believed that people can, and should, transform their character.
14 Williams (1985), 6.
15 Although "*quan*" plays a significant role in ethical consideration in Confucianism (*Analects*, 9.30, *Mencius*, 7A26), I cannot elaborate this idea here. In short, "*quan*" refers to some discretionary weighing exercised in the cases where mere observance of norms might not be the right thing to do. For lengthy discussion, see ch. 4, "The Resolution of Moral Dilemma," and WONG (2005e).
16 Becker has also used "all things considered" to characterize a moral judgement which is similar to the "ethical decision" mentioned here. See Becker (1973).
17 *Mencius*, 4A17; 5A2.
18 Only when *yi* in this passage is understood as the ability for ethical reasoning, are its relations with *li*, modesty and trustworthiness in the following sentences intelligible.

3 Confucian Ethics: Universalistic or Particularistic?

1 Metaphysical assertions as well as views on human nature are closely related to the idea of *ren*, accounting respectively for Confucian ethics' autonomous and altruistic characteristics.
2 A lengthy discussion of this problem can be seen in WONG (2005g), 39–46.
3 Mencius makes this point clearly in 4B11; he has also cited examples from history, as in 4A17.
4 *Mencius*, 4B19.
5 MOU Zongsan has elaborated this point in a very elegant way in many of his writings. Also see WONG (2005f), 143–59.
6 I have argued this case more extensively in WONG (1995c), 116–20.
7 *The Doctrine of the Mean*, 27:3.
8 For example, *yi* (義) is more significant than *xin* (信 "trust"), Cf. *Mencius*, 4B11.
9 Cf. KING (1991), 203–20.
10 See ch. 4, "The Resolution of Moral Dilemma."

11 For example, Stacey in her book claims, "For more than 1,000 years it [Confucianism] was the dominant cosmology, political philosophy, and doctrine of proper ethics and comportment of the Chinese people; Confucianism is nearly synonymous with traditional Chinese civilization." See Stacey (1983), 30.
12 *The Commentaries on I Ching*, "Appended Remarks," part 1, ch. 5.
13 Perhaps there are people who observe Confucian teachings and practices without identifying themselves as Confucians, just as a survey conducted in Korea has shown. (See KOH (1991), 184–96.) I find that in this survey it is reasonable to ask questions about the conviction of respondents in order to measure the degree of their adherence to specific Confucian values, apart from questioning them about their actual behavior and daily practices. Since the problem is not "What do people do?" but "Why do people act this way?" the conviction underlying their practices is significant. Nevertheless, whether the "Confucian values" in the questionnaire truly reflect the core values of Confucian ethics should be carefully investigated. Besides, there is a fundamental question to be solved before we can consider the possibility of there being "Confucian Buddhists," "Confucian Christians," "Confucian Catholics," and the like, namely, "Are there contradictory beliefs in the two philosophies (or religions) which are so basic that they cannot be dismissed?" These questions relate to a more fundamental issue: "What is Confucianism?" This in itself requires in-depth study. However, discussions on this topic have already been commenced. See YU (1991), 31–98 and LIU (1995).
14 Bauman (1993), 8–9 passim.
15 Bauman (1993), 10. Maintaining an epistemological "foundation" for/of certainty is another feature of modern ethical thought which Bauman finds unacceptable from a postmodern perspective. People believe that moral rules are well justified whereas Bauman thinks that they are unfounded.
16 Bauman (1993), 12.
17 Bauman (1993), 8 and 47.
18 Bauman (1993), 50–1.
19 "The thesis of universalizability requires that if we make any moral judgement about this situation, we must be prepared to make it about any of the other precisely similar situations." See Hare (1981), 41–2, quotation here from 42.
20 This was recognized by Hare as one of the battle-cries of situational ethicists. Hare (1981), 39.
21 Hare (1981), 42–108.
22 Hare (1981), 108.
23 Hare (1981), 109.
24 Bauman (1993), 51.
25 Bauman (1993), 51.
26 Bauman (1993), 51.
27 At least it is the case at the first level. We can also conclude that Confucian ethics at the other levels except the first one is in a certain sense "particularistic."

4 The Resolution of Moral Dilemma: From the Confucian Perspective

1 Hare (1981).
2 Related discussions are collected in Gowans (1987). Among the contemporary contributors to the book, Alan Donagan, Richard Hare and Earl Conee deny the

possibility of irresolvable moral dilemmas. On the other side, Bas C. van Fraasser, Thomas Nagel and Bernard Williams assert that there are moral dilemmas. Alasdair MacIntyre also argues for such a view in MacIntyre (1990).

3 Walter Sinnott-Armstrong takes a position that while he agrees that there are irresolvable moral dilemmas, he denies that there is inescapable wrongdoing since it is not morally wrong to violate either moral requirement in a moral dilemma. MacIntyre (1990).
4 Nivison and Roetz have addressed this issue in different approaches. See Nivison (1996), ch. 3; Roetz (1993).
5 In Confucian ethics the term "*quan*" is used to signify such kind of discretionary judgement, which plays a significant role in the moral decision. See *Analects*, 9.30. Another similar example is shown in the case of Shun marrying without telling his father, and in doing so he violated the rite. See *Mencius*, 4A26.
6 *Mencius*, 6B3; 7A15; 7B24.
7 Mencius emphasizes the importance of the extension of love from family to the general public. See *Mencius*, 1A7; 7A15; 7B1.
8 Also see *Mencius*, 5B4.
9 Also see *Analects*, 18.7.
10 MacIntyre (1990), 369.
11 MacIntyre (1990), 369.
12 MacIntyre (1990), 369.
13 The core of the discussion in this passage is whether *yi* is internal.
14 It is questionable how one can distinguish moral values from non-moral values as well as moral virtues from non-moral virtues. I am unable to discuss this question in the present chapter. Generally speaking, moral values are those endorsed by the moral mind for some moral reasons, whereas non-moral values do not have this characteristic. This differentiation does not involve any question-begging descriptions since whether a judgement springs from the moral mind can be well-identified.
15 So far there is no case which shows that moral virtues and non-moral virtues are in conflict.
16 For the detailed discussion of the relationship between the moral and non-moral virtues in Confucian ethics, see ch. 2, "The Moral and Non-moral Virtues in Confucian Ethics."
17 MacIntyre (1990), 369.
18 The conflict between the virtues of "loyalty to the state" and "filial piety" is always considered as a typical case of moral dilemma which has been forming a major theme in Chinese literature and drama for over a thousand years. See Roetz (1993), ch. 7.
19 MacIntyre (1990), 368.
20 Another kind of moral dilemma which occurs frequently is that both the roles from which moral responsibilities derive can be abandoned. This kind of problem can be resolved in the same way as the case of conflicting responsibilities derived from unabandonable roles. See the following discussion.
21 See WONG (1991). In that paper I argue that to view oneself as a human being is the Confucian's reason for one's being moral.
22 Here I borrow the concept of *prima facie* principle from Richard Hare, especially in the sense that these principles will be overridden by principles at the level of critical thinking. Hare (1981).
23 The concept of "moral heart-mind" is signified by the notion of "*xin*" (heart-mind) in Confucianism.

24 Also see *Mencius*, 2A2.
25 There are very many books and papers discussing the problem of utilitarianism; the book written by J.C.C. Smart and Bernard Williams is one of these. See Smart and Williams (1973). Richard Hare tried to defend utilitarianism by introducing two levels of moral thinking (Hare, 1981), but his model produces other problems. See WONG (1988).
26 See Winkler (1996), 50. For the criticism made by anti-theorists, see Clarke and Simpson (1989), 1–3.
27 The situation ethics is criticized by not being able to guide human behaviour. See Sumner and Boyle (1996), 4 and Hare (1996), 25–6.

5 The Unity of Heaven and Man: A New Interpretation

1 The reflecting heart-mind is also named "the original heart-mind" (*ben xin* 本心) in Mencius (*Mencius*, 6A10).
2 This is similar to: "*Ren* and *yi* were natural to Yao and Shun" (*Mencius*, 7A30, 7B33).
3 WONG (2005).
4 Main reference: Wiber (2000).
5 Wilber (2000), 36.
6 Wilber (2000), 37.
7 Wilber (2000), 279. His italics.
8 For detailed exposition, see ch. 13, "The Thought of CHENG Hao."
9 CHENG and CHENG (1981), 16.
10 CHENG and CHENG (1981), 15.
11 CHENG and CHENG (1981), 15.
12 CHENG and CHENG (1981), 74.
13 CHENG and CHENG (1981), 33.
14 CHENG and CHENG (1981), 120.
15 Wilber (2000), 37.
16 Wilber (2000), 37.
17 CHENG and CHENG (1981), 34.
18 CHENG and CHENG (1981), 120.
19 Wilber (2000), 38.
20 Wilber (2000), 38.
21 CHENG and CHENG (1981), 33.
22 CHENG and CHENG (1981), 34.
23 Wilber (2000), 38.
24 Wilber (2000), 38.
25 CHENG and CHENG (1981), 20.
26 CHENG and CHENG (1981), 81.
27 CHENG and CHENG (1981), 15.
28 CHENG and CHENG (1981), 15
29 Wilber (2000), 185.
30 Wilber (2000), 184.
31 CHENG and CHENG (1981), 16.
32 CHENG and CHENG (1981), 120.
33 CHENG and CHENG (1981), 17.
34 Wilber (2000), 211. Wilber's italics.

35 Wilber (2000), 213.
36 Wilber (2000)

6 Human Nature in Confucianism: As Understood and Developed by Contemporary Neo-Confucian Philosophers MOU Zongsan and TANG Junyi

1 MOU (1985).
2 The meaning will be elaborated later in the section on Mou's justification of human nature.
3 MOU (1968), v. 2.
4 MOU (1968), v. 1, 152–3.
5 MOU (1985), 26.
6 MOU (1985), 26.
7 For example, Roetz thought that Mencius' argument for "human nature is good" failed to undermine Gaozi's assertion. Roetz (1993).
8 MOU (1968), v.2, 305.
9 The term "experiential" used here does not convey any sense related to "empirical." It is unavoidably related to experience, which is in a broad sense including spiritual experience. The focus of this usage is placed on the meaning of "by one's own."
10 The term *liangzhi* appears in *Mencius*, 7A15 indicating the capability of distinguishing the bad from the good without learning. Therefore, *liangzhi* is another name for the original heart-mind. The idea of "*liangzhi*" is followed and developed by WANG Yangming 王陽明 (1472–1529) who is one of the most influential philosophers in Neo-Confucianism in the Ming Dynasty.
11 MOU (1985), 36.
12 More detailed explanation in the later section.
13 MOU (1985), 36.
14 Mou said it is helpful for one to have proper understanding by explaining the truth analytically. Moreover, it can help one to direct the understanding to the mind. MOU (1968), v.2, 194.
15 MOU (1968), v. 2, 188. Original emphasis.
16 See below for details.
17 MOU (2015), 414.
18 MOU (2015), 415.
19 For the translation of "*nijue tijing*," see MOU (2015), 414, footnote 9.
20 MOU (1979), 229–30.
21 MOU (1979), 230.
22 MOU (1979), 230.
23 The word "reflect" used here has double meanings, one is in optics.
24 MOU (1979), 231.
25 MOU (1979), 166.
26 Gaozi and CHENG Hao agree on the view that every being possesses the inborn qualities of life to come to exist, but for Gaozi these qualities are composed of natural dispositions, desires, and abilities that make one species different from another, whereas for Cheng Hao the inborn quality refers to the productive power which is commonly shared by all kinds of things.

27 CHENG and CHENG (1981), 1.29.
28 MOU (1968), v. 2, 137.
29 *The Doctrine of the Mean* (*Zongyong*), ch. 1.
30 *Tuan Zhua*, 1:1.
31 MOU (1968), v. 2, 148. Also see ch. 5, "The Unity of Heaven and Man: A New Interpretation" for the detailed exposition of the relationship between the Way and human nature.
32 MOU (1985), 132. Original emphasis.
33 CHENG and CHENG (1981), 33.
34 MOU (1968), v. 2, 158.
35 MOU (1985), 133.
36 MOU (1985), 133. Original emphasis.
37 MOU (1985), 134.
38 CHENG and CHENG (1980), 15.
39 TANG (1977).
40 TANG (1977), v. 1, 101.
41 TANG (1977), 339.
42 TANG (1977), 633.
43 For detailed discussion of the meaning of "transference," see WONG (2005), 201–4, also see ch.7 "*Ren*, Empathy and the Agent-Relative Approach in Confucian Ethics."
44 TANG (1977), v. 1, 633–4.
45 TANG (1977), 634.
46 TANG (1977), 638.
47 TANG (1977), 638–9.
48 TANG (1977), 640.
49 TANG (1991), v. 4.
50 Ames (2011), ch. III.
51 Ames (2011), 133. Ames lists the *Great Learning* as an example. Apparently there are many sources in classical Confucianism such as Mencius as well as Song-Ming Neo-Confucianism which present this idea.
52 TANG (1977), v. 2, 867.
53 TANG (1977), 931–2.
54 The matter is even unable to make such perception.
55 TANG (1977), 932.

7 *Ren*, Empathy, and the Agent-Relative Approach in Confucian Ethics

1 For example, Van Norden (2007); Slote (2010).
2 Slote (2001), 5.
3 Van Norden (2007), 249.
4 WONG (1995a); WONG (2005).
5 Van Norden (2007), 247.
6 Van Norden (2007), 249.
7 Slote (2007), 13.
8 Slote (2007), 13.

9 "Transference" (*gantong*) is different from empathy. See below for discussion.
10 WONG (2005), 201–4.
11 Slote (2007), 13.
12 Slote (2007), 15.
13 Slote (2007), 15.
14 MOU (1968), 223.
15 Slote (2007), 15.
16 MOU (1968).
17 *Mencius*, 2A6.
18 Cf. *Mencius*, 7B31: "For every man there are things he cannot bear. To extend this to what he can bear is *ren*." This can be interpreted as *ren* being the extension of empathy to an unlimited extent.
19 MOU (1968), 305.
20 Therefore it is hard to tell whether the feeling of the Emperor Xuan of Qi towards the ox is empathy or *ceyin*.
21 Slote (2007).
22 *Mencius*, 2A2, 2A9, 5B1.
23 See ch. 2, "The Moral and Non-Moral Virtues in Confucian Ethics".
24 Slote (2010), 55.
25 Empathy is close to *ceyin* as understood by ZHU Xi (朱熹), whose thought deviates from Pre-Qin Confucianism, according to MOU Zhongsan's view, see MOU (1968).
26 Slote (2001), 5.
27 *Mencius*, 4B19.
28 Van Norden (2007), 115.
29 Van Norden (2007), 118.
30 CHENG Hao and CHENG Yi interpret "filial piety and love to the elder brother is the root of *ren*" in *Analects*, 1.2 as "filial piety and love to the elder brother is the root of the realization of *ren*," see CHENG and CHENG (1981), 125. Even though this is the Cheng Brothers' interpretation, it still reflects their understanding of Confucian ethics.
31 Cf. "The Conveyance of Rites," *Book of Rites*.
32 *Mencius*, 7A45.
33 *Analects*, 6.28.
34 "*Ren* is the characteristic element of humanity, and the great exercise of it is in loving relatives. *Yi* is the accordance of actions with what is right, and the great exercise of it is in honoring the worthy. The decreasing measures of the love due to relatives, and the steps in the honor due to the worthy, are produced by the principle of propriety." (*Doctrine of the Mean*, ch. 20).
35 WANG (2008), 124–37.
36 Van Norden (2007), 115.
37 There are numerous discussions on "relatives shielding each other." See GUO (2004).
38 *Mencius*, 6B3.
39 Van Norden (2007), 254–5. This interpretation originally comes from CHENG Hao. See CHENG and CHENG (1981), 16–17; 33.
40 See ch. 17, "The Thesis of Single-Rootedness in the Thought of CHENG Hao".
41 *Analects*, 12.11.
42 *Mencius*, 3A4.
43 *Mencius*, 6A4, 6A5.

8 Confucian Ethics and Virtue Ethics

1 Of those anti-theorists, the following are some of the representatives: John McDowell, Bernard Williams, Alasdair MacIntyre, Annette Baier. See Louden (1992) and Clarke and Simpson (1989).
2 See Louden (1992), ch. 5 and Clarke (1989), "Introduction."
3 McDowell (1989), 105.
4 Louden (1992), ch. 5.
5 Wong (2005a).
6 Wong (2005b).
7 For example, in Statman's classification, there are extreme and moderate versions of virtue ethics. According to the moderate versions, the morality of acts and the morality of character are irreducible to each other. Michael Slote and Robert Louden hold such a view. On the contrary, the extreme versions contend that deontic concepts are either derivative from or replaceable by aretaic concepts. G.E.M. Anscombe, Michael Stocker, Bernard Williams, Richard Taylor, and Alasdair MacIntyre belong to these versions.
8 Slote (1992). The primacy of character is regarded by Statman as the basic idea of virtue ethics. Statman (1997), 7–8.
9 Slote (1992), 89.
10 Slote (1992), 90–1.
11 Slote (1992), 95–6.
12 Slote (1992), xvii.
13 Slote (1992), xvi.
14 The differentiation of these two terms as well as their denotations is also suggested by Williams. See Williams (1985) and (1993).
15 See ch. 3, "Confucian Ethics: Universalistic or Particularistic?" for a detailed exposition.
16 *The Analects*, 17.21.
17 A person of *ren* is always aware of other people's well-being, needs and desires through the transference. This interpretation is explicitly made by some Neo-Confucian thinkers such as CHENG Hao, see ch. 3 "Confucian Ethics: Universalistic or Particularistic?"
18 Here appropriateness has a moral connotation since it is considered from the moral point of view.
19 *Mencius*, 6A4; 6A5.
20 Strictly speaking, *ren* and *yi* refer to the same faculty (the heart-mind of *ren-yi*) since only when transference takes place, can one transcend one's own personal point of view and make impartial judgements.
21 This view is explicitly held by CHENG Hao.
22 *Mencius*, 4B11.
23 An hypothetical case as well as a situation in legend are cited by Mencius as instances to illustrate this view, see *Mencius*, 4A17 and 5A2. There is also a lengthy exposition in WONG (2005c).
24 Only when *li* is used to signify one of the moral roots in human nature (the others are *ren*, *yi*, and *zhi*), does it denote an ability of human beings.
25 See ch. 3, "Confucian Ethics: Universalistic or Particularistic?"
26 Evidence of this understanding can be found in the *Analects*, 3.4 and 9.3.
27 Slote (1992), 3.
28 Slote (1992), 5.

29 Slote (1992), xv.
30 Slote (1992), 91.
31 Slote (1992), 88.
32 Slote (1992), 91.
33 WONG (2005c).
34 It seems that Slote is trying to reduce the opposition between benefit and moral to that of self and others, but he fails to see that there is a broad sense of well-being in which these oppositions do not hold.
35 Values are considered as non-moral when they are not pursued for the sake of morality.
36 WONG (2005c).
37 For example, Mencius makes the King aware that the enjoyment experienced in the company of others is greater than the enjoyment alone. He, however, does not claim that the enjoyment of others is greater than that of oneself, thus, the latter should not give way to the former. *Mencius*, 1B1.

9 Confucian Ethics and Virtue Ethics Revisited

1 See ch. 8, "Confucian Ethics and Virtue Ethics."
2 Here I am not going to repeat the argument and exposition in the "first investigation" but will only briefly summarize its conclusions: first, even though the concepts of deontic concepts are derived from those of aretaic concepts, both are derived from the original heart-mind, namely, *ren*, *yi*, *li*, and *zhi*; therefore *ren*, *yi*, *li*, and *zhi*, understood as the original heart-mind, are the basis of morality. For this reason, it is not suitable to consider Confucian ethics as virtue ethics. Second, it is true that Confucianism emphasizes making evaluations of one's ethical character. The evaluation of acts and choices is only important when they contribute to the enhancement (or destruction) of one's ethical character. Third, it is commonly admitted that Confucian ethics emphasizes virtues, and although most of them are moral virtues, non-moral ones do exist. The former (moral virtues) focus on the perfection of moral character, but not on the happiness of oneself and of others; the latter (non-moral virtues) are required for a holistic life. Neither in the realms of moral virtue nor of non-moral virtue could the problem of "self-other asymmetry" indicated by Michael Slote (1992) be found. Fourth, the concept of interest embedded in the concept of self-other asymmetry, which distinguishes between the systems of principled ethics and virtue ethics, is not applicable in the morality of Confucianism. Based on the above-mentioned reasons, even though Confucian ethics fulfills Slote's criteria of virtue ethics in some respects, it is dubious that essentially it belongs to virtue ethics.
3 Van Norden (2007) thinks that Confucianism can be categorized as Aristotelian virtue ethics whereas Slote (2010, ch. 4) thinks that it is more accurate to conceive Confucianism as taking a Humean/sentimentalist approach to virtue ethics.
4 See ch. 2, "The Moral and Non-Moral Virtues in Confucian Ethics."
5 To follow Bernard Williams' usage, hereafter I will use "ethical" as the broad term to stand for the considerations that bear on answering the question "what should I do, all things considered?" and "moral" as the narrower term to stand for a special system in which duties and obligations are examined. See Williams (1985), 6.
6 Van Norden (2007).
7 Van Norden (2007).

8 Van Norden (2007), 2.
9 Van Norden (2007), 3–34.
10 Van Norden (2007), 37.
11 *Mencius*, 6A1.
12 *Mencius*, 4B28.
13 *The Analects*, 15.18; 17.24; 4.10; 4.16; 4.5; 12.4.
14 Such as *Analects*, 6.28; 12.1; 12.2.
15 Such as *Analects*, 14.42; 13.25.
16 Van Norden (2007), 249.
17 Van Norden does not think that this meaning applies to Confucius and I have argued against this view in ch. 2, "*Ren*, Empathy and the Agent-Related Approach in Confucian Ethics."
18 See ch. 2, "*Ren*, Empathy and the Agent-Related Approach in Confucian Ethics."
19 Also see WONG (2005), 201–4.
20 Van Norden (2007), 102.
21 Van Norden (2007).
22 *Analects*, 3.4; 19.1.
23 *Analects*, 3.3.
24 *Analects*, 17.21.
25 *Analects*, 9.3.
26 *Mencius*, 4B6.
27 *Analects*, 3.3.
28 Slote (1992).
29 See ch. 2, "The Moral and Non-Moral Virtues in Confucian Ethics" for detailed discussion.
30 See note 5 and ch. 2.
31 See also WONG, "Moral Dilemma: A Confucian Perspective," and WONG, "The Confucian Resolution of Moral Conflict, Revisited." These two articles are included in WONG (2005).
32 *Analects*, 18.6.
33 Cf. "The Conveyance of Rites," in *Book of Rites*.
34 "The Conveyance of Rites," in *Book of Rites*.

10 Virtues in Aristotelian and Confucian Ethics

1 Cf. Broadie (1991), 3.
2 Broadie (1991), 57.
3 Aristotle (1985), Introduction, xvii.
4 In fact it is the aim of this chapter to discuss the similarities and differences between "*de*" and "*arete*."
5 *Kuo Yu*, ch. 3.
6 For details, see ch. 3, "Confucian Ethics: Universalistic or Particularistic?"
7 Examples can be found in *The Analects* (e.g. 9.3) and *Mencius* (e.g. 4A17; 4A26; 4B11).
8 The central problems of Confucian ethics are how to be a gentleman and in relation to this what is the ground for making this possible.
9 CHEN (2001).
10 In *the Analects*, there are numerous instances discussing gentlemen, including 1.8, 1.14, 2.13, 2.14, 4.10, 4.11, 4.16, 4.24, 5.16, and 6.18.

11 Aristotle uses "desiderative" to mark off the reason-responsive part from the prescriptive. Cf. Broadie (1991), 69.
12 Broadie (1991), 71–2.
13 Broadie (1991), 241. The italic is hers.
14 Aristotle (1992), 159–60.
15 Broadie (1991), 249.
16 *The Analects*, 7.25.
17 This idea is emphasized by a neo-Confucian, LU Jiuyuan, who claims that one can be a man with dignity, even one does not know a single word.
18 *The Analects*, 1.7.
19 *Mencius*, 1A3.
20 *Xunzi*, ch. 1. "Its [Learning's] real purpose is first to create a scholar and in the end to create a sage." (Knoblock (1994), 139.)
21 *Xunzi*, ch. 1. The translation is mainly from Knoblock (1994), 141, with slight modification.
22 A full analysis and discussion on this topic can be found in MOU (1968).
23 Yu (1998), 323–4.
24 Anthony Kenny argues that for Aristotle the exercise of *kalokagathia* is the supreme human good that constitutes happiness, and this must include both contemplation and morally virtuous activity. Cf. Kenny (1992), ch. 7.
25 Heinaman (1995), 2.
26 McDowell (1995), 204.
27 McDowell (1995), 205.
28 McDowell (1995), 206.
29 McDowell (1995), 208.
30 See ch. 3, "Confucian Ethics: Universalistic or Particularistic?"
31 Aristotle, (1985), 39–40.
32 *Mencius*, 6A4; 6A5.
33 Williams (1995), 13.
34 Williams (1995), 16.
35 Williams (1995), 16.
36 Williams (1995), 18.
37 Williams (1995), 22.
38 *The Analects*, 7.34.
39 *Mencius*, 7B38.
40 *The Analects*, 14.42.
41 *The Analects*, 6.30.
42 *The Analects*, 6.30.
43 *The Analects*, 6.30.
44 Here the "ought" is not necessarily in a moral sense.
45 *The Analects*, 5.16. In another passage (15.18), Confucius attempts to give a characterization to the gentleman where he uses some descriptions that are often understood as virtues, but they should not be so interpreted.
46 See ch. 8, "Confucian Ethics and Virtue Ethics."
47 At least it should be admitted that the significance of principles is no less than that of the virtues in Confucian thought.
48 There are cases in *Mencius* exhibiting such a kind of decision, especially in the cases of moral conflict. For the discussion about moral decision as an act of creation, see WONG (2005).

49 One may worry that this renders ethical judgements subjective and arbitrary. Wong has argued that it is not the case and indeed quite contrary to this view, ethical judgements thus made are universal. She has also discussed different meanings of universality, especially that to ethical judgements. See ch. 3, "Confucian Ethics: Universalistic or Particularistic?"
50 Aristotle would say that a virtuous person can see in a particular situation that a specific act is relevant to a particular virtue.
51 "The sage is simply the man first to discover this common element [*li yi*] in my heart." *Mencius*, 6A7.
52 *Mencius*, 5A7.
53 *Mencius*, 5B1.
54 *Mencius*, 5B1.

11 Aristotle's Practical Wisdom and Mencius's *xin*

1 There are two conditions for a choice to be rational: one is the "cognitive" condition, which practical wisdom is responsible for; another is a moral one, the satisfying of which depends on moral virtues.
2 Aristotle (1998), 142.
3 For example, H. Roetz, see Roetz (1993), ch. 5.
4 Aristotle (1998), 56.
5 Also 1112b 34–35 (Aristotle (1998), 57); 1113b 3–4 (Aristotle (1998), 59).
6 Y is chosen since it is a means to the end Z, and so on, till these ends come to the first cause, which is the supreme end (1112b 15–24, Aristotle (1998), 56. Yu (2007), 157). Through deliberation one can reach the means to an end, which itself is a means to another end.
7 Broadie (1991), especially ch. 1.
8 The idea of "the good," which is desired for its own sake, no matter that it is called the "final end," the "ultimate end," or the "supreme end" by different Aristotle scholars, is shown in 1094a 18–22 (Aristotle, 1998, 1–2). The name "Grand End" is another name for "the good" coined by Broadie. For exposition of this idea, see Yu (2007), 25, especially footnote 7 in ch. 1, 231–2.
9 Broadie (1991), 185.
10 Broadie (1991), 183.
11 This is the problem of descriptivism, which R.M. Hare argues against. Philippa Foot and John McDowell hold this view. See Hare (1965).
12 According to Hare, prescriptivity is one of the logical properties of moral judgment. Cf. Hare (1952) and (1981).
13 1139a 1–15, Aristotle (1998), 137–8.
14 Broadie (1991), 217.
15 Broadie (1991), 217.
16 The drive of an action comes from the non-rational part of the soul, which includes desire or emotion. Although it is non-rational, this part listens to and obeys reason. In this sense reason contributes to the motivational force of an action. Yu (2007), 75–6.
17 If the conclusion is inferred from the premises, it takes almost no time to deliberate. But in a real life situation, special discernment is needed in order to find the way leading to the achievement of the object desired. This does not only involve factual knowledge but also assessment and choice among different values. Therefore, the

conclusion is not a result of mere logical inference nor recognition of causal relation. So it is absurd to think that given the reasons one can attain the choice by inference. Broadie (1991), 227.

18 Broadie (1991), 234.
19 Wiggins holds a similar view. Wiggins (1980), 227.
20 Broadie (1991), 239.
21 Broadie (1991), 239.
22 Broadie (1991), 241.
23 Wiggins (1980), 228. Also see 230.
24 Aristotle (1998), 146.
25 Wiggins (1980), 228.
26 Aristotle (1998), 142.
27 Aristotle (1998), 151.
28 The notion "perfect virtue" appears in 1102a 5–8 (Aristotle (1998), 24). Perfect virtue is, in Aristotle's term, "virtue in the strict sense" (*arête kuria*), which is different from natural virtue (1144b 14–16 (Aristotle (1998), 157)). According to Aristotle, since "good in the strict sense" cannot be achieved without practical wisdom, the latter is indispensable for perfect virtue. In the discussion in Yu, "perfect virtue" is understood as "fully developed virtue." Cf. Yu (2007), 147.
29 Aristotle (1998), 155.
30 Aristotle (1998), 62.
31 In this sense virtue is also concerned with means. "Now the exercise of the virtues is concerned with means." (1113b 5–6, Aristotle (1998), 59).
32 Broadie (1991), 247.
33 Broadie (1991), 251. The function of desiderative part of the soul is explained in Broadie (1991), 62–3. The reference can be found in 1102b 13–14 (Aristotle (1998), 26). Broadie asserts that Aristotle's account of deliberation implies that the human ability to "read" goes far beyond specific desiderative dispositions. However, she admits that Aristotle does not say this clearly.
34 Broadie (1991), 252. Her italics.
35 Broadie (1991), 250. Her italics.
36 Kwong-loi SHUN interprets *Xin* in such a way. SHUN (1997), 136 ff.
37 Also in 6A17.
38 There are several interpretations of what the *xin* will get if it reflects; according to SHUN, "it" in the passage is suitably interpreted as *yi*. SHUN (1997), 149–53.
39 "*Yi*" here is used in its derivative meaning, signifying the result of activating the *xin* of *ren-yi*.
40 Jiyuan YU has made the comparison between practical wisdom and *yi*. He is also aware of the multiple meanings of *yi* which include the meaning of *xin* discussed here. Cf. YU (2007), ch. 5.
41 *Mencius*, 7A27; 7A3.
42 Cf. SHUN (1997), 151.
43 *Yi* in this sense is used in its derivative meaning.
44 Broadie (1991), 250. Her italics.
45 As discussed above, for Mencius, a (morally) great man is one who is guided by *xin*, which can decide what is good (*Mencius*, 6A15). The ability of deciding what is good is possessed by every human being and is not attained by learning (of logical reasoning or empirical knowledge) (*Mencius*, 7A15).

46 *Bu yi* occurred when *xin* is not activated hence the actions or decisions are led by other forces such as desires.
47 Broadie (1991), 189.
48 *Yi* (in its derivative meaning) is the product of practical reasoning in which moral and non-moral reasons have been considered. In other words, *yi* signifies the appropriateness judged in the circumstance, all things considered. See ch. 2, "The Moral and Non-Moral Virtues in Confucian Ethics."
49 Aristotle (1998), 140.
50 Aristotle (1998), 143.
51 Broadie (1991), 225.
52 Williams (1995), 13.
53 See ch. 10, "Virtues in Aristotelian and Confucian Ethics."
54 Wiggins (1980), 236–7.
55 Mou claims, "According to Confucianism, only the moral creation made by human nature and heart-mind (*xin*) signifies the real and true meaning of creation which also represents our real and true creative life." (MOU (1968), v.1, 178–9). "Moral creation" used by Mou resembles Wiggin's "invention" but it has a much more rich and profound meaning. See MOU (1968), v.1, 178–9; 323; 473; v.2, 224.

12 Rethinking the Presuppositions of Business Ethics: From Aristotelian Approach to Confucian Ethics

1 Solomon (1992).
2 Solomon (1994).
3 Solomon (1992), 146; also Solomon (1994), 56.
4 Universality has been thought to be inconsistent with specificity but I have a different view, see WONG (2005h).
5 Solomon (1994), 57.
6 For Solomon's argument, see Solomon (1994), 61–5 and Solomon (1992), ch. 2. Other business ethicists including De George also point out that we do not live in a "dog eat dog" world. De George (1990), ch. 1.
7 Solomon (1992), 27.
8 Solomon (1992), 24.
9 Solomon (1992), 26.
10 Solomon (1992), 26.
11 Solomon (1994), 61.
12 Solomon (1994), 61.
13 Solomon (1992), 103.
14 Solomon (1992), 159.
15 Solomon (1992), 162.
16 Solomon (1992), 180.
17 Solomon (1992), 185.
18 Solomon (1992), 175.
19 Solomon (1992), 111.
20 Solomon (1994), 68–72.
21 For the detailed exposition, see WONG (1995b), 89–105.
22 More discussion of this point can be found in *Mencius*, 1B1 and 1B4.

13 The Thought of CHENG Hao

1 All citations of Cheng Hao in this chapter refer to this work, and unless otherwise indicated, quotations are those of Cheng Hao.
2 MOU (1968), 2:5–9
3 GUO (2006), 44–7
4 ZHU (1986), 5:93.
5 CHENG and CHENG (1981), 638.
6 CHENG and CHENG (1981), 29.
7 CHENG and CHENG (1981), 73.
8 CHENG and CHENG (1981), 4.
9 CHENG and CHENG (1981), 121.
10 CHENG and CHENG (1981), 121.
11 CHENG and CHENG (1981), 21.
12 CHENG and CHENG (1981), 21.
13 CHENG and CHENG (1981), 29.
14 CHENG and CHENG (1981), 34.
15 CHENG and CHENG (1981), 120.
16 CHENG and CHENG (1981), 15.
17 CHENG and CHENG (1981), 15.
18 CHENG and CHENG (1981), 15.
19 CHENG and CHENG (1981), 133.
20 CHENG and CHENG (1981), 16–17.
21 Williams (1995), 16.
22 Williams (1995), 16.
23 Graham (1992).
24 Graham (1992), 127.
25 CHENG and CHENG (1981) 17.
26 CHENG and CHENG (1981), 11.

15 Morally Bad in the Philosophy of the Cheng Brothers

1 Here I use "morally bad" to describe an act performed that deviates from values of a certain system, for instance, a dishonest action is morally bad in many ethical systems. I translate *e* as "the morally bad" rather than the more common "evil" in order to avoid a set of ideas associated with the latter that are inappropriate in the case of the Chinese tradition. For example, actions that are *e* need not be done with understanding or intentionally, nor is the agent normally thought to *enjoy* performing such actions.
2 For the exposition and analysis of Mencius' and Xunzi's views on human nature, see SHUN (1997).
3 Cheng Brothers refer to CHENG Hao 程顥 (CHENG Mingdao) (1032–1085) and CHENG Yi 程頤 (CHENG Yichuan 伊川) (1033–1073). See chs 13, 14.
4 The citation is from *Mencius*, 3A4.
5 In the *Collected Works of the Two Chengs* the authors of many sayings are not identified; therefore, it is difficult to identify whether they are from Mingdao or from Yichuan. MOU Zongsan was the first person who set criteria for distinguishing between sayings by the two brothers, see MOU (1968), vol. 2, 5–9. Although Mou's criteria are not completely convincing for some scholars (GUO (2006), 44–7), they are so far the most reliable ones. For those quotations that are clearly marked or

distinguished, I will use "MD" to stand for Cheng Mingdao and "YC" to stand for Cheng Yichuan. This passage is by MD. CHENG and CHENG (1981), 17.

6 The citation is from the *Analects*, 5.26
7 CHENG and CHENG (1981), 17.
8 *Mencius*, 4A27.
9 CHENG and CHENG (1981), 121.
10 CHENG and CHENG (1981), 123.
11 These bad states of affairs are sometimes considered as metaphysical badness since they are recognized as a necessary component of Heavenly Principle. However, I think it would be more appropriate to regard them as empirical badness, with support from metaphysical being. It is noteworthy that they are in nature different from moral badness because the former are not results of intentional acts and nobody can be responsible for their occurrence whereas the latter are not the case.
12 CHENG and CHENG (1981), 69.
13 *Mencius*, 4A11.
14 Wing-tsit Chan represented people who are "self-destructive" and in "self-denial" as "those who do violence to their own nature" and "those who throw themselves away," respectively. See ZHU and LU (1967), 14–15.
15 ZHU and LU (1967), 1.14.
16 This citation is from the *Analects*, 17.2.
17 CHENG and CHENG (1981), 86; ZHU and LU (1967), 12.25.
18 *Mencius*, 4A15.
19 *Mencius*, 2B12.
20 *Mencius*, 6A6.
21 In Chinese thought, *qi* is a notion signifying a kind of vital energy found in both atmosphere and the human body. In later Chinese philosophy, *qi* was specifically thought of as the fundamental "stuff" out of which everything in the universe condenses and into which it eventually dissipates. See the appendix: "Important Terms" in Ivanhoe and Van Norden (eds) (2003).
22 For the philosophy of ZHANG Zai, see MOU (1968), vol. 1.
23 According to A. C. Graham, the term "material nature" does not appear in the works of the Cheng Brothers except once as a variant for xingzhi zhi xing (性質之性). This variant has superseded the original reading in many texts. See Graham (1992), 59, n. 26.
24 ZHU and LU (1967), 2.80.
25 CHENG and CHENG (1981), 10; ZHU and LU (1967), 1.21.
26 The speaker of this saying has not been specified. Zhu Xi ascribed this to Mingdao in Zhu (1971). Mou also judged it as said by Mingdao, see MOU (1968), 161.
27 See n. 23.
28 YC. CHENG and CHENG (1981), 204. Also see ZHU and LU (1967), 1.40; CHENG and CHENG (1981), 253.
29 This citation is from the *Analects*, 16.9.
30 YC. CHENG and CHENG (1981), 253.
31 YC. CHENG and CHENG (1981), 204–5.
32 Paraphrasing *Mencius*, 6A6.
33 *Mencius*, 6A7.
34 YC. CHENG and CHENG (1981), 207.
35 YC. CHENG and CHENG (1981), 191.
36 CHENG and CHENG (1981), 83.

37 CHENG and CHENG (1981), 393.
38 CHENG and CHENG (1981), 83.
39 CHENG and CHENG (1981), 186.
40 Yichuan thought that the impurity of *qi* not only inclines some people to be bad from early childhood, animals are also endowed with the impure *qi* so that they are distinct from human beings. (CHENG and CHENG (1981), 312.) But since animals are confined by their form, they cannot change whereas bad people can. On the other hand, according to Mingdao since the *qi* of things is impure, they are unable to actualize their own nature, let alone extending their nature to actualize others' by which a person can become a sage. See MOU (1968), vol. 2, 147–60.
41 CHENG and CHENG (1981), 82.
42 CHENG and CHENG (1981), 1257.
43 YC. CHENG and CHENG (1981), 66. Also see ZHU and LU (1967), 5.22.
44 CHENG and CHENG (1981), 33–4. Mou ascribed this saying to Mingdao. See MOU (1968), vol. 2, 55.
45 YC. ZHU and LU (1967), 5.7.
46 MD. CHENG and CHENG (1981), 123.
47 ZHU and LU (1967), 5.24.
48 The citation is from the *Analects*, 6.7.
49 ZHU and LU (1967), 2.63. In the opinion of Zhang Boxing, this is Mingdao's saying. See ZHU and LU (1967), 67.
50 YC. ZHU and LU (1967), 2.8.
51 MD. CHENG and CHENG (1981), 20.
52 *Mencius*, 2A2.
53 YC. CHENG and CHENG (1981), 11. Also see CHENG and CHENG (1981), 78.
54 CHENG and CHENG (1981), 29.
55 ZHU and LU (1978), 2.54.
56 *Mencius*, 7B35.
57 CHENG and CHENG (1981), 18.
58 *Mencius*, 7B35.
59 YC. CHENG and CHENG (1981), 145.
60 SHUN (1997), 220.
61 CHENG and CHENG (1981), 10; ZHU and LU (1967), 1.21.
62 YC. CHENG and CHENG (1981), 204. Also CHENG and CHENG (1981), 252; ZHU and LU, 1.40.
63 The quotation cited above (CHENG and CHENG (1981), 10.) Precedes by the following sentences, "Some are good from infancy; that they are so is due to their endowment of *qi*. The good is of course nature, but the bad must also be recognized as nature." This always creates confusion for some readers since it seems that Mingdao is claiming that the nature is good and simultaneously that the nature also consists of badness. Actually the nature in question signifies two different meanings, one of which signifies the nature that human beings possess before birth and the other signifies that after birth. These two meanings imply different assertions concerning the good or bad attribution to the nature: Regarding the nature before one's birth which will decree to him or her upon his or her birth, it is good (which is "what succeeds to it is goodness" means); regarding that after one's birth which has mixed with *qi*, it can be good or bad. However, Mingdao points out that usually when people speak of the nature, they are only talking about "what succeeds to it is goodness," and he himself also adopts this common practice and thus asserts that the nature is good.

Most importantly, he considers the goodness of nature as in the transcendental sense. See ch. 17.

64 CHENG and CHENG (1981), 10–11; ZHU and LU (1967), 1.21.

65 Here the meaning of goodness is understood along the lines of Shun's interpretation of *ke yi wei shan*.

66 CHENG and CHENG (1981), 207.

67 ZHU and LU (1967), 14.6.

68 The citation is from the *Analects*, 17.2.

69 *Mencius*, 6A8.

70 *Mencius*, 6A6.

71 *Mencius*, 7A30.

72 *Mencius*, 7A30.

73 The citation is from the *Analects*, 17.2.

74 YC. CHENG and CHENG (1981), 291–2.

75 CHENG and CHENG (1981), 292.

76 The role and function of *xin* might differ between Mingdao and Yichuan; nevertheless, both of them agreed that when *xin* is activated, the goodness of *xing* will emerge.

77 CHENG and CHENG (1981), 53.

78 CHENG and CHENG (1981), 411.

16 The Status of *Li* in the Cheng Brothers' Philosophy

1 See Xu (1969), chs 2–3; also see Eno (1990), 22.

2 See the *Analects*, 12.1. For a detailed exposition of the various meanings of *li* in early Confucianism, see ch. 8, "Confucian Ethics and Virtue Ethics."

3 Schwartz (1985), 295.

4 Hall and Ames (1987), 269–71.

5 CHOW (1993), 201.

6 In CHENG and CHENG (1981), the authors of many sayings have not been marked. Therefore it is difficult to identify whether they are from Mingdao or from Yichuan. However, it is asserted by MOU Zongsan that "from the overall direction of the objective thoughts and that of moral cultivation, the Cheng Brothers belong to the same system" (MOU (1968), 2). Besides, at least in the quotations cited in this chapter, the two brothers hold similar views (e.g., on filial piety and fraternal duty, see section 4), though their emphases might differ.

7 As previously mentioned, the notion *li* signifies the meaning of social order, rituals as well as ethical norms and different English words corresponding to these meanings constitute proper translations of it. I use propriety here to characterize the meaning of ethical norms which is the dominant meaning of *li* when understood as external rules in Neo-Confucianism (at least in the Chengs' thought; see the quotations cited below). The meaning of "propriety" (ethical norms or rules of behaviour) comprises "forms of norms and rules" which constitute the meaning of "ritual." Therefore, propriety contains rituals but more than that. There is a rationale underlying the forms or rituals and it is formulated as propriety of behaviour. The rituals themselves and the propriety can be signified by *yi* (儀) and *li* (禮) respectively. On the other hand, I will continue to use the word '*li*' untranslated, in order to maintain its rich meaning (especially the internal aspect).

8 CHENG and CHENG (1981), 22. "MD" hereafter stands for CHENG Mingdao (CHENG Hao) while "YC" stands for CHENG Yichuan (CHENG Yi).

9 CHENG and CHENG (1981), 23.
10 CHENG and CHENG (1981), 87.
11 CHENG and CHENG (1981), 127.
12 CHENG and CHENG (1981), 327.
13 CHENG and CHENG (1981), 82.
14 CHENG and CHENG (1981), 177.
15 Graham (1992), 68.
16 CHENG and CHENG (1981), 127; the translation is Graham's, see Graham (1992), 72.
17 CHENG and CHENG (1981), 152.
18 CHENG and CHENG (1981), 66.
19 Another aspect of *jing* also appears in the *Analects*, 14.42, but does not bear a dominant weight.
20 *Jing* has a greater metaphysical connotation in Cheng Hao's philosophy; see MOU (1968), 349; 386. However, both Chengs understand that one of the meanings of *jing* represents a way of moral cultivation.
21 CHENG and CHENG (1981), 168–69. Graham's translation. (Graham (1992), 70).
22 CHENG and CHENG (1981), 7.
23 CHENG and CHENG (1981), 185.
24 CHENG and CHENG (1981), 157.
25 CHENG and CHENG (1981), 143.
26 CHENG and CHENG (1981), 184.
27 CHENG and CHENG (1981), 184–5.
28 CHENG and CHENG (1981), 27.
29 CHENG and CHENG (1981), 1.
30 CHENG and CHENG (1981), 125.
31 CHENG and CHENG (1981), 183.
32 CHENG and CHENG (1981), 144.
33 CHENG and CHENG (1981), 31.
34 CHENG and CHENG (1981), 38.
35 CHENG and CHENG (1981), 144.
36 CHENG and CHENG (1981), 125.
37 CHENG and CHENG (1981), 9.
38 CHENG and CHENG (1981), 127.
39 CHENG and CHENG (1981), 117.
40 CHENG and CHENG (1981), 118.
41 See ch. 13, "The Thought of CHENG Hao."
42 See ch. 14, "The Thought of CHENG Yi."

17 The Thesis of Single-Rootedness in the Philosophy of CHENG Hao

1 Cheng Hao sometimes uses "heaven and earth" in a metaphysical sense which equates with *Dao*, but sometimes he uses them to signify a material entity. Hereafter I will use upper case for the former meaning and lower case for the latter.
2 CHENG and CHENG (1981), 117–18.
3 CHENG and CHENG (1981), 43.
4 CHENG and CHENG (1981), 81. The speaker of the above two passages has not been specified. The editor of *Song-Yuan Case Studies (Song-Yuan xue an* 宋元學案)

combines them and includes them in the "case study" of Cheng Hao (*Mingdao xue an* 明道學案). Mou Zongsan thinks that the combination is a mistake (MOU (1968), 94). Nevertheless, the ideas are in line with the first passage quoted above and therefore probably should be attributed to Cheng Hao.

5 MOU (1968), 121.

6 MOU (1968), 129.

7 Here the mind refers to an empirical or habitual mind (*xixin* 習心), therefore I use "the mind" to distinguish it from the heart-mind (*benxin* 本心).

8 CHENG and CHENG (1981), 33.

9 CHENG and CHENG (1981), 121.

10 CHENG and CHENG (1981), 18.

11 CHENG and CHENG (1981), 33.

12 CHENG and CHENG (1981), 35. The speaker of this saying has not been specified. *Song-Yuan xue an* includes it into "*Mingdao xue an.*" Judging from the content as well as the style, it should be attributed to Cheng Hao.

13 CHENG and CHENG (1981), 133.

14 CHENG and CHENG (1981), 118.

15 Although sincerity and respect bear different connotations, they can be regarded as constituting a single way to Change.

16 CHENG and CHENG (1981), 119.

17 HUANG Yong understands Mou's view concerning the principle (*Li*) to be "some thing, some entity, some substance, whose fundamental feature is to act." He argues that "*Li* remains a being, although a being that always acts. This is what Mou meant by Cheng Hao's *Li* as 'something with both being and activity' (HUANG (2007), 198). I doubt that Huang's understanding of Mou is accurate. Although Mou sometimes speaks of the substance (*ti* 體) of Change, or heart-mind, or *Dao*, sincerity, human nature, etc., he always emphasizes that this substance can only be understood as function or activity. Therefore the relationship between the substance and activity is not a substance-attribute relationship, rather, they are one thing with different names (MOU (1968), 137).

18 MOU (1968), 15. The speaker is not specified. *Song-Yuan xue an* includes it in "Mingdao xue an." Judging from the content as well as the style, it should be attributed to Cheng Hao (MOU (1968), 95).

19 CHENG and CHENG (1981), 120.

20 CHENG and CHENG (1981), 78.

21 CHENG and CHENG (1981), 392.

22 CHENG and CHENG (1981), 1.4. The speaker of this saying has not been specified. *Song-Yuan xue an* includes it in "Mingdao xue an." Mou Zongsan attributes it to Cheng Hao. (MOU (1968), 22).

23 MOU (1968), 361.

24 Graham (1992), 124.

25 ZHONG Caijun has argued that there was naturalistic element in Cheng Hao's thought. See ZHONG (1992). I will return to this in section 6.

26 CHENG and CHENG (1981), 73. The speaker has not been identified but the views expressed are consistent with Cheng Hao's thought.

27 CHENG and CHENG (1981), 118.

28 CHENG and CHENG (1981), 67.

29 CHENG and CHENG (1981), 128.

30 CHENG and CHENG (1981), 4.

31 CHENG and CHENG (1981), 29. The speaker of these two passages has not been specified. *Song-Yuan xue an* includes it in "Mingdao xue an." Judging from the content as well as the style, it should be attributed to Cheng Hao.
32 CHENG and CHENG (1981), 29.
33 CHENG and CHENG (1981), 121.
34 CHENG and CHENG (1981), 4.
35 CHENG and CHENG (1981), 120.
36 Graham (1992), 111.
37 This is shown in his original notes under the quotation from Gaozi.
38 CHENG and CHENG (1981), 33. The speaker of this saying has not been identified. Both Mou Zongsan and A.C. Graham attribute it to Cheng Hao, see MOU (1968), 55; Graham (1992), 124.
39 CHENG and CHENG (1981), 34. The speaker of this saying has not been identified. Both Mou Zongsan and A.C. Graham attribute it to Cheng Hao, see MOU (1968), 57; Graham (1992), 124.
40 CHENG and CHENG (1981), 120.
41 CHENG and CHENG (1981), 34.
42 CHENG and CHENG (1981), 33.
43 CHENG and CHENG (1981), 29. The speaker of this saying has not been specified. *Song-Yuan xue an* includes it in "Mingdao xue an." A similar passage by Cheng Hao is found at CHENG and CHENG (1981), 135. Both Mou Zongsan and A.C. Graham attribute it to Cheng Hao, see MOU (1968), 136; Graham (1992), 111.
44 CHENG and CHENG (1981), 17.
45 CHENG and CHENG (1981), 121.
46 CHENG and CHENG (1981), 123.
47 ZHONG (1992), 18. One form of naturalism takes things that appear in the realm of phenomena as the entire content of the metaphysical being. In this sense Cheng Hao's thought resembles a kind of naturalism. Nevertheless, for Cheng Hao behind the appearance of the realm of phenomena there is the operation of Principle. Therefore I do not think it is appropriate to attribute naturalism to his thought.
48 CHENG and CHENG (1981), 10–11. The speaker of this saying has not been specified. *Song-Yuan xue an* includes it in "Mingdao xue an."
49 CHENG and CHENG (1981), 10–11.
50 CHENG and CHENG (1981), 10–11.

18 Reflections on the "Confucian Heritage Culture" Learner's Phenomenon

1 Bond (1996a); LAU (1996); Watkins and Biggs (1996, 2001); WONG N.Y. (1998a).
2 Brand (1987).
3 As described by scholars like Biggs (1994, 1996b); and Watkins, Regmi, and Astilla (1991).
4 Robitaille and Garden (1989).
5 Lapointe, Mead, and Askew (1992).
6 Beaton et al. (1996).
7 Ranked first on the medal chart.
8 In 1999, it was held in Taiwan. China did not participate.
9 Brand (1987).

10 Murphy (1987).
11 Murphy (1987), 45.
12 Biggs and Moore (1993).
13 Biggs (1990, 1991, 1994); Chan and Watkins (1994); Kember and Gow (1991); Watkins and Ismail (1994); Watkins, Regmi, and Astilla (1991).
14 Biggs (1994).
15 Marton, Tse, and dall'Alba (1996); Marton, Watkins, and Tang (1997); Watkins (1996).
16 Dahlin and Watkins (2000).
17 Biggs (1994).
18 Hess and Azuma (1991).
19 See also Biggs (1996a, 1996b).
20 GAO and Watkins (2001); HO (2001).
21 Yu (1996).
22 In fact there are two sayings which demonstrate this belief, first, "diligence could remedy mediocracy," second, "familiarity breeds sophistication". Bond (1996b); Bond and Hwang (1986); CHENG (1994); HAU and Salili (1991, 1996); HO (1986); LEE (1996).
23 Bond (1996b).
24 Hofstede (1983).
25 Hofstede (1983).
26 Schwartz (1994).
27 Kim, et al. (1994).
28 Stover (1974).
29 Bond and Hwang (1986), 215.
30 It is believed that though life is perishable, there are "three imperishables," namely, erecting an example of a moral life, contributing to the country or his or her fellow people (or to the welfare of the society), and establishing a school of thought.
31 QIAN (1976), 7–10.
32 ZHANG (1989).
33 Ray and Jones (1983).
34 Other studies include Iwawaki and Lynn (1972); YANG (1987). For details, see ZHANG (1989), 254–69.
35 The First East Asian Regional Conference on Mathematics Education held in South Korea in 1998.
36 CHANG (2000).
37 WONG, N.Y. (1998a).
38 Tracey (1983), 30.
39 LAO (1988), 53.
40 The great Neo-Confucian in the Southern Song Dynasty (960–1279), ZHU Xi (1130–1200), even claimed that "... such a problem was not fixed in the past 1,500 years. Though there had been some better-off times, the ideal preached by Yao, Shun, the Three Kings, Zhou Gong and Confucius had never been successfully realized in this world even for one day" (Vol 36: Responding to the letter of CHEN Tongfu, *Collected Writings of Zhu Xi*; translation: author). See also King (1992), 166.
41 Some academics even denounce the possibility of having such causal relationships, see FUNG (1989).
42 Such as Daoism and Buddhism in the Ming (1368–1644) and Qing (1644–1911) Dynasties, see Yu (1987).
43 ZHANG (1989), 254–60.

44 A school in Buddhism (formally translated as zen Buddhism) which flourished in China since the eleventh century which won high regard from Western scholars such as Fromm (1960) who took it as the blending of Daoism and Buddhism.
45 See WONG, N.Y. (1998b).
46 WONG, N.Y. (2001, 2006).
47 See note 22.
48 Elliot (1999).
49 For details, see WONG, N.Y. (1998b, 2001, 2006).
50 Marton (1997).
51 The other being affliction.
52 For details, see WONG, N.Y. (1998a, 1998b, 2001, 2006).
53 See, e.g., LEE (1996).
54 See, e.g., NAN (1976), 11.
55 This also involves the problems of the method of ideal type, as reckoned by many academics (as seen by YANG (1987)).
56 GU (1996).
57 As undertaken by LIU (1989); see ch. 3 "Confucian ethics: Universalistic or particularistic?"
58 See LEE, ZHANG, and ZHENG (1997).
59 See WONG, N.Y. (1998a, 2001, 2006).
60 Peterson (1979); SIU (1999); SIU and Volkov (1999).
61 CHANG (2000).
62 LEE (1996).

19 Confucianism and Contemporary Education Phenomena

1 Brimer and Griffin (1985); Robitaille and Garden (1989).
2 Lapointe, Mead, and Askew (1992).
3 Japan, South Korea, Singapore, and Hong Kong.
4 Later renamed "Trends in International Mathematics and Science Study."
5 Murphy (1987).
6 Brand (1987), 45.
7 Chen, Stevenson, Hayward, and Burgess (1995); Stevenson, Lee, Chen, Stigler, Hsu, and Kitamura (1990).
8 Stevenson and Stigler (1992).
9 Stigler and Hiebert (1999).
10 Watkins, Regmi, and Astilla (1991).
11 Marton, Tse, and dall'Alba (1992).
12 Kember and Gow (1991).
13 Biggs (1996a).
14 Watkins and Biggs (1996).
15 Watkins and Biggs (2001).
16 Chan and Rao (2009).
17 Ryan and Slethaug (2010).
18 Zhang, Biggs, and Watkins (2010).
19 Bond (1986).
20 Bond (1991).
21 Bond (1996a).

22 Bond (2012).
23 LAU (1996).
24 Fan, Wong, Cai, and Li (2004).
25 Fan, Wong, Cai, and Li (2014).
26 Hattie and Watkins (1981); Watkins and Malimas (1980).
27 Watkins and Ismail (1994).
28 Watkins, Regmi, and Astilla (1991).
29 Watkins, Adair, Akande, et al. (1998); Wong, Lin, and Watkins (1996).
30 See YU (1996).
31 In fact, two sayings demonstrate this belief: first, "diligence could remedy mediocracy"; second, "familiarity breeds sophistication." Bond (1996a); Bond and Hwang (1986); CHENG (1994); Hau and Salili (1991, 1996); HO (1986); LEE (1996).
32 LEUNG (2005).
33 MOK (2010); Stankov (2010).
34 Ha and Li (2014).
35 See, e.g., WONG (2006).
36 Hatano and Inagaki (1998).
37 Ha and Li (2014).
38 LAO (1986).
39 Hatano and Inagaki (1998), 94.
40 Refer to N.Y. WONG.
41 Japanese.
42 Hirabayashi (2006), 55.
43 Yuan and Xie (2013).
44 Ma, Zhou, and Tuo (2004).
45 Lam, Wong, Ding, Li, and Ma (2015).
46 Wang (2013).
47 For more in depth discussions, see Wong, Wong, and Wong (2012).
48 Wong, Han, and Lee (2004).
49 See, e.g. Gram, Jæger, Liu, Qing, and Wu (2013); Nguyen-Phuong-Mai, Terlouw, and Pilot (2012).
50 Chan and Rao (2009).
51 Biggs and Watkins (1996); Hatano and Inagaki (1998).
52 WONG (2004).
53 Biggs (1994).
54 Bowden and Marton (1998).
55 Wong, Marton, Wong, and Lam (2002).
56 Gu, Huang, and Marton (2004).
57 Wong, Lam, Sun, and Chan (2009).
58 Huang and Leung (2006).
59 Lo and Marton (2012).
60 Marton, Tse, and dall'Alba (1996); Marton et al. (1997); Watkins (1996).
61 TAN (2011).
62 Dahlin and Watkins (2000).
63 Li and Cutting (2011).
64 Li and Cutting (2011), 39.
65 See Skemp (1976).
66 Sfard (1991).
67 Tall (1998).

68 Baroody, Reil, and Johnson (2007).
69 See also Cai and Wong (2012).
70 For details, see Lo and Marton (2012).
71 Biggs (1994).
72 Ha (2014).
73 Ha (2014), 401.
74 Hess and Azuma (1991).
75 WONG (2006).
76 Watkins (2008) proposed the notion of "learning-centredness" rather than "learner-centredness."
77 Ausubel (1968).
78 WONG (2006).
79 WONG (2006, 2008).
80 "Exiting the *way*" was used in earlier writings, yet "transcending the *way*" is a more accurate phrase.
81 Cai and Wong (2012).
82 WONG (2006).
83 Taken from "Call of the Cranes, Minor Odes of Kingdom" in the *Book of Ancient Poetry*.

Conclusion

1 MOU (1985), preface, ii.
2 Daoism and Buddhism are instances of teaching, under this characterization.
3 MOU (1985), 153.
4 It should be noted that by education it does not refer to a teaching system in which rules and norms are coercively imposed to students. For the Confucian ideal of education, the teacher/instructor acts as an exemplar of *junzi* who would inspire students to find their own ways which suit them most. See the *Analects*, 12.19.
5 The preference of using moral guidance to using edicts by Confucius is explicitly made in the *Analects*, 2.3.
6 LAO (1968), 41–52.
7 MOU (1968), v.2, 476.
8 MOU (1968), v.2, 444.
9 MOU (1979), 466.
10 MOU (1979), 232.
11 MOU (1968), v.2, 471.
12 MOU (1968), v.2, 435–6.
13 There is a subtle distinction between the mere events of daily affairs and those embodies with *Dao*. They are unable to be distinguished by the outer qualities but the latter can only be experienced by the agent who attributes the meaning to it.
14 MOU (1988), 45.
15 This is also a clue for the Confucian answer to the question "Why be moral?" which cannot be explored here. See WONG (1995b).
16 MOU (1985), preface, ii-vi.
17 Kant (1993), 115.

18 The meaning of the perfect good in Confucianism and the way to achieve it have been discussed in depth by Mou in MOU (1985).

Appendix: Can Two Levels of Moral Thinking Reconcile the Rivalry of Principled Ethics and Contextualism?—A Conversation between Winkler and Hare

1 Winkler (1996), 50.
2 Winkler (1996), 51.
3 Winkler (1996), 53.
4 Winkler (1996), 54.
5 Winkler (1996), 55.
6 Winkler (1996), Winkler's italics.
7 Winkler (1996), 51–2.
8 The abortion issue is one of the issues in these areas. In the abortion issue, the moral status of a fetus is always considered as crucial.
9 Sumner and Boyle (1996), 4.
10 Winkler (1996), 52.
11 Sumner and Boyle (1996), 4.
12 Sumner and Boyle (1996), 4.
13 Winkler (1996), 57.
14 Winkler (1996), 57–8.
15 Hare (1996). In his paper, Hare discusses situation ethics instead of contextualism, but I think his analysis on the former can well apply to the latter in this debate.
16 Hare (1996), 21.
17 Winkler (1996), 73–4
18 Hare (1996), 25–6.
19 Hare (1996), 26; Hare's Italics.
20 Hare (1996), 26.
21 Hare (1981), 38.
22 Hare (1981), 36.
23 Hare (1981), 38.
24 Winkler (1996), 58.
25 Hare (1981), 39.
26 Hare (1996), 30.
27 Hare (1981), 40. There are three logical properties of moral concepts such as "ought," namely, prescriptivity, universality, and overridingness. Hare (1981).
28 Hare (1996), 29–30.
29 Hare (1996), 30.
30 Hare (1996), 33.
31 Hare (1981), 43.
32 Hare (1996), 31.
33 Winkler (1996), 56.
34 Sumner and Boyle (1996), 4.
35 Winkler, (1996), 52–3.
36 Winkler (1996), 56.
37 Winkler (1996), 57–8.

38 Winkler (1996), 65.
39 Winkler (1996), 76. Winkler's italics.
40 Hare (1993), 8.
41 Hare (1993), 8.
42 Hare (1993), 11.
43 Hare (1993), 8.
44 Hare (1993), 13–14.
45 Hare (1993), 9.
46 Hare (1993), 14.

References

Ames, Roger T. (2011), *Confucian Role Ethics: A Vocabulary*, Hong Kong: The Chinese University Press.

Aristotle (1985), *Nicomachean Ethics*, trans. T. Irwin, Indianapolis, Indiana: Hackett Publishing Co.

Aristotle (1992), *Eudemian Ethics*, trans. M. Wood, Book I, II, VIII, Oxford: Clarendon Press.

Aristotle (1998), *The Nicomachean Ethics*, trans. D. Ross, Oxford: Oxford University Press.

Ausubel, D.P. (1968), *Educational Psychology: A Cognitive View*, New York: Holt, Rinehart and Winston.

Baroody, A.J, Y. Reil, and A.R. Johnson (2007), "An Alternative Reconceptualization of Procedural and Conceptual Knowledge," *Journal for Resource in Mathematics Education*, 38(2): 115–31.

Bauman, Zygmunt (1993), *Postmodern Ethics*, Oxford: Blackwell.

Beaton, A.E, I.V.S. Mullis, M.O. Martin, E.J. Gonzalez, D.L. Kelly, and T.A. Smith (1996), *Mathematics Achievement in the Middle School Years: IEA Third International Mathematics and Science Study*, Chestnut Hill, MA: TIMSS International Study Center.

Beauchamp, T.L. and J.F. Childress (1979), *Principles of Biomedical Ethics*, Oxford: Oxford University Press.

Becker, L.C. (1973), "The Finality of Moral Judgments: A Reply to Mrs. Foot," *The Philosophical Review*, 364–70.

Biggs, J.B. (1990), "'Asian Students' Approaches to Learning: Implication for Teaching Overseas Students," in M. Kratzing (ed.), *Eighth Australasian Learning and Language Conference*, 1–51. Brisbane, Australia: Queensland University of Technology Counselling Services.

Biggs, J.B. (1991), "Approaches to Learning in Secondary and Tertiary Students in Hong Kong: Some Comparative Studies," *Educational Research Journal*, 6: 27–39.

Biggs, J.B. (1994), "What Are Effective Schools? Lessons from East and West" (The Radford Memorial Lecture), *Australian Educational Researcher*, 21:19–39.

Biggs, J.B. (1996a), "Learning, Schooling, and Socialization: A Chinese Solution to a Western Problem," in S. Lau (ed.), *Growing Up the Chinese Way*, 147–67, Hong Kong: The Chinese University Press.

Biggs, J.B. (1996b), "Western Misconceptions of the Confucian-Heritage Learning Culture," in D.A. Watkins and J.B. Biggs (eds), *The Chinese Learner: Cultural, Psychological and Contextual Influences*, 45–67. Hong Kong: Comparative Education Research Centre and Victoria, Australia: The Australian Council for the Educational Research.

Biggs, J.B. and P.J. Moore (1993), *The Process of Learning*, New York: Prentice Hall.

Biggs, J.B. and D.A. Watkins (1996), "Insights into Teaching the Chinese Learner," in D.A. Watkins and J.B. Biggs (eds), *Teaching the Chinese Learner: Psychological and Pedagogical Perspectives*, 277–300, Hong Kong: Comparative Education Research Centre, The University of Hong Kong.

Bond, M.H. (1986), *Psychology of the Chinese People*. Hong Kong: Oxford University Press.

Bond, M.H. (1991), *Beyond the Chinese Face*. Hong Kong: Oxford University Press.

Bond, M.H. (1996a), "Chinese Values," in M.H. Bond (ed.), *The handbook of Chinese Psychology*, 208–26, Hong Kong: Oxford University Press.

Bond, M.H. (ed.) (1996b), *The Handbook of Chinese Psychology*, Hong Kong: Oxford University Press.

Bond, M.H. (ed.) (2012), *The Oxford Handbook of Chinese Psychology*, New York: Oxford University Press.

Bond, M.H. and K.K. Hwang (1986), "The Social Psychology of Chinese People," in M.H. Bond (eds), *The Psychology of the Chinese People*, 213–66. Hong Kong: Oxford University Press.

Bowden, J. and F. Marton (1998), *The University of Learning*, London: Kogan Page.

Brand, D. (1987), "The New Whiz Kids: Why Asian Americans are Doing Well, and What It Costs Them" (cover story), *Time*, August, 42–50.

Brimer, A. and P. Griffin (1985), *Mathematics Achievement in Hong Kong Secondary Schools*, Hong Kong: Centre of Asian studies, University of Hong Kong.

Broadie, S. (1991), *Ethics with Aristotle*, Oxford: Oxford University Press.

Cai, J. and N.Y. Wong (2012), "Effective Mathematics Teaching: Conceptualisation, Research and Reflections," in W. Blum, R.B. Ferri, and K. Maaß (eds), *Mathematikunterricht im Kontext von Realität, Kultur und Lehrerprofessionalität*, 294–303, Wiesbaden: Springer Spektrum.

CHAN, K.K. and N. Rao (2009), *Revisiting the Chinese Learner: Changing Contexts, Changing Education*, Hong Kong: Comparative Education Research Centre; Springer.

CHAN, G.Y. and D. Watkins (1994), "Classroom Environment and Approaches to Learning: An Investigation of the Actual and Preferred Perceptions of Hong Kong Secondary School Students," *Instructional Science*, 22: 233–46.

CHAN, Wing-tsit (trans.) (1967), *Reflections on Things at Hand: The Neo-Confucian Anthology*, compiled by Zhu Xi and Lu Zu-qian, New York: Columbia University Press.

CHANG, W.C. (2000), "In Search of the Chinese in All the Wrong Places!" *Journal of Psychology in Chinese Societies*, 1(1), 125–42.

CHEN, C., H.W. Stevenson, G. Hayward, and S. Burgess (1995), "Culture and Academic Achievement: Ethnic and Cross-National Differences," in M.L. Maehr and P.R. Pintrich (eds), *Advances in Motivation and Achievement: Culture, Motivation, and Achievement*, 9: 119–51, Greenwich, CT: JAI Press.

CHEN, Lai (2001), "The Characteristics of Virtue Ethics in *Chun Qiu* Period and Early Confucian Ethics: The Similarities and Differences of Confucius' and Aristotle's Ethics" (in Chinese), paper presented at the 12th International Conference on Chinese Philosophy.

CHEN, Lai (2002), *The Thought and Culture in the Ancient World: The Religion, Ethics and Social Thoughts in Chunqiu* (in Chinese), Beijing: Joint Publishing Co.

CHENG, Hao and CHENG, Yi (1981), *The Works of the Two Chengs* (in Chinese), Beijing: Zonghua Shuju.

CHENG, K.M. (1994), "Quality of Education as Perceived in the Chinese Culture," in T. Takala (ed.), *Quality of Education in the Context of Culture in Developing Countries*, 67–84, Tampere: Tampere University Press.

Chinese Culture Connection (1987), "Chinese Value and the Search or Culture-Free Dimensions of Culture," *Journal of Cross-Cultural Psychology*, 18:143–64.

CHOW, Kwai-wing (1993), "Ritual, Cosmology and Ontology: Chang Tsai's Moral Philosophy and Neo-Confucian Ethics," *Philosophy: East and West*, 43.2: 201–28.

Clarke, S.G. and E. Simpson (eds) (1989), *Anti-Theory in Ethics and Moral Conservatism*, Albany: State University of New York Press.

Dahlin, B. and D. Watkins (2000), "The Role of Repetition in the Processes of Memorizing and Understanding: A Comparison of the Views of German and Chinese Secondary School Students in Hong Kong," *British Journal of Educational Psychology*, 70: 65–84.

De George, Richard T. (1990), *Business Ethics*, 3rd edn, New York: Macmillan.

Elliot, D. (1999), "Now Please Think: As Americans Embrace Testing, Asians Pursue Creativity—Learning to Think" (cover story), *Newsweek*, Sept 6, 38–41.

Eno, Robert (1990), *The Confucian Creation of Heaven*. Albany: State University of New York Press.

Fan, L., N.Y. Wong, J. Cai, and S. Li (eds) (2004), *How Chinese Learn Mathematics: Perspectives from Insiders*, Singapore: World Scientific.

Fromm, E. (1960), *Psychoanalysis and Zen Buddhism*, London: George Allen and Unwin.

FUNG, Yiu-ming (1989), "Religious Ethics and Its Relationship with Economic Behaviour—a conceptual analysis of Weber's theory" (in Chinese), *Humanistic Study Series*, 1:169–89.

FUNG, Yu-lan (1952), *A History of Chinese Philosophy*, vol. 1, trans. Derk Bodde, Princeton: Princeton University Press.

GAO, L., and D.A. Watkins (2001), "Towards a Model of Teaching Conceptions of Chinese Secondary School Teachers of Physics," in D.A. Watkins, and J.B. Biggs (eds) (2001), *Teaching the Chinese Learner: Psychological and Pedagogical Perspectives*, 27–45, Hong Kong: Comparative Education Research Centre, The University of Hong Kong.

Gowans, Christopher W. (1994), *Innocence Lost: An Examination of Inescapable Moral Wrongdoing*, Oxford: Oxford University Press.

Gowans, Christopher W. (ed.) (1987), *Moral Dilemmas*, Oxford: Oxford University Press.

Graham, A.C. (1989), *Disputers of the Tao: Philosophical Argument in Ancient China*. Peru, Illinois: Open Court Publishing Company.

Graham, A.C. (1992), *Two Chinese Philosophers: The Metaphysics of the Brothers Ch'êng*, La Salle, Illinois: Open Court Publishing Company.

Gram, M., K. Jæger, Junyang Liu, Li. Qing, and X. Wu (2013), "Chinese Students Making Sense of Problem-Based Learning and Western teaching—Pitfalls and Coping Strategies," *Teaching in Higher Education*, 18(7): 761–72.

Gu, L., R. Huang, and F. Marton (2004), "Teaching with Variation: A Chinese Way of Promoting Effective Mathematics Learning," in L. Fan, N.Y. Wong, J. Cai, and S. Li (eds), *How Chinese Learn Mathematics: Perspectives from Insiders*, 309–47, Singapore: World Scientific.

GU, Zhung-hua (1996), "Confucian Culture and Economic Ethics" (in Chinese), paper presented at the international conference "Confucianism and the Contemporary World," Taipei, July.

GUO, Qiyong (ed.) (2006), *The collected debates on Confucian ethics: Focusing on "relatives shielding each other (Rujia lunli zhengming ji),"* Wuhan: Wupei Education Press.

Ha, P.L. (2014), "The Politics of Naming: Critiquing 'Learner-Centred' and 'Teacher as Facilitator' in English Language and Humanities Classrooms," *Asia-Pacific Journal of Teacher Education*, 42(4), 392–405.

Ha, P. L. and B. Li (2014), "Silence as Right, Choice, Resistance and Strategy among Chinese 'Me Generation' Students: Implications for Pedagogy," *Studies in the Cultural Politics of Education*, 35(2), 233–48.

Hall, David L. and Roger T. Ames (1987), *Thinking Through Confucius*, Albany, N.Y.: State University of New York Press.

Hare, R.M. (1952), *The Language of Moral*, Oxford: Oxford University Press.

Hare, R.M. (1965), "Descriptivism," in W.D. Hudson (ed.) *The Is-Ought Question*, London: Macmillan.

Hare, R.M. (1981), *Moral Thinking: Its Levels, Method, and Point*, Oxford: Oxford University Press.

Hare, R.M. (1993), *Essays on Bioethics*, Oxford: Oxford University Press.

Hare, R.M. (1996), "Methods of Bioethics: Some Defective Proposals," in L.W. Sumner, and J. Boyle (eds), *Philosophical Perspectives on Bioethics*, Toronto: University of Toronto Press.

Hatano, G., and K. Inagaki (1998), "Cultural Contexts of Schooling Revisited: A Review of *The Learning Gap* from a Cultural Psychology Perspective, in S.G. Paris and H.M. Wellman (eds), *Global Prospects for Education: Development, Culture, and Schooling*, 79–104, Washington, D.C.: American Psychological Association.

Hattie, J., and D. Watkins (1981), "Australian and Filipino Investigations of the Internal Structure of Biggs' New Study Process Questionnaire," *British Journal of Educational Psychology*, 51: 241–44.

HAU, K.T., and F. Salili (1991), "Structure and Semantic Differential Placement of Specific Causes: Academic Causal Attributions by Chinese Students in Hong Kong, *International Journal of Psychology*, 26:175–93.

HAU, K.T., and F. Salili (1996), Achievement Goals and Causal Attributions of Chinese Students, in S. Lau (ed.), *Growing up the Chinese Way*, 121–45, Hong Kong: The Chinese University Press.

Heinaman, Robert (ed.) (1995), *Aristotle and Moral Realism*, Boulder, San Francisco: Westview Press.

Hess, R.D., and M. Azuma (1991), "Cultural Support for Schooling: Contrasts between Japan and the United States," *Educational Researcher*, 20 (9): 2–8.

Hiebert, J., R. Gallimore, H. Garnier, K.B. Giwin, H. Hollingsworth, J. Jacobs, et al, and J. Stigler (2003), *Teaching Mathematics in Seven Countries: Results from the TIMSS 1999 video study*, Washington, D.C.: National Center for Education Statistics.

Hirabayashi, I. (2006), "A Traditional Aspect of Mathematics Education in Japan," in F.K.S. Leung, K.D. Graf, and F.J. Lopez-Real (eds), *Mathematics Education in Different Cultural Traditions: A Comparative Study of East Asia and the West. The 13th ICMI Study*, 51–64, Dordrecht: Springer.

HO, D.Y.F. (1986), "Chinese Patterns of Socialization: A Critical Review," in M.H. Bond (ed.), *The Psychology of the Chinese People*, 1–37, Hong Kong: Oxford University Press.

HO, I.T. (2001), "Are Chinese Teachers Authoritarian?" in D.A. Watkins, and J.B. Biggs (eds), *Teaching the Chinese Learner: Psychological and Pedagogical Perspectives*, 99–114, Hong Kong: Comparative Education Research Centre, The University of Hong Kong.

Hofstede, G.H. (1983), "Dimensions of National Cultures in Fifty Countries and Three Regions," in J.B. Deregowski, S. Dziurawiec, and R.C. Annis (eds), *Expiscations in Cross-Cultural Psychology*, 335–55, Lisse: Swets and Zeitlinger B.V.

HUANG, H.X, M.R. ZHANG and Z.Z. TIAN (1995), *Yi Zhou Shu Hui Jiao Ji Zhu* (in Chinese), Shanghai: Guji Publishing Co.

Huang, R. and K.S.F. Leung (2006), "Cracking the Paradox of Chinese Learners: Looking into the Mathematics Classrooms in Hong Kong and Shanghai," in L. Fan, N.Y. Wong, J. Cai, and S. Li (eds), *How Chinese Learn Mathematics: Perspectives from Insiders*, 348–81, Singapore: World Scientific.

HUANG, Yong (2007), "The Cheng Brothers' Onto-theological Articulation of Confucian Values," *Asian Philosophy*, 17 (3): 187–211.

Ivanhoe, P.J. and Bryan W. Van Norden (eds) (2003), *Readings in Classical Chinese Philosophy*, Indianapolis: Hackett.

Iwawaki, S., and R. Lynn (1972), "Measuring Achievement Motivation in Japan and Great Britain," *Journal of Cross-Cultural Psychology*, 3(2): 219–20.

Kant, I. (1993), *Critique of Practical Reason*, trans. L.W. Beck, 3rd edn, New York: Macmillan Publishing Co.

Kember, D., and L. Gow (1991), "A Challenge to the Anecdotal Stereotype of the Asian Students," *Studies in Higher Education*, 161, 117–28.

Kenny, Anthony (1992), *Aristotle on the Perfect Life*, Oxford: Clarendon Press.

Kim, U., H.C. Triandis, C. Kagitcibasi, S.C. Choi, and G. Yoon (eds) (1994), *Individualism and Collectivism: Theory, Method and Application*, Thousand Oaks, CA: Sage.

KING, A.Y.C. (1991), "The Transformation of Confucianism in the Post-Confucian Era: The Emergence of Rationalistic Traditionalism in Hong Kong," in Weiming TU (ed.), *The Triadic Chord: Confucian Ethics, Industrial East Asia and Max Weber*, Singapore: The Institute of East Asian Philosophies.

King, A.Y.C. (1992), *Chinese Society and Culture*, Hong Kong: Oxford University Press.

Knoblock, John (1994), *Xunzi: A Translation and Study of the Complete Works*, vol. 1–3, Stanford: Stanford University Press.

KOH, Byong-ik (1991), "Confucianism in Contemporary Korea," in Wei-ming TU (ed.), *The Triadic Chord: Confucian Ethics, Industrial East Asia and Max Weber*, Singapore: The Institute of East Asian Philosophies.

Lam, C.C., N.Y. Wong, R. Ding, S.P.T. Li, and Y. Ma (2015), "Basic Education Mathematics Curriculum Reform in the Greater Chinese Region—Trends and Lessons Learned," in B. Sriraman, J. Cai, K. Lee, L. Fan, Y. Shimuzu, L.C. Sam, and K. Subramanium (eds), *The First Sourcebook on Asian Research in Mathematics Education: China, Korea, Singapore, Japan, Malaysia, & India*. Charlotte, New Carolina: Information Age Publishing.

LAO, Siguang (1968), *New Edition of A History of Chinese Philosophy* (*Xinbian Zhongguo Zhexue Shi*) (in Chinese), v.1, Taian: Guangxi Normal University Press.

LAO, Siguang (1986), *Confucian Spirit and the Cultural Direction of the World* (in Chinese), Taipei: China Times Publishing Co.

LAO, Siguang (1988), "Philosophical Thought and Education (in Chinese)," in J.Y. To, S.H. Liu (eds), *Philosophy, Civilisation, and Education*, 3–62, Hong Kong: The Chinese University Press.

Lapointe, A.E., N.A. Mead, and J.M. Askeweds (1992), *The International Assessment of Educational Progress Report No. 22-CAEP-01: Learning Mathematics*, New Jersey: The Center for the Assessment of Educational Progress, Educational Testing Service.

LAU, S. (ed.) (1996), *Growing up the Chinese way*, Hong Kong: The Chinese University Press.

LEE, P.Y., D. ZHANG, and Z. ZHENG (1997), "Examination Culture and the Teaching of Mathematics," (in Chinese), *EduMath*, 4, 96–103.

LEE, W.O. (1996), "The Cultural Context for Chinese Learners: Conceptions of Learning in the Confucian Tradition," in D.A. Watkins and J.B. Biggs (eds), *The Chinese Learner: Cultural, Psychological and Contextual Influences*, 25–41, Hong Kong: Comparative Education Research Centre and Victoria, Australia: The Australian Council for the Educational Research.

LEUNG, F.K.S. (2005), "The implication of the Third International Mathematics and Science Study for mathematics curriculum reform in Chinese communities," in N.Y. Wong (eds), *Revisiting Mathematics Education in Hong Kong for the New Millennium*, 226–53, Hong Kong: Hong Kong Association for Mathematics Education.

Li, X. and J. Cutting (2011), "Rote Learning in Chinese Culture: Reflecting Active Confucian-Based Memory Strategies," in L. Jin and M. Cortazzi (eds), *Researching Chinese Learners: Skills, Perceptions, Intercultural Adaptations*, 21–42, Houndmills: Palgrave Macmillan.

LIU, Shuxian (1989), "Reflection and Critics of Review on the Contemporary Neo-Confucian Thought (in Chinese)," in S.H. LIU (ed.), *Mainland and Overseas: the Reflection and Transformation of Tradition*, 237–71, Taipei: Yuen Zhen Civilisation Company.

LIU, Shuxian (1995), "Transcendental Reflections of Contemporary Neo-Confucian Philosophy" (in Chinese), *Chinese Culture*, 12.

Lo, M.L. and F. Marton (2012), "Towards a Science of the Art of Teaching: Using Variation Theory as a Guiding Principle of Pedagogical Design," *International Journal for Lesson and Learning Studies*, 1(1): 7–22.

Louden, R.B. (1992), *Morality and Moral Theory*, Oxford: Oxford University Press.

Lukes, S. (1991), "Taking Morality Seriously," *Moral Conflict and Politics*, Oxford: Clarendon Press.

Ma, Y., D. Zhou, and Z. Tuo (2004), "Differences within Communalities: How is Mathematics Taught in Rural and Urban Regions in Mainland China," in L. Fan, N.Y. Wong, J. Cai, and S. Li (eds), *How Chinese Learn Mathematics: Perspectives from Insiders*, 413–42, Singapore: World Scientific.

MacIntyre, A. (1990), "Moral Dilemmas," *Philosophy and Phenomenological Research*, Vol. 1, Supplement.

Mackie, J. (1977), *Ethics: Inventing Right and Wrong*, New York: Penguin Books Ltd.

Marton, F. (1997), *Student learning: East and West.* Public lecture presented at The Chinese University of Hong Kong, Hong Kong, 18 March.

Marton, F. and S. Booth (1997), *Learning and Awareness*, Mahwah, New Jersey: Lawrence Erlbaum Associates.

Marton, F., L.K. Tse, and G. dall'Alba (1992), *Solving the Paradox of the Asian Learner?* Paper presented to the 4th Asian Regional Conference, International Association for Cross-Cultural Psychology, Kathmandu.

Marton, F., L.K. Tse and G. dall'Alba (1996), "Memorizing and Understanding: The keys to the Paradox?" in D.A. Watkins and J.B. Biggs (eds), *The Chinese Learner: Cultural, Psychological and Contextual Influences*, 69–83, Hong Kong: Comparative Education Research Centre and Victoria, Australia: The Australian Council for the Educational Research.

Marton, F., D. Watkins, and C. Tang (1997), "Discontinuities and Continuities in the Experience of Learning: An Interview Study of High-school Students in Hong Kong." *Learning and Instruction*, 7, 21–48.

McDowell, J. (1989), "Virtue and Reason," in Stanley G. Clarke and Evan Simpson (eds), *Anti-Theory in Ethics and Moral Conservatism*, Albany: State University of New York Press.

McDowell, J. (1995), "Eudaimonism and Realism in Aristotle's ethics," in R. Heinaman (ed.), *Aristotle and Moral Realism*, 201–18, Boulder, San Francisco: Westview Press.

MOK, M.M.C. (2010), "Alternative Explanations for the Confucian Asian High Performance and High Self Doubt Paradox: Commentary on 'Unforgiving Confucian Culture: A Breeding Ground for High Academic Achievement, Test Anxiety and Self-doubt?'" by L. Stankov. *Learning and Individual Differences*, 20, 564–6.

MOU, Zongsan (1968), *Metaphysical Reality of Original Heart-Mind and Human Nature (Xinti yu Xingti)* (in Chinese), vol. 2, Taibei: Zhengzhong Shuju.

MOU, Zongsan (1979), *From Lu Xiangshan to Liu Jishan (Cong Lu Xiangshan dao Liu Jishan)* (in Chinese), Taipei: Student Bookstore.

MOU, Zongsan (1985), *On Perfect Good (Yuanshan Lun)* (in Chinese), Taipei: Student Bookstore.

MOU, Zongsan (1988), *The Philosophy of History* (in Chinese), 7th edn, Taipei: Student Bookstore.

MOU, Zongsan (2015), *Nineteen Lectures on Chinese Philosophy: A Brief Outline of Chinese Philosophy and the Issues It Entails* (trans. E. C. Su), Create Space: Foundation for the Study of Chinese Philosophy and Culture.

Murphy, D. (1987), "Offshore Education: A Hong Kong Perspective," *Australian Universities Review*, 30(2): 43–44.

NAN, Huai-iin (1976), *The Analects: Another Interpretations* (in Chinese), Taipei: Human World Magazine Press.

Nguyen-Phuong-Mai, M., C. Terlouw, and A. Pilot (2012), "Cooperative Learning in Vietnam and the West-East Educational Transfer," *Asia Pacific Journal of Education*, 32(2): 137–52.

Nivison, D.S. (1996), *The Ways of Confucianism*, Chicago: Carus.

Peterson, W. (1979), "Examination Man," *Bitter Gourd*, 44–63. Yale: Yale University Press.

QIAN, Mu (1976), "Soul and Mind," in *Soul and Mind* (in Chinese), Taipei: Jing Lian Publications.

Ray, J. and J. Jones (1983), "Occupational and Educational Achievement Motivation in Australian and Hong Kong School Children," *The Journal of Social Psychology*, 120: 281–2.

Robitaille, D.F. and R.A. Garden (1989), *The IEA Study of Mathematics II: Contexts and Outcomes of School Mathematics*, Oxford: Pergamon Press.

Roetz, H. (1993), *Confucian Ethics of the Axial Age*, Albany, NY: State University of New York Press.

Ryan, J., and G. Slethaug (2010), *International Education and the Chinese Learner*, Hong Kong: Hong Kong University Press.

Schwartz, S.H. (1985), "Cultural Dimensions of Value: Toward an Understanding of National Differences," in U. Kim, H.C. Triandis, C. Kagitcibasi, S.C. Choi, and G. Yoon (eds), *Individualism and Collectivism: Theory, Method and Application*, 85–119, Thousand Oaks, CA: Sage.

Sfard, A. (1991), "On the Dual Nature of Mathematical Conceptions: Reflections on Processes and Objects as Different Sides of the Same Coin," *Educational Studies in Mathematics*, 22: 1–36.

Shanghai Shifandaxue Guji Zhenglizu (ed.) (1978), *Guoyu*, Shanghai: Guji Publishing Co.

SHUN, Kwong-loi (1977), *Mencius and Early Chinese Thought*, Stanford: Stanford University Press.

SIU, M.K. (1999), "How Did Candidates Pass the State Examination in Mathematics in the Tang Dynasty (618–907)?—Myth of the 'Confucian-heritage-culture' classroom," paper presented at the Third European Summer University in History and Epistemology in Mathematics Education. Louvain-la-Neuve/Leuven, Belgium. 15–21, July.

SIU, M.K. and A. Volkov (1999), "Official Curriculum in Traditional Chinese Mathematics: How did Candidates Pass the Examinations?" *Historia Scientiarum*, 9: 85–99.

Skemp, R.R. (1976), "Relational Understanding and Instrumental Understanding," *Mathematics Teaching* (December): 20–6.

Slote, M. (1992), *From Morality to Virtue*, Oxford: Oxford University Press.

Slote, M. (2001), *Morals form Motives*, Oxford: Oxford University Press.

Slote, M. (2007), *The Ethics of Care and Empathy,* New York: Routledge.

Slote, M. (2010), *Essays on the History of Ethics,* Oxford: Oxford University Press.

Smart, J.C.C. and W. Bernard (1973), *Utilitarianism: For and Against,* Cambridge: Cambridge University Press.

Solomon, R.C. (1992), *Ethics and Excellence: Cooperation and Integrity in Business,* Oxford: Oxford University Press.

Solomon, R.C. (1994), "Business and the Humanities: An Aristotelian Approach to Business Ethics," Donaldson, T.J. and Freeman R.E. (eds), *Business as a Humanity,* Oxford: Oxford University Press.

Stacey, J. (1983), *Patriarchy and Socialist Revolution in China,* Berkeley: University of California Press.

Stankov, L. (2010), "Unforgiving Confucian Culture: A Breeding Ground for High Academic Achievement, Test Anxiety and Self-doubt?" *Learning and Individual Differences,* 20: 55–63.

Statman, D. (1997), "Introduction to Virtue Ethics," in Daniel Statman (ed.), *Virtue Ethics: A Critical Reader,* Washington, D.C.: Georgetown University Press.

Stevenson, H.W., and R. Nerison-Low (1999), "To Sum It Up: Case studies of Education in Germany, Japan, and the United States," Washington: National Institute on Student Achievement, Curriculum, and Assessment, Office of Educational Research and Improvement, U.S. Department of Education. Available online: http://www.ed.gov/pubs/SumItUp [accessed 24 March 2017].

Stevenson, H.W. and J.W. Stigler (1992), *The Learning Gap: Why Our Schools Are Failing and What We Can Learn from Japanese and Chinese Education,* New York: Summit Books.

Stevenson, H.W., S. Lee, C. Chen, J.W. Stigler, C-c. Hsu and S. Kitamura (1990), *Contexts of Achievement: A Study of American, Chinese, and Japanese Children,* Monographs of the Society for Research in Child Development, 221 (55), Chicago: The University of Chicago Press.

Stigler, J. and J. Hiebert (1999), *The Teaching Gap: Best Ideas from the World's Teachers for Improving Education in the Classroom,* New York: Free Press.

Stover, L.E. (1974), *The Cultural Ecology of Chinese Civilization,* New York: New American Library.

Sumner, L.W. and J. Boyle (1996), "Introduction," *Philosophical Perspectives on Bioethics,* in L.W. Sumner and J. Boyle (eds), *Philosophical Perspectives on Bioethics,* Toronto: University of Toronto Press.

Tall, D. (1998), "Information Technology and Mathematics Education: Enthusiasms, Possibilities and Realities," Plenary Lecture, Eighth International Congress on Mathematical Education, Seville, Spain, 14–21 July 1996, in C. Alsina, J.M. Alvarez, M. Niss, A. Pérez, L. Rico, and A. Sfard (eds), *Proceedings of the 8th International Congress on Mathematical Education,* 65–82, Sevilla, Spain: Sociedad Andaluza de Educación Matemática "Thales."

TAN, P.-L. (2011), "Towards a Culturally Sensitive and Deeper Understanding of 'Rote Learning' and Memorisation of Adult Learners," *Journal of Studies in International Education,* 15(2), 124–45.

TANG, Junyi (1977), *Life Existences and the Horizons of the Mind* (*Shengming Cunzai yu Xinling Jingjie*) (in Chinese), Taibei: Xuesheng shuju.

TANG, Junyi (1991), *The Complete Works of Tang Junyi* (*TANG Junyi quanji*) (in Chinese), v. 4, Taibei: Xuesheng shuju.

Tracey, J. (1983), *Patriarchy and Social Revolution in Chinese.* Berkeley: University of California Press.

Ueno, K. (2006), "From Wasan to Yozan," in F.K.S. Leung, K.D. Graf and F.J. Lopez-Real (eds), *Mathematics Education in Different Cultural Traditions: A Comparative Study of East Asia and the West, The 13th ICMI Study*, 65–79, Dordrecht: Springer.

Van Norden, B.W. (2007), *Virtue Ethics and Consequentialism in Early Chinese Philosophy*, Cambridge: Cambridge University Press.

WANG, Guowei (2008), *Wang Guowei Ji* (*Collected works of Wang Guowei*) (in Chinese), v. 4, Beijing: China Social Science Press.

Wang, J. (ed.) (2009), *Mathematics Education in China: Tradition and Reality* (in Chinese), Nanjing: Jiangsu Education Publishing House.

Wang, J. (2013), "Understanding the Chinese Learners from a Perspective of Confucianism," in M. Cortazz and L. Jin (eds), *Researching Cultures of Learning: International Perspectives in Language Learning and Education*, 61–79, Houndmills: Palgrave Macmillan.

Wang, J. and B. Xu (eds) (2004), *Trends and Challenges in Mathematics Education*, Shanghai: East China Normal University.

Watkins, D. (1994), "Memorizing and Understanding: The keys to Solving the Mysteries of the Chinese Learner?" Paper presented at the 23rd Congress of the International Association of Applied Psychology, Madrid, July.

Watkins, D. (1996), "Hong Kong Secondary School Learners: A Developmental Perspective," in D.A. Watkins and J.B. Biggs (eds), *The Chinese Learner: Cultural, Psychological and Contextual Influences*, 107–19, Hong Kong: Comparative Education Research Centre and Victoria, Australia: The Australian Council for the Educational Research.

Watkins, D.A. (2008), "Learning-centered Teaching: An Asian Perspective." Keynote address at the 2nd International Conference on Learner-centered Education, Manila, the Philippines.

Watkins, D.A. and J.B. Biggs (eds) (1996), *The Chinese Learner: Cultural, Psychological and Contextual Influences*, Hong Kong: Comparative Education Research Centre, The University of Hong Kong; Victoria, Australia: The Australian Council for Educational Research.

Watkins, D.A. and J.B. Biggs (eds) (2001), *Teaching the Chinese Learner: Psychological and Pedagogical Perspectives*, Hong Kong: Comparative Education Research Centre, The University of Hong Kong.

Watkins, D. and M. Ismail (1994), "Is the Asian Learner a Rote Learner? A Malaysian Perspective," *Contemporary Educational Psychology*, 19: 483–88.

Watkins, D. and B.C. Malimas (1980), "Faculty and Student Orientations to Tertiary Education: A Case Study of a Filipino University," *Higher education*, 9: 707–20.

Watkins, D., J. Adair, A. Akande, C. Cheng, J. Fleming, A. Gerong, et al, and J. Yu (1998), "Cultural Dimensions, Gender, and the Nature of Self-concept: A Fourteen-Country Study," *International Journal of Psychology*, 33(1): 17–31.

Watkins, D., M. Regmi, and E. Astilla (1991), "The Asian-learner-as-a-rote-learner Stereotype: Myth or Reality?" *Educational Psychology*, 11: 21–34.

Watkins, D.A. and J.B. Biggs (eds) (1996), *The Chinese Learner: Cultural, Psychological and Contextual Influences*, Hong Kong: Comparative Education Research Centre; Victoria, Australia: The Australian Council for the Educational Research.

Wiggins, D. (1980), "Deliberation and Practical Reason," in A.O. Rorty (ed.), *Essays on Aristotle's ethics*, Berkeley: University of California Press.

Wilber, Ken (2000), *A Brief History of Everything*, Boston: Shambhala.

Williams, B. (1985), *Ethics and the Limits of Philosophy*, Cambridge: Harvard University Press.

Williams, B. (1993), *Same and Necessity*, Berkeley: University of California Press.
Williams, B. (1995), "Acting as the Virtuous Persons Acts," in R. Heinaman (ed.), *Aristotle and Moral Realism*, 13–23, Boulder, San Francisco: Westview Press.
Winkler, E. (1996). "Moral Philosophy and Bioethics: Contextualism versus the Paradigm Theory," in L.W. Sumner and J. Boyle (eds), *Philosophical Perspectives on Bioethics*, Toronto: University of Toronto Press.
WONG, N.Y. (1998a), "In Search of the 'CHC' Learner: Smarter, Works Harder or Something More? Plenary lecture," in H.S. Park, Y.H. Choe, H. Shin, and S.H. Kim (eds), *Proceedings of the ICMI—East Asia Regional Conference on Mathematical Education*, 1: 85–98.
WONG, N.Y. (1998b), "The Gradual and Sudden Paths of Tibetan and Chan Buddhism: A Pedagogical Perspective," *Journal of Thought*, 33(2): 9–23.
WONG, N.Y. (2001), "Practice, Rote Learning and Backwash Effect—From Examination to Learning" (in Chinese), in S.K. Leung (ed.), *Holistic Review of the Mathematics Curriculum: What's next?*, 122–127, Hong Kong: Department of Curriculum and Instruction, The Chinese University of Hong Kong and the Hong Kong Association for Mathematics Education.
WONG, N.Y. (2004), "The CHC Learner's Phenomenon: Its Implications on Mathematics Education," in L. Fan, N. Y. Wong, J. Cai, and S. Li (eds), *How Chinese Learn Mathematics: Perspectives from Insiders*, 503–34, Singapore: World Scientific.
WONG, N.Y. (2006), "From 'Entering the Way' to 'Exiting the Way': In Search of a Bridge to Span 'Basic Skills' and 'Process Abilities," in F.K.S. Leung, G-D. Graf, and F.J. Lopez-Real (eds), *Mathematics Education in Different Cultural Traditions: The 13th ICMI Study*, 111–128, New York: Springer.
WONG, N.Y. (2008), "Confucian Heritage Culture Learner's Phenomenon: From 'Exploring the Middle Zone' to 'Constructing a Bridge,'" *ZDM—The International Journal on Mathematics Education*, 40: 973–81.
WONG, N.Y. (2013), "The Chinese Learner, the Japanese Learner, the Asian Learner—Inspiration for the (Mathematics) Learner," *Scientiae Mathematicae Japonicae*, 76(2): 376–84.
Wong, N.Y., J.W. Han and P.Y. Lee (2004), "The Mathematics Curriculum: Towards Globalisation or Westernisation?" in L. Fan, N. Y. Wong, J. Cai, and S. Li (eds), *How Chinese Learn Mathematics: Perspectives from Insiders*, 27–70, Singapore: World Scientific.
Wong, N.Y., C.C. Lam, X. Sun, and A.M.Y. Chan (2009), "From 'Exploring the Middle Zone' to 'Constructing a Bridge': Experimenting the Spiral *Bianshi* Mathematics Curriculum," *International Journal of Science and Mathematics Education*, 7(2): 363–82.
Wong, N.Y., W.Y. Lin and D. Watkins (1996), "Cross-cultural Validation of Models of Approaches to Learning: An Application of Confirmatory Factor Analysis," *Educational Psychology*, 16: 317–27.
Wong, N.Y., F. Marton, K.M. Wong and C.C. Lam (2002), "The Lived Space of Mathematics Learning," *Journal of Mathematical Behavior*, 21: 25–47.
Wong, N.Y., W.Y. Wong and E.W.Y. Wong (2012), "What do Chinese Value in (Mathematics) Education," *ZDM—The International Journal on Mathematics Education*, 44(1): 9–19.
WONG, W.Y. (1988), *The Fundamental Problems of Meta-Ethics* (in Chinese), Taipei: Dong Da Publishing Co.
WONG, W.Y. (1995a), *Caring about Morality* (in Chinese), Taipei: Dong Da Publishing Co.
WONG, W.Y. (1995b), "Why Be Moral: A Confucian Solution" (in Chinese), in *Caring about Morality*, Taipei: Dong Da Publishing Co.

WONG, W.Y. (1995c), "The Direction of The Modernization of Confucian Ethics" (in Chinese), in *Caring about Morality*, Taipei: Dong Da Publishing Book Co.

WONG, W.Y. (2005), *Confucian Ethics: Its Substance and Function* (*Rujia Lunli: Ti yu Yong*) (in Chinese), Shanghai: Shanghai Joint Publishing Co.

WONG, W.Y. (2005a), "An Examination on Moral Theories: A Response to Anti-theorists" (in Chinese), in *Confucian Ethics: Substance and Function*, 3–20, Shanghai: Shanghai Joint Publishing Co..

WONG, W.Y. (2005b), "Moral Theory and Confucian Ethics" (in Chinese), in *Confucian Ethics: Substance and Function*, 39–46, Shanghai: Shanghai Joint Publishing Co.

WONG, W.Y. (2005c), "The Self-Other Relation in Confucian Virtues" (in Chinese), in *Confucian Ethics: Substance and Function*, 63–76, Shanghai: Shanghai Joint Publishing Co.

WONG, W.Y. (2005d), "On the Emphases of Confucian and Mencian Philosophies from the Differentiation between Man and Beast" (in Chinese), in *Confucian Ethics: Substance and Function*, 131–49, Shanghai: Shanghai Joint Publishing Co.

WONG, W.Y. (2005e), "The Concept of *Quan* in *Chun Qiu Gongyang Zhuan*" (in Chinese), in *Confucian Ethics: Substance and Function*, Shanghai: Shanghai Joint Publishing Co.

WONG, W.Y. (2005f), "The Meaning of Moral Creativity: Mou Zongsan's Interpretation of Confucianism" (in Chinese), in *Confucian Ethics: Substance and Function*, Shanghai: Shanghai Joint Publishing Co.

WONG, W.Y. (2005g), "Moral Theory and Confucian Ethics" (in Chinese), in *Confucian Ethics: Substance and Function*, Shanghai: Shanghai Joint Publishing Co.

WONG, W.Y. (2005h), "Universal Moral Maxims and Moral Education" (in Chinese), in *Confucian Ethics: Substance and Function*, Shanghai: Shanghai Joint Publishing Co.

XU, Fuguan (1969), *Chinese Discourse on Human Nature: Pre-Qin Period* (in Chinese), Taipei: Xuesheng Shuju.

YAN, K.S. (1986), "Chinese Personality and its Change," in M.H. Bond (ed.), *The Psychology of the Chinese People*, 227–46, Hong Kong: Oxford University Press.

YANG, Junshi (1987), "Confucian Ethics, Weber's Propositions and Ideology" (in Chinese), in J.S. Yang and N.Z. Tao (eds), *Confucian Ethics and Economic Development*, 227–61, Taipei: Yuen Zhen Civilisation Company.

YU, A. (1996), "Ultimate Life Concerns, Self and Chinese Achievement Motivation," in M.H. Bond (ed.), The Handbook of Chinese Psychology, 227–46, Hong Kong: Oxford University Press.

YU, Jiyuan (1998), "Virtue: Confucius and Aristotle," *Philosophy East & West*, 48(2): 323–47.

YU, Jiyuan (2007), *The Ethics of Confucius and Aristotle: Mirrors of virtue*, New York: Routledge.

YU, Yingshi (1987), *The Religious Ethics and the Spirit of Merchants in Late Imperial China* (in Chinese), Taipei: Lian Jin Publications.

YU, Yingshi (1991), "QIAN Mu and New-Confucians" (in Chinese), in *Remembering when the Wind Whirlpools Water*, Taipei: San Min Book Co. Ltd.

Yuan, Y. and Q. Xie (2013), "Cultures of Learning: An Evolving Concept and an Expanding Field," in M. Cortazz and L. Jin (eds), *Researching Cultures of Learning: International Perspectives in Language Learning and Education*, 21–40, Houndmills: Palgrave Macmillan.

ZHANG, Dexing (1989), *Confucian Ethics and the Order Complex* (in Chinese), Taipei: Great Current Publications.

Zhang, L., J. Biggs, and D. Watkins (2010), *Learning and Development of Asian Students*, Singapore: Prentice Hall.

ZHONG, Caijun (1992), "From Naturalism to Teleology: A Study of the General Principles of the Ontology of the Ch'eng Brothers" (in Chinese), *Bulletin of the Institute of Chinese Literature and Philosophy*, 2: 385–422.

ZHU, Xi (1986), *Topically Arranged Conversations of Master Zhu* (in Chinese), Beijing: Zhonghua shuju.

ZHU, Xi and L.U., Zuqian, trans. with notes by Wing-tsit CHAN (1967), *The Neo-Confucian Anthology* (in Chinese), New York: Columbia University Press.

Index